The Marvels of the World

PENN STUDIES IN LANDSCAPE ARCHITECTURE

John Dixon Hunt, Series Editor

This series is dedicated to the study and promotion of a wide variety of approaches to landscape architecture, with special emphasis on connections between theory and practice. It includes monographs on key topics in history and theory, descriptions of projects by both established and rising designers, translations of major foreign-language texts, anthologies of theoretical and historical writings on classic issues, and critical writing by members of the profession of landscape architecture.

The series was the recipient of the Award of Honor in Communications from the American Society of Landscape Architects, 2006.

THE MARVELS OF THE WORLD

An Anthology of Nature Writing Before 1700

Edited by Rebecca Bushnell

PENN

UNIVERSITY OF PENNSYLVANIA PRESS

PHILADELPHIA

Published by
University of Pennsylvania Press
Philadelphia, Pennsylvania 19104-4112
www.upenn.edu/pennpress

Printed in the United States of America on acid-free paper
10 9 8 7 6 5 4 3 2 1

Library of Congress Cataloging-in-Publication Data

Names: Bushnell, Rebecca W., 1952- editor.
Title: The marvels of the world : an anthology of nature writing before 1700 / edited by Rebecca Bushnell.
Other titles: Penn studies in landscape architecture.
Description: 1st edition. | Philadelphia : University of Pennsylvania Press, [2021] | Series: Penn studies in landscape architecture | Includes bibliographical references and index.
Identifiers: LCCN 2020041082 | ISBN 9780812252842 (hardcover) | ISBN 9780812224733 (paperback)
Subjects: LCSH: Nature—Literary collections. | Nature in literature. | Natural history literature—Early works to 1800.
Classification: LCC PN6071.N3 M37 2021 | DDC 808.8/036—dc23
LC record available at https://lccn.loc.gov/2020041082

Contents

Acknowledgments

The idea for this anthology arose from a graduate seminar I taught in 2017 on the early modern English discourses of nature and natural history seen in the context of ecocriticism and ecotheory. While it was offered as an English course, the students came from fields including religious studies, art history, classical studies, and comparative as well as English literature, and only one student called herself an early modernist. It ended up being one of the most stimulating courses I had ever offered, and I am so grateful for what those students taught me: Tom Elliott, Christopher Fite, Zachary Fruit, Johanna Kaiser, Aylin Malcolm, Paul McBain, Alicia Meyer, and Anna-Claire Stinebring.

I thus had to shape the course for students who were not primarily interested in early modern England. That process eventually led to my planning this collection of texts for a broad audience of readers interested in learning more about the premodern natural world. I reached out to Jerry Singerman, the senior humanities editor for the University of Pennsylvania Press, and he enthusiastically endorsed the idea for the project. I am deeply grateful to him for his consistent and thoughtful support throughout the process of bringing this into print. The editorial staff of the Penn Press also ably steered the complicated manuscript through the publication process.

I owe a profound debt for this project's coming to fruition to John Dixon Hunt, my University of Pennsylvania colleague and the acknowledged master of all scholarship about gardens. John has been a mentor for me since I first started writing on this subject almost two decades ago, and he has been an enthusiastic advocate and wise advisor for this book from the beginning; in many ways it belongs to him.

Because of the anthology's scope from antiquity through 1700, and from plants to animals to natural philosophy, I often had to get advice from other scholars about what to include. I am particularly grateful to Kellie Robertson, a reader for the press and brilliant scholar of medieval natural philosophy, who helped me to strengthen the first part and define the medieval selections. Robert Watson also offered a valuable perspective, reminding me to widen my view as capaciously as possible. I also received critical advice from friends and colleagues deeply steeped in premodern ecocriticism, natural philosophy, and medicine: I would particularly like to thank Rita Copeland, David Wallace, Emily Steiner, Karen Raber, Aylin Malcolm, Jennifer Munroe, Steve Mentz, Todd Borlik, Rebecca Laroche, Jean Feerick, Wendy Wall, Ralph Rosen, Leah Knight, and Liza Blake, for both their recommendations of texts and their collegiality and wisdom. I wasn't able to accommodate every suggestion, but overall everyone influenced the volume's content and approach.

Much of the work of an anthology involves preparing the numerous texts and images. In this process I was so fortunate to have the assistance of Alyssa Mulé while she was an undergraduate English and Classical Studies major at the University of Pennsylvania. Her main duties were transcribing and modernizing many of the excerpts and locating illustrations in the University of Pennsylvania's Kislak Center for Special Collections, Rare Books, and Manuscripts. The transcription work could be especially challenging when she had to decode black letter and manuscript texts, but she handled it masterfully. I simply could not have done this without her help. She undertook the research on the illustrations while she was also working in the Kislak Center. There she was aided by John Pollack, the Curator of Research Services: together they located the images I knew I wanted to use, but they also found new ones. John Pollack himself exemplifies everything a research librarian should be, and I am indebted to him for all the support he has given for my scholarship and teaching over the years.

The University of Pennsylvania is a congenial place to work in premodern studies. I've enjoyed the collegiality of those who come together for our Medieval-Renaissance seminar, including Cary Mazer, David Wallace, Rita Copeland, Phyllis Rackin, Zack Lesser, and Melissa Sanchez, and a talented group of medieval and early modern graduate students who have taught me a lot over the years. As the School of Arts and Sciences Board of Overseers Professor of English (now emerita), I have also benefited tremendously from the research funds provided by my endowed chair, and I must once again thank the School of Arts and Sciences Dean's Office and all of those who made that endowed chair possible.

As always, my husband John Toner and my daughters Ruth and Emily Toner have provided the foundation of happiness and sanity that makes my academic work possible. My own horticultural efforts and my forty years of life with cats have taught me much about being patient and respectful in coexisting with the natural world, a lesson echoed throughout this book.

Introduction

In the first century of the Common Era, the Roman writer Pliny the Elder composed a massive natural history in thirty-seven books covering astronomy, geology, zoology, botany, and minerology and embracing all areas of concern for human existence. The work begins by ecstatically praising earth's indulgence of humankind:

> She receives us at our birth, nourishes us when born, and ever afterwards supports us; lastly, embracing us in her bosom when we are rejected by the rest of nature, she then covers us with especial tenderness. . . . The water passes into showers, is concreted into hail, swells into rivers, is precipitated in torrents; the air is condensed into clouds, rages in squalls; but the earth, kind, mild, and indulgent as she is, and always ministering to the wants of mortals, how many things do we compel her to produce spontaneously! What odors and flowers, nutritive juices, forms and colors! With what good faith does she render back all that has been entrusted to her!

In the same passage, Pliny then condemns those who abuse that earth, complaining that "everything which the earth has produced, as a remedy for our evils, we have converted into the poison of our lives," for "she is continually tortured for her iron, her timber, stone, fire, corn" in our pursuit of superfluous wealth. Then, "inasmuch as all this wealth ends in crimes, slaughter, and war, and that, while we drench her with our blood, we cover her with unburied bones; and being covered with these and her anger being thus appeased, she conceals the crimes of mortals which leads to crime and bloodshed, the expression of earth's anger" (Pliny, Part 1).

In this short span Pliny thus highlights the contradictions that inform so much of our experience of the natural world. We wonder at the earth's extraordinary abundance and variety, how "many things" she generates in a dizzying array of forms, smells, and colors, while complacent in our belief that the earth exists only to serve us, caring for us from birth to death. At the same time, however, Pliny contrasts the earth's "indulgence" with the violence of nature's winds and waters, admitting that our lives are subject to natural forces beyond our control. Finally, he exposes humanity's abuse of the earth and her latent anger; he underlines the point that while we assume the earth's love for us, we are driven to destroy it, and she may undo us in return.

From the very beginning, such a fear of both loss and revenge has always underwritten narratives of human dominion over the natural world. The Bible locates humanity's primal sin in a bountiful garden from which we are soon banished: God tells Adam that "cursed is the ground for thy sake; in sorrow shalt thou eat of it all the days of thy life; thorns also and thistles shall it bring forth to thee; and thou shalt eat the herb of the field" (*King James Bible*, Genesis 3:17–18). In his *Works and Days* (ca. 700 BCE), the Greek poet Hesiod also wrote of a lost golden age, a time when people "had all good things; for the fruitful earth unforced bare them fruit abundantly and without stint. They dwelt in ease and peace upon their lands with many good things, rich in flocks and loved by the blessed gods" (Hesiod ll. 110–21). When these humans failed to honor the gods, Zeus condemned them to the grinding and unrelenting work of husbandry. So much of premodern literature is haunted by such memories of how men and women betrayed the indulgent earth through their own arrogance.

Countless such accounts thus contradict the assumption that an environmental consciousness emerged in the West only in the late eighteenth century. Much recent environmental criticism may give the impression that the concept of "nature" was not invented until modern times, or at least not in the way that we would recognize it. Anthologies of Western nature writing tend to start at best in the early modern age: for example, Bridget Keegan and James C. Kusick's *Literature and Nature: Four Centuries of Nature Writing* may begin at 1600, but of its approximately 1,000 pages, only 160 are devoted to the seventeenth century. The sense that nature writing only takes off after 1800 reflects two dominant trends in mainstream ecocriticism: a focus on ideas of nature derived from Romanticism and a primary interest in American literature and culture. When most people think about "nature writing" today, they just cannot reach back further than Thoreau or Wordsworth.

However, as Robert M. Torrance observes in his own massive anthology of global nature writing before 1800, "for most of human history . . . writing about nature has taken forms very different from the self-conscious nature writing of Romantic and modern Europe and America, which would have been puzzling if not inconceivable to people more fully integrated with the world around them" (Torrance xii). Usually, the story of environmentalism begins with a brutal anthropocentrism dominating early Western thinking about nature for centuries, evolving only in the early eighteenth century. Keith Thomas's account in *Man and the Natural World* detects that shift in England in a new interest in natural history, concern for the suffering of animals, and a growing appreciation of country and wilderness. However, as Thomas himself tells the story, even when belief in human exceptionalism reigned, the deep entanglement of humans in the natural world always undermined that sense of privilege.

Stretching back to antiquity, people have experienced that entanglement materially, spiritually, and intellectually. Expecting the natural world would always provide food, transportation, clothing, labor, and shelter meant profoundly depending on it. Then, as now, people knew they could not survive without faithfully nurturing plants and animals, managing soil and water, and attending to weather and climate. Beginning with Hesiod's *Works and Days*, so much premodern writing about the natural world urges close attention to its needs and its inherent power both to sustain and destroy us. A widely held belief that environmental factors directly influence the human body and character further enhanced that sense of vulnerability. The food you consume could alter your body's "temperature" and humoral balance and thus even your temperament or personality (Siriasi; Schoenfeldt; Paster); the air, winds, and water, and the change of seasons could shape you, or a particular climate define the physical and behavioral characteristics of a race (Floyd-Wilson; Feerick 2010).

Complementing this belief in the material interaction between humans and their environment, the premodern habit of mind saw all that is human reflected in the nonhuman world in a vast network of correspondences and resemblances (Foucault; Nicholson). When people wondered at the beauty and mystery of the marvels of this earth, they also beheld themselves (Daston and Park). This idea that a human being is thus a microcosm had the power to deconstruct the human into those constituent analogies with other creatures and matter (Robertson). As much as theologians and philosophers asserted human exceptionalism and supremacy over all other living things, both in their bodies and in the book of nature, people were all too like those other beings (Bach; Raber 2013; Feerick and Nardizzi; Yamamoto).

In the past twenty-five years, understanding of premodern nature writing's complexity and depth has grown, a change driven by contemporary ecological concerns and new theoretical and interdisciplinary approaches. The recommended reading section at the end of this anthology demonstrates the health of the field (while it has tended to focus on the early modern period). For decades, countless scholars have written individually about premodern natural philosophy, medicine, botany, zoology, and agriculture as well as literary genres like the pastoral and georgic, but only recently have these fields been brought together to inform one another, integrating historical and critical approaches. More radically, the idea of what constitutes "nature writing" now extends beyond the canonical philosophical and literary sources to works like how-to manuals and recipe collections, which offer insight into people's everyday involvement with the stuff of the natural world (Wall 2016; Munroe and Laroche; Harkness; Eamon).

As part of that trend, this anthology aims to broaden and complicate the story of premodern nature writing in the West, whether for a student of early literature and culture or for any reader who wants to go beyond the commonplaces that have dominated so much thinking about the past. Todd Borlik recently published a brilliant and capacious anthology on *Literature and Nature in the English Renaissance*; however, except for its inclusion of the essential classical models, it focuses solely on the early modern period in England. This anthology widens the scope to medieval literature and culture as well as to classical texts, so that readers can follow the evolution of conflicting concepts over the sweep of two millennia.

Not surprisingly, it was hard to choose representative writings from those millennia for one compact volume and to organize them in a way that makes sense for readers with different goals. Several principles have shaped those difficult choices. First, this anthology assumes an Anglophone reader, and many of the selections emphasize the evolution of British writing and thinking about the natural world. However, since that tradition participates in the overall history of Western nature writing, the anthology includes not only classical models but also many excerpts from non-Anglophone texts, allowing readers to trace continuities across Europe from antiquity up through the seventeenth century. Since most anthologies of nature writing tend to choose the well-known literary and philosophical works, this collection favors lesser-known ones that reveal a wider range of thinking about daily encounters with nature in all its forms. Thus, for example, Francis Bacon's famous essay "On Gardens" gave way to permit inclusion of Hester Pulter's poem "The Snail, the Tulip, and the Bee" and the description of the garden of Mary Somerset, Duchess of Beaufort. At some points, an introduction or headnote will simply refer a reader to an easily available text, by Shakespeare or Chaucer, for example.

The volume falls into seven parts covering different ways of thinking about the natural world, including practices of natural philosophy and science, engagement with plants and animals, gardening and gardens, experiencing weather and climate, representations of humans inhabiting the natural world, and encounters with nature outside of Europe. The selections speak to the construction of non-human nature; that is, they do not address "human nature" or the human body on its own, except as interacting with the material world (for example, shaped by the changing seasons, or compared with plants or animals). Further, this anthology limits its scope to living things; its view extends to the stars and the wider cosmos only insofar as they were imagined to influence things on earth. It excludes minerals and stones, even though recently much important scholarship has argued for their vitality (see Cohen 2012; Duckert and Cohen).

While each part begins with a short introduction providing a general context for the texts that follow, the selections themselves appear in chronological order, each with an explanatory headnote. In this way the reader can follow changes and continuities over time, while comparing different genres of nature writing. At the same time, the introductions and headnotes point to interconnections among selections throughout the anthology, guiding the reader by references through those networks: for example, untangling the centuries-long debates on grafting, which addressed the mechanisms and social and philosophical implications of mastering plant reproduction. Selections from several authors, including familiar names such as Aristotle, Pliny, Chaucer, and Shakespeare, as well as less-known ones like John Parkinson and Gervase Markham, appear in several parts; for repeated authors the first headnote presents the general background. Citations from the excerpts occur in the introductions and headnotes, with their sources indicated parenthetically. The most important scholarship on an individual subject informs the introductions and headnotes, but for ease of reading, citations have been kept to a minimum. Instead, readers are referred parenthetically to the list of recommended readings at the end if they want to pursue any subject in greater depth.

The anthology opens by surveying the breadth of premodern concepts of the natural world and natural knowledge, a wide and complicated territory that spans theology, philosophy, magic, medicine, and what we now think of as science. These include the models of the structure of *scala naturae*, or the ladder of nature; the network of correspondences, sympathies, and antipathies that connect all living things and matter; and the understanding that all matter is composed of the elements of earth, fire, air, and water, tempered by the accommodating qualities of heat, cold, wet, and dry, with all animals additionally animated by essential humors. This part begins with the classical models of nature, which medieval and early modern scholars and philosophers then adapted and reinterpreted. However, it extends beyond philosophy and theology into writings that offer ways of knowing nature through interacting with or even outdoing it. Our view of early science can now embrace magic and technology, and even the domestic realm of cookery and recipes. All these practices entailed belief in the plasticity of the natural world and the importance of knowing its secrets.

Parts 2 and 3 explore writing that represents plants and animals in poetry and prose, herbals and natural histories, medical treatises, and manuals for horticulture and animal husbandry. Inevitably, in these texts these nonhuman creatures matter for their relevance to human life: their role is to feed, carry, cure, or please us. Because plants and animals thus assured human survival, they touched every part of daily life, and people knew they must care for them in return. While subjecting them to human needs, writers attributed to plants and animals power over us, not only because we depend on them but because in a world of sympathies and antipathies concerning all living things, they have agency to affect our bodies. Further, in the network of elaborate analogies drawn between human and nonhuman natures, other living things symbolize our lives, and in this sense, they are more like us than different.

Part 4 expands beyond these interactions with living creatures to consider more broadly the environment's impact on human lives. In a time when few could escape the effects of water and wind, or heat and cold, people saw that weather could powerfully influence human society, behavior, and health. Of course, activities ranging from farming to seafaring demanded close attention to the change of seasons or signs of a coming storm. However, believing that the human body and character respond acutely to environmental factors, medical authorities recommended activities and diet to suit meteorological changes, thus betraying anxiety about the stability of the human body mired in an earth beyond our control. In turn, the poetic evocations of seasonal cycles suggest that human beings have their own emotional weather, corresponding with the extremes of that volatile natural world.

The next three parts expand outward from a focus on plants, animals, weather, and climate to survey depictions of human interactions with the natural world they inhabit. This turn begins in Part 5 by introducing the two dominant European poetic genres that figure people living and working in the land: pastorals (narratives and poems about the lives of shepherds) and georgics (the literature celebrating the labor of cultivation). Many scholars consider these works primarily as social or political allegories or even as commentaries on poetry itself, that is, as about anything but nature. However, this anthology treats them seriously as nature writing, putting them into dialogue with the practical texts about pasturing and agriculture. Thus, the selection of pastorals highlights how they map human experience onto the world through possession, loss, or sympathetic interaction, images that clash with contemporary descriptions of the realities of sheep farming. In the same way, the georgic poems are paired with practical handbooks and treatises on agriculture and husbandry; in both the poetry and the prose, insistence on managing the earth conflicts with a recognition of nature's power. Part 6, on gardens and gardening, extends beyond husbandry and agriculture to feature texts that mark the pleasure and intellectual delight added to the profit to be derived from cultivating plants. Gardens and gardening form a special category insofar as gardening was an art as well a kind of labor. At the heart of garden writing thus lies a vexed debate about the relationship between art and nature. Further, like plants themselves, gardens and gardening could function more generally as metaphors for aspects of human society and behavior.

Drawing on travel narratives, literature, and natural histories and herbals, Part 7, "Outlandish Natural Worlds," stretches beyond Europe's borders to follow how the premodern West grappled with the evidence of an unfamiliar natural world. In earlier English usage "outlandish" meant just "foreign," but by early modernity it also began to carry its connotation of "bizarre," conveying the mixed wonder and fear of the exotic. Driven by trade and colonization, Europeans were always on the move, and they were eager to report the natural marvels they found; in turn, historians and writers seized on these stories and circulated them (and often exaggerated them) over the centuries. Those explorations outside the West found a nature unlike anything people knew in their native lands. These different natures were both terrifying and seductive, evoking both Eden and hostile wilderness.

Readers may come to this anthology from various backgrounds, looking for different stories or ideas about the relationship between human beings and their environment. It is meant to serve students as a companion to literary or cultural study of premodern ecological concerns, but I would also hope that modernists would appreciate this view of the complexity of environmental history. Modern science dismisses much of what is written here as fantasy or pseudoscience, but in fact, there is still much to be learned from a time far more engaged with the environment than many people in the developed world today. Even in their most relentless anthropocentrism, many of these approaches to the natural world emphasize reciprocity and the value of knowledge gained from experience and observation—not so much the kind of knowledge gained from the rigors of the scientific method, but rather that earned from everyday experience driven by necessity. Premodern nature writing also asks us to remember our physical and cultural vulnerability to natural forces beyond our control, and that everything that happens in the nonhuman world touches us in some way, whether on a small scale in the plants and animals we consume or in the catastrophe of a storm. At the heart of the now-dismissed theories of medicine lies the important truth that human bodies are influenced by extreme heat and cold, and polluted air and water. One comes away from reading these texts with a sense of the extraordinary openness of premodern thinking about the engagement of human beings in an environment that has such a power to shape us, even as we may seek to control and exploit it.

A Note on Editorial Practices

In order for this anthology to reach the widest possible audience, in most of the excerpts the spelling of primary texts from early modern English has been modernized for ease of reading. The punctuation has also been adapted for clarity, while some of the older punctuation has been retained where the sense is clear. The approach to the medieval poetic texts has been twofold: for some (and particularly Chaucer), the Middle English spellings have been modified for clarity of comprehension, while much of its original form has been retained for the sound of the verse; in other cases, where the Middle English is harder to adapt (e.g., Langland), a full modern translation is provided. Throughout, unfamiliar words or concepts are clarified through glosses in footnotes.

PART I

Natural Philosophy and Natural Knowledge

The effort to describe and understand the world around us is as old as civilization itself. We now think of that work as the province of science, the methodical practice of observation and experimentation. However, like that practice itself, using the word "science" in that way is a comparatively recent phenomenon. The earliest usage of "science" simply conveys the act of knowing something by deliberate study; the term derives from the Latin word *scientia*, which designates knowledge as opposed to belief. Long before the first stirrings of modern experimental science in the seventeenth century, people employed multiple and highly sophisticated methods to explain and interpret the world they inhabited, whether it be through theology, literature, natural history, or philosophy.

Representing fully the history of such premodern Western science and natural history is well beyond this anthology's scope (see, e.g., French; Crombie; Grant; Lindberg 1978 and 1992; Daston and Park for surveys). This first part aims more narrowly to lay the groundwork for the subsequent parts on plants, animals, weather and climate, farming and pastoral life, gardening, and "outlandish" nature. Like the rest of the anthology, it does not confine itself to traditional selections from literature, philosophy, theology, and natural history. Rather, it considers many more ways of knowing about the natural world, those shared by communities of people who studied and experimented with plants and animals through invention, craft, medicine, and cookery (see Wall 2016; Eamon; Harkness; Munroe 2008; Laroche). Of course, much of this knowledge, practiced outside of courts, universities, and monasteries, has been lost, but some survives in manuscript collections handed down for generations or printed in popular "books of secrets" and how-to guides.

This part begins with two foundational texts that would drive much later thinking about the natural world: the Hebrew Bible's account of the Creation and Aristotle's foundational natural philosophy. In the biblical story, God created everything in this world in six days, as is now and forever more, and gave man dominion over all living things. In the classical tradition, responding to Plato's elevation of unchanging forms over realized matter, Aristotle developed a complex theory of immanent nature, in which all living things are understood to move toward a fulfillment or end in order to realize their true nature. Thus, a tree becomes what it is through the process of change, evolving from an acorn to a mature tree until it dies a natural death. As the Bible does, Aristotle posited a hierarchical order in nature, but at the same time he recognized that plants, animals, and humans share qualities fundamental to all living things. In the late middle ages, Christian theologians would attempt to reconcile the newly available Aristotelian natural philosophy with the Bible's by applying reason to knowing the world in a way that leads back to God (on Aristotle and nature in the middle ages, see Robertson). While people also began to explore learning about the natural world through observation and experiment, Christian writers still had to conclude that, in Thomas Aquinas's words, "God acts in nature and willing its actions" (Aquinas, Part 1).

All of the resulting premodern models for constructing the natural world allow that even though humans are meant to control and exploit the environment they inhabit, they intimately touch and are open to it. These models include the structure of the *scala naturae*, or ladder of nature; the network of correspondences, sympathies, and antipathies that connect all living things and matter; and the understanding that all matter is composed of the elements of earth, fire, air, and water, with the accommodating qualities of heat, cold, wet, and dry, and with all animals additionally animated by the essential humors of black bile, yellow bile, blood and phlegm (see Siriasi; Paster; Feerick 2010; Schoenfeldt, Floyd-Wilson).

The concept of the ladder of nature, or what has also been called the "Great Chain of Being," dominates many accounts of the premodern model of the natural world (see Lovejoy; Tillyard; Thomas; Robertson; Borlik 2012). It dates back to Aristotle, who while acknowledging the difficulty of making distinctions, described a hierarchy of lifeless and living things:

> Nature proceeds little by little from things lifeless to animal life in such a way that it is impossible to determine the exact line of demarcation, nor on which side thereof an intermediate form should lie. Thus, next after lifeless things in the upward scale comes the plant, and of plants one will differ from another as to its amount of apparent vitality; and, in a word, the whole genus of plants, whilst it is devoid of life as compared with an animal, is endowed with life as compared with other corporeal entities.... And so throughout the entire animal scale there is a

graduated differentiation in amount of vitality and in capacity for motion. (*History of Animals* 8.1, qtd. in Robertson 58–59)

In turn, Christian theology adapted this notion to mesh with the Bible's teaching that man is superior to all creation, made in God's image, and uniquely capable of reason. This vision grew to constitute a divinely ordained natural order informing human society. For example, in order to bolster a broader argument about good governance, in *The Boke Named the Governor* (1531), Thomas Elyot asked his readers to "behold also the order that God hath put generally in all His creatures, beginning at the most inferior or base, and ascending upward," where "every kind of trees, herbs, birds, beasts, and fishes, beside their diversity of forms, have . . . a peculiar disposition appropered unto them by God their creator: so that in everything is order, and without order may be nothing stable or permanent; and it may not be called order, except it do contain in it degrees, high and base, according to the merit or estimation of the thing that is ordered" (4).

Complicating this insistence on hierarchy was the tendency to see everything human mirrored in the nonhuman world: a human being was a microcosm of all creation. More than symbolic, that concept was rooted in a belief in the profound connectedness of the natural and human worlds, a network of innumerable linkages, called correspondences and sympathies. In this sense, the natural world is not just a ladder but also a book, or what Keith Thomas called "a cryptogram full of hidden meaning for man but awaiting decipherment" (64; see also Robertson). Those linkages are vital and active, when in Michel Foucault's words, "in the vast syntax of the world, the different beings adjust themselves to one another; the plant communicates with the animal, the earth with the sea, man with everything around him," containing all within him (18). Early medicine and magic were both founded on such belief, exploiting the power of those connections: as the popular handbook, the *Secrets of Albertus Magnus*, stated the case, since "every natural kind, and that every particular or general nature hath natural amity and enmity towards an other" (Albertus Magnus, Part 1), these states of attraction can be used to influence nature. In his own work on "natural magic," Giambattista della Porta advised his reader "by the agreement and the disagreement of things, either so to sunder them, or else to lay them so together by the mutual and fit applying of one thing to another, as thereby we do strange works, such as the vulgar sort call miracles" (della Porta, Part 1).

The ladder of nature also teetered when decomposed into the elements of earth, air, fire, and water, tempered by the qualities of hot, cold, wet, and dry. Historians trace the idea that these four essential elements make up the physical world back to the Greek philosopher Empedocles (c. 490–430 BCE), who posited that these elements constantly interact, dynamically merging and dividing. When adapting this concept, Aristotle aligned those elements with the "qualities" of hot and cold, wet and dry. Each element could then be attributed two qualities at any given time: for example, in the Arabic physician and philosopher Avicenna's words, "air is a simple substance, whose position in nature is above the sphere of water, and beneath that of fire. This is due to its relative lightness. In nature it is hot and moist" (Avicenna, Part 1). However, all the elements are constantly in flux and in this the natural world is inherently unstable.

Every living thing, human or nonhuman, in turn, has "qualities" associated with those elements. Thus, for example, for an herbalist like William Turner, "chamomile is hot and dry in the first degree" (Turner, Part 2). In humans and animals, those qualities shape their individual temperament or "complexions." Thus, Gervase Markham writes that a horse, identified with air, can be "known to be hot and moist by his lightness, swiftness, valiantness, and long life, and also to be of a temperate nature, in that he is easily tamed, docile, obedient and familiar with the man" (Markham, Part 3). While such temperaments are intrinsic, elements and qualities interact with each other in the exposed body; a cold climate or a hot herb can alter its temperature. So in the case of chamomile, Turner continues, its heat may be a good antidote to a person's "weariness" associated with cold. The theory of the qualities also explains how climate can affect both body and character. The Hippocratic treatise on "Airs, Places, Waters" started the argument that environment shapes the health and personality of an individual or a community (Hippocrates, Part 4). Avicenna later posited that people who go to hot countries "become aged at thirty, are timid (as the breath is so much dispersed) and the body becomes soft and dark," whereas those "who go live in cold countries become robust and stronger, and bolder and more courageous" (Avicenna, Part 4). Such ideas, with all their variations about exactly how climate influences all bodies, extended far into early modernity in the context of what Mary Floyd-Wilson has called "geohumoralism": for example, in his *Method for the Easy Comprehension of History* (1566), Jean Bodin devoted a whole chapter to global climate differences in bodies and temperament and their influence on the course of history (see also Floyd-Wilson; Feerick 2010).

First the Hippocratic writers and later the Greek physician Galen (died ca. 200 CE) adapted the theory of elements and qualities for medical practices that dominated the field throughout antiquity. In turn, in the middle ages, Islamic scholars and practitioners synthesized and disseminated those core Galenic and Hippocratic ideas, which circulated throughout Europe for centuries to come. To the constellation of elemental "mixtures" and qualities these physicians added the concept that four "humors" govern all animals' physical health and personality. In this theory the state of a person's body and mind depends on the balance of those "humors" or fluids circulating throughout their system, including blood, phlegm (defined as "any whitish secretion" [Siriasi 105]), red or yellow bile, and black bile. Each humor expresses certain qualities. For example, blood was "hot and moist" for Avicenna, and medical literature includes many variations on this theme. Those humors and qualities combine to produce a personality type: for example, excess black bile can make both people and cats melancholic (see Paster; Schoenfeldt; Siriasi).

Thus, while human beings formally occupy the top of the ladder of all earthly things, their entanglement with other matter weakens that position. They are highly vulnerable to internal and external influences, all too like nonhuman creatures in the constitution of elements and qualities, and suspended in the network of material correspondences and sympathies. The following selections in Part 1 trace through the foundations and the consequences of this constellation of beliefs in both theory and practice in human entanglement with the world around them.

Hebrew Bible, Genesis 1

Although the Hebrew Bible's current canon was compiled in the first century CE, its roots go back hundreds of years before the birth of Christ, and its account of the Creation echoes Near Eastern cosmologies. The biblical version emphasizes the power of one god who summons up heaven and earth from darkness and void and then populates them. On earth God begins with plants, followed by sea creatures, birds, beasts, and finally man and woman, who are given dominion over all living things. This human-centered story of Creation grounded centuries of thinking about human habitation of the environment, justifying their exploitation of it. The verses following this excerpt relate how, when man and woman were created, they were placed in a garden in the east of Eden, where God made "to grow every tree that is pleasant to the sight, and good for food; the tree of life also in the midst of the garden, and the tree of knowledge of good and evil." When Adam and Eve disobey God and eat from the tree of the knowledge of good and evil, they are banished from Eden, and Adam is told that "cursed is the ground for thy sake; in sorrow shalt thou eat of it all the days of thy life; thorns also and thistles shall it bring forth to thee; and

Source: The King James Version of the Bible, Genesis Chap. 1:1–31.

thou shalt eat the herb of the field" (3:17–18),: thus, the hard work of agriculture originates in an act of betrayal and arrogance.

1 In the beginning God created the heaven and the earth.
2 And the earth was without form, and void; and darkness was upon the face of
the deep. And the Spirit of God moved upon the face of the waters.
3 And God said, Let there be light: and there was light.
4 And God saw the light, that it was good: and God divided the light from the
darkness.
5 And God called the light day, and the darkness he called night. And the eve-
ning and the morning were the first day.
6 And God said, Let there be a firmament in the midst of the waters, and let it
divide the waters from the waters.
7 And God made the firmament, and divided the waters which were under the
firmament from the waters which were above the firmament: and it was so.
8 And God called the firmament heaven. And the evening and the morning
were the second day.
9 And God said, Let the waters under the heaven be gathered together unto one
place, and let the dry land appear: and it was so.
10 And God called the dry land earth; and the gathering together of the waters
called He seas: and God saw that it was good.
11 And God said, Let the earth bring forth grass, the herb yielding seed, and the
fruit tree yielding fruit after his kind, whose seed is in itself, upon the earth:
and it was so.
12 And the earth brought forth grass, and herb yielding seed after his kind, and
the tree yielding fruit, whose seed was in itself, after his kind: and God saw that
it was good.
13 And the evening and the morning were the third day.
14 And God said, Let there be lights in the firmament of the heaven to divide the day
from the night; and let them be for signs, and for seasons, and for days, and years:
15 And let them be for lights in the firmament of the heaven to give light upon
the earth: and it was so.
16 And God made two great lights; the greater light to rule the day, and the
lesser light to rule the night: he made the stars also.
17 And God set them in the firmament of the heaven to give light upon the earth,
18 And to rule over the day and over the night, and to divide the light from the
darkness: and God saw that it was good.
19 And the evening and the morning were the fourth day.
20 And God said, Let the waters bring forth abundantly the moving creature that
hath life, and fowl that may fly above the earth in the open firmament of heaven.

21 And God created great whales, and every living creature that moveth, which
the waters brought forth abundantly, after their kind, and every winged fowl
after his kind: and God saw that it was good.
22 And God blessed them, saying, Be fruitful, and multiply, and fill the waters
in the seas, and let fowl multiply in the earth.
23 And the evening and the morning were the fifth day.
24 And God said, Let the earth bring forth the living creature after his kind,
cattle, and creeping thing, and beast of the earth after his kind: and it was so.
25 And God made the beast of the earth after his kind, and cattle after their
kind, and every thing that creepeth upon the earth after his kind: and God saw
that it was good.
26 And God said, Let us make man in our image, after our likeness: and let
them have dominion over the fish of the sea, and over the fowl of the air, and
over the cattle, and over all the earth, and over every creeping thing that creep-
eth upon the earth.
27 So God created man in his own image, in the image of God created he him;
male and female created he them.
28 And God blessed them, and God said unto them, Be fruitful, and multiply,
and replenish the earth, and subdue it: and have dominion over the fish of the
sea, and over the fowl of the air, and over every living thing that moveth upon
the earth.
29 And God said, Behold, I have given you every herb bearing seed, which is
upon the face of all the earth, and every tree, in the which is the fruit of a tree
yielding seed; to you it shall be for meat.
30 And to every beast of the earth, and to every fowl of the air, and to every
thing that creepeth upon the earth, wherein there is life, I have given every
green herb for meat: and it was so.
31 And God saw every thing that he had made, and, behold, it was very good.
And the evening and the morning were the sixth day.

Aristotle, *Physics*

The Greek philosopher Aristotle (384–322 BCE) deeply influenced both Arabic and European natural philosophy up through early modernity. A student of Plato, Aristotle established his own academy in Athens, where he taught and wrote prolifically on topics including ethics, art, and politics, as well as all as-

Source: *Physics*, translated by R. P. Hardie and R. K. Gaye. *The Complete Works of Aristotle: The Revised Oxford Translation*, edited by Jonathan Barnes, vol. 1, Princeton University Press, 1984, pp. 329–30, 339–40. Bollingen Series 72.

pects of nature. His writings appear in several parts of this anthology, where they touch on plants, animals, and weather. This excerpt comes from Aristotle's *Physics* (*ta physika*, or things pertaining to nature), his foundational treatise on what constitutes "nature," or the nature of things in this world. Here Aristotle responded to Plato's theory that separates the world we know through our senses from that of changeless invisible forms. Like Plato, he sought to understand universals, but he pursued that goal by studying particular things in this world, believing, for example, that the form of a tree exists in each tree, not in an abstract world of forms. Aristotle also grappled with the question of change in the natural world, observing that that tree becomes what it is by evolving from an acorn to maturity. All natural things thus move toward fulfillment or an end. At this excerpt's end, Aristotle does address the role of art in perfecting nature, and the vexing issue of nature's "mistakes," which potentially complicate the idea that natural phenomena "must be for the sake of something; and that such things are all due to nature." As later transmitted by Arabic philosophers and translators, Aristotle's methods and ideas would be debated and imitated for centuries to come, in particular when they intersected with Christian doctrine.

Book II

1. Of things that exist, some exist by nature, some from other causes. By nature the animals and their parties exist, and the plants and the simple bodies (earth, fire, air, water)—for we say that these and the like exist by nature.

All the things mentioned plainly differ from things which are *not* constituted by nature. For each of them has within itself a principle of motion and of stationariness (in respect of place, or of growth and decrease, or by way of alteration). On the other hand, a bed and a coat and anything else of that sort, *qua* receiving these designations—i.e. in so far as they are products of art—have no innate impulse to change. But in so far as they happen to be composed of stone or of earth or of a mixture of the two, they *do* have such an impulse, and just to that extent—which seems to indicate that nature is a principle or cause of being moved and of being at rest in that to which it belongs primarily, in virtue of itself and not accidentally.

I say "not accidentally," because (for instance) a man who is a doctor might himself be a cause of health to himself. Nevertheless it is not in so far as he is a patient that he possesses the art of medicine: it merely has happened that the same man is doctor and patient—and that is why these attributes are not always found together. So it is with all other artificial products. None of them has in itself the principle of its own production. But while in some cases (for instance houses and the other products of manual labor that principle is in something else external to the thing, in others—those which may cause a change in themselves accidentally—it lies in the things themselves (but not in virtue of what they are).

Nature then is what has been stated. Things have a nature, which have a principle of this kind. Each of them is a substance; for it is a subject, and nature is always in a subject.

The term "according to nature" is applied to all these things and also to the attributes which belong to them in virtue of what they are, for instance the property of fire to be carried upwards—which is not a nature nor has a nature but is by nature or according to nature.

What nature is, then, and the meaning of the terms "by nature" and "according to nature," 'has been stated. *That* nature exists, it would be absurd to try to prove; for it is obvious that there are many things of this kind, and to prove what is obvious by what is not is the mark of a man who is unable to distinguish what is self-evident from what is not. (This state of mind is clearly possible. A man blind from birth might reason about colors. Presumably therefore such persons must be talking about words without any thought to correspond.)

Some identify the nature or substance of a natural object with that immediate constituent of it, which taken by itself is without arrangement, e.g. the wood is the nature of the bed, and the bronze the nature of the statue.

[. . .]

But if the material of each of these objects has itself the same relation to something else, say bronze (or gold) to water, bones (or wood) to earth and so on, *that* (they say) would be their nature and substance. Consequently, some assert earth, others fire or air or water or some or all of these, to be the nature of the things that are. For whatever any one of them supposed to have this character—whether one thing or more than one thing—this or these he declared to be the whole of substance, all else being its affections, states, or dispositions. Every such thing they held to be eternal (for it could not pass into anything else), but other things to come into being and cease to be times without number.

This then is one account of nature, namely that it is the primary underlying matter of things which have in themselves a principle of motion or change.

Another account is that nature is the shape or form which is specified in the definition of the thing.

For the word "nature" is applied to what is according to nature and the natural in the same way as "art" is applied to what is artistic or a work of art. We should not say in the latter case that there is anything artistic about a thing, if it is a bed only potentially, not yet having the form of a bed; nor should we call it a work of art. The same is true of natural compounds. What is potentially flesh or bone has not yet its own nature, and does not exist by nature, until it receives the form specified in the definition, which we name in defining what flesh or bone is. Thus on the second account of nature, it would be the shape or form (not separable except in statement) of things which have in themselves a principle of motion. (The combination of the two, e.g. man, is not nature but by nature.)

The form indeed is nature rather than the matter; for a thing is more properly said to be what it is when it exists in actuality than when it exists potentially. Again man is born from man but not bed from bed. That is why people say that the shape is not the nature of a bed, but the wood is—if the bed sprouted, not a bed but wood would come up. But even if the shape *is* art, then on the same principle the shape of man is his nature. For man is born from man.

Again, nature in the sense of a coming-to-be proceeds towards nature. For it is not like doctoring, which leads not to the art of doctoring but to health. Doctoring must start from the art, not lead to it. But it is not in this way that nature is related to nature. What grows *qua* growing grows from something into something. Into what then does it grow? Not into that from which it arose but into that to which it tends. The shape then is nature.

[. . .]

We must explain then first why nature belongs to the class of causes which act for the sake of something; and then about the necessary and its place in nature, for all writers ascribe things to this cause, arguing that since the hot and the cold and the like are of such and such a kind, therefore certain things *necessarily* are and come to be—and if they mention any other cause (one friendship and strife, another mind), it is only to touch on it, and then bid good-bye to it.

A difficulty presents itself: why should not nature work, not for the sake of something, nor because it is better so, but just as the sky rains, not in order to make the corn grow, but of necessity? (What is drawn up must cool, and what has been cooled must become water and descend, the result of this being that the corn grows.) Similarly, if a man's crop is spoiled on the threshing-floor, the rain did not fall for the sake of this—in order that the crop might be spoiled—but that result just followed. Why then should it not be the same with the parts in nature, e.g. that our teeth should come up of necessity—the front teeth sharp, fitted for tearing, the molars broad and useful for grinding down the food—since they did not arise for this end, but it was merely a coincident result; and so with all other parts in which we suppose that there is purpose? Wherever then all the parts came about just what they would have been if they had come to be for an end, such things survived, being organized spontaneously in a fitting way; whereas those which grew otherwise perished and continue to perish, as Empedocles says his "man-faced oxprogeny" did.[1]

Such are the arguments (and others of the kind) which may cause difficulty on this point. Yet it is impossible that this should be the true view. For teeth and all other natural things either invariably or for the most part come about in a given way; but of not one of the results of chance or spontaneity is this true. We do not ascribe to chance or mere coincidence the frequency of rain in winter, but frequent rain in summer we do; nor heat in summer only if we have it in winter. If then it is agreed that things are either the result of coincidence or spontaneity, it follows that they must be for the sake of something; and that such things are all due to nature even the champions of the theory which is before us would agree. Therefore action for an end is present in things which come to be and are by nature.

Further, where there is an end, all the preceding steps are for the sake of that. Now surely as in action, so in nature; and as in nature, so it is in each action, if nothing interferes. Now action is for the sake of an end; therefore the nature of things also is so. Thus if a house, e.g., had been a thing made by nature, it would have been made in the same way as it is now by art; and if things made by nature were made not only by nature but also by art, they would come to be in the same way as by nature. The one, then, is for the sake of the other; and generally art in some cases completes what nature cannot bring to a finish, and in others imitates nature. If, therefore, artificial products are for the sake of an end, so clearly also are natural products. The relation of the later to the earlier items is the same in both.

This is most obvious in the animals other than man: they make things neither by art nor after inquiry or deliberation. That is why people wonder whether it is by intelligence or by some other faculty that these creatures work—spiders, ants, and the like. By gradual advance in this direction we come to see clearly that in plants too that is produced which is conducive to the end—leaves, e.g., grow to provide shade for the fruit. If then it is both by nature and for an end that the swallow makes its nest and the spider its web, and plants grow leaves for the sake of the fruit and send their roots down (not up) for the sake of nourishment, it is plain that this kind of cause is operative in things which come to be and are by nature. And since nature is twofold, the matter and the form, of which the latter is the end, and since all the rest is for the sake of the end, the form must be the cause in the sense of that for the sake of which. Now mistakes

1. The Greek philosopher Empedocles posited such hybrid monstrous creatures once existed.

occur even in the operations of art: the literate man makes a mistake in writing and the doctor pours out the wrong dose. Hence clearly mistakes are possible in the operations of nature also. If then in art there are cases in which what is rightly produced serves a purpose, and if where mistakes occur there was a purpose in what was attempted, only it was not attained, so must it be also in natural products, and monstrosities will be failures in the purposive effort.

Lucretius, *De rerum natura*, or *On the Nature of Things*

We know little of the life of Lucretius (ca. 99–55 BCE), a Roman philosopher and author of the remarkable *De rerum natura* or *On the Nature of Things*, which is a long poem of some 7,400 lines devoted to interpreting the ideas of the ancient Greek philosopher Epicurus (341–270 BCE), whose extensive works survive only in fragments and his followers' readings. Epicurean philosophy argues that the universe is composed fundamentally of atoms and the void; not the gods, but rather the ever-changing interaction of those atoms causes all that happens in the material world. The poem begins by evoking spring as a time of new birth and joy and calling on humans to release themselves from fear of the gods and of death itself. This excerpt articulates the Epicurean principle that nothing can come of nothing, and conversely, that matter can never be fully annihilated. All things come from "fixed seeds" or "primordial germs of things," each with its own "secret power." The order of the world as we apprehend it derives from these germs. In turn, all things on earth may decay and resolve once again into those germs, only to be reborn. This poem's philosophy was obviously antithetical to the Christian doctrine of Creation, and the text was little appreciated until the Renaissance, when it came to influence other theories of atomism.

This terror, then, this darkness of the mind,
Not sunrise with its flaring spokes of light,
Nor glittering arrows of morning can disperse,
But only Nature's aspect and her law,
Which, teaching us, hath this exordium:
Nothing from nothing ever yet was born.
Fear holds dominion over mortality
Only because, seeing in land and sky

Source: Lucretius. *On the Nature of Things*. Translated by William Ellery Leonard, J. M. Dent, 1921, pp. 8–12. *The Internet Classics Archive*, http://classics.mit.edu/Carus/nature_things.2.ii.html.

So much the cause whereof no wise they know,
Men think divinities are working there.
Meantime, when once we know from nothing still
Nothing can be created, we shall divine
More clearly what we seek: those elements
From which alone all things created are,
And how accomplished by no tool of gods.
Suppose all sprang from all things: any kind
Might take its origin from any thing,
No fixed seed required. Men from the sea
Might rise, and from the land the scaly breed,
And, fowl full-fledged come bursting from the sky;
The horned cattle, the herds and all the wild
Would haunt with varying offspring tilth and waste;
Nor would the same fruits keep their olden trees,
But each might grow from any stock or limb
By chance and change. Indeed, and were there not
For each its procreant atoms, could things have
Each its unalterable mother old?
But, since produced from fixed seeds are all,
Each birth goes forth upon the shores of light
From its own stuff, from its own primal bodies.
And all from all cannot become, because
In each resides a secret power its own.
Again, why see we lavished o'er the lands
At spring the rose, at summer heat the corn,
The vines that mellow when the autumn lures,
If not because the fixed seeds of things
At their own season must together stream,
And new creations only be revealed
When the due times arrive and pregnant earth
Safely may give unto the shores of light
Her tender progenies? But if from naught
Were their becoming, they would spring abroad
Suddenly, unforeseen, in alien months,
With no primordial germs, to be preserved
From procreant unions at an adverse hour.
Nor on the mingling of the living seeds
Would space be needed for the growth of things
Were life an increment of nothing: then

The tiny babe forthwith would walk a man,
And from the turf would leap a branching tree—
Wonders unheard of; for, by Nature, each
Slowly increases from its lawful seed,
And through that increase shall conserve its kind.
Whence take the proof that things enlarge and feed
From out their proper matter. Thus it comes
That earth, without her seasons of fixed rains,
Could bear no produce such as makes us glad,
And whatsoever lives, if shut from food,
Prolongs its kind and guards its life no more.
Thus easier 'tis to hold that many things
Have primal bodies in common (as we see
The single letters common to many words)
Than aught exists without its origins.
Moreover, why should Nature not prepare
Men of a bulk to ford the seas afoot,
Or rend the mighty mountains with their hands,
Or conquer Time with length of days, if not
Because for all begotten things abides
The changeless stuff, and what from that may spring
Is fixed forevermore? Lastly we see
How far the tilled surpass the fields untilled
And to the labor of our hands return
Their more abounding crops; there are indeed
Within the earth primordial germs of things,
Which, as the ploughshare turns the fruitful clods
And kneads the mold, we quicken into birth.
Else would ye mark, without all toil of ours,
Spontaneous generations, fairer forms.
Confess then, naught from nothing can become,
Since all must have their seeds, wherefrom to grow,
Wherefrom to reach the gentle fields of air.
Hence too it comes that Nature all dissolves
Into their primal bodies again, and naught
Perishes ever to annihilation.
For, were aught mortal in its every part,
Before our eyes it might be snatched away
Unto destruction; since no force were needed
To sunder its members and undo its bands.

Whereas, of truth, because all things exist,
With seed imperishable, Nature allows
Destruction nor collapse of aught, until
Some outward force may shatter by a blow,
Or inward craft, entering its hollow cells,
Dissolve it down. And more than this, if Time,
That wastes with eld[1] the works along the world,
Destroy entire, consuming matter all,
Whence then may Venus back to light of life
Restore the generations kind by kind?
Or how, when thus restored, may daedal[2] Earth
Foster and plenish[3] with her ancient food,
Which, kind by kind, she offers unto each?
Whence may the water-springs, beneath the sea,
Or inland rivers, far and wide away,
Keep the unfathomable ocean full?
And out of what does aether[4] feed the stars?
For lapsed years and infinite age must else
Have eat all shapes of mortal stock away:
But be it the long ago contained those germs,
By which this sum of things recruited lives,
Those same infallibly can never die,
Nor nothing to nothing evermore return.
And, too, the selfsame power might end alike
All things, were they not still together held
By matter eternal, shackled through its parts,
Now more, now less. A touch might be enough
To cause destruction. For the slightest force
Would loose the weft of things wherein no part
Were of imperishable stock. But now
Because the fastenings of primordial parts
Are put together diversely and stuff
Is everlasting, things abide the same
Unhurt and sure, until some power comes on
Strong to destroy the warp and woof of each:

1. Age
2. Inventive
3. Fill up
4. An element imagined to fill the upper regions of space

Nothing returns to naught; but all return
At their collapse to primal forms of stuff.
Lo, the rains perish which Aether-father throws
Down to the bosom of Earth-mother; but then
Upsprings the shining grain, and boughs are green
Amid the trees, and trees themselves wax big
And lade themselves with fruits; and hence in turn
The race of man and all the wild are fed;
Hence joyful cities thrive with boys and girls;
And leafy woodlands echo with new birds;
Hence cattle, fat and drowsy, lay their bulk
Along the joyous pastures whilst the drops
Of white ooze trickle from distended bags;
Hence the young scamper on their weakling joints
Along the tender herbs, fresh hearts afrisk
With warm new milk. Thus naught of what so seems
Perishes utterly, since Nature ever
Upbuilds one thing from other, suffering naught
To come to birth but through some other's death.

Pliny the Elder, *Naturalis historia,* or *Natural History,* On the Nature of the Earth

A soldier and lawyer, Pliny the Elder (23–79 CE) also composed a massive *Naturalis historia (Natural History)* in thirty-seven books covering the topics of astronomy, geology, zoology, botany, and minerology and embracing all areas of human life. The work was mostly based on his consulting almost five hundred extant authorities on natural history, while he drew on his own experience when he could. The *Natural History* emphasizes comprehensiveness rather than criticism of any of its sources, including bounteous practical information and observations as well as popular beliefs and magical practices based on sympathies and antipathies. In this excerpt Pliny portrays a loving and feminized natural world created to serve humankind, even praising nature's creation of toxins that can provide an easy death. At the same time, when it comes to luxury and excess, Pliny sternly judges humans' misuse of nature; he condemns those who torture the earth's body in search of iron, gold, and gems to

Source: Pliny the Elder. "Nature of the Earth," *The Natural History of Pliny*. Translated by John Bostock and Henry T. Riley, London, 1855, ch. 63. *Perseus Digital Library*, http://data.perseus.org/citations/urn:cts:latinLit:phi0978.phi001.perseus-eng1:2.63.

decorate their own bodies, or those who drench it with the blood of war. The passage also reminds the reader of the natural forces that threaten humanity (not to speak of the earth's latent anger). While recognizably unreliable, because of its comprehensiveness Pliny's *Natural History* served as an authority for both medicine and natural history for centuries to come. (For Pliny's observations on botany, see the excerpt in Part 2; on zoology, see Part 3).

Next comes the earth, on which alone of all parts of nature we have bestowed the name that implies maternal veneration. It is appropriated to man as the heavens are to God. She receives us at our birth, nourishes us when born, and ever afterwards supports us; lastly, embracing us in her bosom when we are rejected by the rest of nature, she then covers us with especial tenderness; rendered sacred to us, inasmuch as she renders us sacred, bearing our monuments and titles, continuing our names, and extending our memory, in opposition to the shortness of life. In our anger we imprecate her on those who are now no more, as if we were ignorant that she is the only being who can never be angry with man. The water passes into showers, is concreted into hail, swells into rivers, is precipitated in torrents; the air is condensed into clouds, rages in squalls; but the earth, kind, mild, and indulgent as she is, and always ministering to the wants of mortals, how many things do we compel her to produce spontaneously! What odors and flowers, nutritive juices, forms and colors! With what good faith does she render back all that has been entrusted to her! It is the vital spirit which must bear the blame of producing noxious animals; for the earth is constrained to receive the seeds of them, and to support them when they are produced. The fault lies in the evil nature which generates them. The earth will no longer harbor a serpent after it has attacked any one, and thus she even demands punishment in the name of those who are indifferent about it themselves. She pours forth a profusion of medicinal plants, and is always producing something for the use of man. We may even suppose, that it is out of compassion to us that she has ordained certain substances to be poisonous, in order that when we are weary of life, hunger, a mode of death the most foreign to the kind disposition of the earth, might not consume us by a slow decay, that precipices might not lacerate our mangled bodies, that the unseemly punishment of the halter may not torture us, by stopping the breath of one who seeks his own destruction, or that we may not seek our death in the ocean, and become food for our graves, or that our bodies may not be gashed by steel. On this account it is that nature has produced a substance which is very easily taken, and by which life is extinguished, the body remaining undefiled and retaining all its blood, and only causing a degree of thirst. And when it is destroyed by this means, neither bird nor beast will touch the body, but he who has perished by his own hands is reserved for the earth.

But it must be acknowledged, that everything which the earth has produced, as a remedy for our evils, we have converted into the poison of our lives. For do we not use iron, which we cannot do without, for this purpose? But although this cause of mischief has been produced, we ought not to complain; we ought not to be ungrateful to this one part of nature. How many luxuries and how many insults does she not bear for us! She is cast into the sea, and, in order that we may introduce seas into her bosom, she is washed away by the waves. She is continually tortured for her iron, her timber, stone, fire, corn, and is even much more subservient to our luxuries than to our mere support. What indeed she endures on her surface might be tolerated, but we penetrate also into her bowels, digging out the veins of gold and silver, and the ores of copper and lead; we also search for gems and certain small pebbles, driving our trenches to a great depth. We tear out her entrails in order to extract the gems with which we may load our fingers. How many hands are worn down that one little joint may be ornamented! If the infernal regions really existed, certainly these burrows of avarice and luxury would have penetrated into them. And truly we wonder that this same earth should have produced anything noxious! But, I suppose, the savage beasts protect her and keep off our sacrilegious hands. For do we not dig among serpents and handle poisonous plants along with those veins of gold? But the Goddess shows herself more propitious to us, inasmuch as all this wealth ends in crimes, slaughter, and war, and that, while we drench her with our blood, we cover her with unburied bones; and being covered with these and her anger being thus appeased, she conceals the crimes of mortals. I consider the ignorance of her nature as one of the evil effects of an ungrateful mind.

Avicenna, *The Canon of Medicine*, On the Elements

Ibn Sina (ca. 980–1037 CE), later known as Avicenna, was a Persian Muslim philosopher and physician whose works strongly influenced the theory and practice of medicine. He wrote many works on physics and theology, but Western scholars mostly now cite him for *The Book of The Cure* and for *The Canon of Medicine*, a critical medical text used in Europe in the middle ages and the Renaissance. In *The Canon of Medicine*, Avicenna synthesized and expanded on Hippocrates's and Galen's medical theories (see introduction to Part 1), as well as Aristotle, to develop a system for describing the human body and generating treatments. This excerpt from *The Canon of Medicine* provides a con-

Source: *A Treatise on the Canon of Medicine of Avicenna, Incorporating a Translation of the First Book*. Translated by O. Cameron Grune, Luzac, 1930, pp. 34–35.

cise description of the elements of earth, water, air, and fire that make up all living bodies and matter. In turn, those elements align with the "qualities" of hot and cold, wet and dry, said to characterize all material things and environmental phenomena. In *The Canon of Medicine*, Avicenna also categorizes the humors, the fluids essential to all animal bodies. The humors themselves have qualities: the sanguineous humor (or blood) is "hot and moist"; the serous humor (or phlegm) is "cold and moist"; the bilious humor (or red/yellow bile) is "hot and dry"; and the "atrabilious humor" or black bile "cold and dry." The balances of these humors can constantly change, influenced by environmental factors such as diet and climate (see also the passage from Avicenna in Part 4 and also the herbals in Part 2, for example, Turner's *Great Herbal*). Thus, the human body is inextricably tied to the natural world it inhabits.

The elements are simple bodies. They are the primary components of the human being throughout all its parts, as well as of all other bodies in their varied and diverse forms. The various orders of beings depend for their existence on the intermixture of the elements.

Natural philosophy speaks of four elements and no more. The physician must accept this. Two are light, and two are heavy. The lighter elements are fire and air; the heavier are earth and water.

[. . .]

The earth is an "element" normally situated at the center of all existence. In its nature it is at rest, and all others natural tend toward it, at however great a distance away they might be. This is because of its intrinsic weight. It is cold and dry in nature and appears so to our sense as long as it not.

The water is a simple substance whose position in nature is exterior to the (sphere of the) earth and interior to (that of) the air. This position is owing to its relative density. In nature it is cold and moist.

[. . .]

Air is a simple substance, whose position in nature is above the sphere of water, and beneath that of fire. This is due to its relative lightness. In nature it is hot and moist, according to the rule which we have given. Its effect and value in (the world of) creation are to rarefy, and to render things finer, lighter, more delicate, softer, and consequently better able to move to the higher spheres.

Fire is a simple substance, which occupies a position in nature higher than that of the other three elements—namely the hollow of the sublunary world, for it reaches to the (world of the) heavens. All things return to it. This is because of its absolute lightness. In nature it is hot and dry. The part which it plays in the construction of things is that it matures, rarefies, refines, and intermingles with all things.

Hildegard of Bingen, *Causae et curae*, or *Causes and Cures*

Living in what is now Germany, the abbess Hildegard of Bingen (1098–1179) wrote theology, natural philosophy, plays, and music, all while founding and managing her own monastic community and preaching through the land. Among other works, she composed a treatise on medicine, *Causae et curae* (*Causes and Cures*), which covers matters of health in the context of biblical history and a vision of the cosmos composed of the elements of fire, air, earth, and water (see also Avicenna, in Part 1). Where she draws on the Galenic theories of the four humors aligned with the interactions of the four elements, Hildegard intertwines the body with the cosmos. In this excerpt from *Causes and Cures*, she describes the creation of the firmament, explaining the effects of storms, thunder, and lightning, which she compares with both boiling water and human anger. She thus anthropomorphizes the weather, while also describing people as both having their own internal weather and affecting the weather in turn, insofar as "all our deeds touch the elements" when they provoke God's judgment. (Hildegard's interpretation of the weather can be compared with others in Part 4: for example, Thomas Jackson's *The Raging Tempest Stilled* and Shakespeare's *King Lear*.)

The elements and the firmament. And God made the elements of the world. They are within the human, and the human concerns himself with them. They are fire, air, water, earth. These four elements are so intricately joined that they cannot be separated from one another. They hold themselves so tightly together that they are called the firmament.

Sun and stars. The sun is almost supreme among them and sends its brightness and fire through them. Around it, there are some stars of such magnitude and brightness that they extend like mountains through the firmament to the earth. Therefore, the closer they are to the earth, the brighter they seem to be. Around the sun there are also other stars of lesser magnitude and brightness. Compared to the magnitude of the aforementioned stars, they are like lowlands and for that reason they appear less clearly.

Storm. When intense warmth and fiery heat are in the ether,[1] sometimes this ardor causes a sudden bubbling up and a dangerous overflowing of the waters, sending them down to the earth. Storms and cloudbursts originate in this way. It is like a pot over a strong fire suddenly boiling over and emitting foam. And such storms, by God's judgment, occur very often as a result of the

Source: Hildegard of Bingen. *On Natural Philosophy and Medicine: Selections from Cause et cure*. Translated by Margaret Berger, D. S. Brewer, 1999, pp. 24–26.

1. An element thought to fill space

humans' past or more recent wrongdoings or to announce future dangers like wars, famine or sudden death. For all our deeds touch the elements and are shaken up by this, because they are tossed about together with the elements. But when lesser warmth and fiery heat are in the ether, they cause a lesser bubbling up and overflowing of the waters. It is like a pot over a weaker fire, boiling less and emitting less foam. Yet when the air is tempered by fire and water, it sends forth pleasant weather and, like a pot over moderate fire, it is pleasantly warm. But when the sun rises such that its fire burns intensely in the height of the sky, then the air is sometimes dry and parched from the heat of the sun, and the fire of the sun touches, at times, the fire of thunder.

Thunder. Lightning. In thunder is judicial fire [Exodus. 9:23–24], coldness and stench. If at some time the fire of thunder is touched by the fire of the sun, it will be agitated ever so slightly and discharge a weak lightning. It will grumble a little and then stop, like a human who sometimes is angered but does not give in to that anger and suppresses it instead. At other times, however, the fire of thunder is strongly agitated by the heat of the sun and is brought into great turmoil so that it will discharge strong and dangerous lightning and raise its voice loudly, like a human who is extremely angry and brings this anger to an end with a dangerous deed. Then too, on occasion, the thunder's upper fire is touched by the sun's fire and makes the coldness that is in thunder concentrate in one place, like water gathering ice in one place. This coldness sends hail to the clouds, and the clouds receive it, disperse it, and send it forth to the earth.

Hail. Snow. Rain. Hail is like the eye of thunder. But when the sun descends in winter, it does no longer send its fire to the height of the sky; then it burns more beneath the earth than above and glows no longer in the height of the sky. Consequently, as a result of the cold, the waters high up become as if dusted with powder and send forth snow. But when these waters, due to warmth, become mild later on, they will send forth rain. And when, at times, the sun displays neither excessive heat nor excessive cold, then it will, at times, send forth a mild rain, as humans when they are happy will very often shed tears for joy.

The winds. The four cardinal winds support the firmament under and above the sun and hold it together. They enclose, as with a cloak, the entire circle, that is, from the lowest to the highest part of the firmament. The east wind embraces the air and pours a very mild dew over everything dry. The west wind mixes with the floating clouds, to keep the waters from erupting. The south wind keeps the fire under its control and prevents it from burning everything. The north wind controls the outer darkness so that it does not exceed its measure. These four winds are the wings of God's power [Psalms. 104:3]. If they are put into motion all at once, they will fold together all the elements and divide themselves, shake up the ocean, and dry up all the waters.

Judgment Day. But now they are locked up by the key of God's majesty, so that the elements remain in balance. And they will not threaten any human with any danger, except at the end of time [Nehemiah 1:3]. For then everything will be purged. Afterwards they will sing their song in harmony. There is no creature that consists of only one property and has not several.

Nothingness. The firmament and the winds. The collateral winds. But nothingness has no property by which it might subsist, and therefore it is nothing. On account of that, other creatures who join nothingness of their own will, lose their properties and turn into nothing.

The firmament comprises fire, sun, moon, stars, and winds. It exists through all of them and is firmed by their properties so that it may not fall apart. As the soul holds the entire body of a human being, so the winds hold together the entire firmament to prevent its destruction. These winds are invisible, just as the soul, stemming from God's secret place, is invisible. As a house does not stand without the support of cornerstones, so neither the firmament, nor the earth, nor the abyss, nor the entire world with all its components would subsist without these winds, because everything is composed and held fast by them. For the entire earth would break asunder and burst if these winds were not there, just as the entire human being would break apart if he had no bones. The principal east wind holds the entire eastern region together, and the principal west wind the entire western region.

Alain de Lille, *De planctu naturae*, or *The Complaint of Nature*

French theologian and poet Alain de Lille (ca. 1128–1202) studied and taught in Paris and Montpelier until he entered the abbey at Cîteaux later in life. Drawing on Christian theology informed by Neoplatonism, Alain's long poetic works on nature, including *De planctu naturae* (*The Complaint of Nature*) and *Anticlaudianus*, comment passionately on humanity's corruption of nature and in turn, nature's subordination to God. In particular, in *The Complaint* he rails against sodomy and other forms of transgressive sexuality as violating nature's laws. While *The Complaint*'s ethical framework is strictly Christian, it also borrows heavily from classical precedents. In Book 1, Alain introduces an elaborate vision of "Lady Nature," God's surrogate in his Creation, an allegory of "Nature" mediating between the divine and the mundane realms. This ex-

Source: Alain of Lille [Alanus de Insulis]. *De planctu naturae*, translated by Douglas M. Moffat. *The complaint of nature*, 1908. Yale Studies in English 36. *Medieval Sourcebook*, https://sourcebooks.fordham.edu/basis/alain-deplanctu.asp. (Pagination preserved in e-text form.)

cerpt derives from a lengthy description of the virgin Lady's Nature's garments, depicting "a parliament of the living creation," including birds, fish, beasts, and plants. Alain paints these creatures in vivid anthropomorphic terms, echoing ideas about animal behavior found in folklore and bestiaries as well as natural histories like Pliny the Elder's as excerpted in Part 3. While representing the abundance of the natural world, these animals' actions symbolize a nature that has already been torn apart by violence, sin, and vanity.

A garment, woven from silky wool and covered with many colors, was as the virgin's robe of state. Its appearance perpetually changed with many a different color and manifold hue. At first it startled the sight with the white radiance of the lily. Next, as if its simplicity had been thrown aside and it were striving for something better, it glowed with rosy life. Then, reaching the height of perfection, it gladdened the sight with the greenness of the emerald. Moreover, spun exceedingly fine so as to escape the scrutiny of the eye it was so delicate of substance that you would think it and the air of the same nature. On it, as a picture fancied to sight, was being held a parliament of the living creation. There the eagle, first assuming youth, then age, and finally returning to the first, changed from Nestor[1] to Adonis.[2] There the hawk, chief of the realm of the air, demanded tribute from its subjects with violent tyranny. The kite assumed the character of, hunter, and in its stealthy preying seemed like the ghost of the hawk. The falcon stirred up civil war against the heron, though this was not divided with equal balance, for that should not be thought of by the name of war where you strike, but I only am struck. The ostrich, disregarding a worldly life for a lonely, dwelt like a hermit in solitudes of desert places. The swan, herald of its own death, foretold with its honey sweet lyre of music the stopping of its life. There on the peacock Nature had rained so great a treasure store of beauty that you would think she afterwards would have gone begging. The phoenix died in its real self, but, by some miracle of nature, revived in another, and in its death aroused itself from the dead. The bird of concord paid tribute to Nature by decimating its brood. There lived sparrows, shrunk to low, pygmean atoms; while the crane opposite went to the excess of gigantic size. The pheasant, after it had endured the confinement of its natal island, flew into our worlds, destined to become the delight of princes. The cock, like a popular astrologer, told with its voice's clock the divisions of the hours. But the wild cock derided its domestic idleness, and roamed abroad, wandering through the woody regions. The horned owl, prophet of misery, sang psalms of future deep

1. Aged King of Pylos in the *Iliad*
2. The handsome mortal lover of Aphrodite

sorrowing. The night owl was so gross with the dregs of ugliness that you would think that nature had dozed at its making. The crow predicted things to come in the excitement of vain chatter. The dubiously colored magpie kept up a sleepless attention to argument. The jackdaw treasured trifles of its commendable thieving, showing the signs of inborn avarice. The dove drunk with the sweet Dionean[3] evil, labored at the sport of Cyprus[4]. The raven, hating the shame of rivalry, did not confess for its brood its own offspring, until the sign of dark color was disclosed, whereupon, as if disputing with itself it acknowledged the fact. The partridge shunned now the attacks of the powers of the air, now the traps of hunters, now the warning barks of dogs. The duck and the goose wintered, according to the same law of living, in their native land of streams. The turtle-dove, widowed of its mate, scorned to return to love, and refused the consolation of marrying again. The parrot on the anvil of its throat fashioned the coin of human speech. There the trick of a false voice beguiled the quail, ignorant of the deceit of the serpent's figure. The woodpecker, architect of its own small house, with its beak's pick made a little retreat in an oak. The hedge-sparrow, putting aside the role of stepmother, with the maternal breast of devotion adopted as its child the alien offspring of the cuckoo; but the offspring, though the subject of so great a boon, yet knew itself not as own son, but as stepchild. The swallow returned from its wandering, and made with mud under a beam its nest and home. The nightingale, renewing the complaint of its ravishment, and making music of harmonious sweetness, gave excuse for the fall of its chastity. The lark, like a high-souled musician, offered the lyre of its throat, not with the artfulness of study but with the mastery of nature, as one most skilled in the lore of melody; and refining its tones into finer, separated these little notes into inseparable chains. The bat, bird of double sex, held the rank of cipher among small birds. These living things, although as it were in allegory moving there, seemed to exist actually.

Fine linen with its white shaded into green, which the maiden, as she herself shortly afterward said, had woven without a seam, and which was not of common material, but rejoiced in a skilled workmanship, served for her mantle. Its many intricate folds showed the color of water, and on it a graphic picture told of the nature of the watery creation, as divided into numerous species. There the whale fought with cliffs, and rushed on and rammed the forts of ships with the rock of its hugely towering body. The sea-dog, (the noisy sound of the name of which is doubly confusing, since it never barks), hunted the hares of its world in the glades of the sea. The sturgeon offered the excellence of

3. Dione is the mother of Aphrodite.
4. The home of Aphrodite, goddess of love

its flesh to royal tables—as a special blessing. The herring, that most common fish, relieved the hunger of the poor with its body which is shared by all. The plaice atoned by its delectable savor for the absence of meat in the forty days rigor. The mullet, with the sweet spices of its flesh, enticed the palates of those who tasted. The trout was baptized on the open sea and entered into the salt gulfs, and was known by the name of salmon. Dolphins by prophetic appearance foretold to ships the rage of the sea to come. There was a fish with the lower members of a siren, and with the face of a man. The luna, bereft of its own light, revenged, seemingly in spite, its private injury on the shell-fish; but the latter, as if laboring in corporeal new moon, atoned for the loss. To these dwellers in the regions of the brine had been assigned the middle portion of the mantle. Its remaining portion held migratory fish, which wandered in various streams, and had their haunts in their own land of fresher water. There the pike, with tyrannical compulsion and not from warranted necessity, imprisoned its subjects in the dungeon of its belly. The barbel, from its small size not renowned, lived with the common fish on more friendly terms. The shad accompanied the vernal season, and offered with the joys of spring the delights of its savor, greeting the tastes of men with its approach. The small muraena, slit with many an opening, gathered the germs of fever for persons dining. The eel, which copied the nature of the serpent, was thought because of its like trait to be the serpent's descendant. The perch, armored with javelins of spines, shunned the insults of the sea-wolf the less. The cat-fish made up in its swollen head that which it lost in the slimness of its lower body. These pictures, finely drawn on the mantle in the manner of sculpture, seemed by miracle to swim.

A damask tunic, also, pictured with embroidered work, concealed the maiden's body. This was starred with many colors, and massed into a thicker material approaching the appearance of the terrestrial element. In its principal part man laid aside the idleness of sensuality, and by the direct guidance of reason penetrated the secrets of the heavens. Here the tunic had undergone a rending of its parts, and showed abuses and injuries. But elsewhere its parts were united in unbroken elegance, and suffered no discord nor division. On these the magic of a picture gave life to the animals of the earth. There the elephant, of prodigious size, came forward in the field, and doubled the body given by nature by a manifold usury. The camel, misshapen in the ruggedness of its rough frame, ministered to the wants of men like a bought slave. There the forehead of the gazelle was seen to be armed with horns in place of a helmet. The bull, pawing the ground with its feet, and roaring with horrible bellowings, foretold the thunderbolts of its warfare. Oxen, which refused the martial exercise of the bulls, stood gaping like rustics, in servile employment. The horse was carried on by hot courage, and fought in aid of its rider, breaking spear with soldier. The ass offended the ears with horrid noises, like a singer of burlesque perpetrating barbarities on music. The unicorn, lulled to sleep in a virgin's bosom, met in sleep the dream of death by enemies. The lion murmured songs of its roaring in the ears of its offspring, and by a wonderful natural magic aroused in them the spark of life. The she-bear gave birth through the openings of its nostrils to an ill-formed progeny; but by licking and shaping them again and again with its long, pointed tongue brought them to a better figure. The wolf lurked in hiding, assuming the employment of the thief, and deserving of eminence on the airy walk of the gallows. The panther roamed through the woods in more open robbery, and preyed on a flock of sheep, not only for their coats, but also for their very bodies. The tiger did violence to the republic of grazing citizens with frequent shedding of innocent blood. The wild ass threw aside the captivity of the domestic ass, and, emancipated by Nature's command, inhabited bold mountains. There the wild boar, by its murderous weapon of a tusk, sold its death to the dogs for many an injury. The dog rent the winds with unsubstantial wounds, and bit the air with impatient tooth. The stag and doe, light in fleetness of foot, gained life by their running, and cheated the wicked jaws of pursuing dogs. The he-goat, clothed in false wool, seemed to disgust the nostrils with a four days' stench. The ram, robed in a nobler tunic, rejoiced in a plurality of wives, and beguiled the honor of marriage. The little fox cast off the dullness of the brute creation, and strove for the finer sagacity of man. The hare, seized with melancholy dread, not in sleep, but in the stupor of fear, dreamed, terrified, of the approach of dogs. The rabbit, which tempers the wrath of our cold climate by its pelt, fought off the attacks of our hunger with its own flesh. The ermine, scorning to be wedded to a more humble garment, laughed or wept in a splendid marriage with lustrous color. The beaver, lest it should suffer division of its very body by an enemy, cut off its end parts. The lynx rejoiced in such clearness of eyesight that, compared with it, the other animals seemed blear-eyed. The marten and the sable, by the elegance of their fur, brought the half-completed beauty of the coverings of the other animals, when it asked for supplements, to the full. This representation of acting form presented these animal figures, as feasts of pleasure, to the eyes of beholders.

Roger Bacon, *Opus majus*, or *Greater Work*

Educated at Oxford and Paris, Roger Bacon (ca. 1214–1292?) became a Franciscan friar around 1247. When his scholarship then attracted the attention of Pope Clement IV, Bacon produced his *Opus majus*, discourses on language,

Source: Roger Bacon. *Opus majus*, translated and edited by Robert Belle Burke, vols. 1–2, University of Pennsylvania Press, 1928, pp. 583–634.

mathematics, optics, and light (as well as two shorter works). In these treatises Bacon argued for deriving knowledge from direct experience of the natural world, rather than relying solely on written authority and logic as was common in the natural philosophy of his time. For Bacon, "experience" was not the same as modern "experimental science"; rather, it ranged from observation of phenomena to inquiry into the occult forces that animate the material world, thus embracing astrology and alchemy. These interests led to his later reputation as a magician, for example, in his appearing in Robert Greene's play *Friar Bacon and Friar Bungay* (1594) as a master of the occult arts. In this excerpt, Bacon critiques the practices of explaining natural phenomena only through the conclusions of reason, using the examples of false reports about stone, water, and animals, including the beaver, an animal of interest in medieval bestiaries (see *Physiologus* and Anselm Turmeda, *Disputation of the Donkey*, in Part 3).

Having laid down fundamental principles of the wisdom of the Latins so far as they are found in language, mathematics, and optics, I now wish to unfold the principles of experimental science, since without experience nothing can be sufficiently known. For there are two modes of acquiring knowledge, namely, by reasoning and experience. Reasoning draws a conclusion and makes us grant the conclusion, but does not make the conclusion certain, nor does it remove doubt so that the mind may rest on the intuition of truth, unless the mind discovers it by the path of experience; since many have the arguments relating to what can be known, but because they lack experience they neglect the arguments, and neither avoid what is harmful nor follow what is good. For if a man who has never seen fire should prove by adequate reasoning that fire burns and injures things and destroys them, his mind would not be satisfied thereby, nor would he avoid fire, until he placed his hand or some combustible substance in the fire, so that he might prove by experience that which reasoning taught. But when he has had actual experience of combustion his mind is made certain and rests in the full light of truth. Therefore reasoning does not suffice, but experience does.

This is also evident in mathematics, where proof is most convincing. But the mind of one who has the most convincing proof in regard to the equilateral triangle will never cleave to the conclusion without experience, nor will he heed it, but will disregard it until experience is offered him by the intersection of two circles, from either intersection of which two lines may be drawn to the extremities of the given line; but then the man accepts the conclusion without any question. Aristotle's statement, then, that proof is reasoning that causes us to know is to be understood with the proviso that the proof is accompanied by its appropriate experience, and is not to be understood of the bare proof. His statement also in the first book of the *Metaphysics* that those who understand the reason and the cause are wiser than those who have empiric knowledge of a fact, is spoken of such as know only the bare truth without the cause. But I am here speaking of the man who knows the reason and the cause through experience. These men are perfect in their wisdom, as Aristotle maintains in the sixth book of the *Ethics*, whose simple statements must be accepted as if they offered proof, as he states in the same place.

He therefore who wishes to rejoice without doubt in regard to the truths underlying phenomena must know how to devote himself to experiment. For authors write many statements, and people believe them through reasoning which they formulate without experience. Their reasoning is wholly false. For it is generally believed that the diamond cannot be broken except by goat's blood, and philosophers and theologians misuse this idea. But fracture by means of blood of this kind has never been verified, although the effort has been made; and without that blood it can be broken easily. For I have seen this with my own eyes, and this is necessary, because gems cannot be carved except by fragments of this stone. Similarly it is generally believed that the castors[1] employed by physicians are the testicles of the male animal. But this is not true, because the beaver has these under its breast, and both the male and female produce testicles of this kind. Besides these castors the male beaver has its testicles in their natural place; and therefore what is subjoined is a dreadful lie, namely, that when the hunters pursue the beaver, he himself knowing what they are seeking cuts out with his teeth these glands. Moreover, it is generally believed that hot water freezes more quickly than cold water in vessels, and the argument in support of this is advanced that contrary is excited by contrary, just like enemies meeting each other. But it is certain that cold water freezes more quickly for anyone who makes the experiment. People attribute this to Aristotle in the second book of the *Meteorologics*; but he certainly does not make this statement, but he does make one like it, by which they have been deceived, namely, that if cold water and hot water are poured on a cold place, as upon ice, the hot water freezes more quickly, and this is true. But if hot water and cold are placed in two vessels, the cold will freeze more quickly. Therefore all things must be verified by experience.

1. An ointment obtained from glands in a beaver's groin

Saint Thomas Aquinas, *Quaestiones disputatae de potentia dei*, or *Disputed Questions on the Power of God*

A major scholastic theologian and authority on Catholic philosophy, Saint Thomas Aquinas (1224–1274) was both a member of the Dominican order and a professor of theology in Paris. Throughout his life, he traveled between Paris and Italy, consumed with his teaching and prolific writings, including his *Summa contra Gentiles* and his *Summa Theologica*. Thomas rooted his thinking about the created world in Aristotelian reasoning, but he also differentiated between what reason and the senses could understand and knowledge based on faith. When considering God's role in nature, Thomas described him as the first cause of all phenomena, working through the powers or secondary causes with which he endowed natural things. This excerpt on how God acts in nature is taken from Thomas's *Quaestiones disputatae de potentia dei*, or *Disputed Questions on the Power of God*; this treatise reflects the form of scholarly disputation at the time whereby questions are posed, possible objections are considered, and a conclusion is offered, with responses to those objections.

Question 3, Article 7: Is God Active in the Actions of Nature?

We should say that we should absolutely grant that God acts in nature and willing its actions. But some did not understand this and fell into error, attributing the whole activity of nature in such a way that the entirely natural thing did nothing by its own power, and different arguments moved them to hold this position.

[Aquinas then goes on to refute this idea as being contrary to reason, which would demonstrate that "nothing regarding natural things is in vain."]

Therefore, we should understand that, in every natural thing, God is active in the nature or will that acts, not that he is active as if the natural things did nothing, and we need to show how we can understand this.

For we should note that we can in many ways call another thing the cause of a thing's action. One way is that the former gives to the latter the power of acting, as the *Physics*[1] says that the producer moves heavy and light things, inasmuch as it gives them the power by which such movement results. God produces all natural actions in this way, since he gave natural things the powers by which they can act, not only as the producer endowed heavy and light things with their power without further preserving it, but also as keeping the power in

Source: *The Power of God*. Translated by Richard J. Regan, Oxford University Press, 2012), pp. 54–56.

1. The *Physics* of Aristotle

existence. For he causes the power bestowed, both as to being made a power to produce and as to existing, so that we can call God the cause of the action inasmuch as he causes and preserves the natural power in existence.

For we say in a second way that something preserving a power causes action, as we say that medicines preserving sight cause seeing. But nothing moves or acts by itself unless it should be the unmoved cause of motion.

We say in a third way that one thing causes another's action insofar as it moves the other to act, regarding which we understand application of a power to action, not the bestowal or preservation of the active power. For example, a human being causes a knife to cut because one applies the knife's sharpness to cutting by moving it. And an active lower nature acts only when moved to do so, since such lower material substances cause change and are themselves changed. But a heavenly body causes change without undergoing change, although it does not cause motion unless it is moved, and this process does not end until we arrive at God. Therefore, it necessarily follows that God causes the action of any natural thing, as the one moving and applying the power to act.

Pseudo-Albertus Magnus, *The Book of the Secrets of Albertus Magnus*

The Book of The Secrets of Albertus Magnus exemplifies many of the popular premodern books of "secrets" dealing with the magical properties of plants, animals, and minerals. Such books proliferated throughout Europe, the Near East, and North Africa throughout the middle ages and long into the seventeenth century. While dismissed by many scholars, they tapped into long-held traditions and beliefs about the natural world held in pagan, Christian, Jewish, and Islamic cultures. Advertising itself as expounding "The Secrets of the Virtues of Herbs, Stones, and Certain Beasts," *The Book of Secrets of Albertus Magnus* dates back to the late thirteenth century. It is spuriously attributed to the German bishop and prolific philosopher Albertus Magnus, who was mostly misremembered in later centuries as an alchemist and magician. Borrowing from multiple sources, the book compiles recipes for deploying the powers of herbs, beasts, and stones based on sympathetic magic, exploiting the inherent affinities that connect everything in the cosmos. This edition of *The Book of Secrets*, first translated and published in the mid-sixteenth century, also contains "a book of the same author of the marvelous things of the world, and of certain effects caused by certain beasts." In that section, in order to explain the

Source: *The Book of the Secrets of Albertus Magnus*, sig. A3–4, sig. F ff, William Jaggard, 1617.

workings of "marvels," the author articulates the basic principles of sympathies and antipathies in the natural world and within the human body, also aligned with heavenly influences. These excerpts include the introduction to the secrets of herbs, with the example of the marigold; the second excerpt comes from the section on marvels laying out the theory of sympathies and antipathies; the third offers a selection of marvelous and miscellaneous secrets mostly deploying the powers of animal parts.

The First Book of the Virtues of Herbs.

Aristotle the prince of philosophers saith in many places, that every science is of the kind of good things. But notwithstanding, the operation sometime is good and sometime evil, as the science is changed unto a good, or to an evil end, to the which it worketh. Of the which saying, two things are concluded: The first is that the science of magic is not evil, for by the knowledge of it, evil may be eschewed, and good by means thereof, may be followed.

The second thing is also concluded, for so much as the effect is praised and so highly esteemed for the end, and also the end of science is dispraised, when it is not ordained to good or to virtue. It followeth then that every science or faculty, or operation, is sometime good, and sometime evil.

Therefore, because science of magic is a good knowledge (as it is presupposed) and is somewhat evil in beholding of causes and natural things, as I have considered and perceived in very many ancient authors: yea and Albert myself have found out the truth in many things and I suppose or imagine the truth to be in some part of the Book of Chirander,[1] and also the book of Alchorae.[2]

First therefore, I will show and declare natures and virtues of certain herbs. Secondly, the operation and estimation of certain stones, and their virtues. And thirdly of certain beasts, and the virtues of them.

The names of the herbs.

Heliotropia	Marigold
Urtica	Nettle
Virga pastoris	Wild teasel
Celidonia	Celandine
Pervinca	Periwinkle
Nepeta	Calamint or Pennyroyal
Lingua Canis	Hound's tongue[3]

1. *Kirandes,* a book of secrets attributed to the King of Persia
2. Cannot be identified but associated with hermetic writings
3. In the borage family

Jusquiamus	Henbane
Lilium	Lily
Viscum querci	Mistletoe
Centaurea	Centaury
Salvia	Sage
Verbena	Vervain
Melisophylos	Smallage[4]
Rosa	Rose
Serpentina	Snake's-grass

All these forenamed herbs shalt thou find in their several places, with their wonderful operation, and workings, but yet if thou dost not observe the times and reasons, wherein they should be ministered and put in practice, all thy labor is of none effect.

The first herb is called with the men of Chaldee, *Elos*, with the Greeks, *Matuchiol*, with the Latins, *Helitropium* with the Englishmen, Marigold: whose interpretation is of *[h]elion* that is the sun, and *tropos* that is alteration or change, because it is turned according to the sun. The virtue of this herb is marvelous; for if it be gathered, the sun being in the sign Leo in August, and wrapped in the leaf of a laurel, or bay tree, and a wolf's tooth added thereto, no man shall be able to have one word to speak against the bearer thereof, but words of peace. If any thing be stolen, and the bearer of the things before named, lay them under his head in the night, he shall see the thief and all his conditions. Moreover, if the aforesaid herb be put in any church, where women be, which have broken matrimony on their part, they shall never be able to go forth of the church, except it be put away. And this last point hath been proved, and is very true.

[. . .]

Here beginneth the Book of the Marvels of the World,
set forth by Albertus Magnus.

After it was known of philosophers, that all kinds of things move and incline to themselves, because an active and rationable[5] virtue is in them, which they guide, and move as well to themselves as to others, as fire moveth to fire, etc.

Also Avicenna[6] said, when a thing standeth long in salt, it is salt, and if anything stand in a stinking place, it is made stinking: and if anything standeth with a bold man, it is made bold, if it stand with a fearful man, it is made fearful.

4. A kind of celery
5. By proportions
6. See Avicenna.

And if a beast companieth with men, it is made tractable and familiar: and generally it is verified of them by reason, and divers experience, that every nature moveth to his kind, and their verifying is known in the first qualities, and likewise in the second, and the same chanceth in the third. And there is nothing in all dispositions and quality, which moveth to itself according to his whole power. And this was the root, and the second beginning of the works of secrets, and turn thou not away the eyes of thy mind. After that this was grafted[7] in the minds of the philosophers then they found the disposition of natural things. For they knew surely that great cold is grafted in some, in other some, great boldness, in some great wrath, in some great fear, in some barrenness is engendered, in some ferventness of love is engendered, in some is one virtue or another engendered, either after the own kind (as boldness and victory is natural to a lion) or *secundum individium*, as boldness is in a harlot, not by a man's kind, but *per individium*,[8] there are by this great marvels and secrets able to be wrought. And they that understood not the marvelousness, and how that might be, despise and cast away all things in which the labor or wit of philosophers was, whose intent was to their own praise in their posterity that they might by their writing make things called false, be holden in great estimation. It is not hidden to the people, that every like helpeth and strengtheneth his like, and loveth, moveth and embraceth it. And physicians have said, and verified, that the liver helpeth the liver in their writings, and every member helpeth his like. And the turners of one metal into another called alchemists know, that by manifest truth, how like nature secretly entereth and rejoiceth of his like. And every science hath now verified that in like. And note this diligently, for marvelous works shall be seen upon this.

Now it is affirmed and put in all men's minds, that every natural kind, and that every particular or general nature hath natural amity and enmity towards an other. And every kind hath some horrible enemy and destroying thing to be feared. Likewise something rejoicing exceedingly, making glad, and agreeing by nature: as the sheep doth fear the wolf, and it knoweth not only him alive but also dead, not only by sight, but also by taste; and the hare feareth the dog, and the mouse the cat, and all four-footed beasts fear the lion, and all flying birds the eagle, and all beasts fear man, and this is grafted to everyone by nature, and some have this, *secundum individium*, and at a certain time.

And it is the certifying of all philosophers that they which hear others in their life, hate their parents and altogether after they die. For a skin of a sheep

7. Instilled
8. To individuals

is consumed of the skin of the wolf, and a timbrel,[9] tabor, or drumslade,[10] made of the skin of a wolf, causeth that which is made of a sheep's skin, not to be heard, and so it is in all others. And note thou this for a great secret.

And it is manifest to all men, that a man is the end of all natural things, and that all natural things are by him, and he overcometh all things. And natural things have natural obedience grafted in them to man, and that man is full of marvelousness, so that in him are all conditions, that is intemperance in hot and cold, temperate in everything that it will, and in him be the virtues of all things, and all secret acts worketh in man's body itself and every marvelous thing cometh forth of him, but a man hath not all these things at one time but in divers times, and in *diversis individuis*,[11] and in him is found the effect of all things.

Thou shalt note how much reason may see and comprehend, and how much thou mayst prove by the experience, and so understand that which is against man.

There is no man but doth know that everything is full of marvelous operations, and thou knowest not which is the greatest operation, till thou hast proved it. But every man despiseth the thing whereof he knoweth nothing, and that hath done no pleasure to him. And everything hath of hot and cold, that is proper to him, and fire is not more marvelous than water, but they are diverse and after another manner, and pepper is not more marvelous than henbane, but after another manner. And he that believeth that marvelousness of things, cometh from hot and cold, cannot but say that there is a thing to be marveled in everything, seeing that everything hath both of hot and cold that is convenient to it. And he that believeth that the marvelousness of things be in stars, of which all things take their marvelous and hid properties, may know that everything hath his proper figure celestial as agreeing to them, of which also cometh marvelousness in working. For everything which beginneth, beginneth under a determinate ascendant and celestial influence, and getteth a proper effect, or virtue of suffering or working a marvelous thing. And he that believeth the marvelousness of things that come by amity and enmity, as buying and selling cannot be denied so to come: and thus universal everything is full of marvelous things, after every way of searching the natures of them. And after that the philosophers knew this, they began to prove and say what is in things.

[. . .]

And they say, if any man put a diamond under the head of a woman sleeping, she manifesteth if she be an adulterer, for if it be so, she leapeth back out of the bed afraid, and if not, she embraceth her husband with great love.

9. Tambourine
10. Drum
11. Different individuals

And they say, that an ass skin when it is hanged upon children, it letteth them to be afraid.

Architas saith, if the wax of the left ear of a dog, be taken and hanged upon men sick in the fevers, that come by course or fits, it is very profitable, and especially to the fever quartain.[12]

And philosophers say, that some kind or singular, which never had sickness, is profitable to every sickness and he that had never pain, helpeth and healeth a man from it.

And when the house is perfumed with the left hoof of a mule, flies remain not in it. If thou wilt know when a woman telleth to thee a lie, take the tongue of sea pie,[13] and convey it cunningly into the bosom of her.

And if the heart, eye or brain of a lap-wing or black plover, be hanged upon a man's neck, it is profitable against forgetfulness, and sharpeneth man's understanding.

If a woman may not conceive, take an hart's horn, turned into powder, and let it be mixed with a cow's gall, let a woman keep it about her, and let her do the act of generation, and she shall conceive.

A gross and stiff hair of a mare's tail put upon a door, suffereth not zauzales[14] to enter. The tooth of a foal or colt of one year old, put in the neck of a child, maketh his teeth to breed without pain.

The tooth of a mare put upon the head of a man being mad, delivereth him from his fury.

If a woman may not conceive, let a mare's milk be given her not known, let her do the act of generation in that hour and she shall conceive.

The hoof of a horse perfumed in a house driveth away mice: the same chanceth also by the hoof of a mule.

Giambattista della Porta, *Magia naturalis*, or *Natural Magic*

Born into a noble Neapolitan family, the playwright and natural philosopher Giambattista della Porta (1535?–1615) was known across Europe as a professor of secrets, that is, of experiments and recipes for transforming things in the natural world for human uses. His *Magia naturalis* (1558), or *Natural Magic*, a book "wherein are set forth all the riches and delights of the natural sciences," covers a vast number of secrets concerning "the generation of animals," "pro-

12. A fever that recurs every four days
13. An oystercatcher bird
14. Gnats

Source: *Natural Magick by John Baptista Porta, a Neapolitan; in Twenty Books* [. . .] *Wherein are Set Forth All the Riches and Delights of the Natural Sciences*, London: 1658, pp. 2, 59, 64, 68.

duction of new plants," and "strange cures," among many other chapters. Della Porta carefully distinguishes his "natural magic" from "sorcery," though this did not prevent him from having his work censored by the ecclesiastical authorities (compare with *The Book of the Secrets of Albertus Magnus*, above). He argues that natural magic did not mean opposing nature but rather using art to open up the occult powers of natural things, insofar as the "works of magic are nothing else but the works of nature, whose dutiful hand-maid magic is." He envisions an eroticized natural world animated by sympathies or attractions, both love and hate, which the natural magician may manipulate. This excerpt on the generation of plants details how a natural magician can imitate nature's infinite "copulations" and fertility in order to produce new varieties of plants or make plants flourish outside their natural seasons. Despite the Catholic Church's effort to suppress such work, *Natural Magic* continued to influence thinking about the manipulation of nature well into the seventeenth century (see for example, Hugh Platt, and Francis Bacon's *New Atlantis* in Part 1 and Thomas Johnson in Part 3).

The text is from the English translation of 1658.

There are two sorts of magic: the one is infamous, and unhappy, because it hath to do with foul spirits, and consists of enchantments and wicked curiosity; and this is called sorcery, an art which all learned and good men detest. Neither is it able to yield any truth of reason or nature, but stands merely upon fancies and imaginations, such as vanish presently away, and leave nothing behind them, as Iamblichus[1] writes in his book concerning the mysteries of the Egyptians. The other magic is natural, which all excellent wise men do admit and embrace, and worship with great applause; neither is there anything more highly esteemed, or better thought of, by men of learning. The most noble philosophers that ever were, Pythagoras, Empedocles, Democritus, and Plato, forsook their own countries, and lived abroad as exiles and banished men, rather than as strangers, and all to search out and to attain this knowledge; and when they came home again, this was the science which they professed, and this they esteemed a profound mystery. They that have been most skillful in dark and hidden points of learning, do call this knowledge the very highest point, and the perfection of natural sciences; insomuch that if they could find out or devise amongst all natural sciences, any one thing more excellent or more wonderful then another, that they would still call by the name of magic. Others have named it the practical part of natural philosophy, which pro-

1. A third-century CE Syrian Neoplatonist philosopher

duceth her effects by the mutual and fit application of one natural thing unto another. The Platonics,[2] as Plotinus imitating Mercurius, writes in his book of Sacrifice and Magic, makes it to be a science whereby inferior things are made subject to superiors, earthly are subdued to heavenly; and by certain pretty allurements, it fetcheth forth the properties of the whole frame of the world. Hence the Egyptians termed Nature herself a magician, because she hath an alluring power to draw like things by their likes; and this power, say they, consists in love, and the things that were so drawn and brought together by the affinity of nature, those (they said) were drawn by magic. But I think that magic is nothing else but the survey of the whole course of nature. For, whilst we consider the heavens, the stars, the elements, how they are moved, and how they are changed, by this means we find out the hidden secrecies of living creatures, of plants, of metals, and of their generation and corruption; so that this whole science seems merely to depend upon the view of nature, as afterward we shall see more at large. This doth Plato seem to signify in his Alcibiades, where he saith, that the magic of Zoroaster, was nothing else, in his opinion, but the knowledge and study of divine things, wherewith the kings' sons of Persia, amongst other princely qualities, were endued; that by the example of the commonwealth of the whole world, they also might learn to govern their own commonwealth.[3] And Tully,[4] in his book of divinations, saith, That amongst the Persians no man might be a king, unless he had first learned the art of magic, for as Nature governs the world by the mutual agreement and disagreement of the creatures, after the same sort they also might learn to govern the commonwealth committed unto them. This art, I say, is full of much virtue, of many secret mysteries; it openeth unto us the properties and qualities of hidden things, and the knowledge of the whole course of Nature; and it reacheth us by the agreement and the disagreement of things, either so to sunder them, or else to lay them so together by the mutual and fit applying of one thing to another, as thereby we do strange works, such as the vulgar sort of magic was wont to flourish in Ethiopia and India, where was great store of herbs and stones, and such other things as were fit for these purposes. Wherefore, as many of you as come to behold magic, must be persuaded that the works of magic are nothing else but the works of Nature, whose dutiful handmaid magic is. For if she find any want in the affinity of Nature, that it is not strong enough, she doth supply such defects at convenient seasons, by the help

2. Neoplatonic philosophers

3. In the first Platonic dialogue of Alcibiades: Zoroaster (also known as Zarathustra) was said to be an ancient Persian spiritual leader and philosopher.

4. Cicero

of vapors, and by observing due measures and proportions; as in husbandry, it is Nature that brings forth corn and herbs, but it is art that prepares and makes way for them.

[. . .]

We have rehearsed concerning divers kinds of new living creatures; now shall I speak of plants, which ravish with admiration the eyes and minds of those that contemplate on them, with their abundant pleasantness, and wonderful elegancy. These bring more profit, and by these a natural philosopher may seem more admirable. For use made with the earth is more honest and honorable then with other things and the ground never grows old or barren, but is everywhere naturally rank to receive new feed, and to produce new; and is ever unsatisfied in fruitfulness, and brings perpetual increase: and if nature be always admirable, she will seem more wonderful in plants. Copulation was but of one kind, here it is almost infinite; and not only every tree can be engrafted into every tree, but one tree may be adulterated with them all. Living creatures of divers kinds were not easily produced, and those that come from other countries were hard to get: here is no difficulty at all; grafts are fetched and sent, if need be, to any part of the world. And if diversity of creatures are made in Africa, by their copulating when they meet at the rivers, that so new creatures are always produced; here in Italy, where the air is always calm, and the climate very indulgent, strange and wild plants find a good harbor, and ground to grow in, which is the mother and nourisher of all, and so fruitful to produce new and diversity of plants, that it can hardly be exhausted. And we can better write of them, and know the truth more than others, because we have them still before our eyes, and an opportunity to consider of their effects. And if our ancestors found many new things, we by adding to theirs, have found many more, and shall produce more excellent things overpassing them, because daily by our art, or by chance; by nature, or new experience, new plants are made.

[. . .]

As we heard before of divers living creatures, that they might be mingled into one, by copulation; so now we will shew also how to contrive divers kinds of fruits, by grafting into one fruit: for grafting is in plants the same that copulation is in living creatures. Yet I deny not, but there are other means whereby this may be effected, as well as by grafting. But above all other, grafting is most praiseworthy, as being the best and fittest means to incorporate one fruit into another, and so of many to make one, after a wonderful manner. And whereas it may be thought a very toilsome, and indeed impossible matter, here the excellent effect of the work must sweeten all thy labor, and thy painful diligence will take away the supposed impossibility of the thing and perform that which a man would think were not possible to be done. Neither must thou suffer thy self to be discouraged herein by the sayings of rude husbandmen which have attempted this thing, but for want of skill could not perform it, seeing experience teacheth thee that it hath been done. Wherefore against such discouragements, thou must arm thy self with a due consideration of such experiments as the ancients have recorded: as for example, that the fig tree may be incorporated into the plane tree, and the mulberry tree; and likewise the mulberry tree into the chestnut tree, the turpentine tree, and the white poplar, whereby you mayest procure white mulberries; and likewise the chestnut tree into a hazel, and an oak; and likewise the pomegranate tree into all trees, for that it is like to a common whore, ready and willing for all comers; and likewise the cherry tree into a turpentine tree. And to conclude, that every tree may be mutually incorporated into each other, as Columella supposeth. And this is the cause of every composition of many fruits into one, of every adopted fruit which is not the natural child, as it were, of the tree that bare it; and this is the cause of all strange and new kinds of fruits that grow. Virgil makes mention of such a matter, when he saith, that Dido admired certain trees which she saw, that bore new kinds of leaves, and apples that naturally were not their own. And Palladius[5] saith, that trees are joined together as it were, by carnal copulation, to the end that the fruit thereof might contain in it, all the excellencies of both the parents; and the same trees were garnished with two sorts of leaves, and nourished with two sorts of juices, and the fruit had a double relish, according to both the kinds whence it was compounded. But now, as we did in our tract of the commixtion of divers kinds of living creatures; so here also it is meet to prescribe certain rules, whereby we may cause those divers plants which we would intermingle, to join more easily, and to agree better together, for the producing of new and compounded fruits.

[. . .]

Art being as it were Nature's ape, even in her imitation of nature, effecteth greater matters when nature doth. Hence it is that a magician being furnished with art, as it were another nature, searching thoroughly into those works with nature doth accomplish by many secret means and close operations, doth work upon nature, and partly by that which he sees, and partly by that which he conjects and gathers from thence, takes his sundry advantages of nature's instruments, and thereby either hastens or hinders her work, making things ripe before or after their natural season, and so indeed makes nature to be his instrument. He knows that fruits, and flowers, and all other growing things that the world affords, are produced by the

5. Roman writer on agriculture

circuit and motion of celestial bodies; and therefore when he is disposed to hinder the ripening of anything, or else to help it forward, that it may be more rare and of better worth, he effects it by counterfeiting the times and seasons of the year, making the winter to be as the summer, and the spring-time as the winter.

Guillaume du Bartas, *La sepmaine ou creation du monde*, or *Divine Weeks and Works*, On the Seventh Day

La sepmaine ou creation du monde (1578) of Guillaume du Bartas (1544–1590), a distinguished poet and diplomat in the French court of Henry IV, is an epic poem recounting the seven days of Creation from the beginnings of light to the day of rest. It describes in exquisite detail all the elements of the cosmos and natural world. Highly popular in France and throughout Europe up through the mid-seventeenth century, the poem was translated into multiple languages, including Josuah Sylvester's English translation, *Divine Weeks and Works* (1605). In Sylvester's translation, the part on the seventh day when God rests to view his creation begins by evoking a painter admiring his own work, a massive landscape painting including scenes of romantic cliffs and grottos, pigeon-hunting, plowing, shepherding, seafaring, and a city, all post-lapsarian models of humans both peacefully and violently inhabiting the natural world. The passage then shifts to describe God happily contemplating his lovely universe, one in constant motion of wind, fire, and water, while the ball of the earth stands "steady still" at the center. Du Bartas's Creation is thus at once dynamic and completely under God's control.

The Seventh Day of the First Week

In sacred rest, upon this sacred day
Th' Eternal doth his glorious works survey;
His only power and providence persevere
T' uphold, maintain, and rule the world for ever.
Maugre[1] men's malice and Hell's raging mood,
God turneth all things to his children's good.
Sabbath's right use: from all worlds-works to cease;
To pray (not play) and hear the word of peace;

Source: *Bartas: His Divine Weekes and Workes Translated: And Dedicated to the Kings Most Excellent Majestie, by Josuah Sylvester*, London, 1605, pp. 233–35.

1. In spite of

Instructions drawn from dead and living things,
And from our selves, for all estates, for kings.

The cunning painter, that with curious care,
Limning[2] a land-scape, various, rich, and rare,
Hath set a-work, in all and every part,
Invention, judgment, nature, use and art;
And hath at length (t'immortalize his name)
With weary pencil perfected the same,
Forgets his pains, and, inly fill'd with glee,
Still on his picture gazeth greedily.

First in a mead[3] he marks a frisking lamb,
Which seems (though dumb) to bleat unto the dam.
Then he observes a wood, seeming to wave.
Then th' hollow bosom of some hideous cave;
Here a high-way, and there a narrow path;
Here pines, there oaks torn by tempestuous wrath.
Here from a craggy rocks steep-hanging boss
(Thrumm'd[4] half with ivy, half with crisped moss)
A silver brook in broken streams doth gush,
And head-long down the horned cliff doth rush.
Then winding thence above and underground,
A goodly garden it be-moateth round.
There, on his knee (behind a box-tree shrinking)
A skillful gunner with his left eye winking,
Levels directly at an oak hard by,
Whereon a hundred groaning culvers[5] cry;
Down falls the cock,[6] up from the touch-pan[7] flies
A ruddy flash that in a moment dies,
Off goes the gun, and through the forest rings
The thundering bullet, born on fiery wings.
Here, on a green, two striplings, stripped light,
Run for a prize with labor some delight;

2. Painting
3. Meadow
4. Fringed
5. A dove or pigeon
6. Of the gun
7. Part of the gun

A dusty cloud about their feet doth flow
(Their feet, and head, and hands, and all do go)
They swelled in sweat, and yet the following rout[8]
Hastens their haste with many a cheerful shout.
Here, six pied oxen, under painful yoke,
Rip up the folds of Ceres' winter cloak.
Here, in the shade, a pretty shepherdess
Drives softly home her bleating happiness.
Still as she goes, she spins, and as she spins,
A man would think some sonnet she begins.
Here runs a river, there springs forth a fountain,
Here vails a valley, there ascends a mountain,
Here smokes a castle, there a city fumes,
And here a ship upon th' ocean looms.
In brief, so lively, art hath nature shaped,
That in his work the workman's self is rapt,
Unable to look off; for, looking still.
The more he looks, the more he finds his skill.

So th' Architect (whose glorious workmanship
My cloudy muse doth but too-much eclipse)
Having with pain-less pain, and care-less care,
In these six days, finished the table fair
And infinite of th' universal ball,
Resteth this day, t' admire Himself in all;
And for a season eying nothing else,
Joys in His work, sith all His work excels
(If my dull, stutting[9] frozen eloquence
May dare conjecture of His high intents).

One while, He sees how th' ample sea doth take,
God saw that all that he had made, was perfectly good.
The liquid homage of each other lake;
And how again the heav'ns exhale, from it,
Abundant vapors (for our benefit).
And yet it swells not for those tribute streams,
Nor yet it shrinks not for those boiling beams.

8. Crowd
9. Stuttering

There sees He th' ocean-people's plenteous broods;
And shifting courses of the ebbs and floods,
Which with inconstant glances night and day
The lower planets forked front doth sway.
Anon, upon the flowery plains he looks,
Laced about with snaking silver brooks.
Now, He delights to see four brethren's[10] strife
Cause the world's peace, and keep the world in life:
Anon, to see the whirling spheres to roll
In restless dances about either pole,
Whereby, their cressets[11] (carried divers ways)
Now visit us, anon th' Antipodes.[12]
It glads Him now to note how th' orb of flame,
Which girts this globe, doth not enfire the frame;
How th' airs glib-gliding firmless body bears
Such store of fowls, hail-storms, and floods of tears;
How th' high water, pronest to descend,
'Twixt air and earth is able to depend;
And how the dull earth's prop-less massy ball
Stands steady still, just in the midst of all.
Anon His nose is pleas'd with fragrant scents
Of balm, and basil, myrrh, and frankincense,
Thyme, spikenard,[13] hyssop, savory, cinnamon,
Pink, violet, rose, and clove-carnation.
Anon, his ear's charm'd with the melody
Of winged consorts curious harmony:
For, though each bird, guided with artless art,
After his kind, observe a song apart,
Yet the sole burden of their several lays
Is nothing but the heav'n-King's glorious praise.
In brief, th'Almighty's eye, and nose, and ear,
In all His works, doth naught see, scent, or hear,
But shows his greatness, saviors of His grace,
And sounds His glory over every place.
But above all, man's many beauteous features

10. The four winds
11. Lanterns
12. Places on the opposite sides of the globe
13. Aa aromatic plant, possibly valerian

Detain the Lord more than all other creatures:
Man's his own minion; man's His sacred type,[14]
And for man's sake, He loves his workmanship.

Hugh Platt, *Floraes Paradise*

While trained as a lawyer, in his time Hugh Platt or Plat (1552–1608) thrived in London's entrepreneurial culture that sought to produce and profit from innovation in everything from household tasks to energy production. He published over a dozen books: among the most well-known are *The Jewell House of Art and Nature, Containing Divers Rare and Profitable Inventions, Together with Sundry New Experiments in the Art of Husbandry, Distillation, and Moulding* (1594), which is a miscellany of recipes and curious inventions, and *Delights for Ladies* (1600), a compendium of advice on cookery and cosmetics. In this excerpt from his letter to the reader in his *Floraes Paradise* (1608), which collates his thoughts and recommendation on horticultural matters, Platt explains that his book should produce profit for people who want it but also pleasure for the better sort who like "to provoke Nature to play." While he may represent his horticultural knowledge as based on experience, he clearly owed a debt to "natural magicians" like Giambattista della Porta. This excerpt's sample of secrets from *Floraes Paradise* oscillates between a skeptical view of what human beings can do to manipulate the natural world and a belief in art's power to transform it, reflecting Platt's own interest in alchemy. His thoughts on cultivating gillyflowers can be contrasted with other writers' comments on transforming plants, including Della Porta himself, and Gervase Markham, John Parkinson, and Andrew Marvell in Part 6.

Having out of mine own particular experience, as also by long conference with diverse gentlemen of good skill and practice, in the altering, multiplying, enlarging, planting, and transplanting, of sundry sorts of fruits and flowers, at length obtained a pretty volume of experimental observations in this kind, and not knowing the length of my days, nay, assuredly knowing that they are drawing to their period, I am willing to unfold my napkin, and to deliver my poor talent abroad, to the profit of some, who by their manual works, may gain a

14. Figural representation

Source: Hugh Plat[t]. *Floraes Paradise Beautified and Adorned with Sundry Sorts of Delicate Fruites and Flowers, by the Industrious Labour of H. P. Knight*, sig. A3–4, A7r, London, 1608, pp. 78–82; 141–42 :

greater employment, than heretofore in their usual callings; and to the pleasuring of others, who delight to see a rarity spring out of their own labors, and to provoke Nature to play, and to shew some of her pleasing varieties, when she hath met with a stirring workman.

I hope, so as I bring substantial and approved matter with me, though I leave method at this time to schoolmen,[1] who have already written many large and methodical volumes of this subject (whose labors have greatly furnished our studies and libraries, but little or nothing altered or graced our gardens and orchards) that you will accept my skill, in such a habit and form as I shall think most fit and appropriate for it; and give me leave rather to write briefly and confusedly, with those that seek out the practical, and operative part of nature whereunto but a few in many ages have attained, then formally and largely, to imitate her theorists, of whom each age affordeth great store, and plenty.

[. . .]

And thus, gentle reader, having acquainted thee with my long, costly, and laborious collections, not written at adventure, or by an imaginary conceit in a scholar's private study, but wrung out of the earth, by the painful hand of experience; and having also given thee a touch of Nature whom no man as yet ever durst send naked into the world without her veil; and expecting, by thy good entertainment of these, some encouragement for higher and deeper discoveries hereafter, I leave thee to the god of Nature, from whom all the true light of nature proceedeth.

[. . .]

Remove a plant of stock-gillyflowers[2] when it is a little wooded, and not too green, and water it presently; do this three days after the full, and remove it twice more before the change. Do this in barren ground, and likewise three days after the next full moon, remove again; and then remove once more before the change. Then at the third full moon, viz. eight days after, remove again, and set it in very rich ground, and this will make it to bring forth a double flower. But if your stock-gillyflowers once spindle, then you may not remove them. Also, you must shade your plant with boughs for three or four days after the first removing; and so of pinks, roses, daisies, feverfew, etc., that grow single with longstanding. In removing, break not the least root. Make tulips double in this manner. Some think by cutting them at every full moon before they bear, to make them at length to bear double.

1. Scholastic or theoretical writers
2. A form of carnation

By sitting upon a hill late in an evening, near a wood, in a few nights a fire-drake[3] will appear; mark where it lighteth, and there you shall find an oak with mistletoe therein, at the root whereof there is a mistle child, whereof many strange things are conceived. *Beati qui non crediderunt.*[4]

Gather your grapes at the full of the moon, and when they are full ripe, slip each bunch from the stock whereupon it grew, and hang those bunches along by beams, in the roof of a warm chamber, that doth not open to the east, or to the north, and these will keep plump and fresh till our Lady day, or there-about; or else with every bunch, cut off some of the stock whereupon the stalk grew, and then hang up the bunches. Both these ways be true. *Per* S.[5]

[. . .]

All those fantastical conceits,[6] of changing the color, taste, or scent, of any fruit, or flower, by infusing, mixing, or letting in to the bark, or at the roots of any tree, herb, or flower, of any colored, or aromatic substance, Master Hill[7] hath by often experience sufficiently controlled; and though some fruits and flowers, seem to carry the scent, or taste, of some aromatic body, yet that doth rather arise from their own natural infused quality, then from the hand of man.

Francis Bacon, *Novum organum*, or *New Organon*, and *New Atlantis*

Sir Francis Bacon (1561–1626) is credited with developing the scientific method, which emphasizes experiment and observation of natural phenomena as the means to understand and influence them. A lawyer who devoted his life to public service, serving at one point as Lord Chancellor, he also avidly pursued questions of scientific inquiry and the history of natural knowledge in the project he called the "Great Instauration," which appeared in several volumes: first, in English in *The Advancement of Learning* (1605), and later in an expanded Latin version, *De augmentis scientiarum* (1623); and second, in his *Novum organum*, or *New Organon* ("organon" is the term

3. A will-o'-the-wisp, or light appearing in marshland
4. "Blessed those who have not believed."
5. A reference to his source for the hint
6. Ideas
7. Thomas Hill, author of *The Gardener's Labyrinth* (see Part 6)

Source: Translation of *Novum Organum* in *The Work of Francis Bacon*, edited by James Spedding, Robert Leslie Ellis, and Douglas Denon Heat, vol. 8, London, 1858, pp. 68–70, 167, 178–81.

used for Aristotle's logical treatises), published in Latin in 1620. The *New Organon* advocates abandoning scholastic logic in natural philosophy and instead adopting a method of observation and inductive reasoning, proceeding from analyzing particulars to developing axioms of natural knowledge. Bacon wrote in the preface to the plan for the Great Instauration that he aimed to study "nature under constraint and vexed, that is to say, when by art and the hand of man she is forced out of her natural state and squeezed and molded"; at the same time, however, he asserted in his *New Organon* that "Nature to be commanded must be obeyed." The first excerpt below is from Part 1 of the *New Organon*, which combines aphorisms and discursive analysis to deliver Bacon's ideas. These aphorisms depict the seeker of natural knowledge as a "servant and interpreter of nature" and denigrate the application of mere "logic." The second excerpt, from Part 2, clarifies Bacon's distinction between the work of human knowledge, "of a given nature to discover the form, or true specific difference, or nature-engendering nature," and "human power" "to generate and superinduce a new nature or new natures."

During the time that he was laboring on his "Great Instauration," Francis Bacon also composed his *New Atlantis*, an unfinished work of science fiction most likely written around 1614 and published posthumously in 1626. Like Thomas More's *Utopia* (see Part 7), in representing the ideal island world of Bensalem, *New Atlantis* offers an image of a society based on rationality and the pursuit of knowledge. The text culminates in a vision of a College of Knowledge, or "Salomon's House," a collaborative scientific institution that takes all of the natural world as its province for study: there "the end of our foundation is the knowledge of causes and the secret motions of things, and the enlargement of the bounds of human empire, to the effecting of all thing possible." Bacon's vision of Salomon's House would inform later grand plans for the systematic study of the natural world, including the formation of the Royal Society. At the same time that *New Atlantis* thus gazes forward, however, it also looks backward; it was published at the end of Bacon's *Sylva sylvarum, or, a Natural History in Ten Centuries*, an eclectic collection of "experiments" indebted to the previous century's writers of natural "secrets" such as Giambattista della Porta. The types of experiments proposed in the College's enterprise reflect the concerns of those professors of secrets with conserving, preserving, prolonging, converting, and hybridizing things in nature, as well as practices of imitating them, obsessions that would continue to be both advocated and debated later in the seventeenth century (see for example, Hugh Platt, Gervase Markham, John Parkinson, and Andrew Marvell, all in Part 6). (The speaker in this excerpt is the "Father" of Salomon's

House, instructing the narrator, one of a group of Spanish voyagers who happened upon Bensalem.)

Aphorisms

I. Man, being the servant and interpreter of nature, can do and understand so much and so much only as he has observed in fact or in thought of the course of nature: beyond this he neither knows anything nor can do anything.

II. Neither the naked hand nor the understanding left to itself can effect much. It is by instruments and helps that the work is done, which are as much wanted for the understanding as for the hand. And as the instruments of the hand either give motion or guide it, so the instruments of the mind supply either suggestions for the understanding or cautions.

III. Human knowledge and human power meet in one; for where the cause is not known the effect cannot be produced. Nature to be commanded must be obeyed; and that which in contemplation is as the cause is in operation as the rule.

IV. Towards the effecting of works, all that man can do is to put together or put asunder natural bodies. The rest is done by nature working within.

V. The study of nature with a view to works is engaged in by the mechanic, the mathematician, the physician, the alchemist, and the magician; but by all (as things now are) with slight endeavor and scanty success.

VI. It would be an unsound fancy and self-contradictory to expect that things which have never yet been done can be done except by means which have never yet been tried.

VII. The productions of the mind and hand seem very numerous in books and manufactures. But all this variety lies in an exquisite subtlety and derivations from a few things already known; not in the number of axioms.

VIII. Moreover the works already known are due to chance and experiment rather than to sciences; for the sciences we now possess are merely systems for the nice ordering and setting forth of things already invented; not methods of invention or directions for new works.

IX. The cause and root of nearly all evils in the sciences is this—that while we falsely admire and extol the powers of the human mind we neglect to seek for its true helps.

X. The subtlety of nature is greater many times over than the subtlety of the senses and understanding; so that all those specious meditations, speculations, and glosses in which men indulge are quite from the purpose, only there is no one by to observe it.

XI. As the sciences which we now have do not help us in finding out new works, so neither does the logic which we now have help us in finding out new sciences.

XII. The logic now in use serves rather to fix and give stability to the errors which have their foundation in commonly received notions than to help the search after truth. So it does more harm than good.

XIII. The syllogism is not applied to the first principles of sciences, and is applied in vain to intermediate axioms; being no match for the subtlety of nature. It commands assent therefore to the proposition but does not take hold of the thing.

XIV. The syllogism consists of propositions, propositions consist of words, words are symbols of notions. Therefore if the notions themselves (which is the root of the matter) are confused and over-hastily abstracted from the facts, there can be no firmness in the superstructure. Our only hope therefore lies in a true induction.

XV. There is no soundness in our notions whether logical or physical. Substance, quality, action, passion, essence itself, are not sound notions: much less are heavy, light, dense, rare, moist, dry, generation, corruption, attraction, repulsion, element, matter, form, and the like; but all are fantastical and ill defined.

[. . .]

Book 2

I. On a given body to generate and superinduce[1] a new nature or new natures, is the work and aim of human power. Of a given nature to discover the form, or true specific difference, or nature-engendering nature, or source of emanation (for these are the terms which come nearest to a description of the thing), is the work and aim of human knowledge. Subordinate to these primary works are two others that are secondary and of inferior mark; to the former, the transformation of concrete bodies, so far as this is possible; to the latter, the discovery, in every case of generation and motion, of the latent process carried on from the manifest efficient and the manifest material to the form which is engendered; and in like manner the discovery of the latent configuration of bodies at rest and not in motion.

[In the following aphorisms Bacon unfolds the function of the four kinds of causes of natural phenomena, "the material, the formal, the efficient, and the final," and focuses on the methods of inquiry into each of the causes and

1. Add to a preexisting thing

methods and principles underlying the process of "superinduction." He also explores his concept of "Forms" or general and constant causes.]

X. Having thus set up the mark of knowledge, we must go on to precepts, and that in the most direct and obvious order. Now my directions for the interpretation of nature embrace two generic divisions; the one how to educe and form axioms from experience; the other how to deduce and derive new experiments from axioms. The former again is divided into three ministrations; a ministration to the sense, a ministration to the memory, and a ministration to the mind or reason.

For first of all we must prepare a natural and experimental history, sufficient and good; and this is the foundation of all; for we are not to imagine or suppose, but to discover, what nature does or may be made to do.

New Atlantis

The end of our foundation is the knowledge of causes, and secret motions of things; and the enlarging of the bounds of human empire, to the effecting of all things possible. The preparations and instruments are these. We have large and deep caves of several depths. The deepest are sunk 600 fathoms, and some of them are digged and made under great hills and mountains. So that if you reckon together the depth of the hill, and the depth of the cave, they are (some of them) above three miles deep. For we find, that the depth of a hill, and the depth of a cave from the flat, is the same thing; both remote alike, from the sun, and heavens beams, and from the open air. These caves we call the Lower Region. And we use them for all coagulations, indurations,[2] refrigerations, and conservations of bodies. We use them likewise for the imitation of natural mines; and the producing, also of new artificial metals, by compositions and materials which we use and lay there for many years. We use them also sometimes (which may seem strange) for curing of some diseases, and for prolongation of life, in some hermits that choose to live there, well accommodated of all things necessary, and indeed live very long; by whom also we learn many things.

We have burials in several earths, where we put divers cements, as the Chinese, do their porcelain. But we have them in greater variety, and some of them more fine. We also have great variety of composts, and soils, for the making of the

Source: *New Atlantis, a work unfinished written by the Right Honourable Francis, Lord Verulam, Viscount St. Alban*, London, 1658, pp. 29–31.

2. The act of hardening

earth fruitful. We have high towers; the highest about half a mile in height and some of them likewise set upon high mountains, so that the vantage of the hill with the tower, is in the highest of them three miles at least. And these places we call the Upper Region, accounting the air between the high places, and the low, as a middle region. We use these towers, according to their several heights, and situations, for insolation, refrigeration, conservation, and for the view of divers meteors, as winds, rain, snow, hail, and some of the fiery meteors also. And upon them, in some places, are dwellings of hermits, whom we visit sometimes, and instruct what to observe.

We have great lakes, both salt, and fresh, whereof we have use for the fish, and fowl. We use them also for burials, of some natural bodies: for we find a difference in things buried in earth, or in air below the earth and things buried in water. We have also pools, of which some do strain fresh water out of salt; and others by art do turn fresh water into salt. We have also some rocks in the midst of the sea, and some bays upon the shore for some works, wherein is required the air and vapor of the sea. We have likewise violent streams and cataracts, which serve us for many motions; and likewise engines for multiplying and enforcing of winds, to set also on going divers motions.

We have also a number of artificial wells and fountains, made in imitation of the natural sources and baths, as tincted upon vitriol, sulphur, steel, brass, lead, nitre, and other minerals; and again, we have little wells for infusions of many things, where the waters take the virtue quicker and better, than in vessels or basins. And amongst them we have a water, which we call water of Paradise, being, by that we do it, made very sovereign[3] for health and prolongation of life.

We have also great and spacious houses, where we imitate and demonstrate meteors; as snow, hail, rain, some artificial rains of bodies, and not of water, thunders, lightnings; also generations of bodies, in air, as frogs, flies, and divers others.

We have also certain chambers, which we call chambers of health, where we qualify the air as we think good and proper for the cure of divers diseases, and preservation of health. We have also fair and large baths, of several mixtures, for the cure of disease and the restoring of man's body from rarefaction; and others for the confirming of it in strength of sinews, vital parts, and the very juice and substance of the body.

We have also large and various orchards, and gardens, wherein we do not so much respect beauty, as variety of ground and soil, proper for divers trees and herbs; and some very spacious, where trees and berries are set, whereof we

3. Beneficial

make divers kinds of drinks, besides the vineyards. In these we practice likewise all conclusions of grafting, and inoculating, as well of wild trees, as fruit-trees, which produceth many effects; and we make (by art) in the same orchards, and gardens, trees, and flowers, to come earlier or later than their seasons; and to come up and bear more speedily than by their natural course they do. We make them also by art greater much than their nature, and their fruit greater, and sweeter, and of differing taste, smell, color, and figure, from their nature. And many of them we so order, that they become of medicinal use. We have also means to make divers plants rise, by mixtures of earths without seeds; and likewise to make divers new plants, differing from the vulgar; and to make one tree or plant turn into another.

We have also parks, and enclosures of all sorts of beasts, and birds, which we use not only for view or rareness, but likewise for dissections and trials, that thereby we may take light, what may be wrought upon the body of man. Wherein we find many strange effects, as continuing life in them, though divers parts, which you account vital, be perished, and taken forth, resuscitating of some that seem dead in appearance; and the like. We try also all poisons, and other medicines upon them, as well of surgery, as physic. By art likewise we make them greater or taller, than their kind is, and contrariwise dwarf them and stay their growth; we make them more fruitful and bearing than their kind is, and contrary wise barren and not generative. Also we make them differ in color, shape, activity many ways. We find means to make commixtures and copulations of diverse kinds, which have produced many new kinds, and them not barren, as the general opinion is. We make a number of kinds of serpents, worms, flies, fishes, of putrefaction; whereof some are advanced (in effect) to be perfect creatures, like beasts, or birds, and have sexes, and do propagate. Neither do we this by chance, but we know before hand, of what matter and commixture, what kind of those creature will arise.

Hannah Wolley, *The Ladies Directory*

Hannah Wolley or Woolley (1622–ca.1675), often cited as the first Englishwoman to make an income by publishing, brought to print the centuries-old tradition of manuscript recipes for cookery, household management, and medicine, written

Source: *The Ladies Directory in Choice Experiments and Curiosities of Preserving in Jellies, and Candying Both Fruits & Flowers: Also, an Excellent Way of Making Cakes, Comfits, and Rich Court-Perfumes; With Rarities of Many Precious Waters; Among Which, are Doctor Stephens's Water, Dr. Matthias's Palsie-Water; And an Excellent Water Against the Plague; With Several Consumption Drinks, Approved by the Ablest Physicians*, London, 1662, p. 21.

mostly by women for women (see the recipe of Johanna St. John for using plants—and a few woodlice—to cure a cancer). Wolley's first recipe book, *The Ladies Directory* (1661), proved so successful that she wrote several other best-selling books of cookery and household "secrets" that established her international reputation. *The Ladies Directory* offers many recipes for cooking but also "rarities of many precious waters" meant to cure disease. This example, a water to cure consumption (tuberculosis), demonstrates how such recipes combined and distilled everyday and exotic ingredients derived from the natural world, which amounted to a form of experimental science in itself.

A very rare water, which hath restored many (as I can very well witness) out of deep consumptions.

Take a red cock, pluck him alive, then slit him down the back, and take out all his entrails, cut him in quarters, and bruise him in a mortar, put him into an ordinary still, with a pottle[1] of sack, and a quart of milk, new from a red cow, one pound of currants beaten, one pound of raisins in the sun stoned and beaten, four ounces of dates stoned and beaten, two handfuls of penny-royal, two handfuls of pimpernel, or any other cooling herb, one handful of wild thyme, one handful of rosemary, and one handful of borage, one quart of red-rose-water, two ounces of hartshorn, two ounces of chiney;[2] paste up your still very close, and still it with a soft fire; put into the glass wherein it droppeth, one pound of sugar-candy beaten very small, twelve penny-worth of leaf-gold, seven grains of musk, eleven grains of amber-grease, seven grains of unicorn's horns, seven grains of bezoar stone;[3] when it is all stilled, mix all the waters together, and every morning fasting, and every evening when you go to rest, take four or five spoonfuls of it warm, for about a month together. This hath cured many whom the doctors have given over.

Margaret Cavendish, *The Blazing World*

In her time Margaret Cavendish, Duchess of Newcastle (1623–1673), published serious and witty poems, plays, novels, and philosophical treatises while also cutting an eccentric public figure. As an intellectual she immersed herself in

1. A pot with a capacity of a half a gallon of liquid
2. A bit of bacon fat
3. A stone-like formation in the intestines of some animals

Source: *The Description of a New World, Called the Blazing-World Written by the Thrice Noble, Illustrious, and Excellent Princess, the Duchess of Newcastle*, London, 1668, pp. 41–43. *A Celebration of Women Writers*, http://digital.library.upenn.edu/women/newcastle/blazing/blazing.html.

natural philosophy, beginning early with her work on atomism in her *Poems and Fancies* (1653), followed closely by her *Philosophical Fancies* (1653), in which she largely repudiated that atomism. She then published *Philosophical and Physical Opinions* (1655; revised edition 1663) in which she developed her ideas of vitalist materialism (later reprising those ideas in 1668 in her *Grounds of Natural Philosophy* excerpted here in Part 3). In those works she argues that all matter is changing and self-moving and all vital matter is both sensitive and rational, whether animal, vegetable, or mineral; sensitive matter receives impressions, and rational matter orders the forms of the world. While curious about every aspect of nature's working, Cavendish distrusted the experimental work advocated by the members of the Royal Society. Today her best-known work is her utopian romance *The Description of a New World, called the Blazing-World,* published first in 1666 and again as a solo volume in 1668. Here Cavendish imagines that a young woman is abducted to another universe, where she is named empress. There she converses with fantastical creatures, including Bear-men, Fish-men, Bird-men, Ape-men, and Worm-men, who represent different branches of scientific inquiry in Cavendish's time. The Empress asks probing questions about natural causes and effects and critiques many of the answers, which often contradict each other. In this excerpt, she shares her skepticism about what is knowable while she also uses the Worm-men's opinions to express some of her own natural philosophy. When she hears the Ape-men, the chemists, she finally dismisses them to pronounce her own judgment that "Nature is but one infinite self-moving body, which by the virtue of its self-motion, is divided into infinite parts, which parts being restless, undergo perpetual changes and transmutations by their infinite compositions and divisions."

The Empress was so wonderfully taken with this discourse of the Worm-men, that she not only pardoned the rudeness they committed in laughing at first at her question, but yielded a full assent to their opinion, which she thought the most rational that ever she had heard yet; and then proceeding in her questions, inquired further, whether they had observed any seminal principles within the earth free from all dimensions and qualities, which produced vegetables, minerals, and the like? To which they answered, that concerning the seeds of minerals, their sensitive perceptions had never observed any; but vegetables had certain seeds out of which they were produced. Then she asked, whether those seeds of vegetables lost their species, that is, were annihilated in the production of their off-spring? To which they answered, that by an annihilation, nothing could be produced, and that the seeds of vegetables were so far from being annihilated in their productions, that they did rather numerously increase and multiply; for the division of one seed, said they, does produce numbers of seeds out of itself. But replied the Empress, A particular part cannot increase of itself. 'Tis true, answered they: but they increase not barely of themselves, but by joining and commixing with other parts, which do assist them in their productions, and by way of imitation form or figure their own parts into such or such particulars. Then, I pray inform me, said the Empress, what disguise those seeds put on, and how they do conceal themselves in their transmutations? They answered, that seeds did no ways disguise or conceal, but rather divulge themselves in the multiplication of their off-spring; only they did hide and conceal themselves from their sensitive perceptions so, that their figurative and productive motions were not perceptible by animal creatures. Again, the Empress asked them, whether there were any non-beings within the earth? To which they answered, That they never heard of any such thing; and that, if her Majesty would know the truth thereof, she must ask those creatures that are called immaterial spirits, which had a great affinity with non-beings, and perhaps could give her a satisfactory answer to this question. Then she desired to be informed, What opinion they had of the beginning of forms? They told her Majesty, That they did not understand what she meant by this expression; For, said they, there is no beginning in nature, no not of particulars; by reason nature is eternal and infinite, and her particulars are subject to infinite changes and transmutations by virtue of their own corporeal, figurative self-motions; so that there's nothing new in nature, not properly a beginning of anything. The Empress seem'd well satisfied with all those answers, and inquired further, whether there was no art used by those creatures that live within the earth? Yes, answered they: for the several parts of the earth do join and assist each other in composition or framing of such or such particulars; and many times, there are factions and divisions; which cause productions of mixed species; as, for example, weeds, instead of sweet flowers and useful fruits; but gardeners and husbandmen use often to decide their quarrels, and cause them to agree; which though it shews a kindness to the differing parties, yet 'tis a great prejudice to the worms, and other animal-creatures that live under ground; for it most commonly causes their dissolution and ruin, at best they are driven out of their habitations. What, said the Empress, are not worms produced out of the earth? Their production in general, answered they, is like the production of all other natural creatures, proceeding from the corporeal figurative motions of nature; but as for their particular productions, they are according to the nature of their species; some are produced out of flowers, some out of roots, some out of fruits, some out of ordinary earth. Then they are very ungrateful children, replied the Empress, that they feed on their own parents which gave them life. Their life, answered they, is their own, and not their parents; for no part or creature of nature can either give or take away life; but parts do only assist and join with parts, either in dissolution or production of other parts and creatures.

After this, and several other conferences, which the Empress held with the Worm-men, she dismissed them; and having taken much satisfaction in several of their answers, encouraged them in their studies and observations. Then she made a convocation of her chemists, the Ape-men, and commanded them to give her an account of the several transmutations which their art was able to produce. They began first with a long and tedious discourse concerning the primitive ingredients of natural bodies; and how, by their art, they had found out the principles out of which they consist. But they did not all agree in their opinions; for some said, that the principles of all natural bodies were the four elements, fire, air, water, earth, out of which they were composed. Others rejected this elementary commixture, and said, there were many bodies out of which none of the four elements could be extracted by any degree of fire whatsoever; and that, on the other side, there were divers bodies, whose resolution by fire reduced them into more than four different ingredients; and these affirmed, that the only principles of natural bodies were salt, sulfur, and mercury. Others again declared, that none of the aforementioned could be called the true principles of natural bodies; but that by their industry and pains which they had taken in the art of chemistry, they had discovered, that all natural bodies were produced but from one principle, which was water; for all vegetables, minerals, and animals, said they, are nothing else, but simple water distinguished into various figures by the virtue of their seeds. But after a great many debates and contentions about this subject, the Empress being so much tired that she was not able to hear them any longer, imposed a general silence upon them, and then declared herself in this following discourse.

I am too sensible of the pains you have taken in the art of chemistry, to discover the principles of natural bodies, and wish they had been more profitably bestowed upon some other, then such experiments; for both by my own contemplation, and the observations which I have made by my rational and sensitive perception upon nature, and her works, I find, that nature is but one infinite self-moving body, which by the virtue of its self-motion, is divided into infinite parts, which parts being restless, undergo perpetual changes and transmutations by their infinite compositions and divisions. Now, if this be so, as surely, according to regular sense and reason, it appears no otherwise; it is in vain to look for primary ingredients, or constitutive principles of natural bodies, since there is no more but one universal principle of nature, to wit, self-moving matter, which is the only cause of all natural effects.

Thomas Sprat, *History of the Royal Society*

In 1662 Charles II chartered the Royal Society of London for Improving Natural Knowledge to promote "physico-mathematical experimental learning." Deriving much of their approach from the ideas of experimental science advocated by Francis Bacon, this group of scholars, gentlemen amateurs, and collectors of exotica, who made up the Society, met frequently to perform experiments and share their observations of natural phenomena. In 1667 Thomas Sprat (1635–1713), a clergyman and Society fellow, published a *History of the Royal Society* defending their practices against accusations of impiety and lack of productivity, adding reports of experiments and the members' observations. Sprat describes the Society as dedicated to the disinterested pursuit of knowledge, unburdened by either ideology or a desire for profit, for the benefit of England. To illustrate the Society's work, Sprat listed the kind of experiments undertaken on the elements of fire, earth, air, and water, as well as vegetal matter and animals. The list's apparently random nature suggests that, while the fellows were methodologically committed to experimentation, they were largely driven by curiosity and an attraction to marvels and exotica as well as commonplace natural phenomena. For more excerpts from the *History of the Royal Society*, see Robert Hooke's recommendations for measuring the effects of the weather in Part 5 and a report about strange natural phenomena in Java in Part 7.

[Sprat lists four types of experiments concerning fire, air, water, and minerals.]

The fifth kind is of the growth of vegetables in several kinds of water, as river-water, rain-water, distilled-water, May-dew; of hindering the growth of seed corn in the earth, by extracting the air and furthering their growth, by admitting it; of steeping seeds of several kinds; of inverting the positions of roots, and plants set in the ground, to find whether there are values in the pores of the wood, that only open one way; of the decrease of the weight of plants growing in air; of *lignum fossil*;[1] of the growing of some branches of rosemary, by only sprinkling the leaves with water; of camphire wood; of wood brought from the Canaries;[2] of a stinking wood brought out of the East Indies; of the reunion of the bark of trees after it had been separated from the body.

The sixth are experiments medicinal, and anatomical: as of cutting out the spleen of a dog; of the effects of vipers biting dogs; of a chameleon, and its

Source: Thomas Sprat. *The History of the Royal-Society of London for the Improving of Natural Knowledge*, London, 1667, p. 223.

1. Petrified wood
2. Canary Islands

dissection; of preserving animals in spirit of wine, oil of turpentine, and other liquors; of injecting various liquors, and other substances, into the veins of several creatures.

Experiments of destroying mites by several fumes; of the equivocal generation of insects; of feeding a carp in the air; of making insects with cheese, and sack; of killing water-newts, toads, and glow-worms with several salts; of killing frogs, by touching their skin, with vinegar, pitch, or mercury; of a spider's not being enchanted by a circle of unicorn's horn, or Irish earth, laid round about it.

Experiments with a poisoned Indian dagger on several animals; with the Macasser[3] poison: with Florentine poison, and several antidotes against it; of making flesh grow on, after it has been once cut off; of the grafting a spur on the head of a cock, and its growing; of the living of creatures by factitious[4] air; of the reviving of animals strangled, by blowing into their lungs; of flesh not breeding worms, when secur'd from fly-blowings; of the suffocation of animals upon piercing the thorax; of hatching silk-worms eggs in rarified air; of transfusing the blood of one animal into another.

Sor Juana Inés de la Cruz, "First Dream"

Born near Mexico City, Sor Juana Inés de la Cruz (1648–1695) was largely self-educated. Recognized as a child prodigy, she was welcomed into the Viceroy of Mexico's court, where she displayed her acumen in multiple fields of knowledge and her poetic talents blossomed. However, in 1667 she decided to enter a convent and spent the rest of her life as a nun. She was hardly cloistered, however, and maintained her intellectual contacts; by the end of her life she was famous throughout Mexico and Spain. Among her few surviving works is a baroque philosophical poem, "First Dream," in which the speaker imagines her soul freed in sleep to gather together all its intellectual powers and survey from on high all of God's Creation. But the soul struggles to comprehend through mere sight all at once, and so it resolves then to consider all the levels of being, beginning with minerals and ascending to man. Even then, the speaker says, the mind becomes absorbed in the most minute details of the natural world, like the intricate form of a flower. The dream ends at the break of day with the speaker being overwhelmed by the task.

3. From Macasser in Indonesia

4. Artificial

Source: *A Sor Juana Anthology*. Translated by Alan S. Trueblood, Harvard University Press, 1988, pp. 186–90.

In this excerpt Sor Juana weaves together the perspectives of scientific observation, poetics, and cosmology with a depth of poetic detail and expansion. She contemplates both the immense task of comprehending the natural world around us and the powers and limitations of a mind and soul lodged in a human body.

Of this series now my mind
desired to pursue the method:
namely, from the basest level
of being—the inanimate
(the one least favored
by the second productive cause,[1]
yet still not wholly destitute)—
to move on to the nobler hierarchy,
which, in respect to vegetative vigor,
is the firstborn, however rude,
of Thetis[2]—and the first to cling
to her fruitful maternal breasts
and draw by power of suction on the sweet
and gushing springs of that terrestrial humor
which for its natural sustenance
is a sweetest nutriment—
a hierarchy furnished with some four
operations diverging in their action,
now attracting, now excluding carefully
whatever it judges unsuited to itself,
now expelling superfluities and making
the most useful of countless substances its own;[3]
then, this form once examined,
to scrutinize another form,[4] more beautiful—
one that possesses feeling
(and, what is more, equipped with powers
of apprehending through imagination):
grounds for legitimate complaint—
if not indeed for claiming insult—

1. Nature, in Aristotelian philosophy; the first cause is God
2. A sea nymph
3. The four operations of vegetal life, as derived from Aristotle
4. I.e., of animals

on the part of the brightest star
that sparkles, yet lacks all feeling,
however magnificent its brilliant light—
for the lowest, tiniest creature
surpasses even the loftiest of stars,
arousing envy;
and making of this bodily way of knowing
a foundation, however meager,
to move on to the wondrous
composite,[5] triplicate
(set up on three concordant lines)
mysterious compendium
of all the lower forms:[6]
the hinge that makes the link
between the purest nature,
that which occupies the highest throne,[7]
and the least noble of the creatures,
the most abject,
equipped not only with the five
faculties of sense,
but ennobled also by the inner ones,[8]
the three that rule the rest;
for not for nothing was he fitted out
by the powerful and knowing hand
to be supreme over all the others:
the goal of all his works, the circle
clasping heaven and earth in one,
utmost perfection of creation,
utmost delight of its Eternal Author,
with whom well pleased, well satisfied,
His immense magnificence took His rest;
creature of portentous fashioning
who may stretch proud arms to heaven
yet suffers sealing of his mouth with dust;
whose mysterious image might be found

5. I.e., human beings
6. Humans are three-part, because they have vegetal, sensitive, and rational elements.
7. Angels
8. Intellect, memory, and will

in the sacred vision seen in Patmos
by the evangelic eagle,[9] that strange vision
which trod the stars and soil with equal step;
or else in that looming statue
with sumptuous lofty brow
made of the most prized metal,
who took his stance on flimsy feet
made of the material least regarded,
and subject to collapse at the slightest shudder.[10]

In short, I speak of man, the greatest wonder
the human mind can ponder,
complete compendium
resembling angel, plant, and beast alike;
whose haughty lowliness
partook of every nature. Why?
Perhaps that, being more fortunate
than any, he might be lifted high
by a grace of loving union.
Oh, grace repeated often,
yet never recognized sufficiently,
overlooked, so one might think,
so unappreciated is it,
so unacknowledged it remains.

These then were the stages over which
I sometimes wished to range; yet other times
I changed my mind, considering much too daring
for one to try to take in everything,
who failed to understand the very smallest,
the easiest part
of those effects of nature
that lie so close at hand;
who, seeing the laughing brook, could never grasp
the hidden means whereby
she steers her crystal course,
pausing at times for roundabout meanders,

9. St. John the Evangelist
10. See Daniel 2:31–33.

conducting her bright search
through Pluto's grim recesses
and through the frightful caverns
of the deep and terrifying chasm
through lovely countryside,
the pleasant Elysian Fields,
once bridal chamber for his triform wife[11]
(useful inquisitiveness, however trivial,
that brought the goddess of the flaxen hair[12]
sure word of her fair missing daughter
when, searching high and low through woods and hills,
investigating every field and grove,
she sought her very life and all the while
was losing her life from grief);
who, seeing a tiny flower, could not tell
why with an ivory pattern
its fragile beauty is girt about;
why a mixture of colors—
scarlet blending into white of dawn—
tints its fragrant costume,
why its scent is of amber,
why it unravels in the breeze
a wrapping so delicately beautiful
(renewed in its every newborn child)
and makes a bright show of flounces
fluted with golden streaks
which, once the bud's white seal is broken,
boastfully display the tincture
born of the Cyprian goddess'[13] sweet wound,
unless, indeed, the whiteness of the daybreak
or the redness of the dawn
has overwhelmed it, fusing
red snowflake with snow-whitened rose,
such opalescence soon eliciting
acclaim sought from the meadow;
perhaps a tutor in the vanity—

11. Persephone, daughter of Demeter, both queen of the underworld and goddess of agriculture
12. Demeter, goddess of the earth
13. Aphrodite

unless indeed an impious demonstration
of the feminine duplicity which makes
the deadliest poison twice as deadly
in the conspicuous overlay
of the woman who feigns a glowing countenance.[14]

14. Refers to a practice of using cosmetics that were poisonous

PART II

Plants

Modern city-dwellers mostly experience a distant or mediated relationship with plants: their processed vegetables, grains, and fruits arrive packaged in stores; out-of-season flowers come from abroad; and plant-derived drugs are pulverized into powders. Agribusiness cultivates most of our plants used for food and medicine, and even suburban gardeners may depend on commercial nurseries and chemical companies for their efforts. However, in preindustrial cultures, whether cultivating or consuming them, people knew their plants as living in their seasons and places.

From the beginning Western philosophers have asked exactly what kind of living beings plants are, in contrast to animals. In the traditional *scala naturae*, or ladder of nature, they rank above minerals and below animals. When Aristotle defined the boundaries of their existence, he acknowledged that plants reproduce like other living beings and that they move insofar as they grow in all directions, but he averred that they do not feel and certainly do not think. While early philosophers may have thus attributed to plants a "vegetal soul," they denied them the autonomy and agency associated with mobility, as well as the sensitive and reasoning faculties unique to animals and humans (see Marder).

At the same time, however, premodern cultures attributed to plants astonishing powers, expressed in the notion of a plant's "virtues," omnipresent in early natural history, herbal medicine, and magic. The term dates back to the Latin "virtus," a word associated with masculine honor and bravery. According to the *Oxford English Dictionary*, "virtue" may denote "the power inherent in a thing; a capacity for producing a certain effect; an active property or principle; a faculty"; for plants, a virtue is then "power to affect the body in a beneficial manner; strengthening, sustaining, or healing power." The key word here is power, granting plants a form of agency expressed through action in animal bodies. Beginning with Dioscorides' *De materia medica* and extending up through Johanna St. John's manuscript herbal recipes, many excerpts in Part 2 of this anthology track this centuries-old tradition of strongly connecting plants with other living things. Partly those associations are rooted in humoral medicine (see introduction to Part 1 and Avicenna), in which plants have the same hot, dry, wet, and cold properties as animals, and can thus alter properties in other bodies, but those associations also echo beliefs in the sympathies and antipathies that animate all the natural world (see, for example, the *Secrets of Albertus Magnus* in Part 1).

The sense that plants thus mimic or echo the features of human bodies also lent itself to their functioning symbolically in literature and art (see Goody; Hyde 2005). So, for example, Pliny might have recommended twenty-one remedies derived from the lily, but later in Christianity the lily also became a symbol of the Virgin Mary. Medieval and early modern poetry used the rose as a suggestive metaphor for a woman who is an object of desire, ready to be plucked and enjoyed (see *Le roman de la rose* [Part 6] and Pierre Ronsard's "Ode to Cassandra" [Part 2]). More generally, flowers came to symbolize both the beauty and the fragility of human existence in general. In this way, in the poetic imagination the *scala naturae* collapsed through analogy (see Thomas; Feerick and Nardizzi 2012).

As since the beginning of civilization humans have cultivated, altered, and trafficked in everything from cereal crops and fruit trees to exotic flowers, plants have always participated as much in culture, society, and economic life as in nature. When the Greek philosopher Theophrastus argued that a domesticated plant's "true nature" lies in its cultivated rather than its wild form, he articulated a formulation of nature/culture that persisted for millennia. Long before knowledge of plant genetics, farmers and gardeners sought to improve plants for human uses, endlessly speculating about exactly how and why plants grow the way they do and dreaming of controlling that process. This anthology's Parts 5 and 6, on inhabiting the land and on gardening, respectively, explore in more depth the complex history of plant cultivation, especially controversies over grafting that were often coded debates about the natural order of human society (see also, for example, Della Porta, Markham, Marvell and Parkinson in Part 6; on grafting controversies, see Bushnell). In the explosion of the global plant trade and commerce in plants that occurred in the late sixteenth and seventeenth centuries, attention turned in particular to the gardener's and the scientist's powers to shape, name, and categorize a plant, paralleling questions about social change.

In the end, all premodern writing about plants entails reflections about people and our place in the natural order. Plants are seen to be there to serve us, but they also pose a mystery in their very silence and unintelligible force. Not only do we depend on plant life for survival but we also resemble them in so many ways, whether materially when composed of the same elements and qualities, or symbolically, in the brevity and vulnerability of our lives.

Theophrastus, *De causis plantarum*, or *On the Causes of Plants*

After the death of his teacher Aristotle in 322 BCE, Theophrastus (ca. 372–ca. 287 BCE) became the head of the Lyceum and presided there until his own death. Highly respected then for his metaphysics and natural philosophy, he is remembered today for writing the first systematic treatises on botany, *Historia plantarum*, or *On the History of Plants* and *De causis plantarum, or On the Causes of Plants*. *On the History of Plants* undertakes classifying and describing all plants then known, while also exploring their interaction with animals through sympathies and antipathies. In *On the Causes of Plants*, in turn, Theophrastus theorizes how plants grow and recommends the best practices for cultivating them. In particular, he contemplates what art may do to a plant's nature. As this excerpt suggests, he believed that the true "nature" of a domesticated plant inheres in its cultivated form, especially when it provides food for humans. In turn, if such a plant is neglected, it can degenerate and, in fact, become something quite different and in that sense "unnatural." Theophrastus thus fashioned a model for naturalizing culture, which could extend beyond plants to animals and people (see William Lawson [Part 6] on a tendency to degeneration in humans as well as trees).

A General Problem: Is Nature and the Natural to be Seen in What Grows Unaided or in What is Under Cultivation?

But starting from this last point one could perhaps raise a further problem, this time one that applies to all plants and is of general scope: are we to study the nature of a plant in those that grow without human aid or in those growing under various forms of cultivation, and which of the two kinds of growth is natural? (Much the same as this, or rather a part of it, is the question whether we are to study the nature of a given kind from its wild or cultivated form.)

Unaided Growth is Natural

For the nature contains the starting-point in itself, and we speak here of the "natural" (and what we see in plants that grow unaided by man is of this description), contrasting it to what is of external causation, especially

Source: Theophrastus. *De causis plantarum*. Translated by Benedict Einarson and George K. K. Link, vol. 1, Harvard University Press / W. Heinemann, 1976, pp. 139–45.

when it is due to art, for the starting-point is different. And in animals too one must not count as natural those cases where molding or forcing produces small or large size or a general physical outline. The nature instead always sets out to achieve what is best, and about this (one may say) there is agreement.

Cultivation is Natural

But what proceeds from husbandry does this too. For the nature of the plant is also fulfilled when that nature obtains through human art what it happens to lack, such as food of the right kind and in plentiful supply and the removal of impediments and hindrances, all of which evidently is also provided by the regions appropriate to a given plant, the regions in fact where we assert that the natures of plants should be studied. But the appropriate region only provides external help, such as weather, wind, soil and food, whereas husbandry also introduces different movements and arrangements within the plant itself. So if the nature of a plant demands that external aid for the achievement of what is better, it would also accept these internal modifications as appropriate to itself; and it is reasonable that it should demand and seek them, especially since it depends on what is internal and has its starting-points there. In fact in trees that grow without human aid there is this strange and (as it were) unnatural result: produced from seed they deteriorate and even undergo a complete mutation of variety, for this degeneration too is nothing natural, what is natural being instead to achieve similarity in reproduction.

These, then, are the problems (one may say) and such is their character.

The Solution: Two Kinds of Nature

This discussion too makes it appear evident that we must make a prior distinction of the natures just as we say that we must do with the concoctions: so for some plants their nature as it develops unaided by man is more appropriate, for others their nature as developed by care and cultivation, and a few do well in both ways; and we must rest our study on this distinction, just as their natures are distinguished for the domesticated and wild, in animals and plants alike, for each of the two groups has things that are natural and suited to it, conducive not only to preservation and survival and to growth and sprouting, but also to the generation of the fruit. Perhaps within the group of fruitful plants as well one might make the distinction again, letting some bear unaided, the rest only under care and cultivation.

In these matters, then, this is the line to be drawn.

Aristotle, *De anima*, or *Of the Soul*

In *De anima* (or *Of the Soul*) Aristotle attributes to all living things a *psyche* or soul, which supplies them with a purpose. Like all living things, a plant has a "vegetal soul," which drives nutrition and reproduction. While Aristotle thus attributes to plants a kind of "originative power," they still stand at the bottom of a hierarchy of living things insofar as they lack the functions of sensation and motion distinctive to animals. Thus, on the one hand, Aristotle sees plants as enlivened by this "psychic power"; on the other hand, they are debased, low on the ladder of living things (exceeding only stones and minerals). Aristotle extends his discussion of plants in the excerpt in Part 3 from the *History of Animals*, where he notes that within the order of plants "one will differ from another as to its amount of apparent vitality" and observes "a continuous scale of ascent towards the animal." There he acknowledges that the distinction between plants and animals is thus not as sharp as it might first appear.

We resume our inquiry from a fresh starting-point by calling attention to the fact that what has soul in it differs from what has not, in that the former displays life. Now this word has more than one sense, and provided any one alone of these is found in a thing we say that thing is living—viz. thinking or perception or local movement and rest, or movement in the sense of nutrition, decay and growth. Hence we think of plants also as living, for they are observed to possess in themselves an originative power through which they increase or decrease in all spatial directions; they do not grow up but then down—they grow alike in both, indeed in all, directions; and that holds for everything which is constantly nourished and continues to live, so long as it can absorb nutriment.

This power of self-nutrition can be separated from the other powers mentioned, but not they from it—in mortal beings at least. The fact is obvious in plants; for it is the only psychic power they possess.

This is the originative power the possession of which leads us to speak of things as living at all, but it is the possession of sensation that leads us for the first time to speak of living things as animals; for even those beings which possess no power of local movement but do possess the power of sensation we call animals and not merely living things.

[. . .]

Source: *De anima*, or *Of the Soul*, translated by J. A. Smith. *The Complete Works of Aristotle: The Revised Oxford Translation*, edited by Jonathan Barnes, vol. 1, Princeton University Press, 1984, pp. 658–61.

It is necessary for the student of these forms of soul first to find a definition of each, expressive of what it is, and then to investigate its derivative properties, etc. But if we are to express what each is, viz. what the thinking power is, or the perceptive, or the nutritive, we must go farther back and first give an account of thinking or perceiving: for activities and actions are prior in definition to potentialities. If so, and if, still prior to them, we should have reflected on their correlative objects, then for the same reason we must first determine about them, i.e, about food and the objects of perception and thought.

It follows that first of all we must treat of nutrition and reproduction, for the nutritive soul is found along with all the others and is the most primitive and widely distributed power of soul, being indeed that one in virtue of which all are said to have life. The acts in which it manifests itself are reproduction and the use of food, because for any living thing that has reached its normal development and which is unmutilated, and whose mode of generation is not spontaneous, the most natural act is the production of another like itself, an animal producing an animal, a plant a plant, in order that, as far as its nature allows, it may partake in the eternal and divine. That is the goal towards which all things strive, that for the sake of which they do whatsoever their nature renders possible. The phrase "for the sake of which" is ambiguous; it may mean either the end to achieve which, or the being in whose interest, the act is done. Since then no living thing is able to partake in what is eternal and divine by uninterrupted continuance (for nothing perishable can forever remain one and the same), it tries to achieve that end in the only way possible to it, and success is possible in varying degrees; so it remains not indeed as the self-same individual but continues its existence in something like itself—not numerically but specifically one.

The soul is the cause or source of the living body. The terms cause and source have many senses. But the soul is the cause of its body alike in all three senses which we explicitly recognize. It is (a) the source or origin of movement, it is the end, it is the essence of the whole living body.

Dioscorides, *De materia medica*, or *Herbal*

The Greek physician Pendanius Dioscorides' (first century CE) *De materia medica,* a compendium of remedies based on plants, animals, and minerals, founded a tradition of herbals that lasted for centuries (Figure 1). While soon

Source: *The Greek Herbal of Dioscorides.* Translated by John Goodyer (1655) and edited by Robert T. Gunther (1933), Hafner, 1959.

Figure 1. Dioscorides (on the left-hand side) collecting plants, from a fifteenth-century manuscript herbal. Lawrence J. Schoenberg and Barbara Brizdle Manuscript Initiative LJS 62 Fol. 1v. Kislak Center for Special Collections, Rare Books, and Manuscripts, University of Pennsylvania Libraries.

translated into multiple languages across Europe and the Near East, the earliest extant version of this five-book encyclopedia covering over six hundred plants is the magnificent Codex Vindobonensis, dating to the sixth century CE. This entry on hemlock (a flowering plant, not the tree) exemplifies the basic format of the herbal, stating the various names of the plant, its features with its usual habitat, and its "virtues" or powers in medicine, which are often quite extensive. The entry on common basil demonstrates how Dioscorides attributed to this plant both modest and extraordinary powers: for example, it may be a laxative, but it can also cure melancholy and relieve the pain from a scorpion's bite. Basil was also known as the snakeplant (Figure 2) and was later thought to ward off snakes (see excerpt from the *Old English Herbarium* in Part 2). Along with Pliny the Elder, Dioscorides served as an essential authority for later herbal authors; no English translation appeared in print, however, while John Goodyer composed one in manuscript in 1655. This text is based on this translation (first printed in 1933).

Hemlock

Cicuta . . . sends out a knotty stalk, like as fennel, great, but leaves like to ferula,[1] but narrower, and of an heavy smell, and on the tops, excrescencies, and tufts, a whitish flower, the seed like to anise seed whiter, the root hollow, and not deep. And this also is of the venomous herbs, killing by its coldness, but it is helped by unmixed wine. The tops, or the hair, are juiced before that the seed be dry, and being beaten it is pressed out, and thickened by stirring it in the sun, which being dried is of much use for service in cures. The juice being fitly mixed with anodynal collieries,[2] it doth extinguish the herpetas,[3] and the erysipelata[4] being smeared on. And the herb, and the hair being beaten small and smeared on about the stones[5] doth help wanton dreamers, and seed shedders,[6] and doth enfeeble the genitals being smeared on, and drives away milk and forbids the breasts to grow great in time of virginity and makes the stones in children unnourishable. But that is the most potent which grows in Crete, and in Megara and in Attica, then that which grows in Chios and Cilicia.

1. Cane or rod
2. Pain-relieving solid medicines
3. Herpes [?]
4. A skin infection
5. Testicles
6. Those prone to nighttime ejaculations

Figure 2. Sweet basil (or the "snakeplant"), in a fifteenth-century manuscript herbal in the tradition of Dioscorides, in which the plant is shown with snaky roots. Lawrence J. Schoenberg and Barbara Brizdle Manuscript Initiative LJS 62 Fol. 8v. Kislak Center for Special Collections, Rare Books, and Manuscripts, University of Pennsylvania Libraries.

Basil

Ocimum is commonly known, being eaten much it dulls the eyesight, but it is a softener of the belly, a mover of flatulencies, ureticall,[7] and calling out of milk. It is hard of digestion. Being applied with the flour of polenta, and rosaceum,[8] and vinegar, it doth help inflammations, and the stroke of the sea dragon, and of the scorpion. Of itself with Chian wine (it is good) for the griefs of the eyes. But the juice of it, doth take away the dimness that is in the eyes, and dry up the rheums.[9] But the seed being drunk is good for such as breed melancholy, and for the dysuretical[10] and for the flatulent. It causeth also many sneezings, being drawn up by the smell, and the herb doth the like. But the eyes must be shut whilst the sneezing holds. Some also do avoid it and do not eat it, because that being chewed, and set in the sun, it breeds little worms. But the Africans have entertained it, because they which eat it and are smitten of a scorpion, yet remain without pain.

Pliny the Elder, *Naturalis historia*, or *Natural History*, On Flowers

Part 1 introduces Pliny the Elder's (23–79 CE) massive *Naturalis historia* (*Natural History*) as one of the most important authorities on natural history inherited from the classical world.

In the area of botany, Pliny drew a great deal on the Greek natural historian Theophrastus's treatises, the first systematic description of plants (see above), as well as on the Greek herbals, while also including some of his personal observations. His entries on plants include both descriptions of the plants and extensive lists of plant-based remedies. As his entry on flowers for chaplets suggests, he appreciated plants' aesthetic qualities; however, as the following sections on the iris and the lily indicate, flowers were mostly valued or "esteemed" for their uses in cosmetics and medicine. The entry on the iris also reveals the popular beliefs that were often associated with the cultivation of plants; many of these kinds of quasi-magical practices persisted up through the early modern period (see, for example, some of the gardening advice of Thomas Hill in Part 6).

7. Pertaining to urine
8. Of roses
9. Mucous secretions in the head
10. Suffering from dysuria

Source: Pliny the Elder. *The Natural History.* Translated by John Bostock and Henry T. Riley, London, 1855, book 21, chaps. 1, 19. *Perseus Digital Library*, http://www.perseus.tufts.edu/hopper/text?doc=Perseus%3Atext%3A1999.02.0137%3Abook%3D21%3Achapter%3D1.

Book 21, Chapter 1

Cato[1] has recommended that flowers for making chaplets[2] should also be cultivated in the garden; varieties remarkable for a delicacy which it is quite impossible to express, inasmuch as no individual can find such facilities for describing them as Nature does for bestowing on them their numerous tints—Nature, who here in especial shows herself in a sportive mood, and takes a delight in the prolific display of her varied productions. The other plants she has produced for our use and our nutriment, and to them accordingly she has granted years and even ages of duration: but as for the flowers and their perfumes, she has given them birth for but a day—a mighty lesson to man, we see, to teach him that that which in its career is the most beauteous and the most attractive to the eye, is the very first to fade and die.

Book 21. Chapter 19. The iris

There is still another distinction, which ought not to be omitted—the fact, that many of the odoriferous plants never enter into the composition of garlands, the iris and the saliunca,[3] for example, although, both of them, of a most exquisite odor. In the iris, it is the root only that is held in esteem, it being extensively employed in perfumery and medicine. The iris of the finest quality is that found in Illyricum,[4] and in that country, even, not in the maritime parts of it, but in the forests on the banks of the river Drilon and near Narona. The next best is that of Macedonia, the plant being extremely elongated, white, and thin. The iris of Africa occupies the third rank, being the largest of them all, and of an extremely bitter taste.

The iris of Illyricum comprehends two varieties—one of which is the raphanitis, so called from its resemblance to the radish, of a somewhat red color, and superior in quality to the other, which is known as the rhizotomus. The best kind of iris is that which produces sneezing when handled. The stem of this plant is a cubit in length, and erect, the flower being of various colors, like the rainbow, to which circumstance it is indebted for its name. The iris, too, of Pisidia[5] is far from being held in disesteem. Persons who intend taking up the iris, drench the ground about it some three months before with hydromel,[6] as though a sort of atonement offered to appease the earth; with the

1. Cato the Elder, 234–149 BCE, who wrote an important work on agriculture
2. Wreath for the head
3. Probably a form of valerian
4. A region in the Balkans
5. A region of ancient Asia Minor
6. A drink made with honey and water

point of a sword, too, they trace three circles round it, and the moment they gather it, they lift it up towards the heavens.[7] The iris is a plant of a caustic nature, and when handled, it causes blisters like burns to rise. It is a point particularly recommended, that those who gather it should be in a state of chastity.

Book 21. Chapter 74. Twenty-one remedies derived from the lily.

The roots of the lily ennoble that flower in manifold ways by their utility in a medicinal point of view. Taken in wine, they are good for the stings of serpents, and in cases of poisoning by fungi. For corns on the feet, they are applied boiled in wine, not being taken off before the end of three days. A decoction of them with grease or oil has the effect of making the hair grow again upon burns. Taken with honeyed wine, they carry off corrupt blood by stool; they are good, also, for the spleen and for hernia, and act as an emmenagogue.[8] Boiled in wine and applied with honey, they are curative of wounds of the sinews. They are good, too, for lichens, leprous sores, and scurf upon the face, and they efface wrinkles of the body.

The petals of the lily are boiled in vinegar, and applied, in combination with polium,[9] to wounds; if it should happen, however, to be a wound of the testes, it is the best plan to apply the other ingredients with henbane and wheat-meal. Lily-seed is applied in cases of erysipelas, and the flowers and leaves are used as a cataplasm for inveterate ulcers. The juice which is extracted from the flower is called "honey" by some persons, and "syrium" by others; it is employed as an emollient for the uterus, and is also used for the purpose of promoting perspirations, and for bringing suppurations to a head.

Pseudo-Apuleius, *The Old English Herbarium*

In addition to Dioscorides's *De materia medica*, the Latin *Herbarius* was one of the most important herbals circulated in Europe from the fourth to the twelfth century. Attributed to Platonicus Apuleius or Pseudo-Apuleius but most likely a compilation of several authors, the text draws on both Pliny the Elder and

7. Source in Theophrastus
8. Stimulating menstrual flow, potentially an abortifactant
9. A variety of germander

Source: Anne Van Arsdall. *Medieval Herbal Remedies: The Old English Herbarium and Anglo-Saxon Medicine*. Routledge, 2002, pp. 154–55 (dragonswort), pp. 204–5 (basil).

Dioscorides but also adapts its observations for different European regions. Many translations, including this tenth-century Anglo-Saxon version, provided access for those who could not read Latin. In including plants from southern Europe, this herbal betrays its Mediterranean origins (for example, in the account of dragonswort), but it has also been made relevant for more northern climates. In its descriptions and remedies, the herbal often attributes occult powers to plants while offering practical applications; for example, this passage on sweet basil foregrounds its power to antagonize snakes, rather than any more everyday medical applications (compare with the entry on basil from Dioscorides and see Figure 2).

Dragonswort (*Dracunculus vulgaris, Arum dracunculus L.*), *dracontea, Dracentse*

About this plant, which is called *dracontea* and also dragonswort, it is said that it should be grown in dragon's blood. It grows at the tops of mountains where there are groves of trees, chiefly in holy places and in the country that is called Apulia. It grows in stony soil, it is soft to the touch and sweet like green chestnuts in taste, and the root below is like a dragon's head.

1. For all snakebites, take the roots of the *dracontea* [dragonswort] plant, pound it with wine, warm it, and give it to drink. All the poison will disappear.

2. For broken bones, take the roots of this same plant and mix them with grease, just like you make a poultice. The broken bones will appear out of the body.

You should gather the plant in the month called July.

Sweet Basil (*Ocimum basilicum L.*), *basilisca, Nœdderwyrt*

This plant, called *basilica* or basil, grows where the snake is that has the same name, *basilicus.* Indeed, there is not one kind of basil, but three. One is *olocryseis,* that is, as said in our language, that it shines like gold. Another kind is *stillatus,* which is "spotted" in our language; it looks as though its head were golden. The third kind is *sanguineus,* that is blood-red, and also looks as if its head were golden. The basil plant comes in all these kinds. If anyone has this plant with him, none of the following kinds of snakes can harm him. The *olocryssuss* snake is named *eriseos,* and whatever it sees it blows on and sets on fire. The second, *stillatus,* is called *crysocefalus asterites;* whatever it sees dries up and disappears. The third kind is named *hematites* or *crysofalus.* Whatever it sees or touches it destroys so that nothing is left but the bones. The basil plant has all of their strength, and if any person has the plant with him, that person will be strong against all kinds of snakes.

This plant is like rue: it has red milky juice like greater celandine, and it has purple flowers. Anyone who wants to pick it should purify himself and mark around it with gold and silver, with deer horn and ivory, with bear's tooth and bull's horn, and lay around it fruit sweetened with honey.

Geoffrey Chaucer, *The Legend of Good Women*

While remembered as the greatest Middle English poet, Geoffrey Chaucer (ca. 1343–1400) was also steeped in the French and Italian literature of his time. His poem *The Legend of Good Women*, an account of "good women" from literature and history, demonstrates deep connections with both classical and Continental literary traditions, including those representing the natural world. In the prologue Chaucer presents his poem as a dream vision, beginning with his delight in spring flowers, and in particular his worship of the daisy, thus alluding to a contemporary French and English poetic fashion of a daisy cult. His evocation of the "virtuous" daisy transforms into an image of the Greek tragic heroine Alcestis leading the "good women." She appears in the colors of a daisy, crowned in white and dressed in a robe of green. Whereas in *Le roman de la rose* (Part 6) a rose symbolizes a woman an as object of erotic desire, here the daisy symbolizes virtue and love that turns its face to the sun.

The text of this excerpt collates two early manuscript versions of the poem; my version retains some early spellings to give a sense of the poetic rhythm, while many have been modernized for clarity.

But it be other upon the holy-day,
Or else in the jolly time of May;
When that I hear the smalle fowles[1] singe,
And that the flowers ginne for to springe,
Farewell my study, as lasting that season!
Now have I thereto this condition
That of alle the flowers in the mede,[2]
Then love I most these flowers white and rede,
Such as men callen daisies in our town.

Source: *The Complete Works of Geoffrey Chaucer*, vol. 3, *The House of Fame; The Legend of Good Women; The Treatise on the Astrolabe; An Account of the Sources of the Canterbury Tales*. Edited by Walter Skeat, Oxford University Press, 1899, pp. 79–81. *Project Gutenberg*, http://www.gutenberg.org/files/45027/45027-h/45027-h.htm.

1. Birds
2. Meadow

To them have I so great affeccioun,[3]
As I saide erst,[4] when comen is the May,
That in my bed there dawneth me no day
That I nam up,[5] and walking in the mede
To see these flowers again the sunne spreade,
When it upriseth by the morrow shene,
The longe day, thus walking in the greene.
This daisy, of alle flowers flower,
Fulfilled of virtue and of alle honour,
And every like fair and fresh of hewe,[6]
As well in winter as in summer newe.
And when the sunne ginneth for to weste,[7]
Than closeth it, and draweth it to reste.
[. . .]
When passed was almost the month of May,
And I had roamed, all the summeres day,
The greene meadow, of which that I you tolde,
Upon the freshe daisy to beholde,
And that the sunne out of the south gan weste,
And closed was the flower and gone to reste
For darknesse of the night, of which she dreade,
Home to mine house full swiftly I me spede;
And, in a little arbor that I have,
Ybenched newe with turves freshe yrave,[8]
I bad men shoulde me my couche make;
For dainty of the newe summeres sake,
I bad hem strewe flowers on my bed.
When I was laid, and had min eyen hed,
I fell asleepe within an hour or two.
Me mette[9] how I was in the meadow tho,
Til at the last a larke song above:
"I see," quod she, "the mighty god of love!
Lo! yond he cometh, I see his winges sprede!"

3. Affection
4. Before
5. That I am not up
6. Hue
7. Set in the west
8. Fresh-cut turf
9. Dreamed

To seen that flowr, as ye had heard devise,
Tho gan I looken endelong the mede,
And saw him come, and in his hand a queene,
Clothed in royal habite[10] al of grene.
A fret[11] of gold she hadde next her hair,
And upon that a white coroun[12] she bear
With many flowers, and I shall not lie;
For all the world, right as the daisye
Icoroned[13] is with white leaves lite,
Such were the flowers of her coroun white.
For of a pearle fine and oriental
Her white coroun was ymaked all;
For which the white coroun, above the greene,
Made her like a daisie for to seene,
Considered eek[14] the fret of gold above.

Pierre de Ronsard, "Ode to Cassandra"

The French poet Pierre de Ronsard (1524–1585) led the Pléiade, a group of writers steeped in the classics yet dedicated to creating a new vernacular literature. Published in 1552 in his *Amours de Cassandre*, his "Ode to Cassandra" develops the classical "carpe diem" or "seize the day" trope, dating back to the *Odes* of the Roman poet Horace in the first century BCE. In the tradition of *Le roman de la rose* (Part 6), here the rose is eroticized: as the flower, the young woman is imagined unfolding her red robes, blushing, and then fading away in a brief moment. Ronsard's focus on the brevity of the flower's life can be contrasted with George Herbert's celebration of the seasonal renewal of plants in "The Flower."

Dearest, let us see if the rose
That this morning unclosed
Her crimson robe to the sun,
This evening has not lost
The folds of that robe so crimsoned
And its hue so like unto yours.

10. Gown
11. Headband
12. Coronet
13. Crowned
14. Also
Source: Pierre De Ronsard. *Amours de Cassandre*. 1552. Translated by Rebecca Bushnell.

Alas, see how in such a short space,
Dearest, she has in this place
Alas, lost all her loveliness.
Oh, cruel is mother Nature,
That such a flower endures
Only from dawn until dusk.

So, if you trust me, dearest,
While your time still blooms
In its green freshness,
Gather, gather your youth:
For, as with this flower, age
Will blight your beauty.

Leonhart Fuchs, *De historia stirpium*, or *On the History of Plants*

Like Otto Brunfels (1488–1544), the German physician Leonhart Fuchs (1501–1566) transformed the study of botany by basing his observations on life rather than simply on the authority of older botanical texts. Fuchs's *De historia stirpium commentarii insignes* (1542) (*Notable Commentaries on the History of Plants*) discusses 497 plants and includes over 500 extraordinary woodcut illustrations drawn from live specimens (Figure 3). The illustrations and the text work together to present plants as they "really are." Fuchs also claimed to offer a more orderly naming and organizing of the plant world, disposing of fictions of nomenclature and properties associated with older writers such as Dioscorides. He accounted for common plants in his own country, as well as foreign ones, concerned with preserving the story of the plants of his own time, should they disappear in the future. He thus depicted a plant world that is globally diverse and is constantly changing, rather than a static artifact of divine creation.

Now, to come at last to the point at which I was aiming, I have compiled these commentaries on the nature of plants with the utmost care as well as expense, emulating the devotion of the eminent scholars mentioned above. In the first place, we have included whatever relates to the whole history of every plant, with all the superfluities cut out, briefly and, we hope, in the best order, one we

Source: *The Great Herbal of Leonhart Fuchs: De Historia Stirpium Commentarii Insignes, 1542*. Edited and translated by Frederick G. Mayer, Emily Emmart Trueblood, and John L. Heller, vol. 1, Stanford University Press, 1999, pp. 210–13.

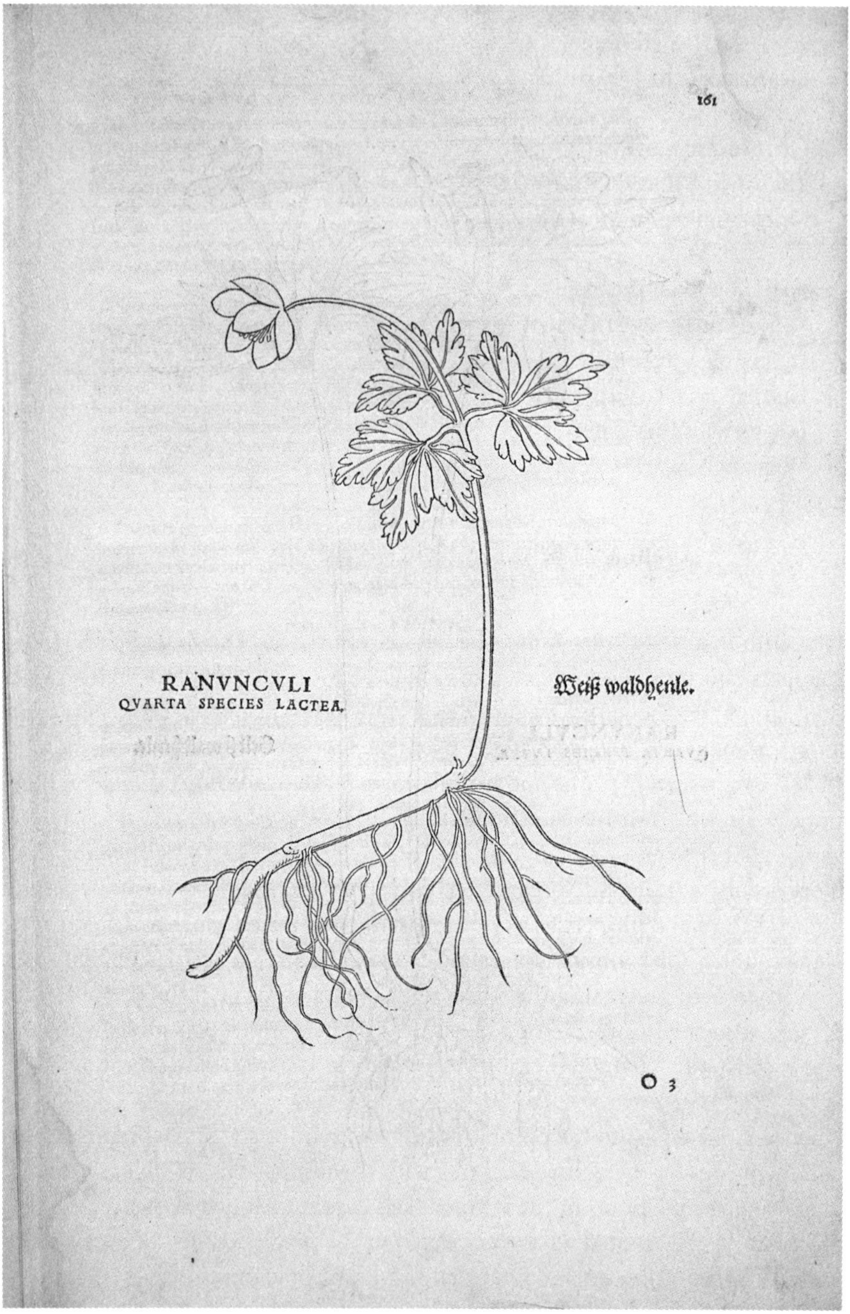

Figure 3. Woodcut of a ranunculus with realistic features, from Leonhart Fuchs, *De Historia Stirpium*, p. 161. Folio 580 F953a. Kislak Center for Special Collections, Rare Books, and Manuscripts, University of Pennsylvania Libraries.

shall follow regularly. Then, to the description of each plant we have added an illustration. These are lifelike and modeled after nature and rendered more skillfully, if I may say so, than ever before. This we have done for no other reason than that a picture expresses things more surely and fixes them more deeply in the mind than the bare words of the text.

Not only have we offered pictures of foreign plants that do not occur naturally in our Germany (although the careful reader will find more than a hundred of these in our commentaries), but also of the common ones, and those that spring up beside hedgerows and thickets everywhere. We have been moved to do this for two reasons especially. First, so that those interested in herbal medicine should have their history, complete and reduced to order, which for the most part has not been handed down by the ancient writers, or, in the more recent ones, has been incomplete and confused. Second, so that what we all know has happened to us will not happen to our descendants—namely, that plants now very familiar to all became altogether unknown to them. For is it not generally agreed that in the time of Dioscorides many plants were so well known that he did not bother to record distinctive marks by which they could be recognized by later ages? For, if you inquire of the most learned students of plants today, you will find no one who recognizes them. And so, lest it should come about from our own neglect or the erosion of time, that plants now common and known to everyone should drop from man's knowledge, we have concluded that their descriptions and pictures too should be included in our commentaries.

And why should we so despise known and common plants, when quite often they have greater medicinal value than those imported from the most distant and remote parts of the earth and sought out at tremendous expense? What is more common than *Polygonum*?[1] What more humble? It is trodden by the feet of all. But if you were willing to try out its power to stop bleeding, you would say there is nothing more effective. I could give many examples like this, but there is no need to waste words on well-known facts.

[. . .]

Furthermore, since we have included in this work the histories of many plants that neither Dioscorides nor any other of the ancients knew (for since they are mostly for treating wounds, and are in daily use by many, especially surgeons, we judged they should by no means be left out), we had to use their common and even barbarous names, since we did not have Latin ones. We have preferred to use tasteless and non-Latin nomenclature rather

1. Knotweed, now an invasive plant

than assign fictitious Greek or Latin names, lest, along with their false nomenclature, we should also ascribe to them fictitious properties. This has happened to some who wrote about herbal matters, as we mentioned before. Therefore, where we were able to find a Greek term corresponding exactly to the German name, we have used it rather than some false one from Dioscorides.

[. . .]

In listing the properties of plants, we have taken the greatest care not to assign to any plant fictitious or unproved properties, a thing that many have done, at the cost of great mischief and loss of human life. And so in the history of plants with which the ancients were familiar, we have kept the properties exactly as they were handed down by Dioscorides, Galen, Pliny, and sometimes even by Aëtius,[2] Paulus,[3] and Simeon Seth.[4] This was for the special reason that all might know that the properties on which these three persons agree are of such sort that reliance can be placed on them, as being most authentic. But if they differ among themselves, then the opinion of Galen[5] should be followed, rather than Dioscorides, and the latter in turn over Pliny.

[. . .]

As for the pictures themselves, every single one of them portrays the lines and appearance of the living plant. We were especially careful that they should be absolutely correct, and we have devoted the greatest diligence that every plant should be depicted with its own roots, stalks, leaves, flowers, seeds, and fruits. Over and over again, we have purposely and deliberately avoided the obliteration of the natural form of the plants lest they be obscured by shading and other artifices that painters sometimes employ to win artistic glory. And we have not allowed the craftsmen so to indulge their whims as to cause the drawing not to correspond accurately to the truth.

William Turner, *A New Herbal*

William Turner (1509/10–1568) was a physician and minister who wrote both Protestant polemics and significant works of natural history. His first English book on plants, *The Names of Herbes* (1548), made Turner's case for writing in the vernacular about English flora. His later masterpiece was his *New Herbal*,

2. A fifth-century CE Byzantine physician
3. A seventh-century CE Byzantine physician
4. An eleventh—century CE Byzantine doctor and scholar
5. The most influential Roman physician and doctor (second century CE)

Source: William Turner. *The First and Second Parts of the Herbal of William Turner Doctor in Physic, Lately Overseen, Corrected and Enlarged with the Third Part*, Cologne, 1568, pp. 46–48.

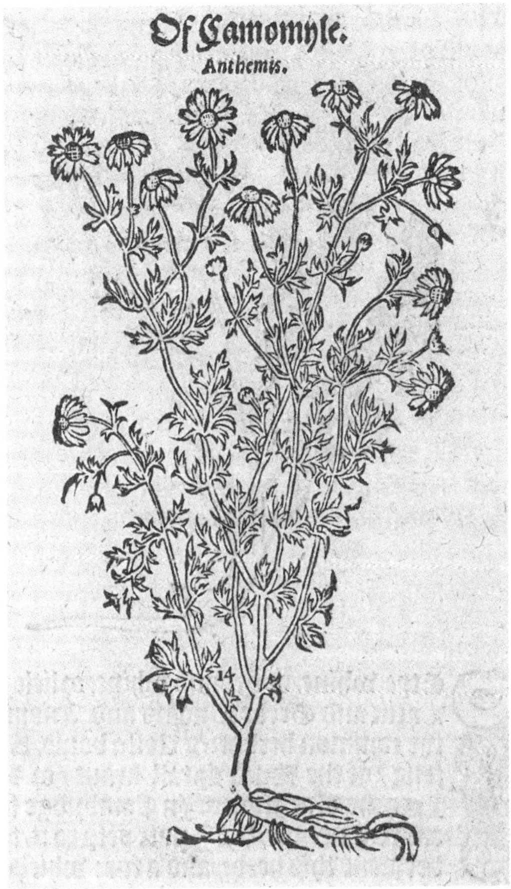

Figure 4. Woodcut of a chamomile, from William Turner's *New Herbal*, p. 46. Rare Book Collection 615.32 T853. Kislak Center for Special Collections, Rare Books, and Manuscripts, University of Pennsylvania Libraries.

published in two parts in 1551 and 1562 (with an addendum in 1568). This book reflects his botanizing in both England and the Continent, where he spent years in exile because of his controversial Protestant polemics. Illustrated with realistic woodcuts borrowed from Leonhart Fuchs's *De historia stirpium*, it broke new ground for English herbals in its claims to originality and specific local botanical knowledge. Turner also insisted on using English so that people without Latin would not have to turn to "old wives" who practiced herbal medicine. Turner's work does otherwise resemble all other early modern herbals in specifying the types, names, and "operations," or virtues, of plants (see Dioscorides). This entry on chamomile exemplifies Turner's detailed attention to the plant's appearance and its varieties in different locales, as well as his extensive knowledge of the plant's virtues, a few of which carry over today, for example, the belief in chamomile tea's calming effects (Figure 4).

Of Chamomile [*Anthemis nobilis*]

Anthemis, otherwise called *Chamemelum*, containeth under it three kinds, which only differ in the color of the flower. The branches are a span long, all bushy with many places like armholes between the stalk and the branches. The branches are thin, small, and many. The little heads are round with yellow flowers in the midst and about the round head, either white flowers stand in order, or purple, or yellow about the greatness of the leaves of rue. The first kind of chamomile is called in Greek *Leucanthemon*, in English chamomile, in Dutch *Roemish camillen*. The apothecaries in Germany call this kind *Chamomillam romanam*. This herb is scarce in Germany, but in England it is so plenteous that it groweth not only in gardens, but also eight miles above London it groweth in the wild field in Richmond Green, in Brentford Green, and in most plenty of all in Hounslow Heath.[1] The second kind is called in Greek *Chrysantemon*. I have seen this herb in High Germany in the fields, but never in England that I remember. It may be called in English, yellow chamomile. The third kind is called in Greek *Heranthemon*. Divers think that *Heranthemon* is the herb which is called of the herbaries, *Amarisca rubra*, and of our countrymen "rede mathe," or red made weed. The thing that seemeth to let this herb to be *Heranthemon* is this: it hath not a yellow head or knob which is compassed about with purple flowers, as the other kinds have yellow knobs set about, one with white flowers and the other with yellow; but the head or knob of this herb is nothing like the knobs of the other, neither in greatness, neither yet in form, nor yet in color; and the seed is as great as spinach seed is but without pricks; in many other points it agrees with the description. The leaves are very small but the flowers are crimson and they should be purple. *Heranthemon* hath the name, because it flowereth in the spring. This have I written of this herb, that learned men should search more diligently for it, which is the true *Heranthemon*.

THE OPERATION OF CHAMOMILE

Chamomile is hot and dry in the first degree.[2] Chamomile in subtleness is like the rose, but in heat it draweth more near the quality of oil, which is very agreeing unto the nature of man, and temperate. Therefore it is good against weariness. It assuageth ache, and unbindeth and looseth it that is stretched out, softeneth it that is but measurably hard, and setting it abroad that was narrowly thrust together. It driveth away and dissolveth agues[3] which come not with an inflammation of any inward part, and specially such as come of

1. All areas in the London vicinity
2. Qualities assigned in humoral medicine
3. Fevers

choleric humors[4] and of the thickness of the skin. Wherefore this herb was consecrated of the wise men of Egypt unto the sun, and was reckoned to be the only remedy of all agues. But in that they were deceived, for it can only heal those agues that I rehearsed, and those when as they be ripe. Howbeit, it helpeth indeed very well, also all other which come of melancholy or of phlegm, or of the inflammation of some inward part. For chamomile is the strongest remedy when it is given after that the matter is ripe; therefore it is most convenient for the midriff, and for the pains under the paps,[5] whether the herb be sodden, or sitten over, or be drunken. It driveth down women's sickness, bringeth forth the birth, provoketh urine, and driveth out the stone.[6] It is good to be drunken against the gnawing and windy swellings of the small guts; it purgeth away the yellow jaundice. It healeth the disease of the liver; it is good for the bladder to be bathed with the broth of this herb. Of all the kinds of chamomile, that kind with the purple flowers is strongest; they with the yellow and white flower do more provoke urine. They heal also laid to emplasterwise, the impostume[7] that is about the corner of the eye. The same chewed, heal the sores of the mouth.

John Gerard, *The Herbal or General History of Plants*

John Gerard's (ca. 1545–1612) *The Herbal or General History of Plants* is now the most well-known early modern English herbal (Figure 5). A barber-surgeon by training, Gerard served as a gardener to William Cecil and later "herbarist" to James I, while also overseeing his own garden in Holborn, where he cultivated hundreds of plants. His 1597 *Herbal* is a massive folio volume covering more than a thousand plants, often illustrated by woodcuts borrowed from earlier publications. Even in its own time, detractors dismissed the *Herbal* as a messy translation that borrows too much from Rembert Dodoen's herbal *Stirpium historiae pemptades sex* (1583) and appropriates unpublished work by the Flemish physician Matthias de L'Obel. In 1633 Thomas Johnson published a critical and "a very much enlarged and amended" version of Gerard's work. However, Gerard did weave into his *Herbal* much of his own observations about plants and the experiences of friends and colleagues. The book also communicates Gerard's appreciation of plants' beauty and their powers to cure

4. An overbalance of yellow bile, in humoral medicine
5. Breasts
6. Kidney stones
7. Swelling or cyst

Source: John Gerard. *The Herball or Generall Historie of Plantes*. London, 1597, dedication and pp. 662–64..

Figure 5. Portrait of John Gerard, from the frontmatter of his *Herbal* (1597). Gerard is holding a potato plant, still considered an exotic item at this time. Call # STC 11750. Used by permission of the Folger Shakespeare Library.

both body and mind. While including the familiar appeal to uses, this excerpt from the *Herbal*'s dedication to Cecil evokes both the sensual delights and the mystical significance of plants. In turn, the entry on borage exemplifies the range of Gerard's capacious interest in a plant's names, varied appearances, and uses (Figure 6).

Dedication to Cecil

Among the manifold creatures of God (right Honorable and my singular good Lord)[1] that have all in all ages diversely entertained many excellent wits, and drawn them to the contemplation of the divine wisdom, none have provoked men's studies more, or satisfied their desires so much, as plants have done, and that upon just and worthy causes. For if delight may provoke men's labor, what greater delight is there than to behold the earth appareled with plants, as with a robe of embroidered work, set with orient pearls, and garnished with great diversity of rare and costly jewels? If this variety and perfection of colors may affect the eye, it is such in herbs and flowers, that no Apelles, no Zeuxis[2] ever could by any art express the like; if odors, or if taste may work satisfaction, they are both so sovereign in plants, and so comfortable, that no confection of the apothecaries can equal their excellent virtue. But these delights are in the outward senses: the principal delight is in the mind, singularly enriched with the knowledge of these visible things, setting forth to us the invisible wisdom and admirable workmanship of almighty God. The delight is great, but the use greater, and joined often with necessity. In the first ages of the world they were the ordinary meat of men, and have continued ever since of necessary use both for meats to maintain life, and for medicine to recover health. The hidden virtue of them is such, that (as Pliny noteth) the very brute beasts have found it out; and (which is another use that he observeth) from thence the dyers took the beginning of their art.

Furthermore, the necessary use of these fruits of the earth doth plainly appear by the great charge and care of almost all men in planting and maintaining of gardens, not as ornaments only, but as necessary provision also to their houses. And here beside the fruit, to speak again in a word of delight; gardens, especially such as your Honor hath, furnished with many rare simples, do singularly delight, when in them a man doth behold a flourishing shew of summer beauties in the midst of winter's force, and a goodly spring of flowers, when abroad a leaf is not to be seen. Beside these and other causes, there are many examples of those that have honored this science: for to pass by

1. The book is dedicated to William Cecil.
2. Apelles and Zeuxis were both famous ancient Greek painters.

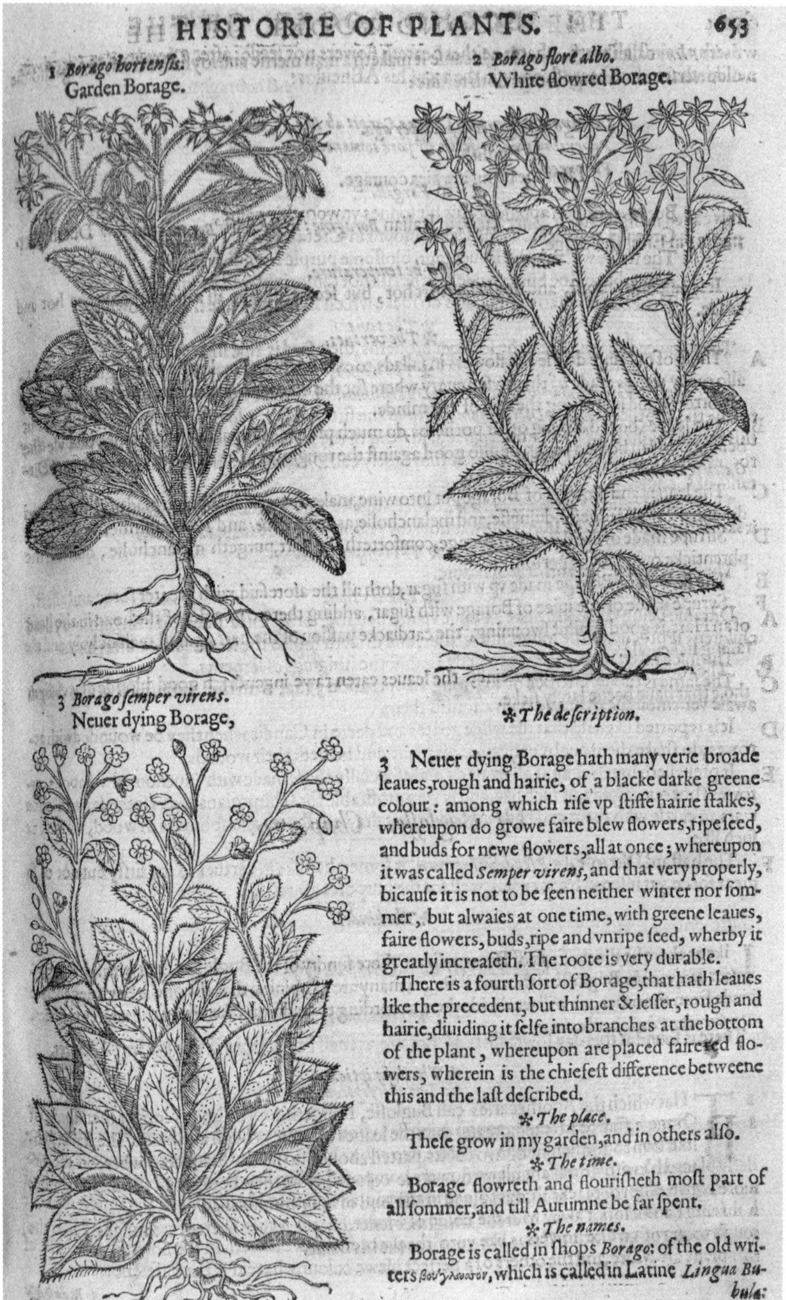
HISTORIE OF PLANTS. 653

1 *Borago hortenſis.*
Garden Borage.

2 *Borago flore albo.*
White flowred Borage.

3 *Borago ſemper virens.*
Neuer dying Borage,

✱ *The deſcription.*

3 Neuer dying Borage hath many verie broade leaues,rough and hairie, of a blacke darke greene colour : among which riſe vp ſtiffe hairie ſtalkes, whereupon do growe faire blew flowers,ripe ſeed, and buds for newe flowers,all at once ; whereupon it was called *Semper virens*, and that very properly, bicauſe it is not to be ſeen neither winter nor ſommer, but alwaies at one time, with greene leaues, faire flowers, buds,ripe and vnripe ſeed, wherby it greatly increaſeth. The roote is very durable.

There is a fourth ſort of Borage,that hath leaues like the precedent, but thinner & leſſer, rough and hairie,diuiding it ſelfe into branches at the bottom of the plant, whereupon are placed faire red flowers, wherein is the chiefeſt difference betweene this and the laſt deſcribed.

✱ *The place.*

Theſe grow in my garden,and in others alſo.

✱ *The time.*

Borage flowreth and flouriſheth moſt part of all ſommer,and till Autumne be far ſpent.

✱ *The names.*

Borage is called in ſhops *Borago*: of the old writers βοὐγλωσσον, which is called in Latine *Lingua Bubula*:

Figure 6. Woodcuts of varieties of borage from John Gerard's *Herbal* (1597), p. 653. Call # STC 11750. Used by permission of the Folger Shakespeare Library.

a multitude of the philosophers, it may please your Honor to call to remembrance that which you know of some noble princes that have joined this study with their most important matters of state. Mithridates the great[3] was famous for his knowledge herein, as Plutarch noteth; Evax also king of Arabia,[4] the happy garden of the world for principal simples, wrote of this argument, as Pliny showeth; Diocletian[5] might he have his praise, had he not drowned all his honor in the blood of his persecution. To conclude this point, the example of Solomon is before the rest and greater, whole wisdom and knowledge was such, that he was able to set out the nature of all plants, from the highest cedar to the lowest moss.

[. . .]

Of borage

THE DESCRIPTION

Borage hath broad leaves, rough, lying flat on the ground of a black or swart green color, among which riseth up a stalk two cubits high, divided into divers branches, whereupon do grow gallant blue flowers, composed of five leaves a piece, out of the middle of which grow forth black threads joined in the top and pointed like a brooch or pyramid. The root is thready and cannot away with the cold of winter.

Borage with white flowers is like unto the precedent, but differeth in the flowers, for those of this plant are white, and the others of a perfect blue color, wherein is the difference. Never dying borage hath many very broad leaves, rough and hairy, of a black dark green color, among which rise up stiff hairy stalks, whereupon do grow fair blue flowers, ripe seed, and buds for new flowers, all at once, whereupon it was called *Semper virens*, and that very properly because it is not to be seen neither winter nor summer, but always at one time, with green leaves, fair flowers, buds, ripe and unripe seed, whereby it greatly increaseth.

[. . .]

THE PLACE.

These grow in my garden and in others also.

3. Mithridates VI, 135–63 BCE, king of Pontus and Armenia Minor

4. We only have indirect evident of Evax, king of Arabia, who was also said to be a master of the lapidary arts.

5. Diocletian 344–311CE was a Roman emperor who notoriously persecuted Christians; he ultimately retired and lived out his final days tending his gardens.

THE TIME

Borage flowereth and flourisheth most part of all summer and till autumn be far spent.

THE NAMES

Borage is call in shops *boragos* of the old writers, which is called in Latine *Lingua bubula*. Pliny calleth it *Euprosumum* because it maketh a man merry and joyful, which thing also that old verse concerning borage doth testify:

Ego Borage gaudia semper ago

In English: I borage bring always courage.

[. . .]

THE TEMPERATURES

It is evidently moist, and not in like sort hot, but seemeth to be in a mean between hot and cold.

THE VIRTUES

Those of our time do use the flowers in salads, to exhilarate and make the mind glad. There be also many things made of them, used everywhere for the comfort of the heart, for the driving away of sorrow, and increasing the joy of the mind.

The leaves boiled among other potherbs do much prevail in making the body soluble, they being boiled in honeyed water be also good against the roughness of the throat and hoarseness, as Galen teacheth.

The leaves and flowers of borage out into wine maketh men and women glad and merry, and driveth away all sadness, dullness, and melancholy, as Dioscorides and Pliny affirm.

Guillaume du Bartas, *La sepmaine ou creation du monde*, or *Divine Weeks and Works*, On Aconite

Part 1 introduces *La sepmaine ou creation du monde*, or *Divine Weeks and Works* (1578) of Guillaume du Bartas (1540–1590) as an ecstatic epic poem describing the seven days of Creation. In the section on the third day Du Bartas describes the formation of the vegetal world, where he celebrates not only the beauty and uses of plants for food but also their extraordinary power to kill and cure. He suggests that the power of plant "virtues" extends

Source: Josuah Sylvester, translator. *Bartas: His Divine Weekes and Workes*, London, 1605), p. 101.

beyond their influence on the human body to galvanize the entire world. This praise of aconite is especially potent in its anthropomorphizing of the plant's virtues, naming the plant a courageous and noble combatant against snake venom.

> Nor, powerful herbs, do we alonely find
> Your virtues working in frail human kind;
> But you can force the fiercest animals,
> The fellest fiends, the firmest minerals—
> Yea, fairest planets, if antiquity
> Have not belied the hags of Thessaly.
> [. . .]
> Moreover, Lord, is't not a work of Thine
> That everywhere, in every turf, we find
> Such multitude of other plants to spring
> In form, effect, and color, differing?
> And each of them, in their due seasons ta'en
> To one is physic, to another bane;
> Now gentle; sharp anon; now good, then ill;
> What cureth now, the same anon doth kill.
> Th'herb, sagapen,[1] serves the slow ass for meat,
> But kills the ox if of the same he eat.
> So branched hemlock for the stares[2] is fit,
> But death to man if he but taste of it;
> And oleander unto beasts is poison
> But unto man a special counter-poison.
> What ranker poison, what more deadly bane,
> Than aconite can there be touched, or ta'n?
> And yet his juice, but cures the burning bite
> Of stinging serpents, if applied to it.
> O valiant venom! O courageous plant!
> Disdainful poison, noble combatant,
> That scorneth aid, and loves alone to fight,
> That none partake the glory of his might,
> For if he find our bodies prepossessed
> With other poison, then he leaves the rest,
> And with his rival enters secret duel,

1. An exotic gum-resin
2. Starlings

One to one, strong to strong, cruel to cruel,
Still fighting fierce, and never overgive
Til they, both dying, give man leave to live.

William Lawson, *A New Orchard and Garden*, On the Cultivation of Trees

The clergyman William Lawson (1553/4–1635) spent most of his life in northern Yorkshire, tending to both his parishioners and his garden. In 1618 he published *A New Orchard and Garden, or, The Best Way for Planting, Grafting, and to Make Any Ground Good for a Rich Orchard; Particularly in the North Parts of England*, with a second part entitled *The Countrie Housewife's Garden* (see also Part 6). Lawson's *New Orchard* offers practical advice for cultivating fruit trees while emphasizing the virtues associated with gardening. He argues that the work itself improves character, while pruning and shaping trees echoes the practice of morally reforming people. For Lawson all living things can be cultivated and improved, although without that care they may degenerate (see also Theophrastus on degeneration in plants). He compares a tree's life with a man's and speculates that with the proper culture and care, a fruit tree might live a thousand years and a timber oak even longer. This acknowledgment of trees' inherent strength and resilience balances out Lawson's copious advice on pruning excerpted in Part 6, where he claims to be able to "bring any tree (beginning by time) to any form."

Every living thing bestows the least part of his age in his growth, and so must it needs be with trees. A man comes not to his full growth and strength (by common estimation) before thirty years, and some slender and clean bodies, not till forty, so long also stands his strength, and so long also must he have allowed by course of nature to decay. Ever supposing that he be well kept with necessaries, and from and without strains, bruises, and all other domineering diseases, I will not say upon true report, that physic holds it possible, that a clean body kept by these three doctors, Doctor Diet, Doctor Quiet, and Doctor Merriman, may live near a hundred years.

[. . .]

Now if a man, whose body is nothing (in a manner) but tender rottenness, whose course of life cannot by any means, by counsel, restraint of laws, or punishment, nor hope of praise, profit, or eternal glory, be kept within any bounds, who is degenerate clean from his natural feeding, to effeminate niceness, and

Source: William Lawson. *A New Orchard and Garden*. London, 1618, pp. 50–52.

cloying his body with excess of meat, drink, sleep, etc., and to whom nothing is so pleasant and so much desired as the causes of his own death, as idleness, lust, etc., may live to that age, I see not but a tree of a solid substance, not damnified by heat or cold, capable of, and subject to any kind of ordering or dressing that a man shall apply unto him, feeding naturally, as from the beginning disburdened of all superfluities, eased of, and of his own accord avoiding the causes that may annoy him, should double the life of a man, more than twice told; and yet natural philosophy, and the universal consent of all histories tell us, that many other living creatures far exceed man in the length of years.

[. . .]

So that I resolve upon good reason, that fruit-trees well ordered, may live and like a thousand years, and bear fruit, and the longer, the more, the greater, and the better, because his vigor is proud and stronger, when his years are many. You shall see old trees put their buds and blossoms both sooner and more plentifully then young trees by much. And I sensibly perceive my young trees to enlarge their fruit, as they grow greater, both for number, and greatness. Young heifers bring not forth calves so fair, neither are they so plentiful to milk, as when they become to be old kine. No good housewife will bred of a young but of an old breed-mother. It is so in all things naturally, therefore in trees.

And if fruit-trees last to this age, how many ages is it to be supposed, strong and huge timber-trees will last? Whose huge bodies require the years of divers Methusalahs, before they end their days, whose sap is strong and bitter, whose bark is hard and thick, and their substance solid and stiff, all which are defenses of health and long life. Their strength withstands all forcible winds, their sap of that quality is not subject to worms and tainting. Their bark receives seldom or never by casualty any wound. And not only so, but he is free from removals, which are the death of millions of trees, whereas the fruit-tree in comparison is little, and often blown down, his sap sweet, easily, and soon tainted, his bark tender, and soon wounded, and himself used by man, as man useth himself, that is either skillfully, or carelessly.

John Parkinson, *Paradisi in Sole: Paradisus Terrestris*, On Auriculas

A practicing apothecary serving both James I and Charles I, John Parkinson (1567–1650) wrote two massive books on plants: first his gardening book, *Paradisi in Sole: Paradisus Terristris* (1629), and then his herbal, *Theatrum*

Source: John Parkinson. *Paradisi in Sole: Paradisus Terrestris*. London, 1629, pp. 8–12, 235–41.

Figure 7. Portrait of John Parkinson, *Paradisi in Sole: Paradisus Terrestris.* Parkinson is holding a rose campion, a mark of his plantsmanship. Folio 630 P222. Kislak Center for Special Collections, Rare Books, and Manuscripts, University of Pennsylvania Libraries.

Botanicum (1640) (Figure 7). Dedicated to Queen Henrietta Maria, *Paradisi in Sole* is an impressive, amply illustrated folio volume offered as "a garden of all sorts of pleasant flowers which our English air will permit to be nursed up with a kitchen garden of all manner of herbs, roots, and fruits, for meat or sauce used with us, and an orchard of all sort of fruit-bearing trees and shrubs fit for our land together with the right ordering, planting, and preserving of them, and their uses and virtues." Parkinson thus emphasizes plants that are suited to England, while he particularly admires those "outlandish" or "stranger" flowers that have been naturalized. In his preface to the reader, Parkinson distinguishes his volume from earlier herbals in its emphasis on aesthetics, advocating flowers that are "chiefest for choice, and fairest for show, from among all the several tribes and kindreds of nature's beauty." At the same time, however, he does not abandon the herbals' concern with "virtues," as evident in this entry on the auriculas or "bears' ears," now called mountain cowslips (Figure 8). Aesthetics thus implicitly compete with use in Parkinson's vision of the plant world. It is instructive to compare Parkinson on auriculas with Samuel Gilbert, in his *Florist's Vade-Mecum*. (On Parkinson, see also entries in Parts 6 and 7.)

Chap. IV. The nature and names of divers outlandish flowers, that for their pride, beauty, and earliness, are to be planted in gardens of pleasure for delight.

Having thus formed out a garden, and divided it into his fit and due proportion, with all the graceful knots, arbors, walks, etc., likewise what is fit to keep it in the same comely order, is appointed unto it, both for the borders of the squares, and for the knots and beds themselves, let us now come and furnish the inward parts, and beds with those fine flowers that (being strangers unto us, and giving the beauty and bravery of their colors so early before many of our own bred flowers, the more to entice us to their delight) are most beseeming it; and namely, with daffodils, fritillaries, jacinthes,[1] saffron-flowers, lilies, flowerdeluces,[2] tulips, anemones, French cowslips, or bears ears,[3] and a number of such other flowers, very beautiful, delightful, and pleasant, hereafter described at full, whereof although many have little sweet scent to commend them, yet their earliness and exceeding great beauty and variety doth so far countervail that defect (and yet I must tell you with all, that there is among the many sorts of them some, and that not a few, that do excel in sweetness, being

1. Hyacinths
2. Irises
3. Auriculas

Figure 8. Woodcuts of varieties of auriculas from John Parkinson, *Paradisi in Sole: Paradisus Terrestris* (1629), p. 237. Folio 630 P222. Kislak Center for Special Collections, Rare Books, and Manuscripts, University of Pennsylvania Libraries.

so strong and heady, that they rather offend by too much than by too little scent, and some again are of so mild and moderate temper, that they scarce come short of your most delicate and daintiest flowers) that they are almost in all places with all persons, especially with the better sort of the gentry of the land, as greatly desired and accepted as any other the most choicest, and the rather, for that the most part of these outlandish flowers, do show forth their beauty and colors so early in the year, that they seem to make a garden of delight even in the winter time, and do so give their flowers one after another, that all their bravery is not fully spent, until that gilliflowers,[4] the pride of our English gardens, do show themselves; so that whosoever would have of every sort of these flowers, may have for every month several colors and varieties, even from Christmas until midsummer, or after; and then, after some little respite, until Christmas again, and that in some plenty, with great content and without forcing; so that every man may have them in every place, if they will take any care of them. And because there be many gentlewomen and others, that would gladly have some fine flowers to furnish their gardens, but know not what the names of those things are that they desire, nor what are the times of their flowering, nor the skill and knowledge of their right ordering, planting, displanting, transplanting, and replanting, I have here for their sakes set down the nature, names, times, and manner of ordering in a brief manner, referring the more ample declaration of them to the work following.

[. . .]

Chap.V. The nature and names of those that are called usually English flowers.

Those flowers that have been usually planted in former times in gardens of this kingdom (when as our forefathers knew few or none of those that are recited before) have by time and custom attained the name of English flowers, although the most of them were never natural of this our land, but brought in from other countries at one time or other, by those that took pleasure in them where they first saw them; and I doubt not, but many other sorts than here are set down, or now known to us, have been brought, which either have perished by their negligence or want of skill that brought them, or else because they could not abide our cold winters. Those only remaining with us that have endured of themselves, and by their increasing have been distributed over the whole land.

4. A type of carnation

AURICULA URSI. BEARS' EARS.

There are so many sundry and several sorts of bears' ears, the variety consisting as well in the differing colors of the flowers, as the form and color of the leaves, that I shall not comprehend and set down unto you all the diversities by many, that are risen up to those that have been industrious in the sowing of the seeds of the several sorts of them. Yet if you accept of these that I do here offer unto you, I shall give you the knowledge of others, as time, occasion, and the view of them shall enable me. And because they are without all question kinds of cowslips, I have set them down before them in the first place, as being of more beauty and greater respect, or at the least of more rarity unto us. To dispose them therefore into order, I shall rank them under three principal colors, that is to say, red or purple, white, and yellow, and show you the varieties of each of them (for so many as are come to my knowledge) apart by themselves, and not promiscuously as many others have done.

[What follows are descriptions of twenty-one different types of auriculas.]

THE PLACE.

Many of these goodly plants grow naturally on mountains, especially the Alps, in divers places; for some kinds that grow in some places, do not in others, but far distant one from the other. There hath likewise some been found on the Pyrenean mountains, but that kind with the blue flower and borage leaf, hath been gathered on the mountains in Spain, and on the Pyreneans next unto Spain.

THE TIME.

They all flower in April and May, and the seed is ripe in the end of June, or beginning of July, and sometimes they will flower again in the end of summer, or in autumn, if the year prove temperate, moist, and rainy.

THE NAMES.

It is very probable, that none of these plants were ever known unto the ancient writers, because we cannot be assured, that they may be truly referred unto any plant that they name [. . .] We in English call them bears' ears, according to the Latin, or as they are called by divers women, French cowslips; they may be called mountain cowslips, if you will, for to distinguish between them and other cowslips, whereof these are several kinds.

[. . .]

THE VIRTUES.

All the sorts of bears' ears are cephalic, that is, conducing help for the pains in the head, and for the giddiness thereof, which may happen, either by the sight of steep places subject to danger, or otherwise. They are accounted also to be helping for the palsy,[5] and shaking of the joints; and also as a sanicle or wound-herb. The leaves of the Cortusa[6] taste a little hot, and if one of them be laid whole, without bruising, on the cheek of any tender-skinned woman, it will raise an orient red color, as if some fucus[7] had been laid thereon, which will pass away without any manner of harm, or mark where it lay.

George Herbert, "The Flower"

A university-educated clergyman once destined for high office, George Herbert (1593–1633) instead retreated to practice his ministry in a small parish near Salisbury. During that time, he composed a volume of poems called *The Temple*, published posthumously in 1633. Like the other "metaphysical" poets, Herbert developed extended "conceits" or strong images to express complicated emotions inherent to profound religious experience. In "The Flower" Herbert uses the flower's life cycle, from winter to spring and back again, to explore the relationship between his heart and soul and God's wrath and forgiveness; it also imagines the garden of God's Paradise, where no flower ever fades. The speaker shares both a plant's strength in its annual renewal and its exposure to heat and cold. (Compare with Pierre de Ronsard's "Ode to Cassandra" [above], which compares a woman's life and loveliness with a rose for its brevity.)

How fresh, O Lord, how sweet and clean
Are thy returns! even as the flowers in spring;
To which, besides their own demean,[1]
The late-past frosts tributes of pleasures bring.
Grief melts away
Like snow in May,
As if there were no such cold thing.

Who would have thought my shriveled heart
Could have recovered greenness? It was gone
Quite underground; as flowers depart

5. Paralysis
6. Variety of auricula
7. Cosmetic, like rouge
Source: George Herbert. *The Temple*. London, 1633, p. 160.
1. Demesne or estate, but also suggests demeanor

To see their mother-root, when they have blown,
Where they together
All the hard weather
Dead to the world, keep house unknown.

These are thy wonders, Lord of power,
Killing and quickening, bringing down to hell
And up to heaven in an hour;
Making a chiming of a passing-bell.[2]
We say amiss,
This or that is:
Thy word is all, if we could spell.

O that I once past changing were,
Fast in thy Paradise, where no flower can wither!
Many a spring I shoot up fair,
Offering at heaven, growing and groaning thither;
Nor doth my flower
Want a spring-shower,[3]
My sins and I joining together.

But while I grow in a straight line,
Still upwards bent, as if heaven were mine own,
Thy anger comes, and I decline.
What frost to that? What pole is not the zone,
Where all things burn,
When thou dost turn,
And the least frown of thine is shown?

And now in age I bud again,
After so many deaths I live and write;
I once more smell the dew and rain,
And relish versing. O my only light,
It cannot be
That I am he
On whom thy tempests fell all night.

2. The church bell that marks the death of a parishioner
3. Both the weather and the speaker's tears

These are thy wonders, Lord of love,
To make us see we are but flowers that glide[4];
Which when we once can find and prove,
Thou hast a garden for us, where to bide.
Who would be more,
Swelling through store,
Forfeit their Paradise by their pride.

Ralph Austen, *A Treatise of Fruit Trees, and The Spiritual Use of an Orchard or Garden of Fruit Trees*

Ralph Austen (ca. 1612–1676) was a self-taught nurseryman and a radical Puritan involved in both the contemporary agricultural revolution and the Commonwealth cause in the English Civil War. He spent most of his working life near Oxford, cultivating trees and plants and contributing to the initiatives led by Samuel Hartlib, who wanted to restore England's prosperity through scientific agriculture. In 1653 Austen published *A Treatise of Fruit Trees*, accompanied by a shorter tract, *The Spiritual Use of an Orchard or Garden of Fruit Trees*. These texts combine a wealth of practical information about growing orchards with meditations on the spiritual values of arboriculture. Like William Lawson (see passages in Parts 2 and 6), Austen compared cultivating trees with moral reformation, expanding that thought to envision the radical reformation of all England. This excerpt represents part of Austen's extensive justification of fruit trees and their cultivation through citation of biblical passages on trees read allegorically to symbolize Christ, the Church, and Christian mysteries.

Arguments of the Dignity of Fruit-trees and Art of Planting.

Another divine argument of the dignity, and value of fruit-trees, and art of planting, is from the frequent use of similitudes between the Church of God and fruit-trees, and between our Savior and fruit-trees. Fruit-trees bear the figure and resemblance of many high and great mysteries held forth to us in parables, tropes, allegories, which represent moral, and spiritual things, under the shape and figure of these corporeal things.

One similitude is between the Church and a vineyard: Isaiah 5.1.2. "My beloved had a vineyard in a very fruitful hill. Verse. 2. And he fenced it, and

4. Pass imperceptibly

Source: Ralph Austen. *A Treatise of Fruit-Trees Shewing the Manner of Grafting, Setting, Pruning, and Ordering of Them in All Respects* [. . .] *Together with the Spiritual Use of an Orchard or Garden of Fruit-Trees*. London, 1653, pp. 14–15.

gathered out the stones thereof and planted it with the choice vine, etc: And he looked that it should bring forth grapes etc."

Secondly, the prophet David useth the similitude of a fruitful tree to express the condition of a godly man. Psalms: 1.3. "He shall be like a tree planted by the rivers of waters, that bringeth forth his fruit in due season, his leaf also shall not wither and look whatsoever he doth it shall prosper." So again Jeremiah: 17.8. "He shall be as a tree planted by the waters, and that spreadeth out her roots by the river, and shall not see when heat cometh, but her leaf shall be green, and shall not be careful in the year of drought neither shall cease from yielding fruit."

Another similitude our Savior useth to express the condition of his church drawn from the vine. John. 15.1. "I am the true vine and my Father is the husbandman: every branch in me that beareth not fruit he taketh away, and every branch that beareth fruit he purgeth it, that it may bring forth more fruit, as the branch cannot bear fruit of itself except it abide in the cine, no more can ye except ye abide in me, Verse 4."

Another similitude is between natural and mystical grafting, Romans: 11.17. "Concerning the calling of the Gentiles, and rejection of the Jews for a time. If some of the branches be broken off, and thou being a wild olive tree were grafted in amongst them, and with them partakest of the root and fatness of the olive tree, Verse. 23. And they also if they abide not still in unbelief shall be grafted in, for God is able to graft them in again, Verse. 24. For if thou wert cut out of the olive tree, which is wild by nature, and wert grafted (contrary to nature) into a good olive tree, how much more shall these which be the natural branches be grafted into their own olive tree."

Fifthly, the condition of the Church is figuratively and by allegories described by Solomon in his Songs, Chap. 4 12.13. "And amongst other figures and resemblances there us'd, one is taken from an orchard or garden of fruit-trees. A garden enclosed is my sister, my spouse. Thy plants are an orchard of pomegranates, with pleasant fruits." And again, the Church compares Christ to a fruit-tree, Chap. 2.3. "Like the apple-tree among the trees of the wood, so is my beloved among the sons: I sat down under his shadow with great delight, and his fruit was sweet to my taste."

Sixtly, A fruit-tree bears the figure and resemblance of our savior Christ in the description of spiritual paradise, Revelations. 22 2. "In the midst of the street of it, and of either side of the river was there the tree of life, which bore twelve manner of fruits, and yielded her fruits every month, and the leaves of the tree were for the healing of the nations." And again Chap. 2.7. "To him that overcommeth I will give to eat of the tree of life, which is in the midst of the Paradise of God."

Johanna St. John, Manuscript Recipes

A supporter of Oliver Cromwell during the Interregnum, Johanna St. John (1631–1705) managed both a London house and a country estate, Lydiard House in Wiltshire, where she maintained substantial gardens. Like so many women of her time, she compiled two recipe books that she valued enough to mention in her will as bequests to her granddaughter and daughter. Now held at the Wellcome Library, the books recommend treating diseases in both human beings and animals with both plant and animal ingredients. Such recipe books reveal women's intimate engagement with the everyday plant world and demonstrate the exchange among women of herbal knowledge (in this case, the recipes are from a "Lady Temple" and "Lady Honywood"; see also Hannah Wolley in Part 1).

An admirable thing for a cancer. Lady Temple. The green leaves of periwinkle, quilt them as thick as one will lie by another upon soft brown paper. It should lie on continually, the leaves next it laying on fresh. As the leaves dry take drying drinks with hoglice[1] in them while you use this, and sometimes purging.

Another for the same. Lady Honywood. Take of the juices of feverfew, celandine, rue, and smallage.[2] Mix the[m] with bean flower and to half a pint as much honey as a small egg. Spread it on the softest brown paper. If it bc broke lay some of the paper next the sore and the juices cold up on it. Change it twice a day and burn the medicine.

Samuel Gilbert, *Florist's Vade-Mecum*, On Auriculas

Samuel Gilbert (died 1692?) was the rector of Quatt in Shropshire and chaplain to Jane, Baroness Gerard, whose garden he planned. He is known today for *The Florist's Vade-Mecum* (1682), "being a choice compendium of whatever worthy notice hath been extant for the propagation, raising, planting, increasing, and preserving the rarest flowers and plants that our climate and skill . . . will persuade to live with us." The book provides a month-by-month guide to flower-gardening tasks (see also his instructions for planting in July in Part 4). Throughout the book, Gilbert closely attends to the status of different flowers, that is, how they are "esteemed." For example, when it comes to auriculas or

Source: Johanna St. John. "Her Booke." 1680. Wellcome Library, MS4338/2. Credit: Wellcome Collection.

1. A woodlouse
2. A form of wild celery

Source: Samuel Gilbert. *Florist's Vade-Mecum*. London, 1682, pp. 44–47.

bears' ears (discussed earlier by John Parkinson in Part 2), Gilbert is mostly concerned with the flower's relative rarity and value, including in monetary terms. He often identifies the different varieties with the men (and some women) who cultivated them and competed for prizes in the now burgeoning "florist societies" of specialists and amateurs. In this sense, for Gilbert flowers serve as both a possession and a commodity for those who cultivate them.

Bears' ears, flowers so much now in esteem (and well deserve it) for their diversity of color and different faces, each adding a new grace to its kind, nature sporting herself so in their various complexions, that we are at a loss, to suit names to the several dyes they offer to our description, either in their self colors, striped or double flowers, some of which are striped also and declare their worth by the prizes given for them from one to two, three, four or five pounds etc. a root, each year producing new faces from the seeds sowed of well-chosen flowers, the best way of performing thereof, not till now made public, shall be faithfully showed after the descriptions of these five plants, as they as flowers offer themselves to our view, dividing them into these sorts, single, self colors, single striped, double self-colored, and double striped flowers.

[. . .]

Single self colors, which as the rest have green thick leaves and broad, some longer some shorter, some of a grass green, others lighter and mealy, some smooth and plain on the edges, others downy and jagged or purled edges. From the middle or sides of the leaves spring up the stalks, from four inches to a shasual[1] in height, round and colored like the leaves, bearing at the top many flowers shaped as the cowslips, consisting of five small leaves, parted at the ends with a white circle or eye in the middle, hollow down to the small caps they stand in, wherein when the flowers fallen appear small round heads with a prick in the middle, which contain the seeds, that are small and brown, having a long, white, stringy root, like that of the primrose or cowslip, that original of these delicate sprigs.

Luteo: The yellow auricula, of which those only are esteemed, that bear the biggest trusses of the deepest yellow, largest and whitest eyes, the rest not worth a farthing, hence came the leather-coats still esteemed, as liver color with a gray eye

[. . .]

Auricula flore purpureo: The purple auricula, of which several sorts, some deeper, some lighter, some bigger, some lesser, some good white eyes, others indifferent.

1. Scavel, or small spade?

One The fair Downam (raised by a divine of that name) bearing many flowers, of a bright murrey[2] or reddish purple color with a white eye.

Tutor Good's purple, bearing a great truss of many fair, rich, purple flowers, with a delicate white eye, that will not wash with rain, but abide so to the last, which many others will not do.

Mrs. Bug's fine purple, like the last, but that the great head of flowers stand more upright, of a deeper purple and broader white eye.

Mr. Whitmore's purple, fair and large great truss of flowers, of a lighter purple than the former, with fine white eyes.

Mr. Rea's purple, like in color brighter, bearing more flowers, good eye.

Purple Fransway, a good flower, bearing a great truss of rich shining purple flowers with a larger white eye than any of the rest

[. . .]

Mrs. Austin's Scarlet, bears a great truss of fine scarlet flowers, with snow-white eyes, yet the best of that kind. There are some of Mr. Jacob Robert's raising, that are good flowers, who keeps the Physic Garden in Oxford, there are others that are raised from seeds of a blood red, as

Mr. Reo's deep scarlet, or rather blood-red auricula, bearing a great truss of flowers, with fair white eyes. Some that are crimson, others carnation, rose color and blushes, with several other colors, the stranger the color, if with good white eyes that will not wash, are of most value.

2. Reddish-purple

PART III

Animals

In constructing his version of the slippery *scala naturae*, or ladder of nature, Aristotle understood that humans share a kind of soul with both plants and animals. For Aristotle, human and nonhuman animals have a "nutritive" or vegetative soul, but they are also sentient and capable of independent motion (see Aristotle in Parts 2 and 3). Humans, in turn, differ from other animals in being capable of calculation and thought (Fudge 2006; Bach). Whether in the biblical construction of God-given human dominance or this Aristotelian hierarchy, this implied superiority of people to other animals as well as plants served to justify exploiting beasts for food, medicine, labor, entertainment, and transportation (see Marder; Thomas).

Yet as much as he insisted on such a hierarchy, Aristotle also acknowledged the difficulty of distinguishing among all living things. Even more so than plants, the category of animals destabilizes rigid boundaries between the human and all other creatures (see Salisbury; Raber 2013; Bach; Boehrer 2010; Feerick and Nardizzi). In a post-Cartesian world, the distinction between human and nonhuman animals lies in privileging reason; however, as Karen Raber has argued, attention only to reason distracts from the awareness of "shared embodiment" characteristic in premodern thinking about animals (Raber 2013). Not only were people then more intimate with other animals but they also believed that the same temperatures and humors that informed the human body and character shaped beasts as well: so, for example, Gervase Markham wrote that, just as in people, when beset with excessive humors, a horse can be "either a hot choleric horse, a cold dull horse, a dry mischievous horse, or a moist cowardly horse, according to the over-flow of that quality which reigneth in him" (Markham, Part 3). Even outside of humoral theory, the notion that animals have characters too dates back to Aristotle, who observed that "in number of animals we observe gentleness or fierceness, mildness or cross temper, courage, or timidity, fear or confidence, high spirit or low cunning, and, with regard to intelligence, something equivalent to sagacity.

Some of these qualities in man, as compared with the corresponding qualities in animals, differ only quantitatively" (Aristotle, Part 3) (see also Paster).

Such observations undergird the centuries-old tradition of the animal fables beginning with Aesop (sixth century BCE), in which stories of anthropomorphized animals teach morality (see the example from Marie de France, Part 3). *Physiologus*, an ancient treatise reading allegorical or Christian meanings into animal physiology and habits, offered a medieval analogue to the animal fable tradition; there, for example, the idea that the panther is a mild creature who breathes a pleasant fragrance leads to comparing this animal with Christ. Elaborations of *Physiologus* and similar works proliferated in the form of bestiaries providing information about animal behavior derived from traditional sources and translated into Christian or moral doctrine. Analogies between animal life and human society also lent themselves to allegorical literature; for example, Chaucer composed a long poem about a *Parliament of Fowls* that gather on Saint Valentine's Day, which critiques the hierarchies of both animal and human society. As with plants, poetic contemplation of animals, even ones as lowly as Richard Lovelace's snail or Hester Pulter's spider could generate revelations about human experience.

Such comparisons of humans and beasts also provoked questioning of humans' innate superiority. Writing in the fourteenth century, Anselm Turmeda playfully but directly challenged the idea that people were really better than animals. Later, when Michel de Montaigne famously speculated on what his cat was doing when he was playing with her (was she playing with him?), he observed how we must "perceive by the greater part of their works what excellency beasts have over us, and how weak our art and short our cunning is, if we go about to imitate them" (Montaigne, Part 3). By the end of the seventeenth century, at the same time that Robert Hooke exposed the secret structure of the smallest animals with his microscope, he also betrayed an intimate understanding of their desires, and Margaret Cavendish more radically claimed a rational as well as sensitive spirit for animals when she speculated on the nature of animal knowledge and cognition. Thus, although in the seventeenth century Descartes began to open up an unpassable abyss between humans and nonthinking animals, the boundaries were still porous.

Aristotle, *Historia animalium*, or *The History of Animals*

Part 1 introduces Aristotle's conception of nature in his *Physics*: there he argues that human and nonhumans alike are created for a purpose, insofar as "action

Source: Aristotle. *The History of Animals*. Translated by D'Arcy Wentworth Thompson, 1907, 487.a1–488b1, 588a.1–588b.1. *Wiki Source*, https://en.wikisource.org/wiki/History_of_Animals_(Thompson).

for an end is present in things which come to be and are by nature." When Aristotle turned his attention to animals (he is said to have examined over five hundred species), he tried to describe and categorize all their forms, sorting creatures out by their differences as well as similarities. In this excerpt from his *History of Animals*, it first seems as if humans are just one category of animals differentiated by "modes of subsistence, in habits, in actions performed." Nonhuman animals are attributed characters and indeed qualities of emotions or personalities just like those of humans. At the same time, Aristotle also establishes the concepts of the "scale" or ladder of nature, which proceeds upwards from lifeless thing to plants and then animals, with humans at its summit. Even then, however, Aristotle acknowledges that it is often hard to draw fine distinctions, for example, in determining when a certain sea creature is a plant or animal. Thus, the scale of nature is revealed to be far less rigid than it first appears. (Compare with Aristotle's *De anima* or *Of the Soul*, on plants, in Part 2.)

Animals differ from one another in their modes of subsistence, in their actions, in their habits, and in their parts. Concerning these differences we shall first speak in broad and general terms, and subsequently we shall treat of the same with close reference to each particular genus.

For instance, some animals live in water and others on land. And of those that live in water some do so in one way, and some in another: that is to say, some live and feed in the water, take in and emit water, and cannot live if deprived of water, as is the case with the great majority of fishes; others get their food and spend their days in the water, but do not take in water but air, nor do they bring forth in the water. Many of these creatures are furnished with feet, as the otter, the beaver, and the crocodile; some are furnished with wings, as the diver and the grebe; some are destitute of feet, as the water-snake. Some creatures get their living in the water and cannot exist outside it: but for all that do not take in either air or water, as, for instance, the sea-nettle and the oyster. And of creatures that live in the water some live in the sea, some in rivers, some in lakes, and some in marshes, as the frog and the newt.

Of animals that live on dry land some take in air and emit it, which phenomena are termed "inhalation" and "exhalation"; as, for instance, man and all such land animals as are furnished with lungs. Others, again, do not inhale air, yet live and find their sustenance on dry land; as, for instance, the wasp, the bee, and all other insects. And by "insects" I mean such creatures as have nicks or notches on their bodies, either on their bellies or on both backs and bellies.

And of land animals many, as has been said, derive their subsistence from the water; but of creatures that live in and inhale water not a single one derives its subsistence from dry land.

Some animals at first live in water, and by and by change their shape and live out of water, as is the case with river worms, for out of these the gadfly develops.

Furthermore, some animals are stationary, and some are erratic. Stationary animals are found in water, but no such creature is found on dry land. In the water are many creatures that live in close adhesion to an external object, as is the case with several kinds of oyster. And, by the way, the sponge appears to be endowed with a certain sensibility: as a proof of which it is alleged that the difficulty in detaching it from its moorings is increased if the movement to detach it be not covertly applied.

Other creatures adhere at one time to an object and detach themselves from it at other times, as is the case with a species of the so-called sea-nettle; for some of these creatures seek their food in the night-time loose and unattached.

Many creatures are unattached but motionless, as is the case with oysters and the so-called holothuria. Some can swim, as, for instance, fishes, mollusks, and crustaceans, such as the crawfish. But some of these last move by walking, as the crab, for it is the nature of the creature, though it lives in water, to move by walking.

Of land animals some are furnished with wings, such as birds and bees, and these are so furnished in different ways one from another; others are furnished with feet. Of the animals that are furnished with feet some walk, some creep, and some wriggle. But no creature is able only to move by flying, as the fish is able only to swim, for the animals with leathern wings can walk; the bat has feet and the seal has imperfect feet.

[. . .]

Furthermore, the following differences are manifest in their modes of living and in their actions. Some are gregarious, some are solitary, whether they be furnished with feet or wings or be fitted for a life in the water; and some partake of both characters, the solitary and the gregarious. And of the gregarious, some are disposed to combine for social purposes, others to live each for its own self.

Gregarious creatures are, among birds, such as the pigeon, the crane, and the swan; and, by the way, no bird furnished with crooked talons is gregarious. Of creatures that live in water many kinds of fishes are gregarious, such as the so-called migrants, the tunny, the pelamys, and the bonito.

Man, by the way, presents a mixture of the two characters, the gregarious and the solitary. Social creatures are such as have some one common object in view; and this property is not common to all creatures that are gregarious. Such social creatures are man, the bee, the wasp, the ant, and the crane.

Again, of these social creatures some submit to a ruler, others are subject to no governance: as, for instance, the crane and the several sorts of bee submit to a ruler, whereas ants and numerous other creatures are every one his own master. And again, both of gregarious and of solitary animals, some are attached to a fixed home and others are erratic or nomad.

[. . .]

Moreover, some creatures are tame and some are wild: some are at all times tame, as man and the mule; others are at all times savage, as the leopard and the wolf; and some creatures can be rapidly tamed, as the elephant.

Again, we may regard animals in another light. For, whenever a race of animals is found domesticated, the same is always to be found in a wild condition; as we find to be the case with horses, kine, swine, (men), sheep, goats, and dogs.

Further, some animals emit sound while others are mute, and some are endowed with voice: of these latter some have articulate speech, while others are inarticulate; some are given to continual chirping and twittering, some are prone to silence; some are musical, and some unmusical; but all animals without exception exercise their power of singing or chattering chiefly in connection with the intercourse of the sexes.

[. . .]

Some, again, are peculiarly salacious, as the partridge, the barn-door cock and their congeners; others are inclined to chastity, as the whole tribe of crows, for birds of this kind indulge but rarely in sexual intercourse.

[. . .]

Furthermore, some are combative under offence; others are provident for defense. Of the former kind are such as act as aggressors upon others or retaliate when subjected to ill usage, and of the latter kind are such as merely have some means of guarding themselves against attack.

Animals also differ from one another in regard to character in the following respects. Some are good-tempered, sluggish, and little prone to ferocity, as the ox; others are quick tempered, ferocious and unteachable, as the wild boar; some are intelligent and timid, as the stag and the hare; others are mean and treacherous, as the snake; others are noble and courageous and high-bred, as the lion; others are thorough-bred and wild and treacherous, as the wolf: for, by the way, an animal is highbred if it come from a noble stock, and an animal is thorough-bred if it does not deflect from its racial characteristics.

Further, some are crafty and mischievous, as the fox; some are spirited and affectionate and fawning, as the dog; others are easy-tempered and easily domesticated, as the elephant; others are cautious and watchful, as the goose; others are jealous and self-conceited, as the peacock. But of all animals man alone is capable of deliberation.

Many animals have memory, and are capable of instruction; but no other creature except man can recall the past at will.

[. . .]

In the great majority of animals there are traces of psychical qualities or attitudes, which qualities are more markedly differentiated in the case of human beings. For just as we pointed out resemblances in the physical organs, so in a number of animals we observe gentleness or fierceness, mildness or cross temper, courage, or timidity, fear or confidence, high spirit or low cunning, and, with regard to intelligence, something equivalent to sagacity. Some of these qualities in man, as compared with the corresponding qualities in animals, differ only quantitatively: that is to say, a man has more or less of this quality, and an animal has more or less of some other; other qualities in man are represented by analogous and not identical qualities: for instance, just as in man we find knowledge, wisdom, and sagacity, so in certain animals there exists some other natural potentiality akin to these. The truth of this statement will be the more clearly apprehended if we have regard to the phenomena of childhood: for in children may be observed the traces and seeds of what will one day be settled psychological habits, though psychologically a child hardly differs for the time being from an animal; so that one is quite justified in saying that, as regards man and animals, certain psychical qualities are identical with one another, whilst others resemble, and others are analogous to, each other.

Nature proceeds little by little from things lifeless to animal life in such a way that it is impossible to determine the exact line of demarcation, nor on which side thereof an intermediate form should lie. Thus, next after lifeless things in the upward scale comes the plant, and of plants one will differ from another as to its amount of apparent vitality; and, in a word, the whole genus of plants, whilst it is devoid of life as compared with an animal, is endowed with life as compared with other corporeal entities. Indeed, as we just remarked, there is observed in plants a continuous scale of ascent towards the animal. So, in the sea, there are certain objects concerning which one would be at a loss to determine whether they be animal or vegetable. For instance, certain of these objects are fairly rooted, and in several cases perish if detached; thus the pinna is rooted to a particular spot, and the solen (or razor-shell) cannot survive withdrawal from its burrow. Indeed, broadly speaking, the entire genus of testaceans have a resemblance to vegetables, if they be contrasted with such animals as are capable of progression.

In regard to sensibility, some animals give no indication whatsoever of it, whilst others indicate it but indistinctly. Further, the substance of some of these intermediate creatures is fleshlike, as is the case with the so-called tethya (or ascidians) and the acalephae (or sea-anemones); but the sponge is in every respect like a vegetable. And so throughout the entire animal scale there is a graduated differentiation in amount of vitality and in capacity for motion.

A similar statement holds good with regard to habits of life. Thus of plants that spring from seed the one function seems to be the reproduction of their own particular species, and the sphere of action with certain animals is similarly limited. The faculty of reproduction, then, is common to all alike. If sensibility be superadded, then their lives will differ from one another in respect to sexual intercourse through the varying amount of pleasure derived therefrom, and also in regard to modes of parturition and ways of rearing their young. Some animals, like plants, simply procreate their own species at definite seasons; other animals busy themselves also in procuring food for their young, and after they are reared quit them and have no further dealings with them; other animals are more intelligent and endowed with memory, and they live with their offspring for a longer period and on a more social footing.

The life of animals, then, may be divided into two acts—procreation and feeding; for on these two acts all their interests and life concentrate. Their food depends chiefly on the substance of which they are severally constituted; for the source of their growth in all cases will be this substance. And whatsoever is in conformity with nature is pleasant, and all animals pursue pleasure in keeping with their nature.

Pliny the Elder, *Naturalis historia,* or *Natural History*, On Animals

The thirty-seven books of Pliny the Elder's (23–79 CE) massive *Naturalis historia* (*Natural History*), introduced in Part 1, depict a capacious natural world, embracing both the familiar and the exotic. When he came to write about animals, Pliny drew on his abundant classical sources to describe in detail creatures he had never seen, sometimes imagined as monstrous combinations of familiar ones (this first excerpt, for example, discusses the mantichora, with parts of man, lion, and scorpion). The distinctions among different animals, including humans, can thus easily collapse. As with plants, Pliny also listed the numerous uses of animals and animal parts to cure human diseases. His recommendations included means to combat the injuries caused by other animals, as in this second excerpt on "remedies against the poison on serpents." It

Source: Pliny the Elder. *The Natural History.* Translated by John Bostock and Henry T. Riley, London, 1855, book 8, chap. 30, and book 28, chap. 42. *Perseus Digital Library*, http://www.perseus.tufts.edu/hopper/text?doc=Perseus:text:1999.02.0137.

was understood that animals had natural antipathies as well as sympathies, which could then be exploited for cures; for example, since deer are naturally destructive to snakes, any part of a deer works as an antidote or a repellent. (For a later version of such thinking, see the *Secrets of Albertus Magnus* in Part 1 and Thomas Johnson's *Cornucopiae* in Part 3.)

Book 8, Chap. 30. The lynx, the sphinx, the crocotta, and the monkey

Ethiopia produces the lynx in abundance, and the sphinx, which has brown hair and two mammae on the breast, as well as many monstrous kinds of a similar nature; horses with wings, and armed with horns, which are called pegasi; the crocotta, an animal which looks as though it had been produced by the union of the wolf and the dog, for it can break any thing with its teeth, and instantly on swallowing it digest it with the stomach; monkeys, too, with black heads, the hair of the ass, and a voice quite unlike that of any other animal. There are oxen, too, like those of India, some with one horn, and others with three; the leucrocotta, a wild beast of extraordinary swiftness, the size of the wild ass, with the legs of a stag, the neck, tail, and breast of a lion, the head of a badger, a cloven hoof, the mouth slit up as far as the ears, and one continuous bone instead of teeth; it is said, too, that this animal can imitate the human voice. Among the same people, there is also found an animal called eale[1]; it is the size of the river-horse, has the tail of the elephant, and is of a black or tawny color. It has also the jaws of the wild boar, and horns that are moveable, and more than a cubit in length, so that, in fighting, it can employ them alternately, and vary their position by presenting them directly or obliquely, according as necessity may dictate. But the wild bulls which this country produces are the fiercest of all; they are larger than our domestic bull, and exceed all the others in swiftness; are of a tawny color, with azure eyes, and the hair turned the contrary way; while the jaws open as far as the ears, and the horns are as moveable as those of the eale. The hide of this animal is as hard as flint, and effectually resists all wounds. These creatures pursue all the other wild beasts, while they themselves can only be taken in pitfalls, where they always perish from excess of rage. Ctesias informs us, that among these same Ethiopians, there is an animal found, which he calls the mantichora; it has a triple row of teeth, which fit into each other like those of a comb, the face and ears of a man, and azure eyes, is of the color of blood, has the body of the lion, and a tail ending in a sting, like

1. Now thought to be a rhinoceros

that of the scorpion. Its voice resembles the union of the sound of the flute and the trumpet; it is of excessive swiftness, and is particularly fond of human flesh.

Book 28, Chap. 42. Remedies using deer parts

We will therefore classify the various remedies, according to the maladies for which they are respectively used; and, first of all, those to which man has recourse for injuries inflicted by serpents. That deer are destructive to those reptiles no one is ignorant; as also of the fact that they drag them from their holes when they find them, and so devour them. And it is not only while alive and breathing that deer are thus fatal to serpents, but even when dead and separated limb from limb. The fumes of their horns, while burning, will drive away serpents, as already stated; but the bones, it is said, of the upper part of a stag's throat, if burnt upon a fire, will bring those reptiles together. Persons may sleep upon a deer's skin in perfect safety, and without any apprehension of attacks by serpents; its rennet too, taken with vinegar, is an effectual antidote to the stings of those reptiles; indeed, if it has been only touched by a person, he will be for that day effectually protected from them. The testes, dried, or the genitals of the male animal, are considered to be very wholesome, taken in wine, and so are the umbles,[2] generally known as the "centipellio." Persons having about them a deer's tooth, or who have taken the precaution of rubbing the body with a deer or fawn's marrow, will be sure to repel the attacks of all serpents.

Physiologus

Physiologus is the name given to an early second-century CE treatise that interweaves descriptions of animals and their behavior with Christian morality and allegories of the life of Christ. First written in Greek, it was translated into Latin in the fourth century and thereafter into numerous Mediterranean and western European vernaculars. The text bears traces of legends derived from ancient natural histories (e.g., Pliny the Elder); however, it emphasizes finding mystical and moral meaning in animals, reflecting the concept that all nature serves as the book of God. Animal characteristics and actions may suggest incidents in biblical history or facets of human morality but sometimes both: thus, the panther is a figure of Christ but also a reminder to fight the dragon that is Satan. The interpretations in *Physiologus* surface in later medieval bestiaries, even where more detailed description of animal

2. Edible viscera

Source: *Physiologus: A Medieval Book of Nature Lore*. Translated by Michael J. Curley, University of Chicago Press, 2009, pp. 15–16, 42, 52.

behavior counterbalances a moral or allegorical reading; see for example, the excerpt on the crocodile from the "second-family" medieval bestiary, Part 3.

On the Viper

John said to the Pharisees, "You brood of vipers."[1] Physiologus says of the viper that the male has the face of a man, while the female has the form of a woman down to her navel, but from her navel down to her tail she has the form of a crocodile. Indeed, the woman has no secret place, that is, genitals for giving birth, but has only a pinhole. If the male lies with the female and spills his seed into her mouth, and if she drinks his seed, she will cut off the male's necessaries (that is, his male organs) and he will die. When, however, the young have grown within the womb of their mother who has no genitals for giving birth, they pierce through her side, killing her in their escape.

Our Savior, therefore, likened the Pharisees to the viper; just as the viper's brood kills its father and mother, so this people which is without God kills its father, Jesus Christ, and its earthly mother, Jerusalem. "Yet how will they flee from the wrath to come?"[2] Our father Jesus Christ and mother church live in eternity while those living in sin are dead.

On the Beaver

There is an animal called the beaver who is extremely inoffensive and quiet. His genitals are helpful as a medicine and he is found in the king's palace. When the beaver sees the hunter hastening to overtake him in the mountains, he bites off his own genitals and throws them before the hunter. If another hunter happens to pursue him later on, he throws himself on his back and shows himself to the hunter. And the hunter, seeing that the beast has no genitals, departs from him.

O, and you who behave in a manly way, O citizen of God, if you have given to the hunter the things which are his, he no longer approaches you. If you have had evil inclinations toward sin, greed, adultery, theft, cut them away from you and give them to the devil. The Apostle said, "Pay all of them their dues, taxes to whom taxes are due, honor to whom honor is due," and so on.[3] Let us first throw the disgraces of sins which are within us before the devil, for they are his works, and let us give to God the things which are God's, prayers and the fruit of our good works. [Separate yourself from the works of the flesh, which are the tax and tribute of the devil, and acquire the spiritual fruits: charity, joy, peace,

1. Matthew 3:7 and Luke 3:7
2. Luke 3:7
3. Romans 13:7

patience, goodness, faith, meekness, continence, chastity in good works, that is, in alms, visitations to the sick, the care of the poor, the praise of God, in prayers and the performance of kindnesses and other acts of God.]

On the Panther

The Prophet says, "I became like a lion to the house of Judah, and like a panther to the house of Ephraim."[4] The panther has this nature: he is a friend of all animals but is an enemy of the dragon. He is entirely variegated and is beautiful like Joseph's cloak. And David said in Psalm 44, "At your right hand stands the queen in a golden dress decked in various hues." The panther is a quiet and most exceedingly mild animal. If, however, he has eaten and is satisfied, he falls asleep immediately in his lair and arises from his sleep on the third day (like our Savior). If the panther awakens from his sleep on the third day, he roars out in a loud voice and many a pleasant fragrance issues from his voice. Those who are far away and those who are near, hearing his voice, follow its pleasant fragrance.

Our Lord and Savior rising up from the dead became a pleasant fragrance for us,[5] peace for those who are far away and those who are near.[6] As the apostle Paul said, "Manifold is the wisdom of God,[7] for it includes virginity, abstinence, mercy, faith, love, harmony, peace, joy, and patience."[8]The heavenly wisdom of Christ who is God is variegated with each form of love. It is wisely said that the panther is an enemy of the dragon in the water. Therefore, Holy Scriptures have said nothing concerning birds and animals without the purpose of our understanding. As the Apostle said about Satan, "We are not ignorant of his cunning,"[9] for he travels every path which is not good.

Bartholomaeus Anglicus, *De proprietatibus rerum*, or *On the Properties of Things*

Outside of bestiaries, medieval readers also consumed information about animals in encyclopedias or vast compendia of extant knowledge about the world. One of the earliest versions, compiled by a French Scholastic writer Bartholomaeus

4. Hosea 5:14
5. Cf. II Corinthians 2:15
6. Cf. Ephesians 2:1
7. Cf. Ephesians 3:10
8. Cf. Galatians 5:22
9. Cf. II Corinthians 2:11

Source: *Batman upon Bartholome his Booke De Proprietatibus Rerum, Newly Corrected, Enlarged and Amended*, London, 1582, p. 201. *Early English Books Online*, https://quod.lib.umich.edu/e/eebo/A05237.0001.001/1:23.28?rgn=div2;view=fulltext.

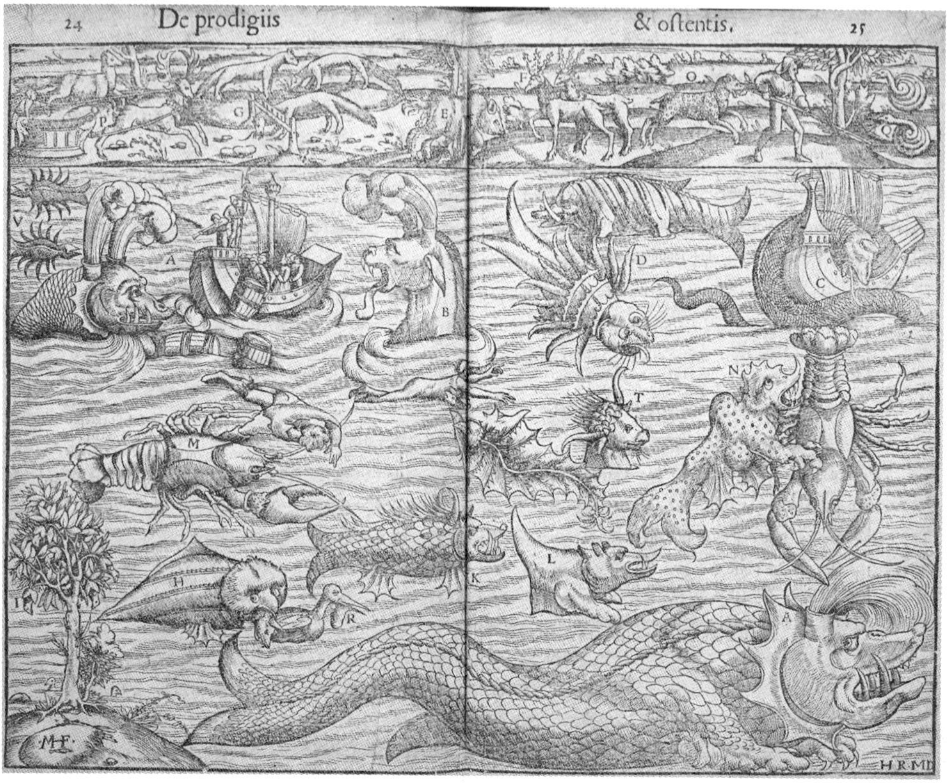

Figure 9. The ocean inhabited by sea monsters, with ships at risk. From Conrad Lycosthenes, *Prodigiorum ac ostentorum chronicon: quae praeter naturae ordinem, motum, et operationem, et in superioribus & his inferioribus mundi regionibus* (1557), pp. 24–25. N.9.7. Kislak Center for Special Collections, Rare Books, and Manuscripts, University of Pennsylvania Libraries.

Anglicus (ca. 1203–1272), *De proprietatibus rerum* (*On the Properties of Things*) begins with angels and humans but also devotes many pages to fish, birds, and other animals among countless other topics. Unlike *Physiologus* or the bestiaries, this popular encyclopedia dwells more on observations about creatures' natural habits. For example, this excerpt on whales notes their wondrous qualities as well as their threats and benefits to humans. This image contrasts with the often-sinister representations of sea creatures found elsewhere: for example, see Figure 9 for a representation of a multitude of such animals overwhelming mariners. Translated into English by John Trevisa (1342–1402) in the mid-fourteenth century, the book's influence lasted for centuries, right up to 1582, when Stephen Batman's augmented edition of the text was printed (the text below is adapted from Batman's edition of Trevisa's translation).

Also the whale and Balena is all one, and Balene be anow great and huge, and be called *Belve ab emittendo*, of outcasting and shedding of water. For they throw water higher than other great fishes of the sea. For Balen is understood outcasting. And the whale is called Cete for hugeness of body, as Isidore sayeth (libro. 22).[1] Also *in libro* Lorath it is said that the whale hath great plenty of sperm. And after that he gendereth with the female, superfluity thereof fleeteth above the water; and if it be gathered and dried, it: turneth to the substance of amber. And when the whale hungereth sore, he casteth out of his mouth a vapor, that smelleth as the smell of amber. And fish have liking in that smell, and for the odor and smell of that vapor, they go into the whale's mouth, and be so deceived and eaten. Also (as he sayeth) in this fish earthly matter hath more mastery then water; and therefore he is soon great and fat. And so in age for greatness of body, on his ridge powder and earth is gathered, and so digged together, that herbs and small trees and bushes grow thereon; so that that great fish seemeth an island. And if ship men come unwarily thereby, unneath they scape without peril. For he throweth so much water out of his mouth upon the ship, that he overturneth it sometime or drowneth it.

Also he is so fat, that when he is smit with fishers' darts, he feeleth not the wound, but it passeth through out the fatness. But when the inner fish is wounded, then he is most easily taken. For he may not suffer the bitterness of the salt water, and therefore he draweth to the shore ward. And also he is so huge in quantity, that when he is taken all the country is the better for the taking. Also he loveth his whelps with a wonderful love, and leadeth them about in the sea long time. And if it happeneth that his whelps be let with heaps of gravel, and by default of water, he taketh much water in his mouth, and throweth upon them, and delivereth them in that wise out of peril, and bringeth them again into the deep sea. And for to defend them, he putteth himself against all things that he meeteth, if it be noiseful[2] to them, and setteth them always between himself and the sun on the more safer side. And when strong tempest ariseth while his whelps be tender and young, he swalloweth them up into his owned womb, and when the tempest is gone and fair weather come, then he casteth them up whole and sound, as he sayeth.

1. A sixth-century Spanish scholar and encyclopedist
2. Harmful

Figure 10. Depiction of a crocodile from the *Ortus Sanitatis* (1491), a late medieval book of medical advice. Shelfmark IB.344 f.262v. Credit: The British Library Board.

Second-Family Bestiary

Indebted to *Physiologus*, medieval bestiaries provided information about animal behavior derived from traditional sources, which was then applied to Christian or moral doctrine. This sample of a medieval bestiary derives from a Latin version, part of the group of the so-called second family bestiaries that proliferated in northern Europe in the twelfth and thirteen centuries. This particular variant also contains borrowings from Isidore of Seville's *Etymologiae*, a medieval encyclopedia of writings about the natural world, as well as other texts. The entry on the crocodile (Figure 10) can be compared with similar entries in the bestiary of *Physiologus*; here the author presents a more detailed description of the beast, in terms of its size, qualities, and mating habits, as well as a nifty detail about the cosmetic uses of crocodile dung. He moralizes the animal's qualities, but not in terms of Christian symbolism, as in *Physiologus*, but rather as bad human behavior.

The crocodile, so called from its yellow (*croceo*) color,[1] is born in the Nile River. It is a four-footed animal capable of being on land and in water. It is

Source: Willene B. Clark. *A Medieval Book of Beasts: The Second-Family Bestiary; Commentary, Art, Text and Translation*, Boydell Press, 2006, pp. 140–41.

1. The name actually comes from the Greek word for lizard *krokodilos*.

more than twenty cubits in lengths, is armed with fierce teeth and claws, and has skin so hard that although a blow with hard stone strikes it back, that does not harm it. It rests by night in the water, and by day on the land. It warms its eggs in the soil: the male and females take turns in this task.

Certain fishes with a saw-like crest can kill [the crocodile], cutting the soft parts of its belly, Now, alone among all animals, it moves the upper jaw and keeps the lower one still. Its dung can be a salve, with which old and wrinkled prostitutes smear their faces, and make themselves beautiful until flowing sweat washes it off.

[The crocodiles] are a figure of the hypocrite, or of dissolute and greedy people who, although they are bloated by the slime of pride, stained by the corruption of riotous life [and] filled with the sickness of greed, yet are esteemed and as if very holy, [and] are seen to move among men in conformance with the law. By night the crocodile rests by night in the water, by day on land, because although the hypocrites live riotously, they nevertheless delight in being said to live virtuously and righteously. Aware of their evil ways, they sing a sad song, even if in practice their way of life always disparages what they have achieved. The upper jaw moves, because in speech they show to others examples and the richness of worlds of the holy fathers, while they exhibit in themselves too little of what they say. A salve is made from their dung, because a lot of evil people are praised for the ignorant for their evil deeds, and puffed up by the applause of the world, as if by a salve. But when the Judge, distressed by the vile deeds increases his anger to the point of striking, then all that beauty of praise vanishes like smoke.

Sir Gawain and the Green Knight

We know little about the composition of the late fourteenth-century Arthurian romance *Sir Gawain and the Green Knight*, except that this Middle English poem's dialect locates it in the English midlands. While being rooted in its present world, in style and theme this poem harks back to an earlier time of Arthurian legend. The plot concerns the adventures of Sir Gawain, one of Arthur's knights who undergoes several trials that challenge his values of chivalry. Among several ways in which it engages nature, the poem presents three scenes of hunting deer, wild boar, and a fox, vividly illustrating the typical premodern aristocratic hunts that took place within an enclosed park or forest belonging to

Source: William Allen Nielson, translator. *Sir Gawain and the Green Knight*, Houghton Mifflin, 1917. *Wiki Source*, https://en.wikisource.org/wiki/Sir_Gawain_and_the_Green_Knight_(Neilson_translation).

Figure 11. Various hunting practices, including of boar, bear, deer, and birds, where animals are also set to prey on other animals. From a sixteenth-century German edition of Cicero's *De Officiis* (1531). PA6312.D5 N48 1531. Kislak Center for Special Collections, Rare Books, and Manuscripts, University of Pennsylvania Libraries.

a lord. This excerpt from the deer hunt begins by evoking the wild excitement and joy surrounding the hunt; after an interlude in which a seduction scene takes place back at the castle (omitted here), the text returns to an unsentimental description of the butchering of the deer and the distribution of meat for all involved, including the hounds and the crows. The passage evokes the pleasure then associated with the slaughter of animals as well as the consumption of their flesh, by humans and beasts alike, while not neglecting exact description of those creatures (Figure 11).

Full early before the day the folk arose;
the guests that would go called their grooms,
and these hastened to saddle the horses,
arrange their gear, and truss their mails.
The great ones arrayed themselves to ride,
leaped up lightly and caught their bridles,
each wight[1] on his way where it well pleased him.

The dear lord of the land was not the last;
arrayed for the riding, with retainers full many,
he ate a sop hastily after he had heard mass,
and took his way quickly with his bugle to the field.
By the time that any daylight gleamed upon the earth,
he with his heroes were mounted on their high horses.
Then these hunters that understood it, coupled their hounds,
unclosed the kennel doors and called them thereout,
blew blithely on bugles three simple calls.
At this the brachets[2] bayed and made a wild noise,
and the hunters chastised and turned back those that wandered off—
a hundred hunters of the best there were, as I have heard tell.
  To their stations the trackers went;
  hunters cast off the couples;
  and then arose for the good blasts
  great uproar in that forest.
At the first noise of the quest the game quaked;
the deer moved down into the dale, dazed for dread;
hurried to the height; but quickly they were
hindered by the beaters, who cried stoutly.
They let the harts with the high head go their way,
the wild bucks also with their broad palms,[3]
for the generous lord had forbidden that there should any man
meddle with the male deer in the close season.
But the hinds were held back with "Hay!" and "Ho!"
and the does driven with great din to the deep glades.
There might one see as they ran the flight of arrows;

1. Person
2. Hounds that follow a scent
3. The flat part of a horn

at each turn under the boughs out flew a shaft,
that savagely bit on the brown hide with full broad heads.
How they leaped and bled and died by the banks!
And ever the hounds with a rush eagerly followed them;
hunters with shrill horn hastened after
with such a resounding cry as if cliffs had cracked.
What game escaped the men who shot
was all run down and torn at the stands.
The deer were pestered at the heights, and worried at the waters;
the people were so alert at the low stations,
and the greyhounds so great, that got them quickly
and pulled them down as fast as a man could see.
  The lord, shouting for joy,
  shot and alighted full oft,
  and passed the day thus with joy
  till the dark night.
[In the interlude: the lord's wife tries to seduce Gawain, but he resists:
    he is the hunted one]
And ever the lord of the land is bound in his sport,
to hunt in holts and heath at barren hinds.
Such a sum of does and of other deer he slew there
by the time the sun was low, that it were a marvel to estimate.
Then eagerly they all flocked together at the last;
and quickly of the slain deer they made a quarry.
The leaders hastened thereto with men enough;
gathered the greatest of grease, and proceeded
properly to undo them as the occasion demands.
Some that were there tried them at the assay
and found two fingers of fat on the leanest of all.
Afterwards they slit the slot,[4] seized the arber,[5]
cut it free with a sharp knife, and tied it up.
Next they cut down along the four limbs and rent off the hide;
then they opened the belly, took out the paunch,
cutting eagerly, and laid aside the knot.
They began at the throat again and skillfully divided
the weasand from the windpipe and threw out the guts.
Then they cut out the shoulders with their sharp knives,

4. Hollow of the breastbone
5. Gullet

and pulled them through by a little hole, so as to have whole sides.
Next they divided the breast, and cut it in two;
and once more they began at the throat,
split the beast quickly right up to the crotch,
took out the advancers, and immediately
severed all the fillets by the ribs,
and took them off properly along the backbone
even to the haunch—all of which hung together.
Then they heaved it up whole and cut it off there;
and that they took for the numbles,[6]
as it is rightly called.
 At the fork of the thighs
 they cut the flaps behind;
 hastily they hewed the carcass in two,
 and severed it along the backbone.
Both the head and the neck they hewed off then,
and afterwards they sundered the sides swiftly from the chine,
and corbie's fee[7] they cast in a green tree.
Then they pierced either thick side through by the rib,
and hung them each by the hocks of the haunches—
each man for his fee, as it befell him to have it.
Upon a skin of a fair beast they fed their hounds
with the liver and the lights, the leather of the paunches,
and bread bathed in blood mingled there among.
Loudly they blew the prize, and bayed their hounds;
then they started to carry home their meat,
blowing full stoutly many loud notes.

Geoffrey Chaucer, *The Parliament of Fowls*

In his allegorical poem *The Parliament of Fowls* (ca. 1381), Geoffrey Chaucer (ca. 1343–1400) conjures up a dream about the nature of love, when all the birds assemble before the goddess of Nature on Saint Valentine's Day to choose their mates. While Chaucer introduces the scene as one of complete natural

6. Entrails or choice cuts
7. Bits for the crows
Source: *The Complete Works of Geoffrey Chaucer*, edited by Walter Skeat, vol. 1, *Romaunt of the Rose; Minor Poems*, Oxford University Press, 1899. *Project Gutenberg*, http://www.gutenberg.org/files/43089/43089-h/43089-h.htm.

harmony, it evolves into a contest and "parliament" in which male eagles contend for the hand of a lovely female. To introduce his parliament, Chaucer offers a catalogue of birds that draws on Alain de Lille's *De planctu naturae*, or *Complaint of Nature*. As Alain did, here Chaucer expresses (more briefly) received ideas about animal behavior while attributing to beasts human emotions or motivations. In his poem, however, Chaucer also explores the shape of bird "society." He initially presents his birds as ordered hierarchically, implying an analogy with the order of human society. However, the debate that follows critiques many of the ideas that undergird that hierarchy; both "natural" orders of human and birds are thus destabilized.

The text below retains much of the early spelling to retain a sense of poetic rhythm (in Middle English all syllables were usually pronounced), while some has been modernized for clarity.

And in a launde,[1] upon an hill of floweres,
Was set this noble goddesse Nature;
Of branches were her halles and her boweres,
Y-wrought after her craft and her measure;
Nor there no fowl that cometh of engendrure,[2]
That they ne were pressed in her presence,
To take their doom and give her audience.

For this was on Saint Valentine's day,
When every fowl cometh there to choose his make,[3]
Of every kinde, that men thinke may;
And that so huge a noise gan they make,
That earthe and sea, and tree, and every lake
So full was, that unnethe[4] was there space
For me to stande, so full was all the place.

And right as Alain, in the *Plaint of Kinde*,[5]
Deviseth Nature of array and face,
In such array men mighten her there finde.
This noble emperesse, full of grace,

1. Glade
2. Engendering
3. Mate
4. Underneath
5. Alain of Lille, *De planctu naturae*

Bad every fowl to take his owne place,
As they were wont always from year to year,
Saint Valentines day, to standen there.

That is to say, the fowles of ravine
Were highest set; and then the fowles smalle,
That eaten as them nature would incline,
As worm, or thing of which I telle no tale;
But water-fowl sat lowest in the dale;
And fowl that liveth by seed sat on the greene,
And that so fell, that wonder was to seene.

There mighte men the royal eagle finde,
That with his sharpe look pierceth the sonne;
And other eagles of a lower kinde,
Of which that clerkes[6] well devisen conne.
There was the tyrant with his feathers dunne
And grey, I meane the gosshawk, that doth pine
To birds for his outrageous ravine.

The gentil falcon, that with his feet distreineth[7]
The kinges hand; the hardy spearhawk eke,
The quailes foe; the merlin that paineth
Himself full ofte, the larke for to seke;
There was the dove, with her eyen meeke;
The jalous[8] swan, against his death that singeth;
The owle eke, that of death the bode bringeth;

The crane the giant, with his trumpets sounde;
The thief, the chough; and eke the jangling[9] pie;
The scorning jay; the eels foe, the herone;
The false lapwing, full of treacherye;
The stare,[10] that the counsel can bewraye;[11]

6. Scholars
7. Clasps
8. Amorous?
9. Talkative
10. Starling
11. Betray

The tame ruddock;[12] and the coward kite;
The cock, that horloge[13] is of thorpe's[14] lighte;

The sparrow, Venus' sone; the nightingale,
That clepeth[15] forth the freshe leaves newe;
The swallow, murderer of the flies[16] smalle
That maken honey of floweres freshe of hue;
The wedded turtle,[17] with her hearte true;
The peacock, with his angels feathers brighte;
The pheasant, scorner of the cock by nighte;

The waker[18] goose; the cuckoo ever unkinde;
The popenjay, full of delicacye;
The drake,[19] destroyer of his owne kinde;
The stork, the wrecker of avouterye;[20]
The hote cormorant of gluttonye;
The raven wise, the crow with voice of care;
The throstle olde; the frosty feldefare.[21]

What shoulde I sayn? of fowles every kinde
That in this worlde han featheres and stature,
Men mighten in that place assembled finde
Before the noble goddesse Nature.
And everich[22] of them did his busy cure
Benignly to choose or for to take,
By their accord, his formel[23] or his mate.

12. Robin
13. Clock
14. Village's
15. Proclaims
16. Bees
17. Turtle dove
18. Vigilant
19. Drake duck
20. Adultery
21. A kind of thrush
22. Everyone
23. Female bird

Marie de France, *Fables*

We know little about the extraordinary poet now called Marie de France, although she appears to have lived in France and Norman England in the late twelfth and early thirteenth centuries. Composed in an early French dialect, her works include her *Lais,* or short narrative poems, and her compendium of versified *Fables.* Marie adapted some fables from Aesop (as transmitted through the *Romulus* collection) and apparently derived others from a variety of folk and popular traditions. While she claimed to have only translated these tales, she clearly adapted them to correspond to the concerns of medieval life and society. Like their classical precedents, her animal fables combine stories of anthropomorphized animals with morals about human behavior. At the same time, her animals live and act in their own recognizable environments. In other versions of the following story of the eagle and the crow, the eagle drops a tortoise rather than a whelk (a kind of sea snail) and then shares the meat with the crow; however, in this version (not only in Marie's), the crow eats the creature's meat alone. Thus, Marie's moral is not about sharing or cooperation but rather more cynically about trickery and competition in both the human and the non-human worlds.

Fable 12. The Eagle and the Crow

This tells how eagle flying went
Along the sea, on fishing bent.
He founds a whelk entire, but now
He just couldn't figure out how
To open up the shell; and so
Back to his nest he thought he'd go.
Just then a crow came up to say
That she could well explain a way
For him to open up the shell
If she could have a share as well.
The crow advised him to climb high,
Until he could no higher fly.
Then when he'd flown and reached the summit,
He should allow the whelk to plummet
Onto hard ground or on a rock:
And thus the shell he'd easily break.
The eagle fervently desired

Source: Marie de France. *Fables*, edited and translated by Harriet Spiegel, University of Toronto Press, 1987, pp. 61–62.

To eat the whelk which he'd acquired.
He bore it high, he let it go;
Lying in wait for it was crow
She ran right up, her beak struck it,
And opened up the shell a tiny bit.
She ate the morsel found inside;
She left the shell, away she hied
Before the eagle had returned
And of her strategy had learned.
The little hole was very small
So eagle saw it not at all.
Thus in this fable of fish
We're shown a man most villainous.
He uses tricks and cunning lies
To give his neighbor bad advice,
Counselling him to do a deed
That cannot possibly succeed.
And even when they get on well
This man deceitfully will steal
All of the goods the other got
Who labored hard for what he bought.

John Lydgate, "The Debate of the Horse, Goose, and Sheep"

A Benedictine monk at St. Bury-upon-Edmond, John Lydgate (ca. 1370–ca. 1451) wrote many literary and religious works, the most well-known being his poems about legendary wars and rulers: *Troy Book*, *The Fall of Princes*, and *Siege of Thebes*. Toward the end of his life he composed a minor poem, "The Debate of the Horse, Goose, and Sheep," staging an argument, judged by an eagle and a lion, as to which of the three "availeth most to man." Each animal argues for its own usefulness to humans in war, agriculture, diet, and medicine. The sheep gets the last word before the judges render their verdict that they are all equally beneficial. The sheep does try to get an edge on the goose and the horse by reminding them that Christ was the Lamb of God, but he does not hesitate to point out more practically that wool is the most valuable English commodity. In any case, down to the guts and sinews, every part of the sheep

Source: *The Minor Poems of John Lydgate*. Edited by Henry Noble MacCracken, Early English Text Society by H. Milford, 1910). *Hathi Trust*, https://catalog.hathitrust.org/Record/002699730. Text has been modernized.

can be converted into something that benefits people. Lydgate's unsentimental image of sheep can be compared, on the one hand, with that in pastoral poetry (see, for example, Edmund Spenser, *The Shephearde's Calendar* in Part 5), and on the other hand, with that in Thomas More's *Utopia* (Part 5), which complains that the practice of sheep farming has impoverished rural England.

[The speaker here is the sheep]
"And to rehearse worldly commodities,
In *republica* make no comparison:
There is no beast which, in all degrees,
Neither tiger, elephant, nor griffon—
All things reckoned through every region—
Doth so great profit, horse, nor goose, nor swan,
As doth the sheep, unto the ease of man.

"Let be thy boast, thou horse, and thy jangling!
Lay down thy trapurs[1] forged of plate and mail!
Cast off thy bridle of gold so fresh shining!
What may thy saddle or boss thee avail?
This ghostly Lamb hath done a great battle;
By His meekness He offered up for man,
Clad in pure purple vanquished hath Satan.

"The goose may gaggle, the horse may prick[2] and prance;
Neither of them in prowess may attain
For to be set or put in remembrance
Against the lamb, though they thereat disdain:
For common profit he passeth both twain,
Weighed and considered they be no thing like
To him in value between poor and rich

"Of Brutus Albion[3] his wool is chief richess,
In price surmounting every other thing
Sauf[4] grain and corn: merchants all express,
Wool is chief treasure in this land growing:

1. Trappings
2. Ride proudly
3. Britain
4. Except

To rich and poor this beast finds clothing:
All nations affirm up to the full,
In all the world there is no better wool.

"Of sheep also cometh pelt and eke fell,[5]
Gathered in this land for a great merchandise,
Carried over sea where men may it sell:
The wool skins maketh men to rise
To great richess in many sundry wise;
The sheep also turneth to great profit,
To help of man beareth furs black and white.

"There is also made of the sheep's skin,
Pilches[6] and gloves to drive away the cold.
Thereof also is made good parchment,
To write on books in quires many fold;
The Ram of Colchis bore a fleece of gold;
The fleece of Gideon of dew delectable[7]
Was of Maria a figure full notable.

"His flesh is natural restoration,
As some men say after great silkiness:
Roasted or sodden,[8] wholesome is mutton,
Welled[9] with gruel, physicians express,
Full nutritious after a great excess.
The sheep also concluding doubtless
Of his nature loveth rest and peace."

Anselm Turmeda, *The Disputation of the Donkey*

While a Franciscan friar in the 1380s Anselm Turmeda (ca. 1355–1423) traveled to Tunis, but there he converted to Islam, taking the name of Abd-Allah

5. Fleece
6. Coats
7. Judges 6:36–40
8. Boiled
9. Boiled

Source: Anselm Turmeda. *The Disputation of the Donkey. Cambridge Translations of Renaissance Philosophical Text*, translated by Neil Kenny and edited by Jill Kraye, vol. 1, Cambridge University Press, 1997, pp. 7–9, 13.

at-Tarjuman. Thereafter his works show the influence of both the Christian and Islamic traditions. Written in Catalan, his *Disputation of the Donkey* (1417–18) adapts a tenth-century Arabic fable from a Christian perspective. In the *Disputation* a friar debates with a donkey as to whether humans are superior to animals. Through eighteen steps, the donkey manages to refute the friar's arguments on behalf of humans; the donkey only loses at the end when the friar recalls that Christ was incarnated in human form. That conclusion aside, the overall weight of the work lies on the donkey's side, resting not only on inherent human weakness and dependence on animals but also on the beast's natural independence and intelligence (this was enough for the Inquisition put it on the list of prohibited books in 1583). Turmeda's skepticism about human excellence anticipates Montaigne's "An Apology for Raymond Sebond."

Friar Anselm Says to the Donkey

"Most worshipful donkey, the argument which proves that we have greater nobility and dignity than you animals and that it is right for us to be your lords is that we sell and buy you, feed and water you, protect you from the cold and heat, from lions and wolves, prepare medicines for you when you are ill. We do all this out of pity and compassion for you. And such works of charity are commonly performed only by lords towards their subjects and slaves."

The Donkey Answers Friar Anselm

"Friar Anselm, your argument has little worth. For if we must be your subjects and slaves, and you our lords, simply because you buy and sell us, then both Christians and Moors must be in a similar position. But such dominion is gained only by force and usurpation, and where force rules, there is no room for either justice or equity. As for what you say about your feeding and watering us, protecting us from the cold and heat and from all ills, you only do this for your own gain, for you profit by our welfare and lose out if we are harmed. And you do none of this out of pity or compassion for us, but you do it for fear that we should die, since by our death you lose the pennies with which you bought us. And without our help you would drink no milk, eat no cheese, butter or cream. You would have no wool to make cloth, nor any lambskins to make furs, but would perish of cold. You would travel on foot and would also carry loads slung over your neck, like porters.

As for what you say about taking pity on us, in fact you take lambs and kids and shut them away, separating them from their mothers and letting them die of thirst so that you can drink and turn into cheese the milk which God provided for their sustenance. You do this despite the fact that you have extremely good water and many different kinds of wine which you can drink. Friar Anselm,

have you ever seen any of us animals drink milk once we have been weaned and are no longer being suckled? But your gluttony and greed are beyond all words and measure. You are old and yet you still consume milk."
[. . .]

Friar Anselm Says to the Donkey

"Sir donkey, without having to think I will prove to you that we sons of Adam have greater dignity and nobility than you animals. The reason is that we eat the animals of the earth, sea and sky, in other words, birds of many different kinds. It is therefore evident and certain that the eater is more noble than the thing eaten. So we are obviously more noble than you."

The Donkey Replies

"'No fly enters a closed mouth,' Friar Anselm. Good God, it would be better for you to keep your mouth closed than to speak foolishly. For if one accepted the force of your argument, worms would be your lords, since they eat you. Lions, vultures and all the other animals and birds and fish of the sea would also be your lords, since they eat you. Wolves, dogs and many other animals would be your lords. And worse still, lice, fleas, bugs, nits, mites and suchlike would be your lords, since all of these eat your flesh. So tell me, in all honesty, whether your case is convincing, given your inability to provide or set out any arguments in favor of it?"
[. . .]

Friar Anselm Speaks to the Donkey

"I still intend to prove to you that we sons of Adam have greater nobility and dignity than you animals. And this is because we have natural intelligence and an intellective soul, whereas you only have a little natural discernment."

The Donkey Answers Friar Anselm, Telling Him about the Nature of Animals and Situating Each Animal within Its Nature

"Friar Anselm, I get the impression that you are a little weak in the head. Dear God, to make you see clearly that we animals have natural intelligence and an intellective soul that is equal, indeed superior, to yours, I'll describe to you certain actions performed by our animals. These will show you plainly that what you say is wrong.

See, Friar Anselm, how the chicks of hens and partridges run after their mother the moment they have hatched. And when they see their mother fleeing with fear, they also flee immediately, keeping to the route taken by their mother, and straightaway they are able to find food for themselves. If they happen to get lost and hear their mother's voice, they run towards it immediately and come to the place where the mother is.

Furthermore, in the case of horses, mules, oxen, sheep, goats, cats and similar animals, see how, as soon as the time has come for them to give birth, the females produce their male and female offspring without pain or labor; the offspring need neither a midwife, nor a woman to wash them, nor someone to cut the umbilical cord, and immediately they search for food. They also take the teat straight away and suck. Moreover, with what discernment and attentiveness do cats and dogs carry their young from one place to another with their teeth, so gently and smoothly that they do not hurt them at all. Whereas when you humans are born, Friar Anselm, far from knowing how to take the nipple, you would die of thirst if your mother did not put it in your mouth; lacking the capacity and the knowledge to eat any food, you continue to live on milk alone for five or six months. After that, your fathers and mothers chew your food for you, so it is already chewed when you eat it. And if your fathers or mothers flee because they are terrified for some reason, you stay in the cradle, lacking the knowledge or capacity to flee after them, in contrast with the chicks of hens and partridges. Besides, your females give birth in great pain and labor; they need midwives and others to cut your children's umbilical cords, and very often they die giving birth. That is because of the curse which God put on them. What's more, once the females of our animals are big-bellied, they would not go near the male for anything in the world, since they know that God's purpose in bestowing the congress of male and female has thus been fulfilled. Yet your women are different, Friar Anselm. The disposition of our females is not at all to their liking. On the contrary, once they are pregnant, they seek out men more than before.

Friar Anselm, what do you think of the true love of the turtle dove for its mate? When he has died she goes into deep mourning, never rests on a green tree, avoids drinking water that is clear rather than murky, and if she cannot find any murky water, she uses her foot to make the water murky before drinking. And then she remains a widow for the rest of her life, not wishing to take another husband. Whereas your women, Friar Anselm, look for other husbands straightaway, with their husband barely rotting in his grave and his bristles still good for a sauce. And it often happens, Friar Anselm, that they will kill their husbands, getting them to eat medicine and poison, so that they can take as husbands men with whom they are in love. See what a difference there is between these two kinds of love.

[. . .]

What do you think of the intelligence of the beaver in knowing, when it sees hunters intent on catching it, that they only want it for its genitals, which are used in many medicines? If it realizes that it will not be able to escape without being caught, then with its teeth it rips off its genitals itself and throws them to the hunters, preferring to lose them than to die and lose its life.

[. . .]

So, do these actions which I have described seem intelligent and reasoned to you? That is certainly what they are. And if you wish to speak the truth, you will agree with me that these animals have intelligence and an intellective soul that is equal, indeed superior, to yours. And I will not even go into the many animals, including some beetles, which, fearing some harm when they see sons of Adam approaching, pretend to be dead, bending their feet and hands so that you would take them for dead; afterwards, when they perceive that there is no longer anyone there, they get up and go about their business."

Michel de Montaigne, "An Apology for Raymond Sebond"

Characterized by both profound learning and a deep personal perspective on human experience and the art of living well, the *Essays* of Michel de Montaigne (1533–92) rank among the most important accomplishments of late Renaissance humanism. Montaigne composed the *Essays* mostly from the 1570s until his death, continually revising and adding to the collection published posthumously in a final edition in 1595. Montaigne's humanism expresses a skepticism that extends to his appreciation of both human and nonhuman creatures. One of his longest essays, his "Apology for Raymond Sebond" (responding to Sebond's treatise on natural theology), explores the values of Pyrrhonism, a version of skepticism questioning all human claims to certain knowledge and allowing only faith in God. In examining human fallibility, Montaigne argues against the idea that the natural order entails human exceptionalism. He decenters human beings in their everyday interactions with beasts, and he speculates about the powers of animal language and cognition. Montaigne's argument was anticipated by Anselm Turmeda's *Disputation of the Donkey*, discussed above.

The text here is John Florio's translation published in 1603.

Presumption is our natural and original infirmity. Of all creatures man is the most miserable and frail, and therewithal the proudest and disdainfullest. Who perceiveth and seeth himself placed here amidst the filth and mire of the world, fast-tied and nailed to the worst, most senseless, and drooping part of the world, in the vilest corner of the house, and farthest from heaven's cope, with those creatures that are the worst of the three conditions; and yet dareth

Source: *The Essayes or Morall, Politike and Millitarie discourses of Lord Michaell de Montaigne*. Translated by John Florio, London, 1603, chap. 12, pp. 260–63.

imaginarily place himself above the circle of the moon, and reduce heaven under his feet. It is through the vanity of the same imagination that he dare equal himself to God, that he ascribeth divine conditions unto himself, that he selecteth and separateth himself from out the rank of other creatures; to which his fellow-brethren and compeers he cuts out and shareth their parts, and allotteth them what portions of means or forces he thinks good. How knoweth he by the virtue of his understanding the inward and secret motions of beasts? By what comparison from them to us doth he conclude the brutishness he ascribeth unto them? When I am playing with my cat, who knows whether she have more sport in dallying with me than I have in gaming with her? We entertain one another with mutual apish tricks. If I have my hour to begin or to refuse, so hath she hers. Plato in setting forth the golden age under Saturn, amongst the chief advantages that man had then, reporteth the communication he had with beasts, of whom enquiring and taking instruction, he knew the true qualities and differences of every one of them, by and from whom he got an absolute understanding and perfect wisdom, whereby he led a happier life than we can do. Can we have a better proof to judge of man's impudence touching beasts? This notable author was of opinion that, in the greatest part of the corporal form which nature hath bestowed on them, she hath only respected the use of the prognostications, which in his days were thereby gathered. The defect which hindreth the communication between them and us, why may it not as well be in us as in them? It is a matter of divination to guess in whom the fault is that we understand not one another. For we understand them no more than they us. By the same reason, may they as well esteem us beasts as we them. It is no great marvel if we understand them not: no more do we the Cornish, the Welsh, or Irish. Yet have some boasted that they understood them, as Apollonius Thyaneus, Melampus, Tiresias, Thales, and others. And if it be (as cosmographers report that there are nations who receive and admit a dog to be their king), it must necessarily follow that they give a certain interpretation to his voice and moving. We must note the parity that is between us. We have some mean understanding of their senses, so have beasts of ours, about the same measure. They flatter and fawn upon us, they threat and entreat us, so do we them. Touching other matters, we manifestly perceive that there is a full and perfect communication amongst them, and that not only those of one same kind understand one another, but even such as are of different kinds. [. . .]

By one kind of barking of a dog, the horse knoweth he is angry; by another voice of his, he is nothing dismayed. Even in beasts that have no voice at all, by the reciprocal kindness which we see in them, we easily infer there is some other mean of intercommunication: their gestures treat, and their motions discourse.

[Montaigne goes on to discuss how human beings communicate silently with signs and gestures.]

[. . .]

And as for other matters; what sufficiency is there in us that we must not acknowledge from the industry and labors of beasts? Can there be a more formal and better ordained policy, divided into so several charges and offices, more constantly entertained, and better maintained, than that of bees? Shall we imagine their so orderly disposing of their actions, and managing of their vocations, have so proportioned and formal a conduct without discourse, reason, and forecast?

[. . .]

The swallows which, at the approach of springtime, we see to pry, to search, and ferret all the corners of our houses; is it without judgement they seek, or without discretion they choose from out a thousand places, that which is fittest for them to build their nest and lodging? And in that pretty cunning contexture and admirable framing of their houses, would birds rather fit themselves with a round than a square figure, with an obtuse than a right angle, except they knew both the commodities and effects of them? Would they (suppose you) first take water and then clay, unless they guessed that the hardness of the one is softened by the moistness of the other? Would they floor their palace with moss or down, except they foresaw that the tender parts of their young ones shall thereby be more soft and easy? Would they shroud and shelter themselves from stormy weather, and build their cabins towards the east, unless they knew the different conditions of winds, and considered that some are more healthful and safe for them than some others? Why doth the spider spin her artificial web thick in one place and thin in another? And now useth one, and then another knot, except she had an imaginary kind of deliberation, fore-thought, and conclusion? We perceive by the greater part of their works what excellency beasts have over us, and how weak our art and short our cunning is, if we go about to imitate them. We see, notwithstanding, even in our grossest works, what faculties we employ in them, and how our mind employeth the uttermost of her skill and forces in them: why should we not think as much of them? Wherefore do we attribute the works which excel whatever we can perform, either by nature or by art, unto a kind of unknown, naturally, and servile inclination? Wherein unawares we give them a great advantage over us, to infer that nature, led by a certain loving kindnesses, leadeth and accompanieth them (as it were by the hand) unto all the actions and commodities of their life; and that she forsaketh and leaveth us to the hazard of fortune, and by art to quest and find out those things that are behovefull and necessary for our preservation, and therewithal deemeth us the means to attain by any institution and contention of spirit to the natural sufficiency of brute beasts; so that their brutish stupidity doth in all commodities exceed whatsoever our divine intelligence can effect. Verily, by this account, we might have just cause and great reason to term her a most unjust and partial step-dame. But there is no such thing, our policy is not so deformed and disordered. Nature hath generally embraced all her creatures; and there is not any but she hath amply stored with all necessary means for the preservation of their being.

John Caius, *Of English Dogges*

A prominent English physician, John Caius (1510–1573) helped to found Gonville and Caius College at Cambridge University. Not only did he publish books on medicine but he also pursued natural history, most notably composing *De canibus Britannicis* (1570), which Abraham Fleming later translated into English as *Of Englishe Dogges: The Diversities, the Names, the Natures, and the Properties* (1576). When writing this work, Caius corresponded with Conrad Gesner, the influential Swiss author of the massive *Historia animalium*, a compendium of all animal species known at the time (see the excerpt from Edward Topsell's *The History of Four-Footed Beasts*, for Gesner). Caius divides dogs into three kinds according to their uses: for hunting, for miscellaneous purposes, and for "toying" or pleasure, of which he does not approve. The two excerpts below contrast his admiration of the English setter's almost miraculous talents with his suspicion of the "pretty, proper, and fine" Maltese dog, doted on by "wanton women." In both cases, the dog plays a role equivalent to that of a human: in the setter's case, as a domestic servant, and for the Maltese, either as a substitute child or lover.

The Dog called the Setter, in Latin *Index*.

Another sort of dogs be there, serviceable for fowling,[1] making no noise either with foot or with tongue, while they follow the game. These attend diligently upon their master and frame their conditions to such becks, motions, and gestures, as it shall please him to exhibit and make, either going forward, drawing backward, inclining to the right hand, or yielding toward the left (in making mention of fowls, my meaning is of the partridge and the quail). When he hath found the bird, he keepeth sure and fast silence, he stayeth his steps and will proceed no further, and with a close, covert, watching eye, layeth his belly to the ground and so creepeth forward like a worm. When he approacheth near to the place where the bird is, he lays him down, and with a mark of his paws be-

Source: *Of Englishe Dogges: The Diversities, the Names, the Natures, and the Properties; A Short Treatise Written in Latine by Johannes Caius*. Translated by Abraham Fleming, London, 1576), pp. 14–15, 20.

1. Hunting birds

trayeth the place of the bird's last abode, whereby it is supposed that this kind of dog is called *Index*, Setter, being in deed a name most consonant and agreeable to his quality. The place being known by the means of the dog, the fowler immediately openeth and spreadeth his net, intending to take them, which being done the dog at the accustomed beck or usual sign of his master riseth up by and by, and draweth nearer to the fowl that by his presence they might be the authors of their own ensnaring, and be ready entangled in the prepared net, which cunning and artificial endeavor in a dog (being a creature domestical or household servant brought up at home with offals of the trencher and fragments of victuals) is not much so be marveled at, seeing that a hare (being a wild and skippish[2] beast) was seen in England to the astonishment of the beholders, in the year of our Lord God, 1564, not only dancing in measure, but playing with his former feet upon a taboret,[3] and observing just number of strokes (as a practitioner in that art) besides that nipping and pinching a dog with his teeth and claws, and cruelly thumping him with the force of his feet. This is no trumpery[4] tale, nor trifling toy (as I imagine) and therefore not unworthy to be reported, for I reckon it a requital of my travail,[5] not to drown in the seas of silence any special thing, wherein the providence and effectual working of nature is to be pondered.

[. . .]

Of the delicate, neat, and pretty kind of dog called the Spaniel gentle or the comforter, in Latin *Melitaeus* or *Fotor.*

There is, besides those which we have already delivered, another sort of gentle dogs in this our English soil but exempted from the order of the residue, the dogs of this kind doth Callimachus call *Melitaeos*, of the Island Melita, in the sea of Sicily, which at this day is named Malta, an island indeed, famous and renowned, with courageous and puissant soldiers valiantly lighting under the banner of Christ their unconquerable captain, where, this kind of dogs had their principal beginning.

These dogs are little, pretty, proper, and fine, and sought for to satisfy the delicateness of dainty dames, and wanton women's wills, instruments of folly for them to play and dally withal, to wile away the treasure of time, to withdraw their minds from more commendable exercises, and to content their corrupted

2. Inclined to skip, or skittish
3. Drum
4. Trickery
5. Work

concupiscences[6] with vain disport (a silly shift to shun irksome idleness). These puppies, the smaller they be, the more pleasure they provoke, as more meet playfellows for mincing mistresses to bear in their bosoms, to keep company withal in their chambers, to succor with sleep in bed, and nourish with meat at board, to lay in their laps, and lick their lips as they ride in their wagons, and good reason it should be so, for coarseness with fineness hath no fellowship, but featness[7] with neatness hath neighborhood enough. That plausible proverb verified upon a tyrant, namely that he loved his sow better than his son, may well be applied to these kind of people who delight more in dogs that are deprive of all possibility of reason, than they do in children that be capable of wisdom and judgment. But this abuse peradventure reigneth where there hath been long lack of issue, or elsewhere barrenness is the best blossom of beauty.

Thomas Johnson, *Cornucopiae*

Cornucopiae or Divers Secrets (1595) belongs to the genre of books of secrets like those of Giambattista della Porta and *The Secrets of Albertus Magnus*. Those books reveal "secrets" for mastering works in nature based on the principle of sympathies and antipathies that animate all Creation. Thomas Johnson's[1] version dispenses with most of the philosophy seen earlier, instead listing a clipped sequence of "rare secrets in man, beasts, fowls, fishes, trees, plants, stones and such like" based on multiple authorities but often claimed to be true by "common experience." These include instructions for curing disease and influencing human behavior with animal parts (compare with Pliny the Elder on animals), as well as observations about animals as omens. While the human is always centered, at the same time a sense of intimacy underlies the principle of likeness between people and other animals. These secrets also imagine connections among the creatures of the nonhuman world that exclude humanity.

Many things are helped by their like, as physicians can tell that the brains of many things are helpful to the brain of man, the lungs to the lungs, the eye to the eye, and foot to the foot, etc.

6. Lusts

7. Elegance

Source: Thomas Johnson. *Cornucopiae, or Divers Secrets wherein is Contained the Rare Secrets in Man, Beasts, Fowles, Fishes, Trees, Plantes, Stones and Such Like*, London, 1595.

1. We know nothing of this Thomas Johnson; he is sometimes confused with another Thomas Johnson, the apothecary who edited Gerard's herbal, but that Johnson was probably just born in 1595.

The right eye of a frog applied to the right eye of one that is purblind, or the left eye to the left healeth the party.

So doth the eye of a crabfish.

The snail applied in the same sort helpeth the gout.

Every barren beast or fowl causeth sterility or barrenness, especially the urine, matrices[2] or stones any ways taken.

So doth the milk of a mule once in a month eaten, cause her that eat it not to conceive.

If you would move love, take such creatures as love most, such are the turtle, the sparrow, the swallow, the wagtail.

If you would move audacity, respect the lion and the cock.

The dog, the raven, the cock, the nightingale, the bat or remouse[3] and such like, especially the head, the heart, and the eyes are said to profit in vigilance, or to keep one from sleeping.

The heart of a crow or a bat borne upon one suffereth not the party to sleep till it be taken away.

[. . .]

In like manner as in plants, so also in fowls and beasts is there a mutual amity, as between the owsell[4] and the felfare;[5] between the crow and the hernshaw;[6] between the dove and the peacock, between the turtle and the popinjay.[7]

Also the fish called *Musculus* loveth the whale so, that he leadeth the whale from danger of rocks: also there is a great amity betwixt it and the chirlepoole.[8]

[. . .]

Neither do plants, herbs, beasts and such like, want a certain kind of hatred or enmities.

[. . .]

There is a beast like a lizard that is called *Stellio* having black spots like stars, which is so contrary unto the scorpion, that his very sight terrifieth him that he presently putrefieth and becometh an oil which is singular to heal hurts received by scorpions or other venomous beasts.

There is also a mortal hate betwixt the mouse and the scorpion, in such sort that a mouse applied to the biting of a scorpion, helpeth the grief.

2. Uterus
3. Another term for bat
4. Unknown?
5. A kind of thrush
6. Heron
7. Parrot
8. Unknown?

Serpents have no greater enemies than crabfishes, and for that cause swine bitten with serpents are helped with crabs.

If a crocodile be touched with a quill or feather of the bird called ibis, it makes immoveable.

There is a bird like a partridge called *Otidis* that cannot abide the sight of a horse.

The hart cannot abide the sight of the raven, neither the sight of the viper.

The elephant is feared most when he heareth the grunting of a swine: the lion when he seeth a cock.

There is also enmity between the wolf, the swan, the bull and the raven.

There is continual war betwixt the crow and the owl, the kite and the crow, the hart and the dragon.

[. . .]

The screech owl and the night-crow evermore prognosticate death, and this also is daily approved.

The finding of a toad in any uncouth place noteth death.

The hawk flying over your head pretendeth death to the party.

The fighting of hawks one with another noteth mutation of kingdoms.

The swallow is a sign of enjoying a patrimony or inheritance.

The meeting of a remouse or bat, signifieth evasion from enemies.

To meet the sparrow flying is a sign of evil luck, but in love matters it noteth good.

Edward Topsell, *The History of Four-Footed Beasts*

Edward Topsell (ca. 1572–1625) was a Cambridge-educated English clergyman who, while writing many sermons and religious tracts, published the amply illustrated *History of Four-Footed Beasts Describing the True and Lively Figure of Every Beast, with a Discourse of Their Several Names, Conditions, Kinds, Virtues (Both Natural and Medicinal) Countries of Their Breed, Their Love and Hate to Mankind, and the Wonderful Work of God in Their Creation, Preservation, and Destruction* (1607). In this book Topsell acknowledged his debt to the Swiss divine Conrad Gesner's monumental *Historia animalium* (1551–1558), as well as to a host of other writers going back to Pliny. He also averred that this work is

Source: Edward Topsell. *The Historie of Four-Footed Beastes Describing the True and Lively Figure of Every Beast, with a Discourse of Their Severall Names, Conditions, Kindes, Vertues (Both Naturall and Medicinall) Countries of Their Breed, Their Love and Hate to Mankinde, and the Wonderfull Worke of God in Their Creation, Preservation, and Destruction*, London, 1607, pp. 102–7.

Figure 12. Image of an enigmatic cat, from Edward Topsell, *The History of Four-Footed Beasts* (1658), p. 103. Founders Collection. 83. F. Kislak Center for Special Collections, Rare Books, and Manuscripts, University of Pennsylvania Libraries.

"necessary for all divines and students, because the story of every beast is amplified with narrations out of scriptures, fathers, philosophers, physicians, and poets." In this sense, Topsell's book owed less to close natural observation and functioned more to collect stories and myths about beasts. At the same time, Topsell wove in his own thoughts and observations when he did know an animal directly. The entry on the cat (Figure 12) exemplifies this mixture of received wisdom and personal experience. There Topsell reveals his ambivalence about this domestic animal at once too close and too dangerous to humankind, both "good and evil." The passage dwells on cats' instinctive cruelty but also casually accepts cruelty towards cats when dismembered to serve for meat and medicine.

Cats are of divers colors, but for the most part grizzled, like to congealed ice, which cometh from the condition of her meat; her head is like unto the head of a lion, except in her sharp ears; her flesh is soft and smooth; her eyes glister above measure, especially when a man cometh to see a cat on the sudden, and in the night, they can hardly be endured, for their flaming aspect. Wherefore Democritus describing the Persian smaradge[1] saith that it is not transparent, but filleth the eye with pleasant brightness, such as is in the eyes of panthers and cats, for they cast forth beams in the shadow and darkness, but in the sunshine they have no such clearness, and thereof Alexander Aphrodisius[2] giveth this reason, both for the sight of cats and of bats, that they have by nature a most sharp spirit of seeing. Albertus[3] compareth their eye-sight to carbuncles in dark places, because in the night, they can see perfectly to kill rats and mice; the root of the herb valerian (commonly called phu) is very like to the eye of a cat, and where so ever it groweth, if cats come thereunto, they instantly dig it up, for the love thereof, as I myself have seen in mine own garden, and not once only, but often, even then when as I had caused it to be hedged or compassed round about with thorns, for it smelleth marvelous like to a cat.

[. . .]

The tongue of a cat is very attractive, and forcible like a file, attenuating by licking the flesh of a man, for which cause, when she is come near to the blood, so that her own spittle be mingled therewith, she falleth mad. Her teeth are like a saw, and if the long hairs growing about her mouth (which some call granons) be cut away, she looseth her courage. Her nails [are] sheathed like the nails of a lion, striking with her forefeet, both dogs and other things, as a man doth with his hand.

This beast is wonderful nimble, setting upon her prey like a lion, by leaping; and therefore she hunteth both rats, all kind of mice, and birds, eating not only them, but also fish, wherewithal she is best pleased. Having taken a mouse, she first playeth with it, and then devoureth it, but her watchful eye is most strange, to see with what pace and soft steps, she taketh birds and flies; and her nature is to hide her own dung or excrements, for she knoweth that the savor and presence thereof, will drive away her sport, the little mouse being able by that stool, to smell the presence of her mortal foe.

[. . .]

The nature of this beast is to love the place of her breeding, neither will she tarry in any strange place, although carried very far, being never willing to forsake the house, for the love of any man, and most contrary to the nature of a dog, who will travel abroad with his master; and although their masters forsake

1. Emerald
2. An Aristotelian philosopher of the second century CE
3. Albertus Magnus

their houses, yet will not these beasts bear them company, and being carried forth in close baskets or sacks, they will yet return again or loose themselves. A cat is much delighted to play with her image in a glass, and if at any time she behold it in water, presently she leapeth down into the water which naturally she doth abhor, but if she be not quickly pulled forth and dried she dieth thereof, because she is impatient of all we[t]. Those which will keep their cats within doors, and from hunting birds abroad, must cut off their ears, for they cannot endure to have drops of rain distill into them and therefore keep themselves in harbor.

[. . .]

It is needless to spend any time about her loving nature to man, how she flattereth by rubbing her skin against one's legs, how she whirleth with her voice, having as many tunes as turns, for she hath one voice to beg and to complain, another to testify to her delight and pleasure, another among her own kind by flattering, by hissing, by puffing, by spitting, insomuch as some have thought that they have a peculiar intelligible language among themselves. Therefore how she beggeth, playeth, leapeth, looketh, catcheth, tosseth with her foot, riseth up to strings held over her head, sometime creeping, sometimes lying on the back, playing with one foot, sometime on the belly, snatching, now with mouth, and anon with foot, apprehending greedily anything save the hand of a man with divers such gestical actions, it is needless to stand upon; insomuch as Coelius[4] was wont to say, that being free from his studies and more urgent weighty affairs, he was not ashamed to play and sport himself with his cat, and verily it may well be called an idle man's pastime. As this beast hath been familiarly nourished of many, so have they paid dear for their love, being requited with the loss of their health, and sometime of their life for their friendship: and worthily, because they which love any beasts in a high measure, have so much the less charity unto man. Therefore it must be considered what harms and perils come unto men by this beast. It is most certain that the breath and savor of cats consume the radical humor and destroy the lungs, and therefore they which keep their cats with them in their beds have the air corrupted and fall into fever hectics and consumptions.

[Next Topsell talks about the dangers of eating cats, because their meat could be contaminated with rat poison.]

It must needs be an unclean and impure beast that liveth only upon vermin and by ravening, for it is commonly said of a man when he sneezeth, that he

4. A Roman historian

hath eaten with cats. Likewise the familiars of witches do most ordinarily appear in the shape of cats, which is an argument that this beast is dangerous in soul and body. It is said that if bread be made wherein the dung of cats is mixed, it will drive away rats and mice. But we conclude the story of this beast with the medicinal observations, and tarry no longer in the breath of such a creature compounded of good and evil. It is reported that the flesh of cats salted and sweetened hath power in it to draw wens from the body, and being warmed to cure the hemorrhoids and pains in the reins and back.

[. . .]

Take the head of a black cat, which hath not a spot of another color in it, and burn it to powder in an earthen pot leaded or glazed within, then take this powder and through a quill blow it thrice a day into thy eye, and if in the night time any heat do thereby annoy thee, take two leaves of an oak wet in cold water and bind them to the eye, and so shall all pain fly away, and blindness depart although it hath oppressed thee a whole year, and this medicine is approved by many physicians both elder and later.

Gervase Markham, *Markham's Masterpiece*

Gervase Markham (1568?–1637) churned out both literary and nonliterary works on an impressive variety of practical matters. Born into a good family, he first followed the royal court, but with the fall from favor of his patron the Earl of Essex, he moved to the country and turned mostly to writing practical manuals to make a living. In these efforts he borrowed from many Continental sources, but he emphasized his own experience, ultimately staking a claim for a particularly English or national culture of both land and animals. He did become notorious for publishing too many recycled books on beasts, claiming to be an expert on riding as well as on horse breeding and care. In *Markham's Masterpiece* (first published 1610), he promised to provide "all knowledge belonging to the smith, farrier, or horse-leech [doctor], touching the curing of all diseases in horses" (Figure 13). He prefaces his recommendations for treating horses by considering the "composition of a horse's body," made up, like the human body, of seven "natural things": "elements, temperaments, humors, members, powers or virtues, actions or operations, and spirits." Markham starts with earth, air, water, and fire to characterize the horse's "temperature" as naturally "hot and dry." He then notes that this temperature, which affects temperament or character, is subject to age and climate. In

Source: *Markham's Masterpiece Containing All Knowledge Belonging to the Smith, Farrier, or Horse-Leech, Touching the Curing of All Diseases in Horses.* 1610. London, 1668, pp. 1–2, 8–9.

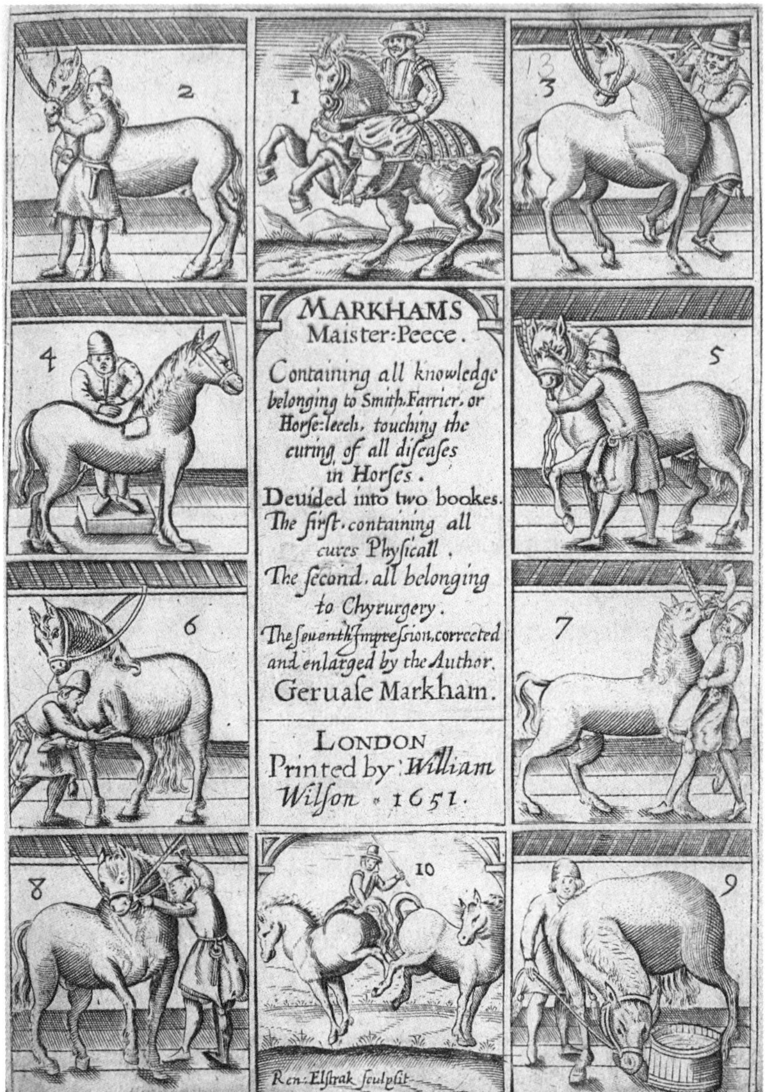

Figure 13. Title page of Gervase Markham's *Markham's Masterpiece: Containing all Knowledge Belonging to the Smith, Farrier, or Horse-Leach* (1610), representing different forms of human interaction with horses. EC.M3418. 610. Kislak Center for Special Collections, Rare Books, and Manuscripts, University of Pennsylvania Libraries.

this, the horse's body and personality do not differ from those of the human (see also Avicenna and Hippocrates in Part 4 on "temperature" in the human body).

These temperaments, or temperatures, which are the second thing in a horse's composition, do spring from the commixture of the four elements, and are nine in number, whereof eight are unequal, and the ninth is equal. Of the eight unequal, four are simple, and those be hot, cold, moist, and dry, which physicians call the first qualities; and of these, the first two be active, and the other two passive. The other four are compound, and they be hot and moist, hot and dry, cold and moist, cold and dry. Now the equal temperament is divided into two, a universal and a special. The equal temperament universal, is, when the four elements are in an equal proportion, generally divided through the whole body, nature enjoying no more from the one, than from the other. The equal temperament especial, is, when the elements are proportioned according as every kind doth most properly require, be it either plant or beast: in plants, when every plant hath that commixture of elements, which are proper to its kind, the hot plant being hot, the cold being cold, etc. Whereas contrariwise, to have a hot plant cold, or a cold hot, to have rue cold, or sorrel hot, were a false and unequal commixture of elements. So likewise of beasts, that horse, that dog, that swine is said to have his due temperament, when he is of such temperature as is most proper unto his kind, which only is best discerned by his actions, or motions. As thus, the horse is known to be hot and moist by his lightness, swiftness, valiantness, and long life, and also to be of a temperate nature, in that he is easily tamed, docile, obedient and familiar with the man. And so long as either horse, or any other thing, continueth in the mediocrity[1] and excellency of his proper temperament, so long as we may truly judge him of a good temper and disposition; but if there be any over-flow of qualities, or excess in his humors, as either heat, coldness, moistness, or dryness, then we say, he is either a hot choleric horse, a cold dull horse, a dry mischievous horse, or a moist cowardly horse, according to the over-flow of that quality which reigneth in him.

Again, every horse is said to have his due temperament, according to his age, and the country wherein he is bred, and sometimes according to the time of the year wherein he liveth. And thus a horse in his foal-age, which is, till he be six years old, is naturally hot and moist. In his middle age, which is till twelve, more hot and dry than moist; and in his old age, which is past eighteen, more cold and dry, than either hot or moist. So likewise, the horses which are bred in southern

1. In the middle between extremes

parts, as either in Spain, Barbary, or Greece, are naturally more hot than those which are bred either in the seventeen lands,[2] Germany, or England; neither is there any horse, which is in good state of body, that is so hot in the spring-time of the year, as in the summer, nor so cold in the summer, as in winter. All which observations are with most curious diligence to be observed of every horse-leech,[3] when he goeth about to cure any sickness: for unless he consider their natures and temperatures, and every other circumstance already declared, he shall right soon be deceived in the administration of his physic. Therefore, I earnestly desire every farrier, before he give any drench or potion, first to inquire the kind, race, and disposition of the horse, next his age, than the country, and lastly, the time of the year: and so according to the truth thereof, to mix his receipts.

Hester Pulter, "The Ugly Spider"

Part 1 introduces Hester Pulter (ca. 1605–1678) as a poet engaged with questions of faith, the natural world, and the social and political turmoil of her time. Her unpublished poems include dozens of "emblems" meditating on different animals and what lessons they might teach about human behavior and our relationship with God. She consulted many different sources, including Edward Topsell's *History of Four-footed Beasts* and Pliny the Elder's *Natural History*. While her emblems anthropomorphize animals' activities, Pulter carefully reports the behavior of animal as animals. The poems tend to focus on the brutality of life in the nonhuman world, matched only by human savagery. In this poem, the cruelty of the spider, killed in turn by a fly, leads her to reflect on how not even tyrants can escape death and humiliation. The poem then surprisingly ends by naming meat-eating humans as the cruelest animals; humans' moral evil is thus expressed in their exploitation of animals.

Behold how many cobwebs doth invest[1]
This ugly spider in her nasty nest,
Where, barricaded, she in ambush lies,
Domitian-like,[2] to murder sportive flies.
Yet such a monstrous spider once I saw

2. The Netherlands

3. Horse doctor

Source: "The Ugly Spider (Emblem 37)." *The Pulter Project: Poet in the Making*, edited by Wendy Wall and Leah Knight, 2018, http://pulterproject.northwestern.edu/poems/ee/the-ugly-spider-emblem-37/.

1. Cover

2. Domitian was a Roman tyrant who said to have loved killing flies.

That would with ease flies, wasps and hornets draw
Most cruelly into her dusty nest;
Then, tyrant-like she on their blood would feast.
Yet did I see a slender azure fly
Make this bloodsucking monster fall and die.
So the most impious tyrants in the world,
Even in a moment, to the grave are whirled.

That king of terrors doth by sentence just
Grind even their very skeletons to dust;
When he upon the pale horse[3] doth appear,
A Julianus[4] then begins to fear,
Throwing his blood and spirits in the skies,
Confessed, yet died, in his apostasies.
What by the wars was Alexander's[5] gains
When guilt his conscience, poison, stung his veins?
So he[6] that hath three kingdoms in his power:
What comfort will they yield that fatal hour
Whenas that sea of innocent blood shall roar
To heaven for vengeance? Who can but implore?
But why do I blame spider's tyranny
Who, forced by hunger, kills a silly[7] fly,
When man's the greatest beast of prey of all?
His house a shamble[8] is, or butcher's stall.
In all those books which I have read, I find
There's none but man doth kill and eat his kind.
The antediluvian patriarchs happy were
That lived by what the earth did freely bear.[9]
The Pythagoreans[10] no blood would spill;
The Banians[11] now no animals do kill
But such as murderers they do esteem

3. The pale horse of death from Revelation
4. Roman emperor known as Julius the apostate
5. Alexander the Great
6. Oliver Cromwell, then ruling England, Scotland, and Ireland
7. Helpless, innocent
8. Slaughterhouse
9. Male authorities before the Flood were thought to be vegetarian.
10. Member of an ancient Greek cult who did not eat meat
11. Hindu traders

And oft will buy those creatures to redeem.
But stay my pen, write no more than is meet,
Lest I forget Noah's license, Peter's sheet.[12]

Richard Lovelace, "The Snail"

A wealthy and witty man, Richard Lovelace (1618–1657) consorted with the "Cavalier poets," Royalist courtiers who wrote of love, honor, and the pleasures of life, as well as of the pain they suffered during the English Civil War and Interregnum. In his collections of poems *Lucasta* (1649) and *Lucasta: Posthume Poems* (1659), Lovelace included several that contemplated small creatures—ants, snails, and grasshoppers, elaborately expanding on the lessons that animal lives and bodies offer humans. In doing so, these poems hark back to the medieval bestiaries and poetry moralizing the lives of animals and flowers, but Lovelace's poetry differs from them in its attention to detail and the heights to which he can elevate the slightest animal. This poem situates the common snail and its trail of slime in the contexts of Euclidean geometry, classical myth and history, popular natural history, and religious imagery. Lovelace's thoughts on the snail can also be compared with Robert Hooke's roughly contemporaneous, painstaking description of the louse preying on his own body.

Wise emblem of our politic world,
Sage snail, within thine own self curl'd;
Instruct me softly to make haste,[1]
Whilst these my feet go slowly fast.

Compendious snail! thou seem'st to me,
Large Euclid's strict epitome;[2]
And in each diagram dost fling

12. From the Pulter project notes: "After the flood, according to the Bible, Noah is given permission to eat animal flesh: 'Every moving thing that liveth shall be meat for you; even as the green herb have I given you all things' (Genesis 9:3). See also God's injunction for Peter to eat meat: 'And he became very hungry, and would have eaten: but while they made ready, he fell into a trance, And saw heaven opened, and a certain vessel descending upon him, as it had been a great sheet knit at the four corners, and let down to the earth: Wherein were all manner of four-footed beasts of the earth, and wild beasts, and creeping things, and fowls of the air. And there came a voice to him, Rise, Peter; kill, and eat' (Acts 10:10–13)."

Source: *Lucasta: Posthume Poems of Richard Lovelace*, London, 1659), pp. 15–16.

1. Refers to a common proverb, *festina lente*, or make haste slowly

2. A summary of Euclid's book on geometry

Thee from the point unto the ring;
A figure now triangular,
An oval now, and now a square;
And then a serpentine dost crawl,
Now a straight line, now crook'd, now all.

Preventing rival of the day,
Th'art up and openest thy ray,
And ere the morn cradles the moon,
Th'art broke into a beauteous noon.
Then when the sun sups in the deep,
Thy silver horns o'er Cynthia's[3] peep;
And thou from thine own liquid bed
New Phoebus[4] heav'st thy pleasant head.

Who shall a name for thee create,
Deep riddle of mysterious state?
Bold Nature that gives common birth
To all products of seas and earth,
Of thee, as earthquakes, is afraid,
Nor will thy dire deliv'ry aid.

Thou thine own daughter then, and sire,[5]
That son and mother art entire,
That big still with thy self dost go,
And liv'st an aged embryo;
That like the cubs of India,
Thou from thyself a while dost play;
But frighted with a dog or gun,
In thine own belly thou dost run,[6]
And as thy house was thine own womb,
So thine own womb concludes thy tomb.

But now I must (analyzéd king)
Thy economic virtues sing;

3. The moon
4. The sun
5. Snails are hermaphroditic.
6. Refers to the popular myth of an animal in India named the "su"

Thou great staid husband still within,
Thou, thee, that's thine dost discipline;
And when thou art to progress bent,
Thou mov'st thy self and tenement,
As warlike Scythians travel'd,[7] you
Remove your men and city too;
Then after a sad dearth and rain,
Thou scatterest thy silver train;[8]
And when the trees grow naked and old,
Thou clothest them with cloth of gold,
Which from thy bowels thou dost spin,
And draw from the rich mines within.

Now hast thou chang'd thee saint; and made
Thy self a fane[9] that's cupola'd;
And in thy wreathed cloister thou
Walkest thine own grey friar too;
Strict, and lock'd up, th'art hood all o'er,
And ne'er eliminat'st thy door.
On salads thou dost feed severe,
And 'stead of beads[10] thou drop'st a tear;
And when to rest, each calls the bell,
Thou sleep'st within thy marble cell,
Where in dark contemplation placed,
The sweets of nature thou dost taste;
Who[11] now with time thy days resolve,
And in a jelly thee dissolve,
Like a shot star, which doth repair
Upward, and rarify the air.[12]

7. Herodotus recounts how the Scythians traveled with their tents on their wagons.
8. Refers to the snail's trail of slime
9. Temple
10. Rosary beads
11. Nature
12. In popular lore, shooting stars were supposed to turn into jelly when they hit the earth, and ascend as air.

Margaret Cavendish, *Grounds of Natural Philosophy*

Part 1 introduces the complex natural philosophy of Margaret Cavendish (1623–73) as a form of vitalist materialism, in which all matter was understood to be composed of self-moving, rational, and sensitive matter, all always in motion and changing. This position meant that she attributed both rational and sensitive spirits, and thus possibly a kind of understanding, to nonhuman living things and minerals. She speculated that, if they could speak, animals could reveal more natural secrets than humans: as she wrote in "Of Fishes" in her collection of *Poems and Fancies*, "Who knows, but fish which in the sea do live /Can a good reason of its saltness give, / And how it ebbs and flows? Perchance they can / Show reasons more than ever yet could man." In her later philosophical work, the *Grounds of Natural Philosophy* (1668) excerpted here, Cavendish offers a more stripped-down and systematized presentation of her thoughts on the capacities of animals as well as vegetables and minerals to sense, perceive, and know. At the same time, she expresses skepticism as to what humans can ever really know about each other or any other creatures, recalling a similar kind of skepticism found in Montaigne's "Apology for Raymond Sebond."

Chap. II. Of knowledge and perception of different kinds and sorts of creatures.

There is not any creature in nature, that is not composed of self-moving parts, (viz. both of rational and sensitive) as also of the inanimate parts, which are self-knowing: so that all creatures, being composed of these sorts of parts, must have a sensitive, and rational knowledge and perception, as animals, vegetables, minerals, elements, or what else there is in nature. But several kinds, and several sorts in these kinds of creatures, being composed after different manners, and ways, must needs have different lives, knowledges, and perceptions; and not only every several kind, and sort, have such differences; but, every particular creature, through the variations of their self-moving parts, have varieties of lives, knowledges, perceptions, conceptions, and the like; and not only so, but every particular part of one and the same creature, have varieties of knowledges, and perceptions, because they have varieties of actions. But, (as I have declared) there is not any different kind of creature, that can have the like life, knowledge, and perception; not only because they have different productions, and different forms; but, different natures, as being of different kinds.

Source: *Grounds of Natural Philosophy Divided into Thirteen Parts: With an Appendix Containing Five Parts / Written by the* [. . .] *Duchess of Newcastle*, London, 1668), pp. 18–21.

Chap. III. Of perception of parts, and united perception.

All the self-moving parts are perceptive; and, all perception is in parts, and is dividable, and compoundable, as being material; also, alterable, as being self-moving. Wherefore, no creature that is composed, or consists of many several sorts of corporeal figurative motions, but must have many sorts of perception; which is the reason that one creature, as man, cannot perceive another man any otherwise but in parts: for, the rational, and sensitive; nay, all the parts of one and the same creature, perceive their adjoining parts, as they perceive foreign parts; only, by their close conjunction and near relation, they unite in one and the same actions. I do not say, they always agree: for, when they move irregularly, they disagree: And some of those united parts, will move after one manner, and some after another; but, when they move regularly, then they move to one and the same design, or one and the same united action. So, although a creature is composed of several sorts of corporeal motions; yet, these several sorts, being properly united in one creature, move all agreeably to the property and nature of the whole creature; that is, the particular parts move according to the property of the whole creature; because the particular parts, by conjunction, make the whole. So that, the several parts make one whole; by which, a whole creature hath both a general knowledge, and a knowledge of parts; whereas, the perceptions of foreign objects, are but in the parts: and this is the reason why one creature perceives not the whole of another creature, but only some parts. Yet this is to be noted, that not any part hath another part's nature, or motion, nor therefore, their knowledge, or perception; but, by agreement, and unity of parts, there is composed perceptions.

Robert Hooke, *Micrographia*

The polymath Robert Hooke (1635–1703) experimented in a wide variety of fields, including geology, surveying, astronomy, and architecture. While serving as a geometry professor at Gresham College and surveyor of London, Hooke joined the Royal Society and for many years served as their "curator of experiments." (For another contribution by Hooke, see his "History of the Weather" in Part 4.) His most famous work, *Micrographia: Or Some Physiological Descriptions of Minute Bodies Made by Magnifying Glasses*, appeared in 1665 as the Royal Society's first official publication. In *Micrographia* Hooke's stunning microscopic images revealed to both scientists and the public never-

Source: *Micrographia: Or Some Physiological Descriptions of Minute Bodies Made by Magnifying Glasses*, London, 1667, pp. 211–13.

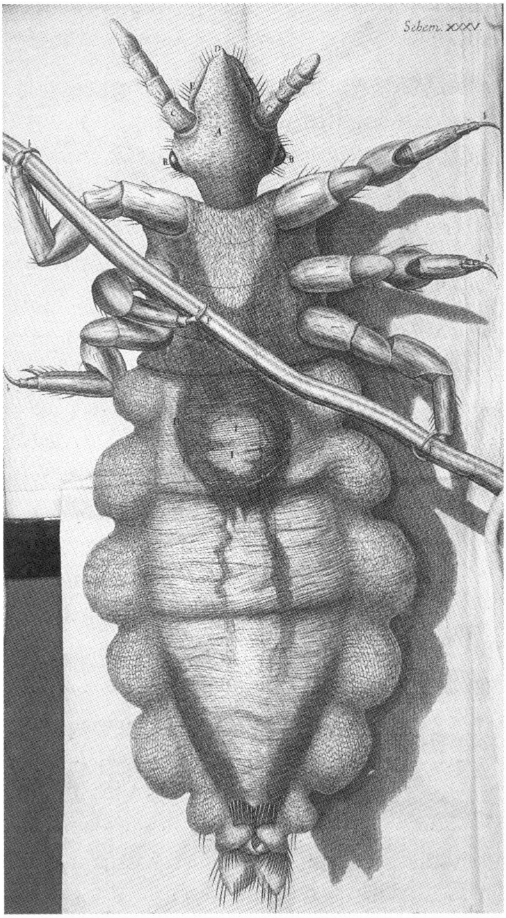

Figure 14. Image of the louse from Robert Hooke, *Micrographia* (1665), p. 212, accompanying the text describing the louse. 578 H76. Kislak Center for Special Collections, Rare Books, and Manuscripts, University of Pennsylvania Libraries.

before-seen details of things in nature. In his representation of the louse (Figure 14), the text that accompanies the intricate drawing precisely evokes in words Hooke's experience of the insect. He goes so far as to observe the louse's motions as it sucks his blood. At the same time that the text and image depict the monstrosity of the louse's body and actions, thus estranging it, Hooke also partially anthropomorphizes the "impudent" and "saucy" insect. (The letters in the text below refers to part of the image in Figure 14.)

Observation. LIV. Of a Louse.

This is a creature so officious, that 'twill be known to everyone at one time or other, so busy, and so impudent, that it will be intruding itself in every one's company, and so proud and aspiring withal, that it fears not to trample on the best, and affects nothing so much as a crown; feeds and lives very high, and that makes it so saucy, as to pull any one by the ears that comes in its way, and will never be quiet till it has drawn blood. It is troubled at nothing so much as at a man that scratches his head, as knowing that man is plotting and contriving some mischief against it, and that makes it often time skulk into some meaner and lower place, and run behind a man's back, though it go very much against the hair; which ill conditions of it having made it better known than trusted, would exempt me from making any further description of it, did not my faithful Mercury, my microscope, bring me other information of it. For this has discovered to me, by means of a very bright light cast on it, that it is a creature of a very odd shape; it has a head shap'd like that expressed in 35. Scheme [Figure 14] marked with A, which seems almost conical, but is a little flatted on the upper and under sides, at the biggest part of which, on either side behind the head (as it were, being the place where other creature's ears stand) are placed its two black shining goggle eyes (BB), looking backwards, and fenced round with several small cilia or hairs that encompass it, so that it seems this creature has no very good foresight. It does not seem to have any eye-lids, and therefore perhaps its eyes were so placed, that it might the better cleanse them with its fore-legs; and perhaps this may be the reason, why they so much avoid and run from the light behind them, for being made to live in the shady and dark recesses of the hair, and thence probably their eye having a great aperture, the open and clear light, especially that of the sun, must needs very much offend them. To secure these eyes from receiving any injury from the hairs through which it passes, it has two horns that grow before it, in the place where one would have thought the eyes should be; each of these (CC) hath four joints, which are fringed, as 'twere, with small bristles, from which to the tip of its snout D, the head seems very round and tapering, ending in a very sharp nose D, which seems to have a small hole, and to be the passage through which he sucks the blood. Now whereas if it be plac'd on its back, with its belly upwards, as it is in the 35. Scheme, it seems in several positions to have a resemblance of chaps, or jaws, as it is represented in the figure by EE, yet in other postures those dark strokes disappear; and having kept several of them in a box for two or three days, so that for all that time they had nothing to feed on, I found, upon letting one creep on my hand, that it immediately fell to sucking, and did neither seem to thrust its nose very deep into the skin, nor to open any kind of mouth, but I could plainly perceive a small current of blood, which came directly from its snout, and past into its belly; and about A there seem'd a contrivance, somewhat resembling a pump, pair of bellows, or heart, for by a very swift systole and diastole the blood seem'd drawn from the nose, and forced into the body. It did not seem at all, though I viewed it a good while as it was sucking, to thrust more of its nose into the skin than the very snout D, nor did it cause the least discernable pain, and yet the blood seem'd to run through its head very quick and freely, so that it seems there is no part of the skin but the blood is dispers'd into, nay, even into the cuticula; for had it thrust its whole nose in from D to CC, it would not have amounted to the supposed thickness of that tegument, the length of the nose being not more than a three hundredth part of an inch. It has six legs, covered with a very transparent shell, and jointed exactly like a crab's, or lobster's; each leg is divided into six parts by these joints, and those have here and there several small hairs; and at the end of each leg it has two claws, very properly adapted for its peculiar use, being thereby enabled to walk very securely both on the skin and hair; and indeed this contrivance of the feet is very curious, and could not be made more commodiously and compendiously, for performing both these requisite motions, of walking and climbing up the hair of a man's head, then it is. For, by having the lesser claw (a) set so much short of the bigger (b) when it walks on the skin the shorter touches not, and then the feet are the same with those of a mite, and several other small insects, but by means of the small joints of the longer claw it can bend it round, and so with both claws take hold of a hair, in the manner represented in the figure, the long transparent cylinder (FFF), being a man's hair held by it.

The thorax seem'd eas'd with another kind of substance than the belly, namely, with a thin transparent horny substance, which upon the fasting of the creature did not grow flaccid; through this I could plainly see the blood, suck'd from my hand, to be variously distributed, and mov'd to and fro; and about G there seem'd a pretty big white substance, which upon the fasting of the creature did not grow flaccid; through this I could plainly see the blood, suck'd from my hand, to be variously distributed, and mov'd to and fro; and about G there seem'd a pretty big white substance, which seem'd to be moved within its thorax. Besides, there appear'd very many small milk-white vessels, which crossed over the breast between the legs, out of which, on either side, were many small branchings, these seem'd to be the veins and arteries, for that which is analogous to blood in all insects is milk-white.

PART IV

Weather, Climate, and Seasons

When people can shelter in air-conditioned or central-heated homes and offices, the weather only gets attention during extreme events. Science tells us that we are experiencing a catastrophic shift in climate, but it is all too easy to ignore that news. Only when the heat scorches or cold immobilizes us, the fierce winds blow, or the water laps at our feet, do we start to notice. However, not even the most privileged people could find refuge from the weather in previous ages. In societies highly dependent on agriculture, a catastrophic storm or frost could ruin a harvest for a year, causing starvation and unemployment. From the thirteenth through the nineteenth centuries, Europe did experience what we now call the Little Ice Age, several periods of significant climatic cooling causing long harsh winters and wet summers, with its peak in the mid-seventeenth century (see Blom; Fagan). Crops failed repeatedly, devastating the rural economy and causing social disruption and discontent, eventually leading to long-range economic and political change.

For millennia people have wondered what causes weather, from seasonal changes to floods, droughts, and storms. Every ancient culture had its own mythology associated with the weather: in Greece, Zeus was the thunder god, and in the Hebrew Bible, God speaks through thunder and lightning and punishes through tempests, heat, or floods. The idea of the weather's divine origins persisted for centuries: thus, in the seventeenth century ministers like Thomas Jackson could still preach of storms at sea as examples of divine wrath. However, at the same time, going back to Aristotle, natural philosophers have also sought to discover the material conditions that make the weather, speculating about how the elements of air, water, and fire interact in constant motion (see also Hildegard of Bingen in Part 1). At the end of the seventeenth century, the members of the Royal Society proposed to develop instruments to measure, record, and analyze meteorological phenomena, making a "history" of the weather based on systematic observations, the culmination of the direction Aristotle set in his work.

Knowing about the causes of weather mattered, because people cared about its impact on everything from living beings to the movement of the oceans. Cultivating plants requires sensitivity to the changes of the seasons, and so horticultural advice was often ordered in monthly calendars (as it is still today). Farmers and gardeners were also warned to watch for the signs of impending disaster, preparing for what Virgil called in his *Georgics* the "armies of wind"—hail, snow, and torrential rains. However, humans and animals were thought to be just as vulnerable to the effects of heat and cold, moisture and dryness. From the very beginning of Western medicine, physicians elaborated on complex theories of how changes of season and variations in climate influence both health and human character (see Totoro; Feerick 2010; Floyd-Wilson). Such concepts persisted for centuries: see, for example, the immensely popular medieval handbook of advice for kings, the *Secreta secretorum*, which offers advice on diet and activity aligned with the "temperament" and qualities of each season of the year. Further, regional climates were understood to shape the body types and characters of different ethnicities and races, often with the possibilities that a change in region could affect that "temperament" (see Hippocrates and Avicenna in Part 4).

As with everything else in the natural world, weather has also long carried symbolic meaning, whether through seasonal cycles of death and renewal or analogies between extreme weather and violent human emotions—torrid or frigid, stormy or temperate. In literature human emotions may be said to reflect or even imaginatively influence the weather. In Amelia Lanyer's poem "The Description of Cookham," the landscape responds to the presence or absence of the women who inhabit it, flourishing when they are there but sinking into winter when they depart (see also Edmund Spenser, *The Shephearde's Calendar* in Part 5). In Shakespeare's *King Lear*, the mad Lear's rage is staged in a scene of a violent thunderstorm, in which the old king's emotional weather is realized materially. The matter of weather and climate surfaces everywhere in this anthology where the health and vitality of all living things are at stake, but even beyond that, weather and climate constantly remind us how we live, exposed to natural forces we do not fully understand that may overwhelm us.

Hippocrates, *Airs, Waters, Places*

The Greek physician Hippocrates (ca. 460–370 BCE) is now considered the founder of the Western medical practice based on observing the human body and its disorders. While we cannot say which of the some sixty ancient medi-

Source: Hippocrates. "Airs, Waters, Places," translated by Francis Adams, 1886. *Internet Classics Archive*, http://classics.mit.edu/Hippocrates/airwatpl.html.

cal texts that form the Hippocratic corpus were written by Hippocrates himself, these texts do present a largely coherent approach to the subject, stressing the importance of describing and systematically interpreting symptoms exactly to achieve a prognosis. Hippocratic theories entail the belief that the elements of earth, water, air, and fire—and their associated qualities—constitute all living things (see Avicenna in Part 1 for synopsis). The interaction of those elements, both internally and externally, affects the flow and quality of the humors circulating in the body. While acknowledging the role of internal factors, the Hippocratic writers also investigated the complex influence of external factors on the human body and character. Treatments thus mostly involve controlling the environment and diet. As the following passages from *Airs, Waters, Places* insist, the physician must take into account the effects of the winds, soil, and water, all of which constantly change with the seasons. Climate shapes the body but also regional personality types, whether weak or strong, slow or fiery. Such thinking had a long afterlife right up through the early modern period, as writers came up with explanations to justify what they saw as the relative qualities of different races and ethnicities, where climate became inscribed in the body and human character (for a medieval example, see Avicenna in Part 4).

Whoever wishes to investigate medicine properly, should proceed thus: in the first place to consider the seasons of the year, and what effects each of them produces for they are not at all alike, but differ much from themselves in regard to their changes. Then the winds, the hot and the cold, especially such as are common to all countries, and then such as are peculiar to each locality. We must also consider the qualities of the waters, for as they differ from one another in taste and weight, so also do they differ much in their qualities. In the same manner, when one comes into a city to which he is a stranger, he ought to consider its situation, how it lies as to the winds and the rising of the sun; for its influence is not the same whether it lies to the north or the south, to the rising or to the setting sun. These things one ought to consider most attentively, and concerning the waters which the inhabitants use, whether they be marshy and soft, or hard, and running from elevated and rocky situations, and then if saltish and unfit for cooking; and the ground, whether it be naked and deficient in water, or wooded and well watered, and whether it lies in a hollow, confined situation, or is elevated and cold; and the mode in which the inhabitants live, and what are their pursuits, whether they are fond of drinking and eating to excess, and given to indolence, or are fond of exercise and labor, and not given to excess in eating and drinking.

From these things he must proceed to investigate everything else. For if one knows all these things well, or at least the greater part of them, he cannot miss knowing, when he comes into a strange city, either the diseases peculiar to the place, or the particular nature of common diseases, so that he will not be in doubt as to the treatment of the diseases, or commit mistakes, as is likely to be the case provided one had not previously considered these matters. And in particular, as the season and the year advances, he can tell what epidemic diseases will attack the city, either in summer or in winter, and what each individual will be in danger of experiencing from the change of regimen. For knowing the changes of the seasons, the risings and settings of the stars, how each of them takes place, he will be able to know beforehand what sort of a year is going to ensue. Having made these investigations, and knowing beforehand the seasons, such a one must be acquainted with each particular, and must succeed in the preservation of health, and be by no means unsuccessful in the practice of his art. And if it shall be thought that these things belong rather to meteorology, it will be admitted, on second thoughts, that astronomy contributes not a little, but a very great deal, indeed, to medicine. For with the seasons the digestive organs of men undergo a change.

But how of the aforementioned things should be investigated and explained, I will now declare in a clear manner. A city that is exposed to hot winds (these are between the wintry rising, and the wintry setting of the sun), and to which these are peculiar, but which is sheltered from the north winds; in such a city the waters will be plenteous and saltish, and as they run from an elevated source, they are necessarily hot in summer, and cold in winter; the heads of the inhabitants are of a humid and pituitous constitution, and their bellies subject to frequent disorders, owing to the phlegm running down from the head; the forms of their bodies, for the most part, are rather flabby; they do not eat nor drink much; drinking wine in particular, and more especially if carried to intoxication, is oppressive to them.

[. . .]

And there are in Europe other tribes, differing from one another in stature, shape, and courage: the differences are those I formerly mentioned, and will now explain more clearly. Such as inhabit a country which is mountainous, rugged, elevated, and well watered, and where the changes of the seasons are very great, are likely to have great variety of shapes among them, and to be naturally of an enterprising and warlike disposition; and such persons are apt to have no little of the savage and ferocious in their nature; but such as dwell in places which are low-lying, abounding in meadows and ill ventilated, and who have a larger proportion of hot than of cold winds, and who make use of warm waters—these are not likely to be of large stature nor well proportioned, but are of a broad make, fleshy, and have black hair; and they are rather of a dark than of a light complexion, and are less likely to be phlegmatic than bilious; courage and laborious enterprise are not naturally in them, but may be engendered in them by means of their institutions. And if there be rivers in the country which carry off the stagnant and rain water from it, these may be wholesome and clear; but if there be no rivers, but the inhabitants drink the waters of fountains, and such as are stagnant and marshy, they must necessarily have prominent bellies and enlarged spleens. But such as inhabit a high country, and one that is level, windy, and well-watered, will be large of stature, and like to one another; but their minds will be rather unmanly and gentle. Those who live on thin, ill-watered, and bare soils, and not well attempered in the changes of the seasons, in such a country they are likely to be in their persons rather hard and well braced, rather of a blond than a dark complexion, and in disposition and passions haughty and self-willed. For, where the changes of the seasons are most frequent, and where they differ most from one another, there you will find their forms, dispositions, and nature the most varied. These are the strongest of the natural causes of difference, and next the country in which one lives, and the waters; for, in general, you will find the forms and dispositions of mankind to correspond with the nature of the country; for where the land is fertile, soft, and well-watered, and supplied with waters from very elevated situations, so as to be hot in summer and cold in winter, and where the seasons are fine, there the men are fleshy, have ill-formed joints, and are of a humid temperament; they are not disposed to endure labor, and, for the most part, are base in spirit; indolence and sluggishness are visible in them, and to the arts they are dull, and not clever nor acute. When the country is bare, not fenced, and rugged, blasted by the winter and scorched by the sun, there you may see the hardy, hardy, slender, with well-shaped joints, well-braced, and shaggy; sharp, industry and vigilance accompany such a constitution; in morals and passions they are haughty and opinionative, inclining rather to the fierce than to the mild; and you will find them acute and ingenious as regards the arts, and excelling in military affairs; and likewise all the other productions of the earth corresponding to the earth itself. Thus it is with regard to the most opposite natures and shapes; drawing conclusions from them, you may judge of the rest without any risk of error.

Aristotle, *Meteorologica*, or *Meteorology*

In his treatise on *Meteorology*, Aristotle derived his analysis of weather from the movement and interaction of the four principles or elements of fire, earth, air, and water, with their corresponding qualities of hot and cold, dry and

Source: *Meteorologica*, translated by E. W. Webster. *The Complete Works of Aristotle: The Revised Oxford Translation*, edited by Jonathan Barnes, vol. 1, Princeton University Press, 1984, p. 596. Bollingen Series LXX2.

wet. Rather than attributing weather phenomena to the actions or will of the gods, Aristotle can thus explain them materially. Aristotle details the various motions of heat and air that can be said to cause thunder and lightning; to help students understand these actions, he compares the motions of moist and dry exhalations or winds with more mundane phenomena, such as the squeezing of a seed that rises or the rowing of oars. In this sense, the most dramatic weather events do not differ in kind from ordinary occurences in human experience.

Let us go on to explain lightning and thunder, and further whirlwinds, fire-wind, and thunderbolts; for the cause of them all must be supposed the same.

As we have said before, there are two kinds of exhalation, moist and dry, and the combination contains them both potentially. It, as we have said before, condenses into cloud, and the density of the clouds is highest at their upper limit. (For they must be denser and colder on the side where the heat escapes to the upper regions and leaves them. This explains why hurricanes and thunderbolts and all analogous phenomena move downwards in spite of the fact that everything hot has a natural tendency upwards. Just as the pips that we squeeze between our fingers are heavy but often jump upwards: so these things are necessarily squeezed out away from the densest part of the cloud.) Now the heat that escapes disperses to the upper region. But if any of the dry exhalation is caught up in the process as the air cools, it is squeezed out as the clouds contract, and is forcibly carried on and collides with the neighboring clouds, and the sound of this collision is what we call thunder. This collision is so analogous, to compare small with great, to the sound we hear in a flame which men call the laughter or the threat of Hephaestus or of Hestia. This occurs when the wood dries and cracks and the exhalation rushes on the flame in a body. So in the clouds, the exhalation is projected and its impact on dense clouds causes thunder: the variety of the sound is due to the irregularity of the clouds and the hollows that intervene where their density is interrupted. This, then, is thunder, and this its cause.

It usually happens that the wind that is ejected is inflamed and burns with a thin and faint fire: this is what we call lightning, where we see as it were the exhalation colored in the act of its ejection. It comes into existence after the collision and the thunder, though we see it earlier because sight is quicker than hearing. The rowing of triremes illustrates this: the oars are going back again before the sound of their striking the water reaches us.

However, there are some who maintain there is actually fire in the clouds. Empedocles says that it is part of the upper ether (which he calls fire) which has descended from above. Anaxagoros that it is part of the upper ether (which he calls fire) which has descended from above. Lightning, then, is the gleam of this fire, and thunder the hissing noise of its extinction in the cloud.

Virgil, *Georgics*, Book 1, On the Storm

Written after Virgil (70–19 BCE) composed his *Eclogues*, his *Georgics* depicts the demanding experience of agriculture and the life of the earth itself. The poem's name derives from the Greek words for earth (*gē*) and work (*ergon*), signaling its concern with both human labor and the natural world's inherent power (for another passage from the *Georgics*, see Part 5). Drawing on both literary sources and the agricultural manuals of his time, Virgil highlights humans' unceasing desire to control their environment and the living things in it, and the eventual futility of that effort. Concerned specifically with the work of farming, Book 1 represents human and non-human encounters as mutual violence, tempered by respect and care on the part of those who cultivate the land. (Book 2 is focused on cultivated trees and vines, Book 3 on animal husbandry, and Book 4 on bees.) This excerpt evokes a violent storm that has the power to obliterate everything, reminding the farmer to carefully read the signs of what is to come. In the context of an emphasis on hard work, the poem thus shows how people are vulnerable to the overwhelming force of wind and water, driven by the force of Jove who hurls thunder and lightning.

Why tell of autumn's storms and stars
and, now days draw in and summer softens, what keeps
men to vigil?—now or when spring falls in downpours
as the sheathed harvest needles through the field
and grain on its green stem swells up with milk?
Often, as the farmer guides the reaper to his golden tract
and shears the barley from its crackling stalk,
I have seen all the armies of wind clash
uprooting plump grain left and right from deepest roots
and hurling it high, then with its whirlwind black
the storm whisks the slight straw and airborne slips away.
And often in the sky looms a tremendous host of waters—
clouds levied from the ether roll a murky squall
of swart[1] rains: shelved heaven tumbles, and with its wet

Source: Virgil. *The Georgics: A Poem of the Land*. Translated and edited by Kimberly Johnson, Penguin, 2009, pp. 23–27

1. Dark

pounding washes off the lilting crop, the oxen's labors.
The gutters fill, the gully swells with rushing,
the sea seethes, its estuaries heaving.
The Father himself, in his midnight of clouds, hurls
with his fulgent[2] fist the thunderbolt, at whose impact
the earth's bulk trembles: critters scatter, terror blasts
all mortal hearts to cowering. He with lancing fire
sunders Athos or Rhodope or the heights of Ceraunia.[3]
The southwind redoubles, and the thronging rain.
Now thickets, now shores moan beneath the savage gale.

Fearing this, observe the months and heaven's constellations—
where Saturn's frozen star runs retrograde,
into which of heaven's orbits wanders Mercury with his fires.
Above all, love the gods, and to exalted Ceres
devote your yearly tribute, performed on the reviving grass
as the last of winter falters, at the crack of clement spring.
Then lambs are fat and wine is mellow,
then sleep is sweet as shadows cluster on the peaks.
Let every farmhand worship Ceres: for her
infuse the honeycombs with milk and well-aged wine,
and thrice around the sprouts parade the blessed sacrifice
whom the chorus of your company trails with cordant jubilation,
with cheers invoking Ceres to dwell beneath their eaves.
Nor should any edge his sickle under the ripe ears
before he wreathes his brows with sprigs of oak,
spins an artless shuffle, and lifts his harvest hymn.

That by sure signs we may anticipate
these heats and torrents, the wind that speeds the ice,
the Father himself ordained the monthly omens of the moon,
at what sign the southwinds fall, at what steady sightings
the farmer keeps his cattle near the stalls.
Always under gusting winds the salty straits
begin to churn and swell and dry thunder sounds
against the mountaintops, or shores resound
a tumult to the distances and the woodland murmur amplifies.

2. Shining brightly
3. All three are mountains

Then the tide restrains not from the curved keel,
when fleet the terns wheel shoreward from mid-ocean
shrieking to the strand, when sea-coots
frolic on dry land, and the heron quits her wonted swamps
to wing above the towering cloud.
Often, when wind freshens, you'll see stars
falling headlong down the sky, through the shades of night
trailing lengths of blanching flame behind.
Often too you'll see fine chaff and fallen leaves fluttering,
or on the water's surface feathers trifling as they skim.
But when from the grim northland levin[4] flares, when
the mansions of the east- and westwind roll thunder,
the countryside entire sloshes under flooding ditches,
and every sea-bound sailor furls his soaked sails.
Never has rain worked ill unwarned: either as it masses
the aerial cranes dive for valleys deep, or the heifer
eyeing heaven tracks the breeze with flaring nostrils,
or the twitting swallow flits around the cisterns
and in the mire frogs croak their immemorial complaint.
More often, from her cloistered crannies the ant drags out
her eggs, wearing a threadlike groove, and a vaulting rainbow
stretches down to drink, and from the pasture departing
in grand array a raven army drums with frequent wings.
Already seabirds variegated, already birds like those
that comb the Asian lees around Cayster's[5] comely oxbows—
see them vie to douse their shoulders in the heavy spray,
now thrusting heads under the stream, now rushing waves,
aimlessly dithered with zeal for bathing.
Then unruly the crow cries down rain with sharp tones
and solitary strolls the thirsty strand.
Even girls engrossed in nightly chores are never unaware
of brewing storms—they mark when in sparking lamps
the oil-light flickers and smutty mold collects.

4. Flash of lightning
5. A river in Ephesus

Pseudo-Aristotle, *Secreta secretorum*, or *The Secret of Secrets*

The *Secreta secretorum*, or *The Secret of Secrets*, takes the form of an imagined letter from Aristotle to Alexander the Great proffering advice on many matters, including statecraft, magic, health, and astrology. The earliest extant Arabic manuscript of this work dates to the tenth century, while the treatise's origins are still unknown. Once it was translated into Latin in the twelfth century, the *Secreta* spread across Europe, appearing in multiple vernaculars, and in 1528 Robert Copeland published it in English. This excerpt from Copeland's translation aligns the four seasons' changes with the human body's needs in diet and medical treatment, thus implying that the human body has its own seasons, and earth's body, its own humors. Such thinking had a long afterlife: compare, for example, to the monthly recommendations on gardening and healthy living in *Rams Little Dodoen*, and also to John Evelyn's description of the seasonal changes in the body of the earth in his *Elysium Britannicum* in Part 6.

Our intention is to treat in this book of the four seasons of the year with the quality, propriety, contrariety, and difference of each of them. And they been certain seasons of the year divided as follows. That is to wit [primetime] springtime or vere beginneth when the sun entereth in the sign of Aries, and lasteth four score and eight days and eighteen hours and the fourth part of an hour. That is to wit from the tenth day in the end of March to the four and twenty day of June. And in this season the days and nights being all of length, the weather is fair. The warm weather cometh. The snows melt, rivers run swift and clear, and wax warm, the moistness of the earth riseth to the height of trees and causeth them to smell sweet. Meadows and grains sprout and corn groweth, all flowers take color, birds been clothed with new robes, and enforce them to sing. Trees be decked with leaves and flowers, and the lands with seeds. Beasts engender and all people take strength and lust. The earth is arrayed goodly and is as a fair bride clothed with jewels of divers[1] colors because she should seem the fairer at her wedding.

Of primetime and what it is.

The primetime is hot and moist temperately as the air. This season the blood moveth and spreadeth to all the members of the body and the body is perfect in temperate complexion. In this season chickens, kids, and poached eggs ought to be eaten with lettuces and goats milk in these three months. Primetime beginneth when the sun entereth the sign of Aries and lasteth ninety-one days

Source: *Thus endeth the secrete of secretes of Aristotle*. London, 1528.

1. Various

and an hour and a half from the tenth day of March to the tenth day of June. In this season is the best letting of blood of any time. And then is good to travail[2] and to be laxative. And to be bathed. And to eat such things as will purge the belly. For all diseases that cometh either by purging or bleeding returneth anon in this primetime.

Of summer and what it is.

Summer beginneth when the sun entereth the first point of the crevice and lasteth ninety-two days and an hour and a half. That is to wit from the tenth day of June to the tenth day of September. In this season the days be long and the nights short. And all regions increaseth and abateth their heat and the sea is calm and the air meek and fair. The flowers wither and the serpents increase and shed their venom and spread their strength. The might of man's body be fortified. And all the world is full of wealth as the fair bride is of goodly stature and in perfect age. The season of summer is hot and dry and then choler[3] is moved. And in this season it is good to beware of all things that be hot and dry of complexion.[4] And take heed of too much eating and drinking for thereby is the kindly heat quenched. In this season eat meats of cold and moist complexion as veal, milk with vinegar, and pottages made with barley meal. Eat fruit of eager savor as pomegranates and drink small[5] wines and use not the company of women. In this season let thee not blood but if great need compel thee. Use little travails and seldom bathing.

Of autumn or harvest.

Harvest entereth when the sun cometh into the first degree of the balance and lastest ninety-one days and an hour and a half. That is to wit from the tenth day of September to the tenth day of December. In this season the day and night be of one length. And then the days wax short and the nights long. The air is dark and the winds enter the northern regions or Septemtrion. The weather changeth and the rivers and spring wax less. The orchards and fruits withereth. The beauties of the earth fadeth. Birds cease their singing. Serpents seek their hole where they assembled their living in summer for the time of winter. The earth is as an old naked woman goeth from youth to age. The season of the harvest is cold and dry; this time black choler is moved. In this season it is good to eat meats that be hot and moist as chickens, lamb, and drink old wines, eat sweet

2. Exertion
3. Yellow bile
4. Humoral composition
5. Weak

raisins. And keep thee from all things that breed black choler as lying with women more than in summer nor bathe thee not but if great need require it be done. In this season if a man have need of vomiting do it at noon in the hottest of the day. For at that time all the superfluities of man's body gathereth together Also, it is good to purge the belly with a medicine ordained therefore and other things that been to expel black choler and retain humors.

Of winter and what it is.

Winter cometh when the sun entereth in the first degree of the sign of Capricorn and lasteth seventy days and an hour and half. And it beginneth the tenth day of December and continueth to the tenth day of March. In this season the nights be long and the days short. It is very cold. The wines be in the press and the leaves fall and herbs lesseth all their strength or the most part. The beast hideth them in caves and pits of hills. The air and the weather are dark. And the earth is like an old, decrepit person that by great age is naked and nigh unto death. Winter is very cold and moist, and then it behooveth thee to use hot meats as chickens, hens, mutton, and other hot and fair flesh, eat figs, nuts, and drink green wines. And beware too much lax and bleeding and eschew the company of women for it will feeble thy stomach, and baths be good. And for the great cold the natural heat entereth into the body, and therefore the digestion is better in winter than in summer. And in harvest the belly is cold and then the pores been open by the heat of the season and reproveth the natural heat of all the parts of the body. And therefore the stomach hath but little heat whereby the digestion is feebled and the humors assemble there.

Avicenna, *The Canon of Medicine*, On Climate

Part 1 introduces *The Canon of Medicine*'s description of the fundamental elements of earth, water, air, and fire, with the qualities of hot, cold, wet, and dry aligned in turn with the nature of the four humors. In the section on the causes of disease, he begins by considering the extra-corporeal factors affecting our bodies, starting with the nature of the air. As long as the air is good, our health prospers, but the air constantly changes, turning hot and cold, or wet or dry, whether in the seasons' passing or travel to different climates (see also Hildegard of Bingen in Part 1 and the pseudo-Aristotelian *Secreta secretorum*, discussed above). Like Hippocrates, Avicenna theorized that different environments have the power to shape both the human body and character. This kind of thinking

Source: *A Treatise on the Canon of Medicine of Avicenna*. Translated by O. Cameron Gruner, Luzac, 1930, pp. 204–5.

about climatic effects persisted for centuries and complicated later ideas about colonization and race: on the one hand, climate theory was used to ground racial difference in the body, but on the other, it was feared that exposure to different climates could also alter that malleable body, undermining the essentializing of racial difference.

Hot countries.

The hair becomes dark or black and frizzly and becomes gathered into tight clumps like pepper-flowers; the digestion is weakened. Old age comes on early, owing to the great dissipation of breath and the draining away of the bodily moisture. This is seen in the land of the blacks (Ethiopia, Abyssinia). Persons who reside in such countries become aged at thirty, are timid (as the breath is so much dispersed) and the body becomes soft and dark.

Cold countries.

Persons who go live in cold countries become robust and stronger, and bolder and more courageous. The digestion improves. If the climate is also damp the people will become obese and fleshly and coarse. The veins will not show under the skin of the hands, and the joints are indistinct in outline. The body become pale and delicate.

Damp wet countries.

Here the summer is not very warm, nor the winter very cold. People living in humid countries have beautiful faces with soft smooth complexions They soon get tired with exercise. They are liable to develop protracted fevers, with looseness of the bowels and menorrhage. Piles, which are common, often bleed.

Wandalbert of Prüm, *On the Names, Signs, Times of Planting, and Qualities of Weather of the Twelve Months*

The practice of giving month-by-month agricultural advice dates back to the Roman writers, including Columella, Varro, and Palladius, and it has never ceased. The most significant extant medieval example is a poem on the twelve months by Wandalbert of Prüm, a Benedictine monk living in the Rhineland in the ninth century. Proceeding month by month, Wandalbert describes each month's corresponding zodiac sign, typical activities in the natural

Source: Carl I. Hammer. *Charlemagne's Months and their Bavarian Labors: The Politics of the Seasons in the Carolingian Empire*, Archaeopress, 1997, pp. 53–54, 61–62. BAR International Series 676.

world, and agricultural labors and human amusements such as hunting, as adapted to the climate of northern parts of Europe. It contrasts with monthly advice that focuses on the dangers of seasonal change for the human body (compare with the *Secreta secretorum*); rather, Wandalbert encourages both the appropriate work and celebrations fitting the moment. Each time of year was understood to have its distinctive human and natural activities (Figure 15).

Concerning January

Which Julius[1] decreed to be observed as the first month of the year,
It is designated by the name of King Janus
Who ruled the people of Saturn in Latium and
Increased the town of Laurentum in authority and in people and in laws.
Over this twin monstrosity preside the stars of Capricorn
Twice twelve in splendor together in one zodiac sign.
In that season, the hares cavort in the snowy fields,
And by various crafts they trap the painted birds
That fly about the fields, the hills and streams.

Then it pleases, free of cares, to indulge the sparrow-hawk
In its taste for capon throughout the winter, and at home
By diverse means to prepare for coming spring.
But then is not the time to chase the fleet stags and hinds,
Nor is it of use to transfix the shoulder of the foaming boar with iron:
They are restrained by Boreas,[2] and leanness
Wastes and shrinks the enfeebled limbs of the beasts.
Nor is it easy to commit seed to the tilled land.
Everything withers in frost, and a terrible hardness stiffens the fields.
Then are trees at their strongest, and it is profitable to fell the fissile wood,
Then to apply axes for dwellings and boats.
[. . .]

Concerning July

Starting with March it marks itself out as the fifth in the year,
And Quirinus[3] commanded his people to call it Quintilis,
Seventh from January, July now occupies the middle of the year,

1. Julius Caesar, who established the Julian calendar
2. The north wind
3. An epithet for the god Janus

Figure 15. February as represented in an illuminated manuscript page from the *Très Riches Heures du Duc de Berry*, showing the typical activities of people and animals in the season, as well as the state of the land. Limbourg Brothers (flo. 1399–1416 CE). Ms. 65, fol. 2 verso. Photo: René-Gabriel Ojéda, Musée Condé, Chantilly, France. Photo credit: © RMN-Grand Palais /Art Resource, NY.

It exults, being named for the Great Caesar,
At the solstice the four stars of blazing Cancer gleam upon it,
And radiate their shine equally in ten-fold flame.
Set on the heavenly axis at equal distances about the center,
The golden light of the sun unites it with the sixth month.

At this time, the fertile fields of grain begin to turn to gold on their
tallest stalks,
And ripe barley, sown at the first frosts of autumn,
Conveys the hope of harvest.
Now also, since, Phoebus[4] does, indeed, warm the fields with perfect
fires,
The favorable breezes grant the wheat harvest.
From now on, also, the skilled hand seeks out the field of flax:
For what was sown in the month of March,
July returns with full ears as ripe, and whatever
Is committed in the month of April to the scattered furrows,
That very thing shall bestow the harvest in the burned field of August.
Also, in this month one can adorn the dessert courses with pears,
And pluck the tiny peaches with luscious taste,
Those with ripen first in the summer's heat,
The rest it is agreed to yield to autumn.

Also, from the first spelt, dedicate it upon the early altars,
Then cease, and demand the pleasant proceeds of the year,
Whenever their seasons bring forth the full harvest:
For the crops there is the entreating countenance of the bright sky.
Henceforth, with zeal the huntsmen pursue the fat stags,
Now with hounds amongst the high woods,
Their bodies now first escaping their prolonged thinness,
Which Venus and the cold by barren fodder begat,
In fresh bloom, after the vines produce certain clusters
For a special favor adorns this month.

William Ram, *Rams Little Dodoen*

In 1606 William Ram (about whom little is known) published what he called an "epitome" or abridgement of Henry Lyte's *New Herbal* (1578), a standard folio herbal in England at that time (itself a translation of the Flemish Rembert Dodoens's *Cruÿdeboeck* [1554]). Ram's preface advertises his book as a cheaper version of Lyte's, but in fact it bears little resemblance to that book. Rather, it contains a random assemblage of "observations" and recipes gath-

4. Sun god

Source: *Rams Little Dodeon* [*sic*] *A Brief Epitome of the New Herbal, or History of Plants*, London, 1606.

Figure 16. Image of life in spring, from Pieter van der Heyden (1570), representing both women and men working in the garden, with aristocrats enjoying eating and drinking in the background. Reproduced by permission of the Metropolitan Museum of Art. Harris Brisbane Dick Fund, 1926. Image Source: Art Resource.

ered from Lyte and Dodoen and other practitioners, including recommendations for gardening, diet, and exercise month by month. The instructions for June suggest that this month demands a certain amount of abstinence in eating and drinking in order to regulate the humors of the body (compare with the *Secreta secretorum*). Along with very specific horticultural and agricultural advice tied to the month's average temperature, as well as to the phases of the moon, the instructions emphasize consumption of cooler foods and exposure to cold water as the weather begins to warm, seeking a balance between the external and internal temperatures. Spring was understood as a time for planting but also for moderate pleasure in food and drink (Figure 16).

Observations in June.

My corn is weeded well enough.
Abstain from drink both sweet and new;
From physic do thy self refrain.
Bid riotous pleasures quite adieu,
Lest that they breed thy endless pain.
Cold herbs in June are very meet,
But such meat shun chiefly,
As shall be either new or sweet.
Take pleasures medicinably.
Abstain from meats that engender phlegm.
Drink the pleasantest wines.
Drink sometime tasting white wine, which purgeth choler.[1]
Eat salads of lettuce prepared with vinegar, to purge humors descending to the kidneys.
Use meats of light digestion.
Arise always from the table somewhat hungry.
Exercise thy body with some long walk.
Use phlebotomy[2] safely.
Eat no milk but that is well sodden.
Beware of eating apples this month.
To bathe is good, but not to tarry long in it.
To wash thy feet often in cold water is commendable.
It is now good time to make syrup of damask roses, conserves of red roses, violets, borage and bugloss, and to distill rose water, and to make oil of roses.
Weed corn and gardens.
When the sun shineth, make hay.
Set gillyflowers, carnations, and rosemary.
Sow salad herbs, and lettuce four days before the full moon, and radish four days after the full moon, in every month from March to September.
Set no herbs, hedges, nor trees in June, July, or August: and have an eye unto ants, emits,[3] and snails in your gardens.

- Sow lettuce, at all times.
- Sow radish, at all times.

1. Yellow bile
2. Blood-letting
3. Mites?

- Sow spinach, and at all times.
- Sow parsnips, at all times.
- Sow pumpkins in the new moon.
- Sow cucumbers in the old moon.
- Gather town cresses.
- Gather peritory.[4]
- Gather lang de bief.[5]
- Gather dragons.[6]
- Gather origanum.[7]
- Gather catmint.
- Gather marigolds the sixteenth day before the sun, without knife.

If thou must needs take physic, take it early in the morning.
Use thin diet of thy meat.
Let no blood, but in extremity.
Drink clarified whey as in May.
Take no great thirst: for the pores of the brain are open.

Thomas Tusser, *An Hundredth Pointes of Good Husbandrie*

Although educated at Eton and Cambridge and once a court musician, Thomas Tusser (1524–1580) spent much of his life as a farmer and a writer of hugely popular versified books about agriculture and husbandry. Over the decades he kept revising his first book, *An Hundredth Pointes of Goode Husbandrie* (1557), and in 1573 he published a longer version, the *Five Hundredth Pointes of Good Husbandrie United to as Many of Good Huswiferie*. The most popular poetry book of its time, that edition (as revised in 1580) was frequently reprinted well into the seventeenth century. Tusser loosely organized his advice around the work that needs to be done according to the agricultural calendar. Unlike earlier classically oriented works on husbandry aimed at the manorial master, his advice targeted the tenant farmer who pays rent to his lord; the 1573 edition marks this by starting the agricultural year in September, when changes of land tenure occurred. Tusser's work appears in this anthology

4. Pellitory
5. Langue de boeuf: a form of borage
6. Unknown reference
7. Oregano

Source: Thomas Tusser. *An Hundredth Pointes of Good Husbandrie* (1557). *Renascence Editions*. 2003, http://www.luminarium.org/renascence-editions/tusser1.html. Transcribed by Risa Bear from Dobell 1909. Spelling modernized.

in two parts: in this excerpt from *An Hundredth Pointes* (1557 edition) on the labors of July, with the short summary of a calendar of the year's work, and also in Part 6 with the brief introduction to the *Five Hundredth Pointes*. This excerpt represents Tusser's concern with seasonal activities at harvest time, when the labor involves managing people and animals as well as the land. Tusser conveys a sense of urgency to act both against and with the rhythms of the weather and the cycle of growth. The excerpt ends with a brief summary of the year's work, counseling the farmer to make the most of time to reap each month's rewards.

July

Then muster thy folk, play the captain thy self,
providing them weapon, and such kind of pelf.[1]
Get bottles and bags, keep the field in the heat;
the fear is not much, but the danger is great.
With tossing and raking, and setting on cox,
the grass that was green, is now hay for an ox.
That done, leave the tithe, load thy cart and away;
the battle is fought, thou hast gotten the day.
Then done with thy headlands,[2] thy corn round about;
leave never a dallop[3] unmown or had out.
Though grass be but thin, about barley and peas,
yet picked up clean, it shall do thee good ease.
Thy fallow betimes,[4] for destroying of weed,
lest thistle and dock fall a blooming and seed.
Such season may hap, it shall stand thee upon,
to till it again, or the summer be gone.
And better thou wert, so to do for thy haste;
then (hardness) for sloth make thy land to lie waste.
A ready good forehorse,[5] is dainty to find;
be hindered at first, and come always behind.
Thy houses and barns would be looked upon,
and all thing amended, or harvest come on.
Things thus set in order, at quiet and rest,
thy harvest goeth forward and prospereth best.

1. Goods
2. Hedge greens
3. Patch of land unmowed
4. Plow fallow land three times
5. Foremost horse in a team

Saint James willeth husbands, get reapers at hand;
 the corn being ripe, do but shed as it stand.
 Be saving and thankful, for that God hath sent,
 he sendeth it thee, for the self same intent.
Reap well, scatter not, gather clean that is shorn:
 bind fast, shock apace, pay the tenth of thy corn.
 Load safe, carry home, lose no time, being fair;
 goife[6] just, in the barn, it is out of despair.
This done, set the poor over all for to glean,
 and after thy cattle, to eat it up clean.
 Then spare it for pasture, till rowen[7] be past;
 to lengthen thy dairy no better thou hast.
Then welcome thy harvest folk, servants and all;
 with mirth and good cheer, let them furnish thine hall.
 The harvest lord nightly, must give thee a song;
 fill him then the black bowl, or else he hath wrong.
Thy harvest thus ended, in mirth and in joy,
 please every one gently, man, woman, and boy.
 Thus doing, with always, such help as they can,
 thou winnest the name, of a right husbandman.
 Finis.
 Now think upon God, let thy tongue never cease;
 from thanking of him, for his mighty increase.
 Accept my good will, find no fault till thou try;
 the better thou thrivest, the gladder am I.

A sonnet, or brief rehearsal of the properties of the twelve months afore rehearsed.

As January fryse[8] pot, broth corn keep him low;
 And February fill dyke, doth good with his snow;
 A bushel of March dust, worth ransoms of gold;
 And April his storms, be too good to be told;
 As May with his flowers, give ladies their lust;
 And June after blooming, set carnels[9] so just;

6. Stack
7. Aftermath of mown meadows
8. Freeze
9. Hips and haws of plants

As July bid all thing, in order to ripe;
And August bid reapers, to take full their gripe;
September his fruit, biddeth gather as fast;
October bid hogs to come eat up his mast;
As dirty November, bid thresh at thine ease;
December bid Christmas to spend what he please;
So wisdom bid keep, and provide while we may;
For age creepeth on as the time passeth away.

William Shakespeare, *King Lear*

William Shakespeare's *King Lear* stages early Britain's descent into civil war, catalyzed by the aging Lear's abdication of his throne. The play explores themes of familial loyalty and treachery through Lear's suffering at the hands of his daughters, Goneril and Regan, and with that, his own descent into madness. At the play's heart, accompanied by his Fool and later his banished servant Kent in disguise, Lear rages on a desolate heath in a spectacular thunderstorm. There Lear calls on the winds, rain, and thunder to obliterate the earth and nature itself, identifying the storm's power with his own fury against "ungrateful man." Lear may associate the weather with divine anger, yet at the same time, the Fool reminds us that, in the end, the rain just makes you wet and cold. At the passage's end, Lear descends from his rhetorical heights to recognize those real effects of the storm. Overall, conflicting ideas of nature underpin this play, where "nature" signals both a conservative natural order and a raw and ravening menace.

Act 3, scene 2.

Storm still. Enter Lear, and Fool.
Lear. Blow winds, and crack your cheeks; Rage, blow
You cataracts,[1] and hurricanoe's spout,[2]
Till you have drench'd our steeples, drown the cocks.
You sulph'rous and thought-executing fires,
Vaunt-couriers[3] of oak-cleaving thunderbolts,
Singe my white head. And thou all-shaking thunder,
Strike flat the thick rotundity o't'world,

Source: *King Lear* has come down to us in two different versions: an individual quarto text from 1609 (and 1619) and the text as printed in the First Folio edition published in 1623. The text below is based on the First Folio.

1. Floods from the sky
2. Water spouts
3. Forerunners

Crack Nature's molds, all germens[4] spill at once
That makes ungrateful man.

Fool. O nuncle, court holy-water[5] in a dry house is better than this rain-water out o' door. Good nuncle, in, ask thy daughters' blessing, here's a night pities neither wisemen, nor fools.

Lear. Rumble thy belly full: spit fire, spout rain;
Nor rain, wind, thunder, fire are my daughters.
I tax[6] not you, you elements with unkindness.
I never gave you kingdom, call'd you children;
You owe me no subscription.[7] Then let fall
Your horrible pleasure. Here I stand your slave,
A poor, infirm, weak, and despis'd old man.
But yet I call you servile ministers,
That will with two pernicious daughters join
Your high-engender'd battles, 'gainst a head
So old, and white as this. O, ho! 'tis foul.

Fool. He that has a house to put's head in, has a good head-piece. The codpiece that will house, before the head has any; The head, and he shall louse: so beggars marry many.[8] The man that makes his toe, what he his heart should make, shall of a corn cry woe, and turn his sleep to wake. For there was never yet fair woman, but she made mouths in a glass.

Enter Kent.

Lear. No, I will be the pattern of all patience,
I will say nothing.

Kent. Who's there?

Fool. Marry here's grace,[9] and a codpiece, that's a wiseman, and a fool.

Kent. Alas, sir, are you here? Things that love night,
Love not such nights as these. The wrathful skies
Gallow[10] the very wanderers of the dark
And make them keep their caves. Since I was man,
Such sheets of fire, such bursts of horrid thunder,

4. Seeds
5. The water of blessings for courtiers
6. Blame
7. Obedience
8. The sense of the Fool's speech is someone who houses his penis (a cod-piece is the covering for the male genitalia) before finding a proper house will end up poor and infested with lice.
9. The king
10. Frighten

Such groans of roaring wind, and rain, I never
Remember to have heard. Man's nature cannot carry
Th'affliction, nor the fear.

Lear. Let the great gods
That keep this dreadful pudder[11] o'er our heads,
Find out their enemies now. Tremble thou wretch,
That hast within thee undivulged crimes
Unwhipped of justice. Hide thee, thou bloody hand,
Thou perjured, and thou simular[12] of virtue
That art incestuous. Caitiff,[13] to pieces shake
That under covert, and convenient seeming
Has practiced on man's life. Close[14] pent-up guilts,
Rive[15] your concealing continents, and cry
These dreadful summoners[16] grace. I am a man,
More sinn'd against than sinning.

Kent. Alack, bare-headed?
Gracious my Lord, hard by here is a hovel,
Some friendship will it lend you 'gainst the tempest.
Repose you there, while I to this hard house,
(More harder then the stones whereof 'tis rais'd,
Which even but now, demanding after you,
Deny'd me to come in) return, and force
Their scanted[17] courtesy.

Lear. My wits begin to turn.
Come on my boy. How dost my boy? Art cold?
I am cold myself. Where is this straw, my fellow?
The art of our necessities is strange,
And can make vile things precious. Come, your hovel;
Poor fool, and knave, I have one part in my heart
That's sorry yet for thee.

Fool. He that has and[18] a little-tiny wit,[19]

11. Pother or trouble; the word is thundering in Quarto 2
12. Pretender
13. Villain
14. Secret
15. Split open
16. Those seeking justice
17. Paltry
18. Even
19. Intelligence

With heigh-ho, the wind and the rain,
Must make content with his fortunes fit,
Though the rain it raineth every day.

Amelia Lanyer, "The Description of Cookham"

The daughter of Italian musicians, Amelia Lanyer (1569–1645) sought to prosper at Queen Elizabeth's court, but she eventually suffered disappointment when she became pregnant and had to be married off to the profligate Captain Lanyer. For all her trials, she was also an accomplished poet, and in 1611 she published her *Salve Deus Rex Judaeorum*, the first printed book of poems by an Englishwoman. In the early 1600s Lanyer spent time with Margaret Clifford, Countess of Cumberland, and her daughter Anne at a country estate at Cookham, and the last poem of *Salve Deus Rex Judaeorum*, "The Description of Cookham," celebrates that estate and the women who lived there for a short but happy interlude. Lanyer's poem contrasts with Ben Jonson's "To Penshurst," which summons up a fantasy of aristocratic privilege, fertility, and generosity expressed through features of a country house and its land. Lanyer's poem neglects the house; instead, she explores a conceit in which the estate's landscape responds to the women who inhabit it; their presence animates the spring and summer, and their leaving brings on the winter. Like Jonson, Lanyer includes herself in the circle of the aristocrats identified with the estate, while she never forgets that she is an outsider. Since the Cliffords and Lanyer were never to return to Cookham, this poem of dispossession also evokes pastorals that mourn the loss of land (see Virgil's *Eclogue 1* in Part 5).

Farewell (sweet Cookham) where I first obtain'd
Grace from that grace[1] where perfect grace remain'd;
And where the muses gave their full consent,
I should have power the virtuous to content;
Where princely palace will'd me to endite,[2]
The sacred story of the soul's delight.
Farewell (sweet place) where virtue then did rest,
And all delights did harbor in her breast.

Source: "The Description of Cookham." *Salve Deus Rex Judaeorum*, sig. H2-Ii', London, 1611. *Perseus Digital Library*, http://www.perseus.tufts.edu/hopper/text?doc=Perseus%3Atext%3A1999.03.0077.

1. Both God's grace and "Her Grace," the Countess of Cumberland
2. Write

Never shall my sad eyes again behold
Those pleasures which my thoughts did then unfold;
Yet you (great lady) mistress of that place,
From whose desires did spring this work of grace,
Vouchsafe to think upon those pleasures past
As fleeting worldly joys that could not last;
Or, as dim shadows of celestial pleasures,
Which are desir'd above all earthly treasures.
Oh how (me thought) against[3] you thither came,
Each part did seem some new delight to frame!
The house receiv'd all ornaments to grace it,
And would endure no foulness to deface it.
The walks put on their summer liveries,[4]
And all things else did hold like similes;
The trees with leaves, with fruits, with flowers clad,
Embrac'd each other, seeming to be glad,
Turning themselves to beauteous canopies,
To shade the bright sun from your brighter eyes;
The crystal streams with silver spangles graced,
While by the glorious sun they were embraced;
The little birds in chirping notes did sing,
To entertain both you and that sweet spring.
And Philomela[5] with her sundry lays,[6]
Both you and that delightful place did praise.
Oh how me thought each plant, each flower, each tree
Set forth their beauties then to welcome thee!
The very hills right humbly did descend,
When you to tread upon them did intend,
And as you set your feet, they still did rise,
Glad that they could receive so rich a prize.
The gentle winds did take delight to be
Among those woods that were so grac'd by thee.
And in sad murmur uttered pleasing sound,
That pleasure in that place might more abound;

3. In preparation

4. The special clothes worn by servants to aristocratic families

5. The mythical Philomela was raped by Tereus, who tore out her tongue; she then turned into a nightingale.

6. Songs

The swelling banks deliver'd all their pride,
When such a phoenix[7] once they had espied.
Each arbor, bank, each seat, each stately tree,
Thought themselves honor'd in supporting thee.
The pretty birds would oft come to attend thee,
Yet fly away for fear they should offend thee;
The little creatures in the burrow by
Would come abroad to sport them in your eye,
Yet fearful of the bow in your fair hand
Would run away when you did make a stand.
Now let me come unto that stately tree,
Wherein such goodly prospects you did see;
That oak that did in height his fellows pass,
As much as lofty trees, low growing grass;
Much like a comely cedar straight and tall,
Whose beauteous stature far exceeded all.
How often did you visit this fair tree,
Which seeming joyful in receiving thee,
Would like a palm tree spread his arms abroad,
Desirous that you there should make abode;
Whose fair green leaves much like a comely veil,
Defended Phoebus[8] when he would assail;
Whose pleasing boughs did yield a cool fresh air,
Joying his happiness when you were there.
Where being seated, you might plainly see,
Hills, vales, and woods, as if on bended knee
They had appeared, your honor to salute,
Or to prefer some strange unlooked for suit;[9]
All interlac'd with brooks and crystal springs,
A prospect fit to please the eyes of kings;
And thirteen shires appear'd all in your sight,
Europe could not afford much more delight.
What was there then but gave you all content,
While you the time in meditation spent,
Of their creators power, which there you saw,
In all his creatures held a perfect law;

7. A mythical bird thought to die in fire and be reborn in its ashes
8. God of the sun
9. Petition

And in their beauties did you plain descry,
His beauty, wisdom, grace, love, majesty.
In these sweet woods how often did you walk,
With Christ and his apostles there to talk.
Placing his holy writ in some fair tree,
To meditate what you therein did see;
With Moses you did mount his holy hill,
To know his pleasure, and perform his will.
With lovely David did you often sing,
His holy hymns to heaven's eternal King.
And in sweet music did your soul delight,
To sound his praises, morning, noon, and night.
With blessed Joseph you did often feed
Your pined brethren, when they stood in need.
And that sweet lady sprung from Clifford's race,[10]
Of noble Bedford's blood, fair stem of grace,
To honorable Dorset now espous'd,
In whose fair breast true virtue then was hous'd;
Oh what delight did my weak spirits find,
In those pure parts of her well framed mind;
And yet it grieves me that I cannot be
Near unto her, whose virtues did agree
With those fair ornaments of outward beauty,
Which did enforce from all both love and duty.
Inconstant Fortune, thou art most too blame,
Who casts us down into so low a frame,
Where our great friends we cannot daily see,
So great a difference is there in degree.[11]
Many are placed in those orbs of state,
Parters[12] in honor, so ordain'd by fate;
Nearer in show, yet farther off in love,
In which, the lowest always are above.
But whither am I carried in conceit?
My wit too weak to conster[13] of the great.
Why not? although we are but born of earth,

10. Anne Clifford, Margaret's daughter, who married Richard Sackville, Earl of Dorset
11. Rank
12. Separators
13. Construe

We may behold the heavens, despising death;
And loving heaven that is so far above,
May in the end vouchsafe us entire love.
Therefore sweet memory do thou retain
Those pleasures past, which will not turn again;
Remember beauteous Dorset's[14] former sports,
So far from being toucht by ill reports;
Wherein my self did always bear a part,
While reverend love presented my true heart;
Those recreations let me bear in mind,
Which her sweet youth and noble thoughts did find;
Whereof depriv'd, I evermore must grieve,
Hating blind fortune, careless to relieve.
And you sweet Cookham, whom these ladies leave,
I now must tell the grief you did conceive
At their departure; when they went away,
How every thing retained a sad dismay;
Nay long before, when once an inkling came,
Me thought each thing did unto sorrow frame;
The trees that were so glorious in our view,
Forsook both flowers and fruit, when once they knew,
Of your depart, their very leaves did wither,
Changing their colors as they grew together.
But when they saw this had no power to stay you,
They often wept, though speechless, could not pray you,
Letting their tears in your fair bosoms fall,
As if they said, Why will ye leave us all?
This being vain, they cast their leaves away,
Hoping that pity would have made you stay;
Their frozen tops, like age's hoary hairs,
Shows their disaster, languishing in fears;
A swarthy riveled rind[15] all over spread,
Their dying bodies half alive, half dead.
But your occasions call'd you so away,
That nothing there had power to make you stay;
Yet did I see a noble grateful mind,
Requiting each according to their kind,

14. Referring to Anne (as the wife of Dorset)
15. Bark

Forgetting not to turn and take your leave
Of these sad creatures, powerless to receive
Your favor, when with grief you did depart,
Placing their former pleasures in your heart,
Giving great charge to noble memory,
There to preserve their love continually;
But specially the love of that fair tree,
That first and last you did vouchsafe to see,
In which it pleas'd you oft to take the air,
With noble *Dorset*, then a virgin fair;
Where many a learned book was read and scanned
To this fair tree, taking me by the hand,
You did repeat the pleasures which had past,
Seeming to grieve they could no longer last.
And with a chaste, yet loving kiss took leave,
Of which sweet kiss I did it soon bereave,
Scorning a senseless creature should possess
So rare a favor, so great happiness.
No other kiss it could receive from me,
For fear to give back what it took of thee,
So I ungrateful creature did deceive it,
Of that which you vouchsafed in love to leave it.
And though it oft had giv'n me much content,
Yet this great wrong I never could repent:
But of the happiest made it most forlorn,
To show that nothing's free from fortunes scorn,
While all the rest with this most beauteous tree,
Made their sad consort sorrows harmony.
The flowers that on the banks and walks did grow,
Crept in the ground, the grass did weep for woe.
The winds and waters seem'd to chide together,
Because you went away they knew not whither;
And those sweet brooks that ran so fair and clear,
With grief and trouble wrinkled did appear.
Those pretty birds that wonted were to sing,
Now neither sing, nor chirp, nor use their wing,
But with their tender feet on some bare spray,
Warble forth sorrow, and their own dismay.
Faire Philomela leaves her mournful ditty,
Drown'd in dead sleep, yet can procure no pity;

Each arbor, bank, each seat, each stately tree,
Looks bare and desolate now for want of thee,
Turning green tresses into frosty gray,
While in cold grief they wither all away.
The sun grew weak, his beams no comfort gave,
While all green things did make the earth their grave:
Each briar, each bramble, when you went away,
Caught fast your clothes, thinking to make you stay;
Delightful Echo wonted to reply
To our last words, did now for sorrow die;
The house cast off each garment that might grace it,
Putting on dust and cobwebs to deface it.
All desolation then there did appear,
When you were going whom they held so dear.
This last farewell to Cookham here I give,
When I am dead thy name in this may live
Wherein I have perform'd her noble hest,[16]
Whose virtues lodge in my unworthy breast,
And ever shall, so long as life remains,
Tying my heart to her by those rich chains.

William Shakespeare, *The Tempest*

William Shakespeare's play *The Tempest* (ca. 1611) brings travelers across seas to an island ambiguously located either in the Mediterranean or in the Atlantic on the way to the Americas. The island is ruled by Prospero, the exiled Duke of Milan, and the travelers include Alonso, the King of Naples and his brother Sebastian, complicit in the plot to usurp Prospero, as well as Alonso's young son Ferdinand; also on the ship are the usurper Antonio, who is Prospero's brother, and Gonzalo, "an honest old councilor." The play begins in a spectacular fashion by representing a storm at sea and the wreck of the travelers' ship; it turns out in the end that Prospero has produced this illusion, and all are actually saved. This opening powerfully evokes everyone's helplessness in the grip of a storm; here, no political authority matters, and water and wind swallow all. When the Boatswain castigates his betters and Antonio betrays his lack of loyalty to Alonso, it is also suggested that the tempest's chaos echoes the social disorder on board. (Compare with Thomas Jackson's

16. Command
Source: William Shakespeare. *The Tempest,* act 1, scene 1.

The Raging Tempest Stilled, which identifies the power of a storm at sea with God's majesty.)

Act 1, Scene 1.

Noise of thunder and lightning heard

Enter a Master and a Boatswain

Master. Boatswain!

Boatswain. Here, master. What cheer?

Master. Good, speak to the mariners: fall to't, yarely,[1] or we run ourselves aground. Bestir, bestir!

Exit

Enter Mariners

Boatswain. Heigh, my hearts! Cheerly, cheerly, my hearts! Yare, yare! Take in the topsail. Tend to the master's whistle. Blow, till thou burst thy wind, if room enough!

Enter Alonso, Sebastian, Antonio, Ferdinand, Gonzalo, and others

Alonso. Good boatswain, have care. Where's the master? Play[2] the men.

Boatswain. I pray now, keep below.

Antonio. Where is the master, boatswain?

Boatswain. Do you not hear him? You mar our labor: keep your cabins, you do assist the storm.

Gonzalo. Nay, good, be patient.

Boatswain. When the sea is. Hence! What cares these roarers[3] for the name of king? To cabin: silence! Trouble us not.

Gonzalo. Good, yet remember whom thou hast aboard.

Boatswain. None that I more love than myself. You are a councilor; if you can command these elements to silence, and work the peace of the present, we will not hand a rope more. Use your authority. If you cannot, give thanks you have lived so long, and make yourself ready in your cabin for the mischance of the hour, if it so hap. Cheerly, good hearts! Out of our way, I say.

Exit

Gonzalo. I have great comfort from this fellow. Methinks he hath no drowning mark upon him; his complexion[4] is perfect gallows. Stand fast, good fate, to his hanging: make the rope of his destiny

1. Nimbly
2. Ply, employ
3. The roaring sea, but also a term for unruly men
4. Appearance

our cable, for our own doth little advantage. If he be not born to be hanged, our case is miserable.

Exeunt

Re-enter Boatswain

Boatswain. Down with the topmast! Yare! Lower, lower! Bring her to try with main-course.[5]

(*A cry within*)

A plague upon this howling! They are louder than the weather or our office.

(*Re-enter Sebastian, Antonio, and Gonzalo*)

Yet again! Hang, you whoreson, insolent noisemaker! We are less afraid to be drowned than thou art.

Gonzalo. I'll warrant him[6] for drowning, though the ship were no stronger than a nutshell and as leaky as an unstanched[7] wench.

Boatswain. Lay her a-hold, a-hold! Set her two courses off to sea again. Lay her off.

Enter Mariners, wet

Mariners. All lost! to prayers, to prayers! all lost!

Boatswain. What, must our mouths be cold?

Gonzalo. The King and prince at prayers! Let's assist them,
For our case is as theirs.

Sebastian. I'm out of patience.

Antonio. We are merely cheated of our lives by drunkards:
This wide-chopp'd[8] rascal—would thou mightst lie drowning
The washing of ten tides!

Gonzalo. He'll be hang'd yet,
Though every drop of water swear against it
And gape at widest to glut him.

A confused noise within

Voices. Mercy on us!—
We split, we split!—
Farewell, my wife and children!—
Farewell, brother!—
We split, we split, we split!

Antonio. Let's all sink with the king.

5. Keep the ship close to the wind
6. Guarantee him against
7. Leaking fluids
8. Wide jawed

Sebastian. Let's take leave of him.
Exeunt Antonio and Sebastian
Gonzalo. Now would I give a thousand furlongs of sea for an acre of barren ground, long heath, brown furze,[9] any thing. The wills above be done! But I would fain die a dry death.
Exeunt

Thomas Jackson, *The Raging Tempest Stilled*

While a busy Church of England clergyman serving many parishes, Thomas Jackson (1570/71–1646) also managed to write eight volumes of sermons that preached of man's sinfulness and God's almighty power. In 1623 he published a sermon, *The Raging Tempest Stilled: The Historie of Christ His Passage, with His Disciples, over the Sea of Galilee, and the Memorable and Miraculous Occurrents Therein,* interpreting the biblical story of Christ's calming a storm at sea in Galilee that threatened to sink his ship. In this sermon Jackson develops the trope of a storm expressing God's awful majesty. He exclaims at the vanity of those who see tempests as merely caused by conjurers, or those who fall to cursing the storm and who attempt to curb or control its power. This passage can be compared with Shakespeare's conjuror Prospero's summoning up a tempest in *The Tempest*, where the storm generates fear and suggests the failure of human authority in the face of winds and waves (see also Lear's raging with and against the storm in *King Lear*, above).

Therefore God himself often urgeth his dominion over the aea, that unruly and boisterous element, for declaration of his great Majesty, as unto Job; Who shut up the sea with doors, who set bars, and said, Hitherto shalt thou come, and no further, and here shalt thou stay thy proud waves? And again, Fear ye not me, saith the Lord, will ye not tremble at my presence, which have placed the sand for the bound of the sea, by a perpetual decree, that it cannot pass it, and though the waves thereof toss themselves, yet can they not prevail, though they roar, yet can they not pass over it? Who ever saw tempest on sea, whose heart was not smitten with fear, and reverence of the majesty of that God, who hath made, and doth govern it? And again, thus saith the Lord, who divideth the sea, when the waves thereof roar, the Lord of hosts is his name. As God himself

9. Gorse

Source: Thomas Jackson. *The Raging Tempest Stilled: The Historie of Christ His Passage, with His Disciples, over the Sea of Galilee, and the Memorable and Miraculous Occurrents Therein*, London, 1623, pp. 77–79.

doth urge it, so holy David specially, was very frequent in the meditation thereof. He gathered the waters of the sea together, as on an heap, and layeth up the deep as in store houses. Let all the earth fear the Lord, let all the inhabitants of the world stand in awe of him. And again, it is God, that stilleth the raging of the sea, and the noise of its waves; and again, He turned the sea into dry land, he ruleth by his power for ever: And again, I will meditate of all thy works, and talk of thy doings, thou art the God that dost wonders; the waters saw thee, O God, the waters saw thee, and were afraid, the depths also were troubled; and again, God is greatly to be feared in the assembly of the saints, and to be had in reverence of all them that are round about him, O Lord God of hosts, who is a strong Lord like unto thee, thou rulest the raging of the sea, and stillest the waves thereof, when they arise. The floods, O God, have lift up their voice, the floods have lift up their waves, but the Lord on high is mightier than the noise of many waters, yea than the mighty waves of the sea. Many such like there are in the book of the Psalms, whereof these are but a taste.

But now if we come to our selves; who but hath seen, or heard of a tempest on the sea? But who so religious and devout, as thence to take occasion, to meditate, or talk of the greatness, power, and majesty of God? Oh the atheism, I say again, the atheism, which lurketh in our hearts, and then doth specially break out, and bewray it self, when there are extraordinary winds, storms, and tempests, by sea and land, with thunder, lightning, hail, rain! But specially, if therein we sustain hurt and loss, in our houses, lands, cattle, goods; then as if God were on sleep, and minded no such thing, they will say, there is conjuring, and witches are abroad, or else fall to cursing and banning, and blaspheming; almost as mad, as Herodotus reporteth Xerxes the Persian monarch to have been, who having received a great loss, by the tempestuous rage of Hellespont, he caused abundance of fetters and manacles to be cast into it, as if he would make it his prisoner, and bind it with links of iron at his pleasure. And another no wiser than he, who because the river Ginde had drowned him a white horse, threatened the river to divide it into so many streams, that a woman great with child should go over it dry-shod. Alas, alas, men may be more tempestuous, raging and mad, than the sea, but the sea will know none, but him that made it. What manner of man is this, that both winds and seas obey him? Pharaoh King of Egypt asked proudly, Who is the Lord? and the sea might ask, Who is Pharaoh? It did acknowledge the rod of God, in Moses his hand, and gave way, but drowned Pharaoh and his host. Oh, look we up unto God; for from him, all winds and weather, by sea and land, thunders and lightnings, hail-stones and stormy tempests, all are at his assignment, be they for a blessing or a curse; and therefore let all flesh give glory unto God, and fear that majesty which shineth herein.

Thomas Sprat and Robert Hooke, *History of the Royal Society*, On Weather

Thomas Sprat's *History of the Royal Society for Improving Natural Knowledge* is introduced in Part 1 for its advocating experimental approaches to understanding the natural world. While some of the experiments introduced there seem more ad hoc than systematic, they mark a shift not only to direct observation but also toward the methodical measurement of natural phenomena. Thus, Sprat includes in his book "a method for making a history of the weather," attributed to Robert Hooke, the renowned natural philosopher (and author of *Micrographia*). Hooke calls for the fashioning of instruments to measure temperature, humidity, and barometric pressure (much of which work he had done himself), but he also recommends closely watching the movement of clouds, thunder and lightning, and wind and water, and their effects on other things in the natural world. Such attention is a familiar theme in writing about the weather, going back to Virgil's *Georgics*, but Hooke promotes careful study in order to understand the weather itself; observations are to be recorded systematically in a comparative schema, as a means to interpret those mysteries scientifically.

A Method For Making a History of the Weather. By Mr. Hooke

For the better making a history of the weather, I conceive it requisite to observe,

1. The strength and quarter of the winds, and to register the changes as often as they happen, both which may be very conveniently shown, by a small addition to an ordinary weather-clock.
2. The degrees of heat and cold in the air, which will be best observed by a sealed thermometer, graduated according to the degrees of expansion, which bear a known proportion to the whole bulk of liquor, the beginning of which gradation, should be that dimension which the liquor hath, when encompassed with water, just beginning to freeze, and the degrees of expansion, either greater or less, should be set or marked above it or below it.
3. The degrees of dryness and moisture in the air, which may be most conveniently observed by a hygroscope, made with the single beard of a wild oat perfectly ripe, set upright and headed with an index,[1] after the

Source: Thomas Sprat. *The History of the Royal-Society of London for the Improving of Natural Knowledge*, London, 1667, p. 173.

1. Pointer

way described by Emanuel Magnan, the conversions and degrees of which, may be measured by divisions made on the rim of a circle, in the center of which, the index is turned round; the beginning or standard of which degree of rotation, should be that, to which the index points, when the beard, being thoroughly wet, or covered with water, is quite unwreathed, and becomes straight. But because of the smallness of this part of the oat, the cod[2] of a wild vetch may be used instead of it, which will be a much larger index, and will be altogether as sensible of the changes of the air.

4. The degrees of pressure in the air, which may be several ways observed, but best of all with an instrument with quicksilver,[3] contrived so, as either by means of water or an index, it may sensibly exhibit the minute variations of that action.
5. The constitution and face of the sky or heavens; and this is best done by the eye. Here should be observed, whether the sky be clear or clouded; and if clouded, after what manner, whether with high exhalations or great white clouds, or dark thick ones. Whether those clouds afford fogs or mists, or sleet, or rain, or snow, etc. Whether the underside of those clouds be flat or waved and irregular, as I have often seen before thunder. Which way they drive, whether all one way, or some one way, some another; and whether any of these be the same with the wind that blows below; the color and face of the sky at the rising and setting of the sun and moon; what haloes or rings may happen to encompass those luminaries, their bigness, form, and number.
6. What effects are produced upon other bodies, as what aches and distempers in the bodies of men: what diseases are most rife, as colds, fevers, agues, etc. What putrefactions or other changes are produced in other bodies as the sweating of marble, the burning blue of a candle, the blasting[4] of trees and corn; the unusual sprouting, growth, or decay of any plants or vegetables; the putrefaction of bodies not usual; the plenty or scarcity of insects; of several fruits, grains, flowers, roots, cattle, fishes, birds, anything notable of that kind. What conveniences or inconveniences may happen in the year, in any kind, as by floods, droughts, violent showers, etc. What nights produce dews and hoarfrosts, and what not?

2. Seed pod
3. Liquid mercury
4. Withering

7. What thunders and lightnings happen, and what effects they produce; as souring beer or ale, turning milk, killing silk-worms, etc.?
8. Anything extraordinary in the tides; as double tides, later or earlier, greater or less tides than ordinary. Rising or drying of springs; comets or unusual apparitions, new stars, *Ignes fatui*[5] or shining exhalations, or the like.

These should all or most of them be diligently observed and registered by someone, that is always conversant in or near the same place.

Now that these and some other, hereafter to be mentioned, may be registered so as to be most convenient for the making of comparisons, requisite for the raising axioms, whereby the cause or laws of weather may be found out; it will be desirable to order them so, that the scheme of a whole month, may at one view be presented to the eye; and this may conveniently be done on the pages of a book in folio, allowing fifteen days for one side, and fifteen for the other. Let each of those pages be divided into nine columns, and distinguished by perpendicular lines; let each of the first six columns be half an inch wide, and the three last equally share the remaining of the side.

Samuel Gilbert, *Florist's Vade-Mecum*, Instructions for July

Part 2 introduces the reader to the clergyman and "florist" Samuel Gilbert's *Florist's Vade-Mecum* (1682), with its elaborate attention to specific flowers for their rarity and value. The book is structured as a month-by-month guide to flower-gardening tasks, especially for plants that are dear to the "florist," the person who cultivates flowers for pleasure while competing with other gardeners. Gilbert's instructions for July focus on the cultivation and propagation of the *Caryophyllus hortensis,* or July-flowers, now called carnations. His description of the difficulties growing seed imported from the Netherlands and the process of propagating carnations through layering of slips attends carefully to fluctuations in seasonal temperature, humidity, and air circulation. The delicacy and specificity devoted to understanding the work and its relationship to the season contrast boldly with the broad view of July's field work in Thomas Tusser's *An Hundredth Pointes of Good Husbandrie* more than a hundred years earlier.

5. Will-o'-the-wisp, a phosphorescent light on swampy ground

Source: Samuel Gilbert. *Florist's Vade-Mecum*, London, 1682, pp. 186–91.

JULY.

Caryophyllus hortensis, called July-flowers from the month they blow[1] in, and are indeed the summer's glory, as tulips the pride of spring, deserving a florist's care in their propagation and preservation, especially the nobler sorts, which are called Dutch July-flowers, or more vulgarly carnations, raised from seeds in the Netherlands, and other parts adjoining to the sea, and thence conveyed to us. Our inland endeavors to raise them seldom countervail our trouble, none or very few raising good ones, that have not the neighborhood of the sea, which annually produce new mixtures, though seldom new colors; and though their dyes not many, as red, purple, scarlet, tawny, and white, and of those deeper or paler, yet so recompensing that defect in their delicate variegations, various mixtures, and pleasing scents, as to vie with any species whatsoever, considering the usefulness of some of them as the best cordials, extremely comforting the noblest part of man, the heart, either in the conserve of the cloves made with sugar, or in syrups; the single colors as flowers little esteemed, in comparison of those striped, flaked, or powder'd upon white or blush, with darker or lighter red, crimson or carnation, sadder or brighter, purple, deeper or paler scarlet; so that the chief July-flowers may be brought under these four sorts: red and white, crimson and white, purple and white, and scarlet and white. Some whereof shall be named, that those unacquainted may the better know how to collect them, being such sorts as a florist ought not to want,[2] viz.

[. . .]

From the middle of June, till the same time in July, is the prime time of laying July-flowers, which is thus performed.

Make choice of such slips as are strongest, having joints sufficient for laying; prune off the side and end of the top-leaves, cut the undermost part of the middlemost joint half through, from thence slit the stalk through the middle upwards to the next joint; open the earth underneath to receive it, then gently bend it down therein, with a small hook-stick stuck in the earth to keep it down, keeping up the head of the slip, that the slit may be open, and so pressed down and earthed up, which as soon as performed, must be sure to be water'd, which must be often reiterated, especially if the season dry, it will make them root the sooner, and shoot forth fibers sufficient to be removed with earth about them the beginning of September following, into pots or beds of the aforementioned prepared earth, which must be shaded and gently watered. But take heed of too much moisture, lest it rot their young and tender fibers; therefore

1. Blossom
2. Lack

for preventing great rains, shelter them under boards supported by forks and sticks laid on them, but not too near them, lest on the other hand they perish for want of air, in a freedom of which they chiefly delight, many having been suffocated for want thereof, as too close housing in winter hath showed the experience, and in transplanting your layers, set them not too deep, for that hath rotted and spoiled many.

PART V

Inhabiting the Land

In writings about plants, animals, weather, and climate, humans are never absent from the scene, where texts foreground our needs, bodies, and feelings in interactions with the world around us. That world is always imagined as *our* environment, even when recognizing our vulnerability when immersed in it. Building from the excerpts on Parts 1–4, Part 5 groups together two contrasting literary models of how people inhabit the land: the pastoral, representing the life of shepherds, and the georgic, portraying the labors and virtues of farming. Both genres entail the interplay of nature and culture, which can never be fully disentangled from each other.

The Hellenistic poet Theocritus first shaped the pastoral in his *Idylls* (which he called bucolics), highly wrought poems that imagine a half-real, half-artificial life of shepherds given to love and song. The Latin poet Virgil then adapted this tradition in his *Eclogues*; in so doing, he transformed them into reflections on both the Roman landscape and the art of poetry, while also alluding to contemporary politics. Since Virgil, the genre of pastoral poetry and prose has had a complicated history, in which it expanded to address just about everything but nature (see Alpers; Williams; Kermode). In *The Country and the City*, Raymond Williams traces this shift of the pastoral's depiction of rural life and song into a form of sophisticated Renaissance romance, "in which the shepherd is an idealized mask, a courtly disguise" (20). The pastoral did thus evolve to function as a veiled version of a court or urban world that the pastoral world rejects. However, as Kent Hiltner observes, "Renaissance pastoral poetry is more often a form of nature writing than one may think" (1), emerging as it did amid early modern crises of deforestation, air pollution, and urbanization. The pastoral does still ask us to remember the animals and the groves that are its setting. To sharpen this point, Part 5 juxtaposes literary pastorals with contemporary accounts of sheep farming, which was critical to the English economy when it depended on the wool trade. Raising and pasturing sheep remained controversial when it entailed landowners' enclosure of common and agricultural land to convert it for grazing, a practice whereby, as Thomas More wrote, "sheep, which are naturally mild, and easily kept in order, may be said now to devour men and unpeople, not only villages, but towns" (*Utopia*, Part 5).

The pastoral's counterpart is the georgic, a genre that the eighteenth-century essayist Joseph Addison dryly described as "some part of the science of husbandry put into a pleasing dress and set off with all the beauties and embellishments of poetry" (cited in McRae 198). Addison was reflecting on the poetry that emerged from what Anthony Low has called "the georgic revolution" of the seventeenth century, a transformation in English society elevating the social, religious, cultural, and political value of labor and farming. The georgic mode rejected the denigration of labor that was filtered through the pastoral but was also inherent to aristocratic culture (McRae; Low). While it flowered in the seventeenth century, the georgic mode has deep roots in a variety of modes of writing about agriculture. The tradition of farming poetry goes back to Hesiod's *Works and Days* (ca. seventh century BCE), which recounts the poet's incessant efforts to cultivate his lands throughout all the seasons of the year. Here the story begins with Virgil's *Georgics*, his four evocative long poems on animal husbandry, agriculture, and beekeeping. While the *Georgics* did not undergo extensive postclassical adaption until its late revival, it did set a pattern for writing about farming as an ennobling activity.

Part 5 thus includes a diverse group of writings about the work of agriculture, stemming from both Virgil's poems and Latin agricultural manuals, which demonstrate the complex interactions of farmer and field. Critics commenting on georgics and husbandry manuals have generally focused on the farmer's exploiting animals and plants toward the end of improvement of nature and productivity. Since Roman times, husbandry had also been associated with good moral character, in Andrew McRae's terms, as a sign of "order, economic stability, and social hierarchy" (151). As in Ben Jonson's country house poem, "To Penshurst," in georgics the master's virtue is vested in his estate and lands. However, as the excerpts in Part 5 suggest, much of premodern writing about agriculture also demonstrates an awareness of human weakness when facing the forces of nature, as the material world resists us. As Virgil advises, the farmer must always be aware of nature's power and volatility and watch the environment for signs of change to come. As Gervase Markham notes, the productive husbandman must be an effective "helper and interpreter of nature" as well as a master. In the end, the georgic mode is as much one of reciprocity as it is of dominance.

Theocritus, *Idyll 7*

Born in Syracuse around 300–250 BCE, the Greek poet Theocritus composed bucolics, or songs of herdsmen, as he travelled throughout Magna Graecia. Now called "idylls," these sophisticated poems represent herdsmen speaking and singing of their loves and their country lives, not in any particular place, but in a beautifully detailed landscape animated by the spirits of Pan and the gods. The singers intimately inhabit that world, which responds to the actions and sorrows of the humans who dwell in and feed on it. This excerpt is from the seventh idyll, representing a song competition between two herdsmen, Simichidas and Lycidas, travelling to a harvest festival in honor of the goddess Demeter. It includes first the song of Lycidas, who imagines first a voyage of his beloved Ageanax and then how he will celebrate when he learns Ageanax has returned. Simichidas follows by singing of his own desires, and the idyll concludes with Lycidas's departure and a celebration at a harvest festival. Throughout the poem, while the natural world is potentially threatening, the herdsmen luxuriate in its gifts by the end, and they fall silent, immersed in the sounds of the trees, insects, and birds.

"Ageanax shall have a calm voyage to Mytilene,
When the Kids appear in the evening sky and the
South wind chases the sea's waves, and Orion
Sets his foot upon Ocean,[1] if only he saves Lycidas
From Aphrodite's blast; hot desire for him burns me up.
Halcyons[2] shall soothe the sea's waves, and shall calm
The south wind and the east, which churns the wrack
In the sea's lowest depths—halcyons, most loved of birds by the
Grey-green Nereids,[3] and those who seek their catch in the sea.
As he sails for Mytilene may Ageanax's ship
Enjoy fair weather and bring him safe to harbor.
When that day comes, I'll make myself a garland
Of anise, roses, or stocks, and set it on my head.
I'll ladle out Ptelean wine from the bowl, and sprawl
By the fire, while beans roast in the embers.

Source: Theocritus. *Idylls*. Translated by Anthony Verity, Oxford University Press, 2002, pp. 25–29.

1. Both constellations are associated with stormy weather.
2. A fabled bird thought lay its nest in sea around the winter solstice, calming the winds and sea
3. Sea nymphs

My couch shall be piled elbow-deep with fleabane,
Asphodel, and pliant wild celery. Drinking at ease
I shall remember Ageanax, as I lift the cup
And press my lips even to the dregs. Two shepherds
Will play their pipes for me: one from Acharnae, and one
From Lycopa. Nearby Tityrus will sing how once
Daphnis the cowherd fell in love with Xenea, and how
The mountain grieved over him, and the oaks
Which grow on the banks of Himera sang a dirge.[4]
He was wasting away like the snow which melts under
Lofty Haemus or Athos, Rhodope or remote Caucasus.
He will sing how once the goatherd was shut up alive
In a wide chest, through a king's high-handed arrogance;
In his fragrant cedar chest he was fed by snub-nosed bees,
Who came from the meadows to bring him tender flowers,
Because the Muse had poured sweet nectar over his mouth.
O Comatas, long gone! These pleasures were yours:
A chest was your prison, too; you too were fed
On honeycombs while you toiled through the year's springtime.
I wish you had been on earth in my lifetime;
I would have pastured your fine goats on the hills,
Listening to your voice, while you, divine Comatas, lying at ease
Under oaks or pines sang your honey-sweet song."

Here he ended his song. Then I answered him, and said,
"Lycidas, my friend, I too have learned much from the Nymphs
As I grazed my cows on the hills: excellent songs,
Whose fame perhaps has reached the throne of Zeus.
This is the best of them by far—so listen, please, while I
Begin to pay you honor, for you are dear to the Muses.

"The Loves sneezed[5] for Simichidas; so he, poor wretch,
Yearns as much for Myrto as goats yearn for the spring.
But as for Aratus, my dearest friend of all, he desires
A boy, deep in his entrails. Aristis knows all this—
A good man, the best of men; Phoebus himself

4. In Greek mythology, Daphnis is said to be the first pastoral singer: there are different versions of his story, but in all he died young for love.

5. Traditionally a good omen

Would allow him into his sanctuary, to sing to his lyre—
How Aratus burns in his bones with love for the boy.

"O Pan, patron of Homole's lovely plains, I beg you, bring
Him unsummoned and press him into my friend's arms,
Whether it is dainty Philinus or yet some other lad.
Pan,[6] if you bring this about, may your back and shoulders
Be spared a beating with squills[7] by the boys of Arcadia,
When they are short of game. But if you refuse,
May you scratch yourself all over, covered in bites,
And may you go to your rest on a bed of nettles.
Midwinter shall find you on Edonian mountains,
On your way to the Hebrus, close by the North Pole.
May Ethiopia's marches be your summer pasture,
Under the Blemyan cliff, beyond sight of the Nile.
But you, O Loves, with cheeks as rosy as apples,
Leave the sweet waters of Byblis and Hyetis, and Oecus,
Shrine of golden-haired Dione. Wound, I pray you,
Desirable Philinus with your arrows. Wound him,
Since he, cruel boy, can find no pity for my friend.
He is ripe, riper than a pear, and women shout after him
'Ah, Philinus, your beauty's bloom is fading away!'
So, Aratus, let us abandon guard duty at his door,
And give our feet a rest. Let the morning cockcrow
Rouse someone else to numbing pain. It's Molon's turn,
And his alone, my friend, to be caught in *that* headlock.
All we should hope for is a tranquil life, and an old crone
To spit on us and keep all nastiness away."

I finished my song; and he, with a cheerful laugh as before,
Gave me the stick, pledging friendship in the Muses,
Then slanted off to the left, taking the road to Pyxa.
Eucritus and I and pretty Amyntas turned aside
To the farm of Phrasidamus, where we sank down
With pleasure on deep-piled couches of sweet rushes,
And vine leaves freshly stripped from the bush.
Above us was the constant quiet movement of elm

6. A god of nature, and of flocks and shepherds
7. Sea onion plants

And poplar, and from the cave of the Nymphs nearby
The sacred water ran with a bubbling sound as it fell.
Soot-black cicadas chattered relentlessly on
Shady branches, and the muttering of tree-frogs
Rose far off from the impenetrable thorn bush.
Larks and finches were singing, the turtle-dove moaned,
And bees hummed and darted about the springs.
Everything smelt of the rich harvest, smelt of the fruit-crop.
Apples and pears rolled all around us, enclosing
Our bodies with plenty; branches reached to the ground,
Bent with the weight of plums. Men broke for us
Four-year-old seals from the mouths of their wine jars.
O Nymphs of Castalia, haunters of steep Parnassus,
Was it such a bowl as this that the old man Chiron
Set before Heracles in the rocky cave of Pholus?[8]
Was it nectar like this that once on Anapus' banks
Impelled that shepherd, the mighty Polyphemus,
The one who bombarded ships with mountains, to
Dance about his sheepfolds?[9] This was the wine, Nymphs,
You mixed for us on that day, by the altar of Demeter,
Queen of the threshing-floor. May I once again
Plant the great winnowing-fan[10] in her heap of grain,
While she smiles, her hands laden with poppies and sheaves.

Virgil, *Eclogue 1*

In both his pastorals and georgics the Roman poet Virgil (70–19 BCE) fundamentally shaped Western poetry about inhabiting the natural world. While Virgil himself had adapted Theocritus's *Idylls*, for centuries the Virgilian eclogue defined the essential features of literature representing rustic figures singing of love, loss, and poetry itself (Figure 17). Literary critics generally associate the pastoral with an idealized landscape and life in harmony with nature, but Virgil's eclogues diverge from that stereotype. Virgil wrote during a civil war and Octavius Caesar's ascension to power, and his poetry about the

8. Chiron, the wisest centaur, and Heracles were tempted by the marvelous wine of centaur Pholus.

9. Polyphemus, the one-eyed monster of the *Odyssey,* whom Odysseus makes drunk

10. An instrument for winnowing grain, which was set upright to mark the end of the harvest

Source: *Virgil's Eclogues.* Translated by Len Krisak, University of Pennsylvania Press, 2012, pp. 1–9.

Figure 17. A sixteenth-century pastoral image, with shepherds singing and sheep at leisure, from an Italian translation of Virgil's *Georgics*, Bernardino Daniello's *La Georgica di Virgilio: nuouamente di latina in thoscana fauella* (1549). LatC V5874 Ei5 1549. Kislak Center for Special Collections, Rare Books, and Manuscripts, University of Pennsylvania Libraries.

natural world reflects that time of change. *Eclogue 1* is a dialogue between two herdsmen: Meliboeus, who has lost his land because of the war, and Tityrus, who has retained his land, thanks to an unnamed benefactor usually identified with Caesar. Thus, the pastoral landscape functions as more than background when it is lost, abandoned, or consumed. That natural world can be as hostile as it is inviting, and it is intimately tied to the herdsmen's conditions, even feeling their presence, as when the forest is said to call for Tityrus when he is absent. In the end, the poem sounds a melancholy note, as "shadows drop."

Meliboeus. Under a beech's stretching branches, there you lie,
Tityrus, trying, on the slimmest reed, to court
The forest muse, while I must leave, saying good-bye
To home, with its dear fields. But you, in shady ease,

Make "Lovely Amaryllis" echo through the trees.
Tityrus. Well, Meliboeus, one who's like a god to me
Gave me this peace.[1] His altar stone will always be
Bloodstained from spring lambs barely in the pen a day,
Because he lets my cattle roam, as you can see,
And lets me play my panpipe—any melody.
Meliboeus. I'm far less jealous than amazed, my friend. The land
Is crying havoc, and I'm sick at heart, for driving
My goats just now, I couldn't budge this nanny caught
In hazel thickets, struggling as twins were arriving.
She dropped the future of the flock on naked flint!
I would have realized the signs had meant bad luck
If I had had my wits when heaven's lightning struck
That oak. Still, tell me, Tityrus: who *is* this "god"?
Tityrus. I thought, "Rome must be like our little town." But Rome
Was proof that I was wrong; it's nothing like our home,
This place where we would wean the little newborn lambs.
(I learned there pups resemble dogs and kids their dams;
That small forms mimic bigger ones.) Rome's not like those,
However. Rising over every city, she's
A cypress towering above a guelder rose.[2]
Meliboeus. What made it possible for you to visit Rome?
Tityrus. The goddess Liberty. Though late, she smiled on me—
A slug whose barbered beard was white when it was sheared.
She smiled on me when Galatea finally
Was gone and Amaryllis here. I must confess,
While Galatea still possessed me, liberty
Was hopeless, and I couldn't save a blessed thing
Despite the untold victims sold from my sheepfold,
And fat rich cheeses pressed for an ungrateful town.
Not once did I come home with coins that weighed me down.
Meliboeus. So *that's* why you so sadly begged the deities,
Amaryllis, leaving ripe apples on the trees:
Your Tityrus was gone! And Tityrus, the pines
And springs and orchards all were calling you back home.
Tityrus. What could I do, indentured in my weightless chains?
And where else could I find such ready gods? For there

1. Understood to allude to Octavius Caesar
2. Viburnum shrub

I saw him, Meliboeus. Now, throughout the year—
Each month—my altar smokes for that young man, the first
Who listened to my prayer and spoke: "My children, graze
Your cattle as you used to—bulls to breed and raise."
Meliboeus. Old man, you're lucky, since these acres stay with you—
More than enough, though naked stones pave every patch,
And reeds from muddy marshes make for plastered pastures.
At least no toxic fodder tempts the pregnant ewe;
No neighboring flocks infect your sheep with scab or pox.
Old man, you're lucky. Here, amid familiar brooks
And sacred springs, you'll search out cool, refreshing shade.
And near your neighbor's boundary, as it always did,
The hedge that keeps the bees of Hybla[3] willow-fed
Will often lull you to your sleep with soft susurrus.
Below the bluff, a pruner tunes the air with airs,
While all along, the doves who are your special care
Coo with the moaning doves in immemorial elms.
Tityrus. The gentle deer will crop the firmament, therefore;
The waves will wash the fish they've stranded on the shore;
The vagrant Parthians[4] will drink the Arar,[5] or
The Germans race to drain the Tigris[6] long before
The precious memory of *his* face will be no more.
Meliboeus. But *we* must leave here, some for searing Africa,
Some, Scythia or the Oaxes,[7] sluicing Crete.
A scant few, Britain—where all severance is complete.
Long years from now, when I recall my native land—
My poor man's roof piled thick with sod—what will I see?
The realm I called my own when it was eared with wheat?
Will some ungodly soldier claim these plowed up furrows,
Some foreigner these crops? You see where civil war
Has led? These are the sorts of men we planted for.
Go, Meliboeus. Plant your pear trees; set your vines.
My flock once blessed with luck, come on. Come, little ones.
I'll never lie at length again in some green dell

3. An area in Sicily famous for honey
4. Persian nomads
5. The Saône, a river in France
6. A river in Persia
7. Area in Southern Russia

To watch you rooted to the distant, leafy bluff.
I'll sing no more, kids; now your grazing days are over;
Your browsing on the bitter willows or the clover.
Tityrus. Well, here's a place to sleep. Come join me; take your rest
On still-green grasses for a bed. I have soft chestnuts,
Ripe apples, and a good supply of cheese just pressed.
Already, smoke curls from the highest chimney top,
As from the mountain summits, longer shadows drop.

Virgil, *Georgics*, On Farming

In a passage describing the farmer's fear of extreme weather and his need to constantly watch the earth and sky for what is to come, Part 4 introduces *Georgics*, the masterful four-book poem by Virgil (70–19 BCE) about agriculture and the life of the earth. Overall, however, Book 1 is devoted to the hard world of farming (Figure 18). It is said that after a Golden Age of environmental harmony, Jove created a resistant earth, wanting to spur ingenuity in man in his efforts to subdue it; so humans had to invent tools to manage hostile and unruly plants and animals. However, not only does farming demand creativity and hard labor but the farmer must also learn from the land and those animals, understanding that he is ultimately subject to their needs.

In new spring, when from snowy peaks the run-off
flows, and the moldering clod crumbles under the Zephyr,[1]
straightaway I'd hitch my bull to groan before the deep-
driven plough, its blade scoured to gleaming by the furrow.
That field alone fulfils the keen farmer's prayer
which twice sun and twice frost has felt:
its teeming harvests burst the granaries.
But before our iron carves an unknown plain,
let our study be to learn its wind and fickle sky,
the local tricks, the temper of the land,
what each zone yields, what each refuses.
Here corn, there grapes will sprout more exuberantly,
there fruited trees, or herbs unbidden flourish.

Source: Virgil. *The Georgics: A Poem of the Land*. Translated and edited by Kimberly Johnson, Penguin, 2009, pp. 7–9, 11–13.

1. West wind

Figure 18. A sixteenth-century image of Virgil's farming, including grafting, plowing and sowing, from an Italian translation of Virgil's *Georgics*, Bernardino Daniello's *La Georgica di Virgilio: nuouamente di latina in thoscana fauella* (1549), p. 33. LatC V5874 Ei5 1549. Kislak Center for Special Collections, Rare Books, and Manuscripts, University of Pennsylvania Libraries.

See how Tmolus[2] offers up saffron fumes,
India sends ivory, and the soft Sabaeans[3] incense,
but the bare Chalybes[4] export iron, Pontus[5] the pungent musk
of beavers, and Epirus[6] the palms of Olympian mares?
From the first has Nature fixed for discrete climes
these laws and compacts everlasting, from the moment
Deucalion[7] sowed stones upon the empty world

2. Mount Tmolus in Lydia (modern Turkey)
3. The people of Saba, in the southern Arabian Peninsula
4. People in northern Anatolia
5. Area on the south coast of the Black Sea
6. Region in northwestern Greece
7. Son of Prometheus, he and his wife survived a great flood and repopulated the earth by sowing stones.

from which sprang men, a gritty race. Up then, where soil
is rich make haste and let your oxen hale upturn it
in the year's first months, then let the clods lie
for dusty summer to bake with ripening suns.
But if your earth's not fertile, it will do
to furrow up a shallow ridge as Arcturus rises,[8]—
here lest weeds choke off a fat harvest, elsewhere
lest the scant moisture desert the barren sand.
[. . .]
For humid summers and winters mild, pray,
O farmers: wheat delights in winter's dust,
our field is flush—no tillage makes Mysia flaunt
as richly, and Gargara's[9] agape at her own harvests.
Why mention him who, having cast his seeds,
grapples hand to soil and razes fruitless sandheaps,
then leads in the stream and its eddying ripples?
When the heatstruck field swelters, shoots withering,
look!—from a hillcrest ditch he taps a runlet
which falling sounds a low racket through sleek stones
and with its gushing slakes the thirsty earth.
And what of him who, lest stalks droop with corpulent ears,
mows the rampant grain in its green delicacy
when first the crop grows even with the furrow?
Or him who drains the marsh's hoard of water
into the sumping absorbency of sand, especially if
in capricious months the swollen river floods
and swathes the wide scape in a skin of silt,
so that the land's hollows seep with warm droplets?

And yet, though seasoned men and oxen struggle thus
to turn the soil, still the fractious gander spoils their work,
or Thracian cranes, or bitter-leaved chicory,
or shade harms the crops. The Father himself willed the way
of husbandry to be severe, first stirred by ingenuity
the fields, honing mortal skill with tribulation,
and suffered not his realm to laze in lumpish sloth.
Before Jove no yeoman groomed the soil: to mark

8. In September
9. Both Mysia and Gargara are fertile regions in Asia Minor.

the ground or to divide with fences was sacrilege.
In fellowship men strove, and the earth herself,
unpestered, more freely fruited her abundance.
But he put dire venom into vipers black, bade wolves
to raven and the sea to heave, shook honey from the leaves,
secreted fire, stanched the wine that ran everywhere in streams,
so that need with contemplation might forge sundry arts
in time, might seek in furrows the blade of wheat
and strike from flinty veins the hidden spark.
Then first did rivers heft the hollowed alder,
then the sailor plotted out the stars, numbering and naming:
Pleiades, Hyades, and radiant, royal Arctos.
Then . . . what discovery!—how to catch game in snares, to dupe
with birdlime, to encircle great woods with hounds.
Now one whips a wide river with a dragnet, probing
the depths, and one through the sea trawls his wet gear.
Then came hard iron, and the shrill sawblade
(for earliest men with wedges split the splintered timber),
and then myriad arts. Toil subdued the earth,
relentless toil, and the prick of dearth in hardship.

Ceres[10] first taught men to turn the earth with iron
when arbutes[11] and acorns dwindled in the sacred grove
and Dodona[12] withheld her provender. But soon trouble grew
with crops, as mildew's blight devoured the stalks
and lazy thistles bristled in the fields: grain fails, a scraggly wood
springs up with burrs and caltrops, and among the bronzing acres
the contrary tares and feckless reed are despots.
If you harry not with tireless rake the weeds,
if with your voice you do not terrify the birds
or with your sickle prune the canopy shading the land,
if with no prayers you call down rain,
O! how you'll gaze in vain at another's ample stockpile
and shake the forest oak to soothe your famine.

10. Goddess of agriculture
11. Arbutus tree
12. The sacred oracle at Delphi

Columella, *Res rustica*, or *On Agriculture*, On Farming

Born in the area of the Roman empire that is now Spain, Lucius Junius Columella (ca. 70 CE) later extensively cultivated his own estates in central Italy. Drawing on previous writers, including Varro and Virgil, as well as his own experience, he composed *Res rustica*, a twelve-book treatise on agriculture covering topics ranging from building and labor to raising crops, animals, and bees. (He also provided a poem on gardening, excerpted in Part 6.) His treatise begins by complaining about the neglect of agriculture in his time, which has led to barren lands, and he asks Rome's best men to take up farming as an antidote to corruption and vice. While calling on them to use their own intelligence and learning, Columella also directed those men to closely attend to the specific qualities of plants and animals, according to various situations and climates. Columella's agricultural advice and his view of farming's moral benefits proved highly influential when revived in Italy in the early fifteenth century and spread across Europe for the next two centuries.

Again and again I hear leading men of our state condemning now the unfruitfulness of the soil, now the inclemency of the climate for some seasons past, as harmful to crops; and some I hear reconciling the aforesaid complaints, as if on well-founded reasoning, on the ground that, in their opinion, the soil was worn out and exhausted by the over-production of earlier days and can no longer furnish sustenance to mortals with its old-time benevolence. Such reasons, Publius Silvinus,[1] I am convinced are far from the truth; for it is a sin to suppose that Nature, endowed with perennial fertility by the creator of the universe, is affected with barrenness as though with some disease; and it is unbecoming to a man of good judgment to believe that earth, to whose lot was assigned a divine and everlasting youth, and who is called the common mother of all things—because she has always brought forth all things and is destined to bring them forth continuously—has grown old in mortal fashion. And, furthermore, I do not believe that such misfortunes come upon us as a result of the fury of the elements, but rather because of our own fault; for the matter of husbandry, which all the best of our ancestors had treated with the best of care, we have delivered over to all the worst of our slaves, as if to a hangman for punishment.

[. . .]

Source: Columella. *On Agriculture: Res rustica*, translated by Harrison Boyd Ash, vols. 1–4, Harvard University Press, 1941, pp. 3–27. Loeb Classical Library.

1. The treatise is written to Publius Silvinus.

If good men are to shun these pursuits and their kind, there remains, as I have said, one method of increasing one's substance that befits a man who is a gentleman and free-born, and this is found in agriculture.

[. . .]

But for my part, when I review the magnitude of the entire subject, like the immensity of some great body, or the minuteness of its several parts, as so many separate members, I am afraid that my last day may overtake me before I can comprehend the entire subject of rural discipline. For one who would profess to be a master of this science must have a shrewd insight into the works of nature; he must not be ignorant of the variations of latitude, that he may have ascertained what is suitable to every region and what is incompatible. He should tell over in his mind the rising and setting of the stars, that he may not begin his operations when rains and winds are threatening, and so bring his toils to naught. He must observe the behavior of the current weather and season, for they do not always wear the same habit as if according to a fixed rule; summer and winter do not come every year with the same countenance; the spring is not always rainy or the autumn moist. These matters I cannot believe that any man can know beforehand without the light of intelligence and without the most accurate instruction. Indeed, it is granted to few to discern what the very diversity of land and the nature of each soil may deny us, or what they may promise us. Of how many, in fact, is it the lot to survey all parts of this science, so as thoroughly to understand the practice of cropping and ploughing and to have an accurate knowledge of the varied and very unlike types of soil (of which some deceive us by their color, some by their texture; in some lands the black soil which they call pulla, as in Campania, is commended; in others a fat, glutinous soil answers better; in some countries, as in Africa and Numidia, a crumbling, sandy soil surpasses in fertility even the strongest land; while in Asia and Mysia[2] a stiff and viscous soil is especially productive)? Of how many is it the lot to have an understanding in the matter of these soils, as to what crop a hillside will refuse to yield, what a level situation, what a cultivated land, what a wooded land, what a land that is moist and grassy or dry and blasted; to discern also the method of planting and tending trees and vineyards, of which there are endless varieties; and of acquiring and keeping cattle, since we have admitted this as a part of agriculture, though the herdsman's art is distinct from husbandry? And yet even this is not of one pattern; for a stud of horses requires one kind of management; a herd of cattle another; a flock of sheep still another, and of these the Tarentine breed[3] demands a different method from the

2. In Asia Minor
3. From southern Italy

coarse-wooled; a still different treatment is required by the goat kind, and of these the hornless and thin-haired are cared for in one way, the horned and shaggy-haired, as in Cilicia,[4] in another way. Moreover, the business of the swine-breeder and swineherd is different, their method of feeding is different; nor do light-coated and heavy-coated swine require the same climate, rearing, and care. And, to take my leave of cattle, as a part of which the care of farmyard poultry and bees is reckoned, who has extended his studies so far as to be acquainted, in addition to the points which I have enumerated, with the many methods of grafting and pruning? To put in practice the cultivation of the many fruits and vegetables? To devote his attention to the many varieties of figs as well as to rose-gardens, when even greater things are neglected by most people even though they have now begun to be, for many farmers, not the least part of their revenue? For meadows and willow-thickets, broom-plants and reeds, though they require little attention, still require some.

Walter of Henley, *Dite de hosbondrie*, or *Boke of Husbandrye*

This treatise on husbandry attributed to Walter of Henley was widely read from its mid-thirteenth-century composition in French as the *Dite de hosbondrie* up through the sixteenth century; it was revised and printed in England in 1510 by Wynkyn de Worde as *The Boke of Husbandrye* (Figure 19). The guidance is presented in the form of a father advising his son about the management of an estate, including its crops, animals, and people. The treatise calls for constant and detailed attention to the requirements of cultivating the land and the proper treatment of animals, all in the name of maximizing productivity and profitability. The excerpt below gives very specific instructions about raising sheep, revealing an intimate knowledge of the animal's habits. The ugly images of disease and alimentation contrast sharply with the often-idealized image of sheep herding offered in pastoral poetry (see, for example, Jacopo Sannazaro's *Arcadia*).

See that your shepherd be not hasty, for by an angry man some may be badly overdriven, from which they may perish there where your sheep are pasturing and the shepherd comes among them.

Sort out your sheep once a year, between Easter and Whitsuntide,[1] and cause those which are not to be kept to be sheared early and marked apart from

4. In Asia minor

Source: Elizabeth Lamond. *Walter of Henley's Treatise on Husbandry*, Longman, Green, 1890. *Martha Carlin*, https://people.uwm.edu/carlin/walter-of-henleys-husbandry/.

1. Seventh Sunday after Easter

Figure 19. Clearing the forest with curious sheep looking on, from Walter of Henley's *The Boke of Husbandrye*, a translation of the *Dite de hosbondrie*. Cambridge University Library SeL.5.13. Licensed by Creative Commons.

the others, and put them in enclosed wood or in other pasture where they can fatten, and about St. John's Day sell them, for then will the flesh of sheep be in season. And the wool of these may be sold by itself with the skins (of those) which died of the murrain.[2] And when the sheep are sold, for them and their wool and the skins as foresaid replace as many head.

Some men replace others for those which died of murrain. How? I will tell you. If a sheep die suddenly they put the flesh in water for as many hours are between midday and three o'clock, and then hang it up, and when the water is drained off they salt it and dry it. And if any sheep begin to fall ill they see if it

2. Infectious disease

be because the teeth drop, and if the teeth do not fall out they cause it to be killed and salted and dried like the others, and then they cut it up and distribute it in the household among the servants and laborers, and they shall then yield as much as they cost, for by this means and with the skins they can replace as many. But I do not wish you to do this.

See that your sheep are in houses between Martinmas[3] and Easter, I say not if the weather be dry and the fold be properly prepared and strewed, and if the weather be fine your sheep may lie there, and let those that are in houses have more or less hay, according to the weather. And marl[4] the ground of the sheepfold every fortnight, as I have said before, and let it be strewed on the top, and you shall have from these more profit than if they lie in the fold.

And if wethers[5] be in the house for a storm let them be by themselves, and let them have the coarsest hay or hay mixed with wheat or oat straw, well threshed. Why? I will tell you. They are driven for the night in the fold, and by chance the morrow also, that they cannot pasture, and then come to the manger starving, and push back the weak and choke themselves without chewing the small hay. And when the sheep has eaten its fill it ruminates, and that which is not chewed cannot be chewed again, but remains within its body, and wastes unnaturally, whereby several have perished. And if straw be mixed with the hay they will chew it better because of the coarseness of the straw. And if you have a lack of hay the pods and straw of peas are good for sheep.

William Langland, *Piers Plowman*

Little is known of the life of William Langland (ca.1325–ca.1390), the author of the powerful and complex allegorical poem *Piers Plowman*, dated to the late fourteenth century when England was ravaged by plague and social and political unrest. The poem recounts the dream of a narrator named Will who wishes to live as a true Christian, represented in a dizzying mix of religious allegory, realism, and biting social and clerical satire. In the poem's first part, Will envisions thousands of people in search of Saint Truth, symbolizing the truth of God and the Christian life. In their journey a group of them meet Piers, a plowman who says he will guide them if they first help him to plow his half acre of land (Figure 20). In this excerpt we see that those who shirk the work end up

3. November 11
4. Apply marl, a clay-rich soil
5. Castrated rams

Source: William Langland. *Piers Plowman*. Edited by Elizabeth Robertson and Stephan H. A. Shepherd, based on the translation of the B text by E. Talbot Donaldson, Norton Critical Edition, 2006, pp. 101–3.

Figure 20. A medieval image of a plowman, with a man who leads a horse drawing a harrow; following behind is a slinger, as one of his shots passes midway between two crows. From the Luttrell Psalter (ca. 1325–1335). Add. 42130, f.171. Credit: The British Library Board.

mocked and attacked by the allegorical figure of Hunger. Langland thus moralizes agricultural labor, while he also connects it to the urgency of providing food for a starving land. As a model for later social satire and complaint, *Piers Plowman* also fashioned the durable image of the plowman as a type of Christian morality and reform.

[Piers says]
"As for the residue and the remnant, by the Rood of Lucca,[1]
I will worship Truth with it all my lifetime,
And be his pilgrim at the plow for poor men's sake.
My plowstaff shall be my pikestaff[2] and push at the roots
And help my coulter[3] to cut and cleanse the furrows."
Now Perkin[4] and the pilgrims have put themselves to plowing.
Many there helped him to plow his half-acre.
Ditchers and diggers dug up the ridges;
Perkin was pleased by this and praised them warmly.
There were other workmen who worked very hard:
Each man in his manner made himself a laborer,
And some to please Perkin pulled up the weeds.
At high prime[5] Piers let the plow stand
To oversee them himself; whoever worked best

1. A popular pilgrimage site
2. Staff with a metal tip
3. The iron blade in the front of a plow
4. A nickname for Piers
5. Nine in the morning

Should be hired afterward, when harvest-time came.
Then some sat down and sang over ale
And helped plow the half-acre with "Ho! trolly-lolly!"
"Now by the peril of my soul!" said Piers in pure wrath,
"Unless you get up again and begin working now,
No grain that grows here will gladden you at need,
And though once off the dole you die let the Devil care!"
Then fakers were afraid and feigned to be blind;
Some set their legs askew as such loafers can
And made their moan to Piers, how they might not work:
"We have no limbs to labor with, Lord, we thank you;
But we pray for you, Piers, and for your plow as well,
That God of his grace make your grain multiply,
And reward you for whatever alms you will give us here,
For we can't strain and sweat, such sickness afflicts us."
"If what you say is so," said Piers, "I'll soon find out.
I know you're ne'er-do-wells, and Truth knows what's right,
And I'm his sworn servant and so should warn him
Which ones they are in this world that do his workmen harm.
You waste what men win with toil and trouble.
But Truth shall teach you how his team should be driven,
Or you'll eat barley bread and use the brook for drink;
Unless you're blind or broken-legged, or bolted with iron—
Those shall eat as well as I do, so God help me,
Till God of his goodness gives them strength to arise.
But you could work as Truth wants you to and earn wages and bread
By keeping cows in the field, the corn from the cattle,
Making ditches or dikes or dinging on sheaves,
Or helping make mortar, or spreading muck afield.
You live in lies and lechery and in sloth too,
And it's only for suffrance[6] that vengeance has not fallen on you.
But anchorites[7] and hermits that eat only at noon
And nothing more before the morrow, they shall have my alms,
And buy copes[8] at my cost—those that have cloisters and churches.
But Robert Runabout shall have no rag from me,
Nor 'Apostles' unless they can preach and have the bishop's permission.

6. Indulgence
7. A religious recluse
8. A cloak worn by priests or other religious figures

They shall have bread and boiled greens and a bit extra besides,
For it's an unreasonable religious life that has no regular meals."
Then Waster waxed angry and wanted to fight;
To Piers the Plowman he proffered his glove.
A Breton, a braggart, he bullied Piers too,
And told him to go piss with his plow, peevish wretch.
"Whether you're willing or unwilling, we will have our will
With your flour and your flesh, fetch it when we please,
And make merry with it, no matter what you do."
Then Piers the Plowman complained to the knight
To keep him safe, as their covenant was, from cursed rogues,
"And from these wolfish wasters that lay waste the world,
For they waste and win nothing, and there will never be
Plenty among the people while my plow stands idle."
Because he was born a courteous man the knight spoke kindly to Waster
And warned him he would have to behave himself better:
"Or you'll pay the penalty at law, I promise, by my knighthood!"
"It's not my way to work," said Waster, "I won't begin now!"
And made light of the law and lighter of the knight,
And said Piers wasn't worth a pea or his plow either,
And menaced him and his men if they met again.
"Now by the peril of my soul!" said Piers, "I'll punish you all."
And he whooped after Hunger who heard him at once.
"Avenge me on these vagabonds," said he, "that vex the whole world."
Then Hunger in haste took hold of Waster by the belly
And gripped him so about the guts that his eyes gushed water.
He buffeted the Breton about the cheeks
That he looked like a lantern all his life after.
He beat them both so that he almost broke their guts.
Had not Piers with a pease loaf[9] prayed him to leave off
They'd have been dead and buried deep, have no doubt about it.
"Let them live," he said, "and let them feed with hogs.
Or else on beans and bran baked together."
Fakers for fear fled into barns
And flogged sheaves with flails from morning till evening,
So that Hunger wouldn't be eager to cast his eye on them.
For a potful of peas that Piers had cooked

9. Cheap bread

A heap of hermits laid hands on spades
And cut off their copes and made short coats of them
And went like workmen to weed and to mow,
And dug dirt and dung to drive off Hunger.
Blind and bedridden got better by the thousand;
Those who sat to beg silver were soon healed,
For what had been baked for Bayard[10] was boon to many hungry,
And many a beggar for beans obediently labored,
And every poor man was well pleased to have peas for his wages,
And what Piers prayed them to do they did as sprightly as
sparrowhawks.
And Piers was proud of this and put them to work,
And gave them meals and money as they might deserve.

Second Shepherd's Play, from the *Wakefield Mystery Plays*

In the late fourteenth and early fifteenth centuries, cycles of plays dramatizing the biblical events played an important part in English urban culture. Amateurs performed these plays (now called "mystery plays" after the "mysteries," the guilds that sponsored them) on wagons drawn through the city streets at festival times. While retelling biblical stories, they also humorously depicted aspects of contemporary social life. The cycle called the Wakefield plays, transmitted in the Townley manuscript, includes the "Second Shepherd's Play," staging the shepherds' worship of Christ at the Nativity. That part of the story begins with a comic subplot concerning the stealing of a lamb, later found hidden in a manger, presented as a counterpart to the Christ Child's birth. Complaining about the hardships of their life, the shepherds describe how they were driven from their farms by the recent conversion of fields to pasture that benefited wealthy landlords (see also Thomas More's *Utopia* on enclosure and the conversion to an economy based on the wool trade). Their complaints offer a wintery, bleak vision of the shepherd's lot, in contrast to the greater security of life as a tenant farmer, and one that is certainly unlike any idealized version of pastoral leisure.

First Shepherd. Lord, but this weather is cold, and I am ill wrapped,
My hands in frost's hold, so long have I napped;

10. A generic name for a horse

Source: *Second Shepherd's Play. The Wakefield Mystery Plays*, edited by Martial Rose, 1961, pp. 207–9.

My legs they fold, my fingers are chapped,
It is not as of old, for I am lapped
    In sorrow.
In storms and tempest,
Now in the east, now in the west,
Woe to him who has no rest
    Now or tomorrow.
But we simple shepherds that walk on the moor,
Are soon by richer hands thrust out of door;
No wonder as it stands, if we be poor,
For the tilth of our lands lies as fallow as the floor,
    As you know.
We are so lamed,
Overtaxed and maimed,
And cruelly tamed,
    By our gentlemen foe.
Thus they rob us of our rest, may ill-luck them harry!
These proud men are our pest, they make the plough tarry.[1]

What men say is for the best, we find it contrary:
Thus are ploughmen oppressed, no hope now to carry
    Alive.
Thus hold they us under,
Thus bring us into blunder;
It were great wonder,
    If ever we should thrive.
If one gets a modish sleeve or a brooch nowadays,
Take care if you him grieve or once cross his ways![2]
Dares no man bid him leave the power that he sways,
And yet may not believe one word that he says
    The better
He grasps for his gain
In his bragging vein,
And boasts men maintain
    Him, who are far greater.
There shall come a swain, a proud peacock you know,

1. These men (who work for the lords) hinder their farming.
2. This refers to the livery of the lord's retainers.

He must borrow my wain,[3] my plough also,
This for my gain I must grant ere he go.
Thus live we in pain, anger and woe;
    By night and day
He craves what comes to his head,
And I give in great dread;
I were better be dead,
    Than once say him nay.
It does me good as I walk thus on my own,
Of this world for me to talk, and so make my moan.
To my sheep will I stalk and listen anon;
There abide on a balk[4] or sit on a stone
    Full soon.
For believe you me,
True men, if they be,
We get more company
    Ere it be noon.

Second Shepherd *enters.*

Second Shepherd. Benedicite dominus![5] What may this mean?
The world faring thus, how oft have we seen?
Lord, this weather works through us, and the wind is so keen
And frost will undo us, fast blind I have been,
    No lie.
Now in dry, now in wet,
Now in snow, now in sleet,
When my shoes freeze to my feet,
    It's not at all easy.

Jacopo Sannazaro, *Arcadia*

The *Arcadia* of the Neapolitan Jacopo Sannazaro (1458–1530) profoundly influenced the Renaissance pastoral tradition. As was customary for a man of noble birth, Sannazaro's humanist education would have exposed him to the classical pastoral tradition, including the works of Theocritus and Virgil. He

3. Wagon
4. A strip of grass separating fields
5. The Lord bless

Source: Jacopo Sannazaro. *Arcadia and Piscatorial Eclogues*. Translated by Ralph Nash, Wayne State University Press, 1966, pp. 29–33.

composed his first Arcadian eclogues while a member of a humanist academy in Naples; the full work appeared first in 1502 (in an unauthorized edition) and then in 1504, and thereafter it was frequently reprinted and circulated across Europe. Presented in prose and poetry, the story is narrated by Sincero (a figure for the poet), who has left his city to live in the idealized land of Arcadia, a place inhabited by shepherds singing sadly of their loves and losses. While it has some realistic features, Arcadia's natural world is almost universally pleasant, lovely, and innocent, except in the experience of unhappy lovers. The narrator contrasts the pastoral landscape's beauty with that of the art and artificial gardens associated with city and court. Sannazaro's image of Arcadia shaped many later representations of this imagined world, in the European Renaissance and beyond (see, for example, Mary Wroth's *Urania*, below).

More often than not the tall and spreading trees brought forth by nature on the shaggy mountains are wont to bring greater pleasure to those who view them than are the cultivated trees pruned and thinned by cunning hands in ornamented gardens. And the birds of the woodland singing upon the green branches in the solitary forests give much more pleasure to him who hears them than do those birds that have been taught to speak from within their lovely and decorated cages in the crowded cities. For this reason it happens, as I judge, that woodland songs carved on the rugged barks of beeches no less delight the one who reads them than do learned verses written on the smooth pages of gilded books. And the wax-bound reeds of shepherds proffer amid the flower-laden valleys perhaps more pleasurable sound than do through proud chambers the polished and costly boxwood instruments of the musicians. And who has any doubt that a fountain that issues naturally from the living rock, surrounded by green growth, is more pleasing to the human mind than all the others made by art of whitest marble, resplendent with much gold? Certainly no one, to my thinking. Therefore relying on that, I shall among these deserted places recount to the listening trees, and to those few shepherds that will be there, the rude eclogues issued from a natural vein, setting them forth just as naked of ornament as I heard them sung by the shepherds of Arcady under the delightful shades, to the murmuring of crystal fountains.

[. . .]

There lies on the summit of Parthenius, a not inconsiderable mountain of pastoral Arcadia, a pleasant plateau, not very spacious in extent, since the situation of the place does not permit it, but so filled with tiny and deep-green herbage that, if the wanton herds with their greedy nibbling did not pasture there, one could always find green grasses in that place. There, if I am not mistaken, there are perhaps a dozen or fifteen trees of such unusual and exceeding beauty that any who saw them would judge that Mistress Nature had taken special delight in shaping them. These trees, standing somewhat apart and arranged in non-artificial order, with their rarity ennoble beyond measure the natural beauty of the place. There without any gnarl is seen the fir tree, wholly straight, born to endure the perils of the deep; and with more open branches the sturdy oak and the lofty ash and the most pleasant plane tree there dispread themselves, covering with their shade no little part of the rich and beautiful meadow. And there with shorter leaf is the tree with which Hercules was wont to be crowned, into whose trunk the wretched daughters of Clymene were transformed. On one side may be seen the knotty chestnut, the leafy box tree, and with its pointed leaves the towering pine laden with the hardest fruits: on the other the shady beech, the incorruptible linden and the fragile tamarisk, together with the oriental palm, the welcome and honored reward of the victors. But in their midst, near a limpid fountain, soars toward heaven a straight cypress, a most accurate imitator of the lofty obelisks, into which not only Cyparissus[1] but, if one may say it, Apollo himself would not disdain to endure a transformation.

Nor are the trees of which I speak so discourteous that with their shade they altogether forbid the rays of the sun to enter the pleasant little grove; on the contrary, so graciously do they admit them in divers places that rare is that tree that does not receive from them the greatest invigoration: and though it be at all times a pleasant spot, in the flowery spring more than in all the rest of the year it is most pleasing. In this so lovely a place the shepherds with their flocks will often gather together from the surrounding hills and exercise themselves there in various strenuous contests, such as hurling the heavy stake, shooting with bows at a target, and making proof of their skill in light leaping and stout wrestling, full of rustic trickery; and most often in singing and in playing the shepherd's pipe in rivalry one with another, not without praise and reward for the victor.

Thomas More, *Utopia*

The *Utopia* of Sir Thomas More (1478–1535) presents a controversial version of an ideal commonwealth, a world without private property yet undergirded by slavery, distinguished by freedom of thought yet without privacy. A humanist and lawyer, Thomas More served as Lord Chancellor to Henry VIII; however,

1. In Ovid, a youth loved by Apollo, who was transformed into a cypress tree

Source: Thomas More. *Utopia*. Edited by Henry Morley and translated by Gilbert Burnet, Cassell, 1901.

he also was an ardent Roman Catholic, which led him to oppose his king when Henry broke from the church in Rome, ultimately ending in his execution for treason. More wrote and published *Utopia* in Latin in 1515, intending it for an audience of fellow humanists; it was not translated and printed in English until 1551 (by Ralph Robinson). In its first book, More prefaces the later description of the Utopian commonwealth by discussing the current state of Europe. In explaining why he chose not to be involved in public affairs, Ralph Hythloday, the voyager returned from Utopia, offers a dark picture of an England rife with crime and poverty. He partially attributes that poverty to a shift from agriculture to sheep farming, whereby land was diverted from agriculture to pasture, and common lands were enclosed, dispossessing and impoverishing countless people (see also *The Second Shepherd's Play*, above). This opposition between agriculture and sheep farming provides a sharp counterpoint to the pastoral and georgic poetic modes.

"But I do not think that this necessity of stealing arises only from hence; there is another cause of it, more peculiar to England." "What is that?" said the Cardinal: "The increase of pasture," said I, "by which your sheep, which are naturally mild, and easily kept in order, may be said now to devour men and unpeople, not only villages, but towns; for wherever it is found that the sheep of any soil yield a softer and richer wool than ordinary, there the nobility and gentry, and even those holy men, the abbots, not contented with the old rents which their farms yielded, nor thinking it enough that they, living at their ease, do no good to the public, resolve to do it hurt instead of good. They stop the course of agriculture, destroying houses and towns, reserving only the churches, and enclose grounds that they may lodge their sheep in them. As if forests and parks had swallowed up too little of the land, those worthy countrymen turn the best inhabited places into solitudes; for when an insatiable wretch, who is a plague to his country, resolves to enclose many thousand acres of ground, the owners, as well as tenants, are turned out of their possessions by trick or by main force, or, being wearied out by ill usage, they are forced to sell them; by which means those miserable people, both men and women, married and unmarried, old and young, with their poor but numerous families (since country business requires many hands), are all forced to change their seats, not knowing whither to go; and they must sell, almost for nothing, their household stuff, which could not bring them much money, even though they might stay for a buyer. When that little money is at an end (for it will be soon spent), what is left for them to do but either to steal, and so to be hanged (God knows how justly!), or to go about and beg? And if they do this they are put in prison as idle vagabonds, while they would willingly work but can find none that will hire them; for there is no more occasion for country labor, to which they have been bred, when there is no arable ground left. One shepherd can look after a flock, which will stock an extent of ground that would require many hands if it were to be ploughed and reaped. This, likewise, in many places raises the price of corn. The price of wool is also so risen that the poor people, who were wont to make cloth, are no more able to buy it; and this, likewise, makes many of them idle: for since the increase of pasture God has punished the avarice of the owners by a rot among the sheep, which has destroyed vast numbers of them—to us it might have seemed more just had it fell on the owners themselves. But, suppose the sheep should increase ever so much, their price is not likely to fall; since, though they cannot be called a monopoly, because they are not engrossed by one person, yet they are in so few hands, and these are so rich, that, as they are not pressed to sell them sooner than they have a mind to it, so they never do it till they have raised the price as high as possible. And on the same account it is that the other kinds of cattle are so dear, because many villages being pulled down, and all country labor being much neglected, there are none who make it their business to breed them. The rich do not breed cattle as they do sheep, but buy them lean and at low prices; and, after they have fattened them on their grounds, sell them again at high rates. And I do not think that all the inconveniences this will produce are yet observed; for, as they sell the cattle dear, so, if they are consumed faster than the breeding countries from which they are brought can afford them, then the stock must decrease, and this must needs end in great scarcity; and by these means, this your island, which seemed as to this particular the happiest in the world, will suffer much by the cursed avarice of a few persons: besides this, the rising of corn makes all people lessen their families as much as they can; and what can those who are dismissed by them do but either beg or rob?"

Thomas Tusser, *Five Hundredth Pointes of Good Husbandrie*

The ideas of Thomas Tusser (1524–1580) on farming and husbandry circulated first in *The Hundredth Pointes of Good Husbandrie* in 1557 (excerpted in Part 4). In his subsequent enlarged edition, the *Five Hundredth Pointes of Good Husbandrie United to a Many of Good Huswiferie* (1573, with many reprintings), he added a brief introduction to his work that succinctly expresses his georgic vision from the point of view of the tenant farmer rather than manorial lord. With that shift, however, Tusser still emphasizes exacting as much profit as

Source: Thomas Tusser. *Five hundredth pointes of good husbandrie*, sig. B4r, London, 1580.

possible from the land and animals. Thrift, local knowledge, and unceasing labor are necessary to reap "a thousand things as richly worth, as any pearl is worthy gold."

Good husbandmen must moil and toil,
to lay to live by labored field:
Their wives at home must keep such coil,[1]
as their like acts, may profit yield,
    For well they know,
    as shaft from bow,
    or chalk from snow,
A good round rent their lords they give,
and must keep touch in all their pay;
With credit cracked, else for to live,
or trust to legs, and run away.

Though fence well kept, is one good point,
and tilth well done, in season due;
Yet needing salve, in time to anoint,
is all in all and needful true,
    As for the rest,
    thus think I best,
    as friend doth jest,
With hand in hand to lead thee forth,
to Ceres[2] camp, there to behold:
A thousand things as richly worth,
as any pearl is worthy gold.

William Harrison, *Description of England*

In his *Description of England* the clergyman William Harrison (1534–1593) participates in the genre of chorography, the detailed depiction of the natural and social features of a specific place or country. The book's eminent British forerunners include the preface to Bede's *Ecclesiastical History* (ca. 730) and Ranulf Higden's monumental *Polychronicon* (fourteenth century). Designed to

1. Bustle
2. Roman goddess of agriculture

Source: William Harrison. *The Description of England: The Classic Contemporary Account of Tudor Social Life*. Edited by Georges Edelen, Folger Shakespeare Library, 1994, pp. 275–76.

complement Raphael Holinshed's history of England, Harrison's *Description* was published first in 1577 as part of Holinshed's *Chronicles of England, Scotland and Ireland* and then in a revised version in 1587. While Harrison borrowed from other writers, his text also reflects his own observations of the state of the land in his time. He exuded national pride in England's prosperity and wealth of natural resources, but he could criticize what he saw as change for the worse. His chapter on "woods and marshes" opens with his concern about Britain's deforestation caused by farming, clearing for pasture, and the pillaging of trees to build houses of oak, which Harrison sees as an unnecessary luxury.

It should seem by ancient records and the testimony of sundry authors that the whole countries of Loegria and Cambria, now England and Wales, have sometimes been very well replenished with great woods and groves, although at this time the said commodity be not a little decayed in both, and in such wise that a man shall oft ride ten or twenty miles in each of them and find very little or rather none at all, except it be near unto towns, gentlemen's houses, and villages, where the inhabitants have planted a few elms, oaks, hazels, or ashes about their dwellings for their defense from the rough winds and keeping of the stormy weather from annoyance of the same.

This scarcity at the first grew (as it is thought) either by the industry of man, for maintenance of tillage (as we understand the like to be done of late by the Spaniards in the West Indies, where they fired whole woods of very great compass, thereby to come by ground whereon to sow their grains), or else through the covetousness of such as, in preferring of pasture for their sheep and greater cattle, do make small account of firebote[1] and timber, or, finally, by the cruelty of the enemies, whereof we have sundry examples declared in our histories. Howbeit, where the rocks and quarry grounds are I take the sward[2] of the earth to be so thin that no tree of any greatness, other than shrubs and bushes, is able to grow or prosper long therein, for want of sufficient moisture wherewith to feed them with fresh humor, or at the leastwise of mold, to shroud, stay upright, and cherish the same in the blustering winter's weather till they may grow unto any greatness and spread or yield their roots downright into the soil about them; and this either is or may be one other cause wherefore some places are naturally void of wood. But to proceed.

Although I must needs confess that there is good store of great wood or timber here and there even now in some places of England, yet in our days it is far unlike to that plenty which our ancestors have seen heretofore, when stately

1. Firewood
2. Upper layer of the ground

building was less in use. For albeit that there were then greater number of messuages[3] and mansions almost in every place, yet were their frames so slight and slender that one mean dwelling house in our time is able to countervail very many of them, if you consider the present charge with the plenty of timber that we bestow upon them. In times past men were contented to dwell in houses builded of sallow,[4] willow, plum tree, hardbeam,[5] and elm, so that the use of oak was in manner dedicated wholly unto churches, religious houses, princes' palaces, noblemen's lodgings, and navigation, but now all these are rejected and nothing but oak any whit regarded.

And yet see the change, for when our houses were builded of willow, then had we oaken men; but now that our houses are come to be made of oak, our men are not only become willow, but a great many, through Persian delicacy crept in among us, altogether of straw, which is a sore alternation.

Edmund Spenser, *The Shepheard's Calendar*

While Edmund Spenser (1552/3–1599) is mostly celebrated for his spectacular allegorical epic, *The Faerie Queene* (excerpted in Part 6), his first work was a set of eclogues, *The Shephearde's Calendar* (1579). Spenser's eclogues echo Virgilian pastoral but are organized differently; imitating the older almanac form of the *Kalendar of the Shepheardes*, each eclogue corresponds to a month of the year. Each is also preceded by a woodcut emblem representing the scene evoked in the poem and a sign of the zodiac (Figure 21). In blending Virgilian themes and tropes with religious ones, the Italian humanist Mantuan's Latin eclogues most directly influenced Spenser's approach, while stylistically Spenser adapted his diction from Chaucer's Middle English, seeking to give his poems an archaic and rustic gloss. Most of Spenser's eclogues have a specific allegorical structure, alluding to political controversies and figures of the time. However, they also function as a form of nature writing in Theocritus's pastoral tradition, and not just as a veil for human affairs. In the January eclogue, "Colin Clout" (a stand-in for the poet) complains of his unrequited love for Rosalind. While the poem links Colin's emotions with the weather, we see the human body responding to the cold, but the poem also suggests that Colin's unhappiness itself influences the weather (compare with Amelia Lanyer, "A Description

3. Dwellings with their outbuildings and land
4. A kind of willow
5. Hornbeam

Source: Edmund Spenser. *The shepheardes calender conteyning twelve aeglogues proportionable to the twelve monethes*, London, 1579, pp. 1–2.

Figure 21. Woodcut preceding the January eclogue, representing both a sad shepherd and mournful sheep, from Edmund Spenser, *The Shepehearde's Calendar*. From *The Faerie Queene: The Shepheardes Calendar: together with the other works of England's arch-poët, Edmund Spenser, collected into one volume and carefully corrected* (London: 1611), p. 1. PR2350 1615. Kislak Center for Special Collections, Rare Books, and Manuscripts, University of Pennsylvania Libraries.

of Cookham" [Part 4]). Colin's sheep, too, suffer for his pain, but mostly from his neglect. (The poems were published with interpretive notes provided by a mysterious "E. K.," who some scholars think was a front for Spenser himself; these notes are represented in the glosses.)

In this first Eclogue Colin Clout a shepherd's boy complaineth him of his unfortunate love, being but newly (as seemeth) enamoured of a country lass called Rosalind: with which strong affection being very sore traveled, he compareth his careful case to the sad season of the year, to the frosty ground, to the frozen trees, and to his own winterbeaten flock. And lastly, finding himself robbed of all former pleasance and delights, he breaketh his pipe in pieces, and casteth himself to the ground.

Colin Clout.
A shepherd's boy (no better do him call)
When winters wasteful spite was almost spent,

All in a sunshine day, as did befall,
Led forth his flock, that had been long ypent.[1]
So faint they wax, and feeble in the fold,
That now unnethes[2] their feet could them uphold.

All as the sheep, such was the shepherd's look,
For pale and wan he was (alas the while,)
May seem he loved, or else some care he took;
Well couth[3] he tune his pipe, and frame his style.
Tho to a hill his fainting flock he led,
And thus him plained,[4] the while his sheep there fed.

Ye gods of love, that pity lovers' pain,
(If any gods the pain of lovers pity)
Look from above, where you in joys remain,
And bow your ears unto my doleful ditty.
And Pan thou shepherds God, that once didst love,
Pity the pains, that thou thy self didst prove.

Thou barren ground, whom winter's wrath hath wasted,
Art made a mirror, to behold my plight;
Whilom thy fresh spring flowered, and after hasted
Thy summer proud with daffadillies dight.[5]
And now is come thy winter's stormy state,
Thy mantle marred, wherein thou maskedst late.

Such rage as winters, reigneth in my heart,
My life blood freezing with unkindly cold:
Such stormy stoures[6] do breed my baleful smart,[7]
As if my year were waste, and waxen old.
And yet alas, but now my spring begun,
And yet alas, it is already done.

1. Pent up
2. E. K.: scarcely
3. E. K.: had the skill
4. Complained
5. Arrayed
6. Fit
7. Pain

You naked trees, whose shady leaves are lost,
Wherein the birds were wont to build their bower;
And now are cloth'd with moss and hoary frost,
Instead of blossoms, wherewith your buds did flower;
I see your tears, that from your boughs do rain,
Whose drops in dreary icicles remain.

All so my lustful leaf is dry and sere,[8]
My timely buds with wailing all are wasted:
The blossom, which my branch of youth did bear,
With breathed sighs is blown away, and blasted,
And from mine eyes the drizzling tears descend,
As on your boughs the icicles depend.

Thou feeble flock, whose fleece is rough and rent,
Whose knees are weak through fast and evil fare,
Mayst witness well by thy ill government,
Thy masters mind is overcome with care.
Thou weak, I wan; thou lean, I quite forlorn;
With mourning pine I, you with pining mourn.

A thousand sithes[9] I curse that careful hour
Wherein I long'd the neighbor town to see;
And eke ten thousand sithes I blesse the stoure,
Wherein I saw so fair a sight, as she.
Yet all for naught: [such] sight hath bred my bane.
Ah God, that love should breed both joy and pain.

It is not Hobbinol[10] wherefore I plain,
Albee my love he seek with daily suit;
His clownish gifts and curtsies[11] I disdain,
His kids, his cracknels,[12] and his early fruit.

8. E. K.: Withered

9. E. K.: times

10. E. K writes, "A fained country name, whereby, it being so commune and usual, seemeth to be hidden the person of some his very special and most familiar friend, whom he entirely and extraordinarily beloved, as peradventure shall be more largely declared hereafter. In this place seemeth to be some savor of disorderly loue, which the learned call paederastice [pederasty]: but it is gathered beside his meaning."

11. Courtesies

12. Crackers

Ah foolish Hobbinol, thy gifts been vain:
Colin them gives to Rosalind[13] again.

I love thilke lass, (alas why do I love?)
And am forlorn, (alas why am I lorn?)
She deigns not my good will, but doth reprove,
And of my rural music holdeth scorn.
Shepherd's devise she hateth as the snake,
And laughs the songs, that Colin Clout doth make.

Wherefore my pipe, albee rude Pan thou please,
Yet for thou pleasest not, where most I would;
And thou unlucky Muse, that wantst to ease
My musing mind, yet canst not, when thou should;
Both pipe and Muse, shall sore the while abye.
So broke his oaten pipe, and down did lye.

By that, the welked[14] Phoebus gan availe,[15]
His weary wain,[16] and now the frosty night
Her mantle black through heaven gan overhail.[17]
Which seen, the pensive boy half in despite
Arose, and homeward drove his sonned[18] sheep,
Whose hanging heads did seem his careful case to weep.

Gervase Markham, *The English Husbandman*, On Farming

Part 3 introduces the prolific and ubiquitous writer Gervase Markham in his discussion of horses. This excerpt lays out the broader context of Markham's approach to managing the environment as outlined in his *The English Husbandman* (1613), which he boasts contains "the knowledge of the true nature of

13. E. K. notes: "'Rosalind' is also a feigned name, which being well ordered, will bewray the very name of his love and mistress, whom by that name he coloureth."

14. Faded

15. E. K.: Bring down

16. Chariot or wagon

17. E. K.: draw over

18. Exposed to the sun

Source: *The English Husbandman: The First Part; Contayning the Knowledge of the True Nature of Every Soyle within this Kingdome; How to Plow It; And the Manner of the Plough, and Other Instruments Belonging Thereto; Together with the Art of Planting, Grafting, and Gardening After our Latest and Rarest Fashion*, sig. A1–A3; C2v–C3r, London, 1613.

every soil within this kingdom: how to plow it; and the manner of the plough, and other instruments belonging thereto." Markham represented himself as writing plainly for "the honest plain English husbandman," since he himself had experienced that life (while that claim should be regarded with some skepticism). He lays out the "utility" and "necessity" of a husbandman to serve his land in feeding the people and curbing the earth's tendency to run wild. In his epistle to his reader, Markham also insists that his book differs from other agricultural manuals insofar as he writes specifically for Englishmen, considering the conditions of their land and climate. He thus links vernacular horticulture with experience and the belief that his "kingdom" is unique; a growing political consciousness thus merges with attention to the soil's "true nature" in each of England's regions. The last excerpt on plowing and cultivating black clay soil illustrates that sense of regional specificity.

The Epistle to the General and Gentle Reader.

[. . .]

Now for the motives which first drew me to undertake the work, they were divers: as first, when I saw one man translate and paraphrase most excellently upon Virgil's *Georgics*, a work only belonging to the Italian climate, but nothing agreeable with ours another translates Libault and Stevens,[1] a work of infinite excellency, yet only proper and natural to the French, and not to us; and another takes collections from Xenophon,[2] and others: all foreigners and utterly unacquainted with our climates. When this I beheld, and saw with what good liking they were entertained of all men, and that every man was dumb to speak anything of the husbandry of our own kingdom, I could not but imagine it a work most acceptable to men, and most profitable to the kingdom, to set down the true manner and nature of our right English husbandry, our soil being as delicate, apt, and fit for increase as any foreign soil whatsoever, and as far outgoing other kingdoms in some commodity, as they us in other some.

[. . .]

The Utility of the Husbandman.

A husbandman is the master of the earth, turning sterility and barrenness, into fruitfulness and increase, whereby all commonwealths are maintained and upheld; it is his labor which giveth bread to all men and maketh us forsake the society of beasts drinking upon the water springs, feeding us with a much more nourishing liquor. The labor of the husbandman giveth liberty to all vocations,

1. A French treatise on agriculture
2. Ancient Greek philosopher who wrote a dialogue on household management

arts, mysteries and trades, to follow their several functions, with peace and industry, for the filling and emptying of his barns is the increase and prosperity of all their labors. To conclude, what can we say in this world is profitable where husbandry is wanting, it being the great nerve and sinew which holdeth together all the joints of a monarchy?

Of the Necessity of a Husbandman.

Now for the necessity, the profit inferreth it without any larger amplification: for if of all things it be most profitable, then of all things it must needs be most necessary, since next unto heavenly things, profit is the whole aim of our lives in this world; besides it is most necessary for keeping the earth in order, which else would grow wild, and like a wilderness, brambles and weeds choking up better plants, and nothing remaining but a chaos of confusedness.

[. . .]

Of all soils in this our kingdom there is none so rich and fruitful, if it be well handled and husbanded, as is that which we call the stiff, black, clay, and indeed is more blacker to look on than any other soil, yet some times it will turn up very bluish, with many white veins in it, which is a very special note to know his fruitfulness; for that bluish earth mixt with white is nothing else but very rich marl, an earth that in Cheshire, Lancashire, and many other countries, serveth to manure and make fat their barrenist land in such sort that it will bear corn seven years together. This black clay as it is the best soil, well husbanded, so it is of all soils the worst if it be ill husbanded; for if it lose but one ardor, or seasonable plowing, it will not be recovered in four years after, but will naturally of itself put forth wild oats, thistles, and all manner of offensive weeds, as cockle, darnel, and such like: his labor is strong, heavy, and sore, unto the cattle that tilleth it, but to the husbandman is more easy than any other soil, for this asketh but four times plowing over at the most, where divers other soils ask five times, and six times, as shall be showed hereafter.

Ben Jonson, "To Penshurst"

In his time, Ben Jonson (1571/2–1637) was as well known as Shakespeare. A son of a bricklayer, he became a brilliant playwright in the public theater and a poet who mixed with the best literary coteries. While his plays burst with eccentric and excessive characters, he fashioned himself as a classicist, advocating an aesthetic of "natural" plainness and order. He also aspired to royal patronage, and with Inigo Jones he composed elaborate celebratory masques

Source: *The Workes of Benjamin Jonson*, London, 1616, pp. 819–21.

performed at the courts of James I and Charles I. Along with Amelia Lanyer's "Description of Cookham" (Part 4), "To Penshurst" launched the tradition of the country house poem, paeans to landed estates meant to symbolize the owners' natural virtues, whether or not they possessed them. This one describes the estate of Robert Sidney, younger brother of the celebrated poet Sir Philip Sidney, contrasting its status as an "ancient pile" with those properties built with new money; in fact, the Sidney family had only owned this estate for some fifty years, and they had recently renovated the house in neo-Gothic style to sustain the idea of its antiquity. In contrast to the georgic poetry and husbandry manuals that describe farming labor, the poem delivers a fantasy of a classicized, golden-age natural world produced without work or violence, one that offers itself up generously to the Sidney family to be consumed. Like those plants and animals, the farmers and peasants are imagined giving of themselves and their work freely. Nature's excessive generosity implicitly corresponds to the family's hospitality to both the visiting King James and the poet; in this economy, Jonson the poet can insert himself into this house and estate as if he "reigned here," equally benefitting from that natural bounty.

Thou art not, Penshurst, built to envious show
Of touch,[1] or marble; nor canst boast a row
Of polish'd pillars, or a roof of gold.
Thou hast no lantern whereof tales are told,
Or stair, or courts; but stand'st an ancient pile,
And these grudg'd at, art reverenced the while.
Thou joy'st in better marks, of soil, of air,
Of wood, of water; therein thou art fair.
Thou hast thy walks for health, as well as sport;
Thy mount, to which thy Dryads[2] do resort,
Where Pan and Bacchus their high feasts have made,
Beneath the broad beech, and the chestnut shade;
That taller tree, which of a nut was set,
At his great birth, where all the Muses met.[3]
There, in the writhed bark, are cut the names
Of many a sylvan,[4] taken with his flames;

1. Touchstone, an expensive building material
2. Classical wood nymphs
3. Sir Philip Sidney, born at Penshurst
4. Forest dweller

And thence the ruddy satyrs oft provoke
The lighter fauns, to reach thy lady's oak.[5]
Thy copse too, named of Gamage,[6] thou hast there,
That never fails to serve thee season'd deer,
When thou wouldst feast or exercise thy friends.
The lower land, that to the river bends,
Thy sheep, thy bullocks, kine,[7] and calves do feed;
The middle grounds thy mares and horses breed.
Each bank doth yield thee conies; and the tops
Fertile of wood, Ashore and Sidney's copse,
To crown thy open table, doth provide
The purpled pheasant, with the speckled side.
The painted partridge lies in ev'ry field,
And for thy mess is willing to be kill'd.
And if the high-swoln Medway[8] fail thy dish,
Thou hast thy ponds, that pay thee tribute fish;
Fat aged carps that run into thy net,
And pikes, now weary their own kind to eat,
As loth the second draught or cast to stay,
Officiously at first themselves betray.
Bright eels that emulate them, and leap on land,
Before the fisher, or into his hand.
Then hath thy orchard fruit, thy garden flowers,
Fresh as the air, and new as are the hours.
The early cherry, with the later plum,
Fig, grape, and quince, each in his time doth come;
The blushing apricot, and woolly peach
Hang on thy walls, that every child may reach.
And though thy walls be of the country stone,
They're rear'd with no man's ruin, no man's groan;
There's none, that dwell about them, wish them down;
But all come in, the farmer and the clown;[9]
And no one empty-handed, to salute
Thy lord and lady, though they have no suit.

5. A lady of the house was said to have gone into labor under this tree.
6. Named after Barbara Gamage, wife of Sir Robert Sidney, the current lady of the house
7. Cattle
8. Local river
9. Peasant

Some bring a capon, some a rural cake,
Some nuts, some apples; some that think they make
The better cheeses, bring them; or else send
By their ripe daughters, whom they would commend
This way to husbands, and whose baskets bear
An emblem of themselves in plum, or pear.
But what can this (more than express their love)
Add to thy free provisions, far above
The need of such? whose liberal board doth flow
With all that hospitality doth know!
Where comes no guest, but is allow'd to eat,
Without his fear, and of thy lord's own meat;
Where the same beer and bread, and self-same wine,
That is his lordship's, shall be also mine.
And I not fain to sit (as some this day,
At great men's tables) and yet dine away.
Here no man tells my cups; nor standing by,
A waiter, doth my gluttony envy,
But gives me what I call, and lets me eat;
He knows, below, he shall find plenty of meat.
Thy tables hoard not up for the next day,
Nor, when I take my lodging, need I pray
For fire, or lights, or livery; all is there,
As if thou then wert mine, or I reign'd here;
There's nothing I can wish, for which I stay.
That found King James, when hunting late, this way,
With his brave son, the prince; they saw thy fires
Shine bright on every hearth, as the desires
Of thy Penates[10] had been set on flame,
To entertain them; or the country came,
With all their zeal, to warm their welcome here.
What (great, I will not say, but) sudden cheer
Didst thou then make 'em! and what praise was heap'd
On thy good lady, then! who therein reap'd
The just reward of her high huswifry,
To have her linen, plate, and all things nigh,
When she was far, and not a room, but dressed,

10. Roman household gods

As if it had expected such a guest!
These, Penshurst, are thy praise, and yet not all.
Thy lady's noble, fruitful, chaste withal.
His children thy great lord may call his own:
A fortune, in this age, but rarely known.
They are, and have been taught religion; thence
Their gentler spirits have suck'd innocence.
Each morn, and even, they are taught to pray,
With the whole household, and may, every day,
Read in their virtuous parents' noble parts,
The mysteries of manners, arms, and arts.
Now, Penshurst, they that will proportion thee
With other edifices, when they see
Those proud ambitious heaps, and nothing else,
May say, their lords have built, but thy lord dwells.

Mary Wroth, *Urania*

Mary Wroth (1587–1651) was born into the distinguished literary family of the Sidneys, but she blazed her own way into fame by writing the sonnet sequence *Pamphilia and Amphilantus* and the massive prose romance, *The Countess of Montgomery's Urania* (1621), the first published by an Englishwoman. Wroth composed her *Urania* with an eye to her uncle Philip Sidney's *Arcadia* (composed in two parts and published posthumously in 1593 by his sister Mary Sidney as *The Countess of Pembroke's Arcadia*). Sidney's romance is set in an imagined world of Arcadia, expanding far beyond the sylvan landscape and poetic complaints of Sannazaro's *Arcadia* to embrace war, rebellion, and political conflict. Nor does Wroth's *Urania* remain in Arcadia alone; rather, her romance world of love, betrayal, and politics is set in a Europe ravaged by war. However, *Urania* begins by evoking pastoral conventions, in this case, not with male shepherds speaking of their loves (as at the beginning of Sidney's *Arcadia*), but rather with the sad song of a shepherdess Urania, mourning because she has discovered that she was not born to a shepherd at all (rather, we find out later, she is the daughter of the King of Naples). Here Wroth adapts the pastoral convention of nature's responding to the singer's sorrow, but this time the singer is a woman.

Source: *The Countesse of Montgomeries Urania*, London, 1621, pp. 1–2.

When the spring began to appear like the welcome messenger of summer, one sweet (and in that more sweet) morning, after Aurora[1] had called all careful eyes to attend the day, forth came the fair shepherdess Urania, (fair indeed; yet that far too mean a title for her, who for beauty deserved the highest style could be given by best knowing judgements). Into the mead she came, where usually she drove her flocks to feed, whose leaping and wantonness showed they were proud of such a guide; but she, whose sad thoughts led her to another manner of spending her time, made her soon leave them, and follow her late begun custom, which was (while they delighted themselves) to sit under some shade, bewailing her misfortune, while they fed, to feed upon her own sorrow and tears, which at this time she began again to summon, sitting down under the shade of a well-spread beech, the ground (then blessed) and the tree with full, and fine leaved branches, growing proud to bear, and shadow such perfections. But she regarding nothing, in comparison of her woe, thus proceeded in her grief: Alas, Urania, said she, (the true servant to misfortune); of any misery that can befall woman, is not this the most and greatest which thou art fallen into? Can there be any near the unhappiness of being ignorant, and that in the highest kind, not being certain of mine own estate or birth? Why was I not still continued in the belief I was, as I appear, a shepherdess, and daughter to a shepherd? My ambition then went no higher than this state, now flies it to a knowledge; then was I contented, now perplexed. O ignorance, can thy dullness yet procure so sharp a pain? And that such a thought as makes me now aspire unto knowledge? How did I joy in this poor life being quiet? Blessed in the love of those I took for parents, but now by them I know the contrary, and by that knowledge, not to know myself. Miserable Urania, worse art thou now then these thy lambs; for they know their dams, while thou dost live unknown of any. By this were others come into that mead[2] with their flocks, but she esteeming her sorrowing thoughts her best, and choicest company, left that place, taking a little path which brought her to the further side of the plain, to the foot of the rocks, speaking as she went these lines, her eyes fixed upon the ground, her very soul turned into mourning.

Unseen, unknown, I here alone complain
To rocks, to hills, to meadows, and to springs,
Which can no help return to ease my pain,
But back my sorrows the sad echo brings.

1. Goddess of the dawn
2. Meadow

Thus still increasing are my woes to me,
Doubly resounded by that moanful voice,
Which seems to second me in misery,
And answer gives like friend of mine own choice.
Thus only she doth my companion prove,
The others silently do offer ease;
But those that grieve, a grieving note do love.
Pleasures to dying eyes bring but disease;
And such am I, who daily ending live,
Wailing a state which can no comfort give.

Robert Herrick, "The Hock-Cart, or Harvest Home"

In his early years as a poet, Robert Herrick (1591–1674) belonged to the group affiliated with Ben Jonson, writing English lyrics in the tradition of Latin poetry. He was ordained as a minister, serving both the court and a parish in Devonshire. In 1648, he published *Hesperides*, a book of poems that covers a wide range of themes, including some that are startlingly erotic for a clergyman. A staunch Royalist during the time of the English Civil War, Herrick celebrated the pleasures of life and traditional rituals that the Puritans condemned. Dedicated to the Earl of Westmoreland, "The Hock-Cart, or Harvest Home" invites Westmoreland to the annual procession of the hock-cart, where his workers observe the harvest's end with traditional prayers as well as merriment and feasting. In suggesting that the agricultural workers are "lords of wine and oil," the poem initially suggests a classical landscape, but it then turns distinctly English, conjuring up nostalgia for old English rituals of blessing the animals and the land, based on a belief in a mystical connection between humans and the natural world. However, the poem also ends by reminding the laborers that they must return to their work of "ripping up" and reaping the land to feed their lord, as he feeds them.

Come, sons of summer, by whose toil
We are the lords of wine and oil;[1]
By whose tough labors, and rough hands,
We rip up first, then reap our lands.

Source: *Hesperides, or, The works both humane & divine of Robert Herrick*, London, 1648, pp. 113–15.

1. The produce of Mediterranean farming

Crowned with the ears of corn,[2] now come,
And to the pipe sing harvest home.
Come forth, my lord, and see the cart
Dressed up with all the country art;
See here a maukin,[3] there a sheet,
As spotless pure as it is sweet,
The horses, mares, and frisking fillies,
Clad all in linen white as lilies.
The harvest swains[4] and wenches bound
For joy, to see the hock-cart crowned.
About the cart, hear how the rout
Of rural younglings raise the shout;
Pressing before, some coming after,
Those with a shout, and these with laughter.
Some bless the cart, some kiss the sheaves,
Some prank them up with oaken leaves;
Some cross the fill-horse,[5] some with great
Devotion stroke the home-borne wheat,
While other rustics, less attent[6]
To prayers than to merriment,
Run after with their breeches rent.
Well, on, brave boys, to your lord's hearth,
Glitt'ring with fire, where, for your mirth,
Ye shall see first the large and chief
Foundation of your feast, fat beef,
With upper stories, mutton, veal
And bacon (which makes full the meal),
With sev'ral dishes standing by,
As here a custard, there a pie,
And here all-tempting frumenty.[7]
And for to make the merry cheer,
If smirking[8] wine be wanting here,
There's that which drowns all care, stout beer,

2. Grain
3. A scarecrow, but also a term for a country girl
4. A young man, usually of the country
5. Horse between the shafts of the cart
6. Attentive
7. A pudding made of wheat boiled in milk
8. Sparkling

Which freely drink to your lord's health,
Then to the plough, the commonwealth,
Next to your flails, your fans,[9] your vats,
Then to the maids with wheaten hats;
To the rough sickle, and crook'd scythe,
Drink, frolic, boys, till all be blithe.
Feed, and grow fat; and as ye eat
Be mindful that the lab'ring neat,[10]
As you, may have their fill of meat.
And know, besides, ye must revoke
The patient ox unto the yoke,
And all go back unto the plough
And harrow, though they're hanged up now.
And, you must know, your lord's word's true,
Feed him ye must, whose food fills you;
And that this pleasure is like rain,
Not sent ye for to drown your pain,
But for to make it spring again.

Walter Blith, *The English Improver Improved*

A farmer himself, Walter Blith (1605–1654) rose up the social ladder through his services to the Puritan side during the English Civil War and his role as a surveyor under Oliver Cromwell. His first book on the husbandry was *The English Improver, or, A New Survey of Husbandry* (1649); that text was substantially revised as *The English Improver Improved* (1652). Blith focuses on how to better the land by water management, enclosure, proper tilling, and planting new crops like hops, saffron, licorice, rape, coleseed, hemp, and flax. Like so many other authors on farming and gardening, he links improving land with moral self-improvement in people, both individually and collectively (see for example, Columella in Part 5 and William Lawson in Part 2). In this excerpt Blith first blames ignorance, indolence, and vice in men for the failures of the land to thrive, and then turns to the causes of barrenness inherent in the land itself, sometimes suggesting analogies with the human body and behavior. After this discussion Blith classifies categories of land in terms of their monetary value, from the poorest at one shilling an acre to the richest at four pounds

9. Both instruments used for threshing
10. Cattle
Source: Walter Blith. *The English Improver Improved*, London, 1653, pp. 6–10.

an acre (compare with Samuel Gilbert, on the monetary value of flowers, in Part 2).

Chap. II. Showeth forth the causes of barrenness upon all lands.

They are usually two.

1) In man himself.
2) In the land itself.

In man himself it was occasionally, who by his sin procured a curse upon the land, even barrenness itself, which by the sweat of his brows must be reduced, if he will eat bread, and so now is. In man naturally, which is the main and capital cause of all, and is in him as I conceive the cause of causes, which is ignorance, occasioning the prejudice men bear against improvement, especially that which is not of their own devising, as all men naturally hate the true light of God, because it discovers their darkness, and is contrary to their light, which is that of nature and reason only, the great enemies of gospel light.

[. . .]

The second hindrance as in respect of the owner, or occupier thereof, is idleness, improvidence, and a slavish custom of some old form, or way of husbandry, exercised therein ever since they were born, which begets so much the ill husbandry of these days, never affecting ingenuity in any particulars of their husbandry, which is contrary to the mind and will of God in making us, and the end wherefore we were made, good husbandry commanded, and so experimented by God himself, and charged on us therein, and so commended by Solomon the wisest of men, with ingenuity and activity, to the putting out the utmost of our spirits, in subordination to our spiritual calling, in our particular callings to serve our generations, and improve our principles for the common good, which two aforesaid causes if they be not removed, will never admit of the removal of the subsequent causes.

A third particular cause in man of the earth's unfruitfulness, is want of severe punishment of idleness, the mother, and drunkenness, the daughter, or the putting in execution of such good and wholesome laws as both God and man have provided therein; as also not raising stocks in all countries, as a magazine or treasury of work, and labor, for those that want it; and those other laws for punishing of rogues and vagrants, that wander the country, and compelling and constraining youth, and idle people, to some callings, all which would both put them on to more ingenuity, and the gentry, and yeomanry of the nation would be much induced to invention, and expatiating themselves in charge and treasure, to maintain them, whereby these horrid sins of idleness, lust, and lasciviousness would be checked, and those drones, and caterpillars, the bane of a Christian state, and shame of a Christian nation, would not so swarm amongst us.

[. . .]

The second general cause of barrenness is in the earth itself, and the principal causes of her barrenness are very many; some are obvious to the judgement, and understanding of all, as tilling land till it bear no corn. And mowing ground till it graze no more, or yield no grass, all which are easily to be remedied if men would learn moderation.

But my design lies not so much in reproving, as improving, and discovering that there are many causes which lie more obscure, and are either not discerned at all, or else not adjudged any cause of barrenness, or hindrance of the earth her fertility, and so not at all endeavored to be removed; and they are in some lands: extreme coldness of nature; having a moist springing water lying near, or just under the surface or superficies of the earth, which doth either eat away or devour the sap, fruit, and strength of the said lands, or else breed and increase the rush, and flag[1], which groweth in the room of grass, and eateth away the same.

Another cause is rockiness, stoniness, and graveliness, all which many times lie so near the surface of the land, that they devour much of the earth, and so make that little left so weak, that it can scarce bring forth any fruit.

Another cause is lying mountainous, sometimes so near the sea, that the vapors and fogs, that come from thence, annoy the same. Also lying far from the sun and in shady parts occasioneth barrenness.

Another cause of barrenness is the unsuitable, unnatural laying down of land to graze, a cause scarce imagined so to be; or the present ill lying of; and, that hath lain long, and was ancient enclosure, all which are infinitely more prejudicial to the fertility thereof than can be imagined, till contrary experience hath discovered it.

[. . .]

Also another cause is the standing of the winter water upon the land, or the rain of heaven; I say not the running over lands, so that it may be laid dry at pleasure, but the standing, soaking water breeds the rush and foulness, and likewise gnaws out the heart and strength of it, like the worm at the stomach, and devoureth the strength of it, as experience will shew in many parts of the

1. Rush and flag are weeds

land, where great balks[2] betwixt lands, hades,[3] meres,[4] or divisions betwixt land and land are left, and one furlong butting, or hadlanding,[5] upon other furlongs, makes such a stoppage of the free passage of the water, that a great part of that land lieth as it were drowned a great part of the year, that it overcomes not that backing many times till near midsummer, when other sound lands have yielded a full half year's profit, and so for half a year yields little or no profit at all.

2. Ridges
3. Unplowed strips of land
4. Standing water or marshes
5. Bordering

PART VI

Gardens and Gardening

As Aristotle argued, the essence of *physis*, or nature, is change, and the natural world is ever in motion. Like husbandry, gardening strives to control such change as both a threat and a power to be harnessed. While acknowledging nature's sway and responding to place and season, gardeners rely on work (or workers) as well as on tools and techniques to aid them in their efforts. However, unlike husbandry, gardening introduces aesthetics into the familiar discourse of the pleasure and profit to be gained from cultivation. While the pastoral and georgic modes do consider pleasure, gardening offers a particular kind of delight, beyond that of shady groves or the taste of ripe fruit, that excites what Thomas Hill called "the recreation and delight of minds." In time, writing about gardening came to divide the common gardener's experience from that of the "better sort" who seek to gratify both the senses and their "curiosity."

When gardening thus entails both intellectual and sensual delight, a garden itself can be a work of art, whether a grand design for a princely estate or the more pedestrian knot garden of the "country housewife" (see Hunt 2000; Miller; Bushnell). As Mara Miller notes, gardens always sit ambiguously between "the poles of 'art' and/or the 'artificial' on the one hand and 'Nature' on the other, between art and craft, and between fine and applied art" (72). Premodern gardeners in particular aspired to create an art which, in John Dixon Hunt's words, "feigned a nature, and as Shakespeare's Touchstone puts it, 'The truest poetry is the most feigning'" (Hunt 2000, 42); while "feigning" might be defined differently over time, there was never any question that gardening was a kind of art, even for its most common practitioners. Because of this special status, not only could garden work evoke the moral virtue implied in the georgic mode but it might also suit those who did not need to work, those who as Hugh Platt writes, only "delight to see a rarity spring out of their own labors, and to provoke Nature to play" (Platt, Part 1).

Like flowers and other individual plants, gardens have functioned symbolically, to represent states of human life, politics, and society, as well as the divine order, or even the human body. The Bible's description of the Garden of Eden powerfully influenced the Western imagination of the garden as a paradise lost: "And the Lord God planted a garden eastward in Eden; and there he put the man whom he had formed. And out of the ground made the Lord God to grow every tree that is pleasant to the sight, and good for food; the tree of life also in the midst of the garden, and the tree of knowledge of good and evil. And a river went out of Eden to water the garden" where God "took the man, and put him into the garden of Eden to dress it and to keep it" (*King James Bible*, Genesis 2:8–10). Complementing the construction of paradise in Islamic gardens, this image of Eden and Paradise inspired garden writers with dreams of a nature before the fall, a time of eternal spring, the equivalent of the agricultural dream of the Golden Age, whether in the enclosed medieval gardens of the middle ages or in the new Renaissance botanical gardens designed to represent the bounty of God's creation (Carroll; Prest).

However, echoing the Garden of Eden's loss through Eve's seduction and Adam's betrayal, the enclosed pleasure garden also figured as a feminine, erotic space. Just as women themselves were associated with flowers, in the symbolic framing of gardens the fertility and pleasure associated with femininity posed both a temptation and a danger (see, for example, Spenser's Bower of Bliss in *The Fairie Queene*). While from the beginning garden writing did address the reality that women worked in and designed gardens, most literature and garden advice written by men objectified women (but see the description of the garden of Mary Somerset, Duchess of Beaufort, and Hester Pulter's "The Snail, the Tulip, and the Bee"; Munroe).

The discourse of gardening and gardens thus weaves in many of the obsessions and concerns articulated throughout this anthology in which people saw themselves reflected in every aspect of the natural world, being both creators of that world and made in its image. People sought to remake nature through gardening, but in so doing they may also have been seeking to remake themselves, insofar as gardens, the product of both art and nature, reflected the structures of the human condition.

Columella, *Res rustica,* or *On Agriculture,* On Gardens

Within his massive twelve-book treatise on agriculture, *Res rustica* (also excerpted in Part 5), Lucius Junius Columella addressed gardening, which he believed earlier writers had neglected. Book 10 begins with his version of a short history of gardening that links gardening's beginnings to differences be-

Source: Columella. *On Agriculture and Trees.* Translated by E. S. Forster and Edward H. Heffner, vol. 3, Harvard University Press, 1955, pp. 2–5, 13–15.

tween the poor and rich and their various cultures of sustenance and luxury. Then, emulating Virgil, Columella turned to hexameter poetry to address the matter of how to grow a garden. The poem itself combines practical advice based on the tasks of the gardening year (such as dunging the earth with human waste) with poetic and mythological flourishes. This passage also conjures up a vision of a Roman plant empire stretching in all directions.

So the subject which has still to be dealt with is horticulture, which the husbandman of old carried out in a half-hearted and negligent fashion but which is now quite a popular pursuit. Though, indeed, among the ancients there was a stricter parsimony, the poor had a more generous diet, since highest and lowest alike sustained life on an abundance of milk and the flesh of wild and domestic animals as though on water and corn. Very soon, when subsequent ages, and particularly our own, set up an extravagant scale of expenditure on the pleasure of the table, and meals were regarded as occasions not for satisfying men's natural desires but for the display of wealth, the poverty of the common people, forced to abstain from the more costly foods, was reduced to an ordinary fare. The cultivation, therefore, of gardens, since their produce is now in greater demand, calls for more careful instruction from us than our forefathers have handed down.

[. . .]

But when bright Zephyr[1] with his sun-warmed breeze
Thaws the Riphaean[2] winter's numbing frost,
And Orpheus' Lyre[3] deserts the starry pole
And dives into the deep, and swallows hail
Spring's advent at their nests, the gardener
Should with rich mold or asses' solid dung
Or other ordure glut the starving earth,
Bearing full baskets straining with the weight,
Nor should he hesitate to bring as food
For new-ploughed fallow-ground whatever stuff
The privy vomits from its filthy sewers.
Now let him with the hoe's well-sharpened edge
Again attack earth's surface packed with rain
And hard with frost; then with the tooth of rake

1. West wind
2. Mountain far in the north
3. A northern constellation

Or broken mattock mix the living turf
With clods of earth and all the crumbling wealth
Of the ripe field set free; then let him take
The shining hoe, worn by the soil, and trace
Straight, narrow ridges from the opposing bounds
And these across with narrow paths divide.
Now when the earth, its clear divisions marked
As with a comb, shining, from squalor free,
Shall claim her seeds, 'tis time to paint the earth
With varied flowers, like stars brought down from heaven,
White snow-drops and the yellow-shining eyes
Of marigolds and fair narcissus-blooms,
Fierce lions' gaping mouths[4] and the white cups
Of blooming lilies and the hyacinths,
Snow-white or blue. Then let the violet
Be planted, which lies pale upon the ground
Or blooms with gold and purple blossoms crowned,
Likewise the rose too full of maiden blush.
Next scatter all-heal with its saving tear,
And celandines with their health-giving juice,
And poppies which will bind elusive sleep;
Let onion's fruitful seed from Megara come,
Which sharpen men's desires and fit them for the girls,
And those which Sicca[5] gathers, hidden deep
Beneath Gaetulian[6] clods and rocket, too,
Which, sown beside Priapus rich in fruits,
May rouse up sluggish husbands to make love.
Next lowly chervil plant and succory
Welcome to jaded palates, lettuce too
With fibers soft, garlic with much-cleft heads,
Or Cyprian scented[7] strong, and all that a skilled cook
Mixes with beans to make a laborer's meal.
'Tis time for skirwort[8] and the root which, sprung

4. Possibly snapdragons
5. A town in Numidia
6. From an area near the Atlas mountains
7. A form of garlic
8. A root vegetable

From seeds Assyrian,[9] is sliced and served
With well-soaked lupines to provoke the thirst
For foaming beakers of Pelusian[10] beer.

Piero de' Crescenzi, *Liber ruralium commodorum*, or *Book of Rural Commodity*

A Bolognese lawyer, Piero de' Crescenzi (ca. 1235–ca. 1320) (whose name has been spelled differently in various languages) is remembered now for his Latin treatise on gardening and agriculture entitled *Liber ruralium commodorum*, or "a book of rural benefits or commodity." After Charles V of France commissioned its translation into French in 1371 while using it to design his own princely gardens, the text appeared in multiple European languages up through the fifteenth century. Its twelve books cover a wide variety of subjects concerning agriculture, borrowing from ancient writers like Columella, Cato, and Varro, as well as later writers and Crescenzi's own experience. Book 8 focuses on the cultivation of pleasure gardens, sorting them out as to what would suit different ranks and needs (Figure 22). In each case pleasure is related to health, reflecting current ideas of the interaction between the environment and the human body (for example, see *Secreta secretorum* in Part 4, *The Secrets of Albertus Magnus* in Part 1, and *Rams Little Dodoen* in Part 4). While the modest gardens are more practically designed, the princely garden includes enclosures for animals and birds as well as bowers within the garden walls, representing a kind of miniature paradise of living things.

Preface

1. In the previous books, trees and herbaceous plants were discussed according to how they can be useful to the human body; but now the same ones must be discussed according to how they give pleasure to a rational soul and consequently preserve the health of the body, since the humoric state of the body is always closely related to the disposition of the soul.

9. Radish
10. Pelusium was an Egyptian port

Source: Johanna Bauman. "Tradition and Transformation: The Pleasure Garden in Piero de' Crescenzi's *Le Livre des Prouffitz champestres et ruraulx*." *Studies in the History of Gardens & Designed Landscapes* vol. 22, no. 2, 2002, pp. 99–141.

Figure 22. Planting the medieval enclosed flower and herb garden, from *Le Livre de Rustican des prouffiz ruraulx, compile par Maistre Pierre Croissens, Bourgoiz de Boulongne, or The treatise of Piero de' Crescenzi, "de agricultura, sive de commodis ruralibus,"* translated into French, late fifteenth century. Shelfmark Add. 19720, f.165. Credit: The British Library Board.

On small gardens of herbs

1. Certain gardens may be made only of plants, others of trees and yet others of both. When consisting only of plants they require fine and compact soil, so that they may yield fine and delicate plants that greatly please the sight. Therefore, the place which is prepared for such a garden should first be freed of weeds, which is difficult to do, unless first, after the space has been cleared of roots, it is well leveled and then the space is thoroughly soaked with scalding water, so that the remaining roots and seeds lying hidden in the ground will be altogether incapable of sprouting. And then the whole plot should be filled with a fine turf of thin grass,

and the turfs themselves completely compressed with wooden mallets and the blades of grass trodden underfoot, until hardly any of them are visible. Then it [the grass] will burst forth gradually like hair and cover the surface like a green cloth.

2. The site of the garden should be of such a measure as may suit those plants that are expected to exist in it. Along the edge of the garden should be planted fragrant herbs of all kinds, such as rue, sage, basil, marjoram, mint, and the like, and also flowers of every type, such as violet, lily, rose, gladiola, and the like. Between these plants and the level turf raise and form [another] turf in the fashion of a seat, flowering and pleasant. Plant trees or train vines on the turf against the heat of the sun; the turf will have a pleasant and cool shade from their leaves, in the manner of an overhang. Shade more than fruit is sought from those trees, and therefore they should not be dug or manured, activities that might harm the turf.

3. But care must be taken that the trees are not exceedingly thick or too many in number, which, by removing air, damage health; and this is because a garden needs free air and excessive shade breeds impurities. Furthermore, the trees should not be noxious, such as nut trees and some others, but sweet, fragrant in flower and pleasant in shade, such as vines, pears, apples, pomegranates, laurels, cypresses, and the like. Behind the turf there should be a great number and variety of medicinal and aromatic herbs, since they not only delight by their odor, but their flowers also refresh the sense of sight by their variety. Disperse rue among them in many places, because of its beautiful green color and because its bitterness drives poisonous animals from the garden.

4. There should be no trees in the middle of the turf, but this level place should rather enjoy free and pure air, since that air is healthier, and also since spiders' webs stretched from one branch to another would block the way and contaminate the faces of those passing through, as would be the case if the garden or the turf had trees planted in the middle of it. And, if possible, a very pure spring should be diverted into the middle of the garden, because its purity produces much pleasantness. The garden should be open to the north and the east because of the health and purity of these winds. It should be closed in the direction of the opposing winds, namely the south and west, on account of their violence, impurity, and unhealthy quality. Although the northeast wind may hinder fruit, it marvelously preserves the spirits and ensures health. For delight and not fruit is sought in the garden.

On large and moderate gardens of persons of moderate means

1. Let the space of the earth set aside for the garden be measured according to the means and rank of persons of moderate means, namely, two or three or four or more *iugera* or *bubulcae*. The space should be surrounded with ditches

and hedges of thorns and roses, and moreover, in warm places a hedge of pomegranates should be made and in cold places of nuts or plums and quinces. Again, plough the space and make it flat on all sides with a rake or with hoes; afterwards, mark out the entire space where trees are to be planted with a cord. Plant lines of pears and apples in it, and, in warm places, lines of palms and lemons. Or plant lines of mulberries, cherries, plums, and lines of such noble trees as figs, nuts, almonds, quinces, and pomegranates, each one clearly in its own line or row according to type.

2. The lines or rows should be spaced twenty feet apart, more or less, or forty feet or more, according to the will of the master. The large trees should be spaced in a line twenty feet from the other and the small trees should be spaced ten feet from each other. Noble vines of different types that provide delight and utility may be planted between the trees. Hoe the lines of trees so that the trees and vines grow stronger, and treat the intervals as meadows and weed them often. Mow the meadows of the garden twice a year, so that they may remain beautiful. Trees should be planted and shaped, as was stated above in Book V, in rows of each kind. Again, pergolas formed in the manner of a house or a tent should be made in the most suitable part [of the garden].

On gardens of kings and other illustrious and wealthy lords

Because such persons by reason of their riches and power are able to satisfy their own will in all earthly things and almost nothing is wanted by them, except the labor of setting workers to task, they should know they are able to make gardens having many delights in this manner. They should, therefore, choose a flat place, not marshy or screened from the flow of good winds, in which there is a spring flowing through the place. And the spot should be twenty *iugera* or more, according to the will of the master. Suitably high walls should surround it, and in the northern part it should be planted with a grove of various trees, in which wild creatures placed in the garden may flee and hide.

In the southern part there should be built a handsome palace, in which the king or queen may linger when they wish to escape from heavy thoughts and to renew the spirit by means of joy and solaces. For from this area it [the palace] will create shade for the garden in the hot season and its windows facing onto the temperate garden will enjoy a view unhindered by the heat of the sun. An enclosure for animals, which is discussed above, should be made in another part of the garden; in this vivarium should be made a fish pond in which various types of fish are raised; and hares, stags, roebucks, rabbits and similar non-predatory beasts should be put in it.

And above certain bushes placed near the palace, a kind of house should be made that has a roof and walls densely woven from thick boughs, in which are placed pheasants, partridges, nightingales, blackbirds, goldfinches, linnets, and all other kinds of singing birds. In the garden there should be rows of trees spaced far apart from the palace to the distant grove, so that the animals placed in the garden may be seen easily from the palace.

In this garden there should also be a palace with walks and powers made from nothing but the trunks of trees, in which the king and queen can meet with the barons and lords when it is not the rainy season. And a palace of this type can be made easily in such a manner: the whole space of the walks and bowers should be measured out and demarcated and, if it pleases, fruit trees that grow easily, such as cherries and apples, should be planted in the place of walls; or what is better, willows or elms or birch trees should be planted there, and their growth should be controlled for several years, both by grafting and by stakes, poles, and ties, so that walls and a roof might be formed from them.

The aforesaid palace or house may be made more quickly and easily of wood, and vines may be planted around it on all side and cover the entire structure. Large shelters of dead wood or living trees covered with vine can be made in the garden itself. Furthermore, much pleasure will be provided if marvelous and various grafts are made on the same trees in the garden, which the attentive cultivator of the garden is able to know easily from what is said extensively in the second book.

Guillaume de Lorris and Jean de Meun, *Le roman de la rose*, or *The Romance of the Rose*

The long allegorical poem *Le roman de la rose* (*The Romance of the Rose*) influenced generations of European poets writing of love, desire, courtly behavior, and morality. Guillaume de Lorris (ca. 1200–ca. 1240) composed the first 4,000 lines sometime between 1225 and 1230, and later, between 1269–1278, Jean de Meun (ca. 1240–1305) continued the poem with some additional 17,700 lines. The text was extraordinarily popular in its time; it was translated and circulated across Europe in hundreds of manuscripts extant today, as well as in print up through the seventeenth century. The poem's central symbol is a rose representing the woman who is the object of the narrator-lover's desire. With many moral and philosophical digressions, the poem follows the lover's pursuit to possess that rose, with clear erotic implications; in so doing the poem both describes and critiques the art of courtly love and the nature of desire. The lover

Source: Guillaume de Lorris and Jean de Meun. *The Romance of the* Rose. Translated by Frances Horgan, Oxford University Press, 1994, pp. 21–22.

Figure 23. Experiencing the enclosed pleasure garden with a fountain and fruit trees, from a manuscript illustration of *Le roman de la rose* (1490–1500). Harley 4425, f.12v. Credit: The British Library Board.

finds the rose by first entering an enclosed garden, led through the wicket by a personification of Idleness. Ruled by the figure of Pleasure, the garden is inhabited by lords and ladies disporting themselves (Figure 23). There the narrator meets the god of Love, who eventually wounds him when he glimpses the image of the rosebud in a crystal mirror in water. The garden, which includes features of the gardens described by Piero de'Crescenzi, such as trees, flowers, waterworks, and grassy spaces, as well as animals and birds, is also touched with sensuality and is thus morally ambiguous. (Compare with the garden in Edmund Spenser's Bower of Bliss in *The Faerie Queene.*)

The garden had been laid out in a perfect square, being as long as it was wide. Except for a few hideous ones, there was no fruit-bearing tree of which there were not two or three or more in the garden. I well remember that there were trees bearing pomegranates, excellent fruit for the sick, and abundant nut-trees, which, at the proper season, bore fruit such as nutmeg, which is neither bitter or bland. Many almond trees had been planted in the garden, and he who had need of them could find many fig-trees and good date-palms. There were many spices in the garden, cloves and licorice, fresh cardamom, zedoary, anise, and cinnamon, and many delicious spices good to eat after a meal.

[The passage continues with an elaborate catalog of the trees of the garden.]

There were fallow deer and roe-deer in the garden and a great number of squirrels climbing among the trees. There were rabbits, continually coming out of their burrows and engaged in more than forty different games on the fresh green grass. Here and there were bright springs, free from insects and frogs and shaded by the trees, but I cannot say how many. Little streams ran in channels constructed by Pleasure, and the water made a sweet and pleasant sound. Around the stream and the banks of the bright and lively springs the fresh grass grew thickly, so that one could have lain with one's mistress as if on a feather bed, for the earth was soft and cool, and because of the springs, the grass was as abundant as could be. But the beauty of all was greatly enhanced by the place itself, which was of a kind that the flowers were always plentiful, both in winter and in summer: there were beautiful violets, blooming, fresh and new; there were white flowers and red, and yellow one, in great profusion. That ground was extremely pretty, for it was decorated, and as it were, painted with sweet-smelling flowers of various colors.

Nicolas Bollard, *On Planting and Grafting*

In the middle ages, all monasteries housed gardens to sustain their communities. An English manuscript (ca. 1350–1400) attributed to a Benedictine monk, Nicolas Bollard (possibly from Flanders), records practical advice for "a man to know which times of the year is the best to graft or to plant trees and to make a tree bear [all] manner of fruit," apparently reflecting that monk's practical ex-

Source: W. L. Braekman. "Bollard's Middle English Book of Planting and Grafting and Its Background." *Studia Neophilogica* vol. 57, 1985, pp. 19–39.

perience as well as his knowledge of classical sources. As typical of the time, Bollard was particularly concerned with tying gardening practice to the influence of the zodiac and the phases of the moon, a concern that persisted for centuries. At the same time, he shows sensitivity to differences in climate and types of ground, based on local knowledge. In this excerpt he, like many other writers, also offers directions on how one may achieve horticultural marvels through artful grafting, which requires knowledge, technical skill, and specific tools (Figure 24). By the time of Bollard's writing, English gardening practice was thus already a sophisticated affair. (For later thoughts on grafting, see Giambattista della Porta in Part 1, Gervase Markham in Part 6, Shakespeare's *The Winter's Tale*, John Parkinson in Part 6, and Andrew Marvell.)

This chapter asketh the places of the moon and his age, but for there be but few that know the place of the moon in the zodiac. Therefore us behooveth to pass forth the other things more common. Therefore know thou that are an expert, that when the moon is in Taurus, it is good time to plant trees of greynes [?] and pepins.[1] When it is Cancer or Leo or in Libra, it is good to work on trees that be new sprung. When the moon is in Virgo, it is good time to sow all manner of things. To borel[2] folk I say that from the middle of September unto the middle of December is open time of planting, and right so from the middle of January to the middle of March. But it is good in these times to choose when the moon is of 5 or 6 or 7 or 8 or 9 days old before the full moon. And after the full, when it is 21or 22 or 23 or 24 or 25 days old, for in these quarters the conjunction is most temperate.

Of disposition of the place and arraying of the earth.

In every planting it is to dispose it so that the sun beams may come to the root or to the earth from the hour of terce[3] unto noon. And then be they planted in the best manner, and that the trees that be bearing and of great height, that party that stood toward the north be set again the north wind and the north west wind. But the high north wind and the west wind have kind to kill and dry too much trees that be new set for their unmeasurable greatness.

The earth must be ordained so that it be neither too fat nor too gravely and that proportionally. For if thou wilt bring forth trees declining, whether it be more to heat or to coldness, to moistness or to dryness, thou must consider the region and the air in the best wise thou might and adapt the place after the air

1. A kind of apple
2. Unlearned
3. The third canonical hour, i.e., 9:00 a.m.

Figure 24. Tools for grafting, from *Le vinti giornate dell'agricoltura et de'piaceri della villa di M. Agostino Gallo* (from the sixteenth century; printed Venice, 1629). S515 .G35 1629. Kislak Center for Special Collections, Rare Books, and Manuscripts, University of Pennsylvania Libraries.

thereabout and after that the kind of the tree is. And ordain to every thing it that accordeth thereto for the disposition of the air is in every manner after the diverse affluence of the higher body in every parts of the climates. For it were but idle to sit olive trees in Flanders, since they may neither bring forth the tree, bearing nor not bearing.

[. . .]

Of marvelous grafting.

To have fruits without cores, look thou have a sufficient plant and stock and do therewith as is said before. Chose a graft of a good merle [?] tree, and cut it on this manner that the end of the graft that was upward next the firmament, must be whittled like the nether end of a common graft and the nether end turned upward. It is to do slyly, as it is said before in the first chapter. This rule is true in all trees that have stones and kernels. But a vine it behooveth to cut that is downward next the earth with great cunning and sleight.

That one tree may bear divers fruits of
divers color and divers savor.

In the first year graft in divers branches of a cherry tree divers apples to thy liking, and leave some of the branches ungrafted. The second year make holes through the cherry tree, and draw through one hole a vine branch, the outer rind shaven away, as it is before said. And in the same manner through another hole a red rose branch, and through another hole a white rose branch. And do as is said before in the chapter that goeth next before. And this diversity thou may do thine own liking and therefore I betake it to thy discretion.

Thomas Hill, *The Gardener's Labyrinth*

Thomas Hill (ca. 1529–ca. 1574) was a prolific writer on topics ranging from astrology and physiognomy to cooking. He is often credited with compiling the first popular English gardening book, "a most brief and pleasant treatise, teaching how to dress, sow, and set a garden." It was followed by the bestselling *Profitable Art of Gardening* (1568), and then by his most extensive version, *The Gardener's Labyrinth* (1577), published under the name Didymus Mountain, which was reprinted up through the mid-seventeenth century. Throughout, Hill expresses his conviction that gardening produces both profit and pleasure,

Source: *The Gardeners Labyrinth Containing a Discourse of the Gardeners Life, in the Yearly Travels to be Bestowed on His Plot of Earth, for the Use of a Garden* [. . .] *by Didymus Mountaine*, London, 1577, pp. 48–49, 75–76.

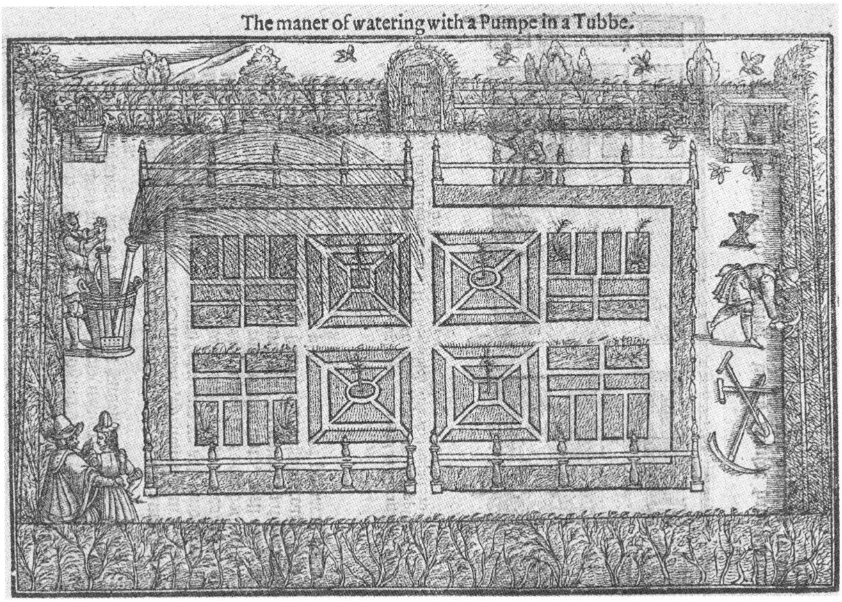

Figure 25. An early modern English enclosed garden, with a formal design, railings, and a beehive, being watered with a clever pump system. From Thomas Hill (Dydimus Mountain), *The Gardener's Labyrinth* (1586), p. 54. Call # STC 13487. Used by permission of the Folger Shakespeare Library.

a theme repeated in many of the gardening books of the era (see, for example, William Lawson in Parts 2 and 6). Divided into two parts, the first on general gardening practice and the second on cultivating specific plants and their uses, the text combines what Hill cites as many years of experience in the garden with comments gathered from classical writers, including Pliny the Elder and Columella. The advice integrates specific practical recommendations, as suggested in the first excerpt on methods of watering (Figure 25), with concepts derived from astrology and sympathetic or natural magic: for example, the second excerpt's thoughts about animal parts protecting a garden from hail and storms (compare with Pliny on animals in Part 3).

[Watering gardens]

The beds being furnished with seeds in due age of the moon, requireth diligence (if the air sufficiently moisteneth not) in the watering of them, least the ground being very dry of the proper nature, may through the drith[1] for the

1. Drought

lack of rain, cause both the seeds and tender plants shoot up, to perished and dry. For which cause, every gardener ought carefully to consider the condition and property of the earth of his garden, whether of it self the same be very moist, or over dry, which two extremes learned, he may with the more diligence, bestow pains about the watering of the garden beds, so often as need shall require.

[. . .]

And this watering of the beds ought rather be done (as Pliny witnesseth) in the morning, soon after the sun rising) and at the evening when the sun possesseth a weak force above the earth. The reason this author allegeth of the same, is that by watering at the hot time of the day as at noon, the water then made hot by heat of the sun, would so burn the young and tender roots of the plants. And in this watering of the beds, the gardener must have a special care and regard, that he moisten not the plants too much, least cloying them too much with water, they after wax feeble and perish.

[. . .]

The age also of the plants, shall greatly direct the gardener to know how much and how small he ought to moisten them at each time needful, for the tender young plants new come up, require a lesser watering, and the same gently, where the herbs more growen, will joy to be plentifully moistened with the water temperate warm. And this water ought gently to be sprinkled forth on the beds, with a watering pot, and by other means, which after shall be demonstrated, that the roots of the young herbs may alike drink in of the water, and not to be cloyed, through over fast, or too much moisture sprinkled on them, by which doing, these they rather retain the spirit vanquishing, procured to pass through the exhalation of the earth. For which cause, the beds at one instant shall not fully be watered, but as the earth and plants drink in, so gently sprinkle forth the water, in feeding the plants with this moisture, as by a breast or nourishing pap, which like handled, shall greatly prosper the tender plants coming up, where they otherwise by the hasty drowning with water, are much annoyed, and put in a hazard of perishing.

[. . .]

The skillful practices and remedies, against hail, lightnings and tempests, beating down, and spoiling the kitchen herbs, trees, and fruits.

For the hail, which for the more part destroyeth both the labors of the oxen and men, conceive these few remedies following. That if the husbandman, would avoid the same danger at hand or ready to fall, then let him draw about the ground (whether it be field, orchard or garden) the skin of a seal, or crocodile, or hyena, and hang it after at the entry or coming in of the place, as the worthy Philostratus,[2] in his Greek commentaries of husbandry, hath noted. Others there be, which seeing the hail at hand, by holding up a mighty glass, do so take the image of the dark cloud, directly over the place, to the end, the object by the same remedy (as Rutilius reporteth) may offend, whereby as doubled, it may give place to the other, and on such wise be speedily averted and moved away.

[. . .]

To utter here the popular help against thunder, lightnings, and the dangerous hail, when the tempest approacheth through the cloud arising, as by the loud noise of guns shot here and there, with the loud sound of bells, and such like noises which may happen: I think the same not necessary, nor properly available to the benefit of the garden.

The famous learned man Archibius which wrote unto Antiochus king of Syria, affirmeth, that tempests shall not be harmful to plants nor fruits, if the speckled toad enclosed in a new earthen pot, be buried in the middle of the garden or field.[3] Others there are, which hang the feathers of the eagle, or seal's skin, in the middle of the garden or at the four corners of the same.

Robert Laneham, Description of the Garden at Kenilworth

In the summer of 1575, when Queen Elizabeth I visited the estate of Robert Dudley, Earl of Leicester, at Kenilworth, he staged a series of magnificent pageants and furnished a garden of pleasure, in a failed effort to woo Elizabeth and promote his own power. A letter attributed to Robert Laneham (or Langham), a minor official and keeper of Elizabeth's privy chamber, details how the garden appeared at that time. In the style of the Italian garden, the architectural elements that were designed to assert Leicester's status and claims to authority dominated the plants; they included obelisks, an elaborate aviary, and a central fountain with statuary of two Atlas-like figures and carvings of scenes from Ovid's *Metamorphoses* (as well as a trick spigot to spray water on the unsuspecting visitor). At the same time, the garden was still populated by living things, familiar and strange: exotic birds in the aviary, fish in the fountain basin, fruit

2. He may mean Philo of Judea, who wrote a treatise on husbandry.

3. A story from Pliny

Source: John Nichols. *The Progresses and Public Processions of Queen Elizabeth I: A New Edition of the Early Modern Sources*, vol. 1, London, 1823, pp. 472–77. *Google Books*, https://play.google.com/books/reader?id=h2gNAAAAIAAJ&hl=en&pg=GBS.PA477.

trees, and unidentified sweet-smelling flowers. Aspects of Laneham's description have been substantiated by recent archaeological research, and the garden has been recreated with as much attention to those details as possible.

Unto this, his honor's exquisite appointment of a beautiful garden. [An] acre or more of quantity that lieth on the north there, wherein hard all along the castle wall is reared a pleasant terrace of a ten foot high and a twelve broad. Even underfoot and fresh of fine grass, as is also the side thereof toward the garden, in which by sundry equal distances with obelisks, spheres, and white bears[1] all of stone upon their curious bases, by goodly show were set; to these, two fine arbors redolent by sweet trees and flowers, at each end one. The garden plot under that, with fair alleys green by grass, even voided from the borders at both sides, and some (for change) with sand, not light or too soft, or solely by dust, but smooth and firm, pleasant to walk on, as a sea shore when the water is availed, then, much gracified by due proportion of four even quarters. In the midst of each, upon a base a too foot square and high, seemly bordered of itself, a square pilaster rising pyramidally of a fifteen foot high, symmetrically pierced through from a foot beneath, until a two foot of the top; whereupon, for a capitol an orb of a ten inches thick, every of these (with his base) from the ground to the top of one whole piece, hewn out of hard porphyry, and with great art and heed (thinks me) thither conveyed and there erected. Where further also by great cast and cost the sweetness of savor on all sides, made so respiring from the redolent plants and fragrant herbs and flowers, in form, color and quantity so deliciously variant, and fruit trees bedecked with their apples, pears and ripe cherries.

[What follows here is the description of an elaborate aviary, decorated with jewels and inhabited by "lively birds, English, French, Spanish, Canarian, and . . . African."]

In the center (as it were) of this goodly garden, was there placed, a very fair fountain, cast into an eight square, reared a four foot high, from the midst whereof a column up set in shape of two Athlants[2] joined together a back half, the one looking east, the other west, with their hands, upholding a fair formed ball of a three foot over, from whence sundry fine pipes, did lively distill continual streams into the receipt of the fountain, maintained still two foot deep by the same fresh falling water, wherein pleasantly playing to and fro and round about carp, tench, bream, and for variety, perch and eel, fish fair-liking all and large. In the top, the ragged staff[3] which, with the ball, the pillar, and

1. Heraldic symbol associated with Leicester
2. Atlas-like figures
3. Another heraldic symbol for Leicester

eight sides beneath, were all hewn out of rich and hard white marble. A one side, Neptune with his tridental fuskin[4] triumphing in his throne, trailed into the deep by his marine horses. On another, Thetis in her chariot drawn by her dolphins. Then Triton by his fishes. Here Proteus herding his sea bulls. There Doris and her daughters solacing a sea and sands. The waves surging with froth and foam, intermingled in place, with whales, whirlpools, sturgeons, tunas, conchs and whelks, all engraven by exquisite device and skill, so as I may think this not much inferior unto Phoebus' gates, which (Ovid says) and peradventure a pattern to this that Vulcan himself did cut, whereof such was the excellency of art, that the work in value surmounted the stuff, and yet were the gates all of clean massy silver.

Here were things ye see, might enflame any mind too long after looking; but who so was found so hot in desire, with the wrest of a cock was sure of a cooler, water spurting upward with such vehemence, as they should by and by be moistened from top to toe.

Edmund Spenser, *The Faerie Queene*

Edmund Spenser (1552–1599) wrote his allegorical epic *The Faerie Queene* after writing his pastoral *The Shephearde's Calendar* (Part 5). *The Faerie Queene* (1590 and 1596) follows the adventures of five heroes representing Temperance, Chastity, Friendship, Justice, and Courtesy in a magical land of monsters and mysterious places, all of which bear a complex symbolic meaning. Book 2 tells the story of Guyon, the knight who represents temperance, or self-control, aided by reason. Throughout his adventures Guyon faces temptations including sexual pleasure, which is allegorized in the Bower of Bliss, a garden inhabited by the female figure of Acrasia (whose name means both excess and disorder). This garden evokes the common association of gardens and flowers with female sexuality (compare Pierre Ronsard's "Ode to Cassandra" in Part 2 and *Le roman de la rose* in Part 6). At the same time, its fences, gates, portraits, fountains, and statuary suggest the Italianate garden style of the time (compare with Robert Laneham's description of the garden at Kenilworth, above). Spenser's representation of the Bower of Bliss also plays out the contemporary ambivalence in valuing both art and nature, the pleasure in artifice contesting with the purity of nature, unforced and unadorned, where nature and art strive to outdo each other.

4. Three pronged spear

Source: Edmund Spenser. *The Faerie Queene Disposed into Twelve Books*, London, 1590, book 2, canto 12, stanzas 42–63.

Here much of Spenser's original spelling is maintained.

Thence passing forth, they shortly do arrive,
Whereas the Bowre of Blisse was situate;
A place pickt out by choice of best alive,
That nature's worke by art can imitate,
In which whatever in this worldly state
Is sweet, and pleasing unto living sense,
Or that may daintiest fantasy aggrate,[1]
Was poured forth with plentifull dispence,
And made there to abound with lavish affluence.

Goodly it was enclosed round about,
As well their entred guestes to keepe within,
As those unruly beasts to hold without;
Yet was the fence thereof but weake and thin;
Nought feard their force, that fortilage[2] to win,
But wisdomes power, and temperaunces might,
By which the mightiest things efforced bin;
And eke the gate was wrought of substaunce light,
Rather for pleasure, then for battery or fight.
[. . .]
Thus being entred, they behold around
A large and spacious plaine, on every side
Strowed with pleasauns,[3] whose faire grassy ground
Mantled with greene, and goodly beautifide
With all the ornaments of Floraes pride,
Wherewith her mother art, as halfe in scorne
Of niggard Nature, like a pompous bride
Did decke her, and too lavishly adorne,
When forth from virgin bowre she comes in th'early morne.

Thereto the Heavens alwayes joviall,
Lookt on them lovely, still in steadfast state,
Ne suffred storme nor frost on them to fall,
Their tender buds or leaves to violate,

1. Gratify
2. Fortress
3. Pleasure grounds

Nor scorching heat, nor cold intemperate
T'afflict the creatures, which therein did dwell,
But the milde air with season moderate
Gently attempred, and disposd so well,
That still it breathed forth sweet spirit and wholesome smell.

More sweet and wholesome, then the pleasaunt hill
Of Rhodope, on which the nymphe, that bore
A giant babe, her selfe for griefe did kill;[4]
Or the Thessalian Tempe, where of yore
Faire Daphne Phoebus hart with love did gore;[5]
Or Ida,[6] where the Gods lov'd to repaire,
When ever they their heavenly bowres forlore;
Or sweet Parnasse, the haunt of Muses faire;
Or Eden selfe, if ought with Eden mote compare.

Much wondred Guyon at the faire aspect
Of that sweet place, yet suffred no delight
To sincke into his sense, nor mind affect,
But passed forth, and lookt still forward right,
Bridling his will, and maistering his might;
Till that he came unto another gate,
No gate, but like one, being goodly dight[7]
With boughes and braunches, which did broad dilate
Their clasping armes, in wanton wreathings intricate.

So fashioned a porch with rare device,
Archt over head with an embracing vine,
Whose bunches hanging downe, seemed to entice
All passers by, to taste their luscious wine,
And did themselves into their hands incline,
As freely offering to be gathered:
Some deepe empurpled as the hyacint,[8]

4. The nymph Rhodope bore a giant child to Neptune; in mythology, Rhodope was also an arrogant queen who was turned into a mountain by Zeus.

5. A valley in Thessaly, Greece, where Apollo was struck with love for Daphne (She fled him and was transformed into a laurel tree.)

6. Where Ganymede was raped and Paris gave the apple of discord to Aphrodite

7. Adorned

8. A precious blue stone, but also an allusion to the plant

Some as the rubine,[9] laughing sweetly red,
Some like faire emeraudes, not yet well ripened.

And them amongst, some were of burnisht gold,
So made by art, to beautifie the rest,
Which did themselves amongst the leaves enfold,
As lurking from the view of covetous guest,
That the weake bowes, with so rich load opprest,
Did bow adowne, as over-burdened.
Under that porch a comely dame did rest,
Clad in faire weedes,[10] but foule disordered,
And garments loose, that seemd unmeet[11] for womanhead.

[. . .]

There the most daintie paradise on ground,
It selfe doth offer to his sober eye,
In which all pleasures plenteously abound,
And none does others happinesse envie;
The painted flowres, the trees upshooting hye,
The dales for shade, the hilles for breathing space,
The trembling groves, the christall running by;
And that, which all faire workes doth most aggrace,[12]
The art, which all that wrought, appeared in no place.

One would have thought, (so cunningly, the rude,
And scorned parts were mingled with the fine,)
That nature had for wantonesse ensude[13]
Art, and that art at nature did repine;[14]
So striving each th'other to undermine,
Each did the others worke more beautifie;
So diff'ring both in willes, agreed in fine:
So all agreed through sweete diversitie,
This garden to adorne with all varietie.

9. Ruby
10. Clothing
11. Unsuitable
12. Favor
13. Imitated
14. Complain

And in the midst of all, a fountaine stood,
Of richest substaunce, that on earth might bee,
So pure and shiny, that the silver flood
Through every channell running one might see;
Most goodly it with curious imageree
Was over-wrought, and shapes of naked boyes,
Of which some seemd with lively jollitee,
To fly about, playing their wanton toyes,[15]
Whilest others did them selves embay in liquid joyes.

And over all, of purest gold was spred,
A traile of ivie in his native hew:
For the rich mettall was so coloured,
That wight,[16] who did not well avis'd it view,
Would surely deeme it to be ivie trew:
Low his lascivious armes adown did creepe,
That themselves dipping in the silver dew,
Their fleecy flowres they tenderly did steepe,
Which drops of christall seemd for wantones to weepe.

Infinite streames continually did well
Out of this fountaine, sweet and faire to see,
The which into an ample laver[17] fell,
And shortly grew to so great quantitie,
That like a little lake it seemd to bee;
Whose depth exceeded not three cubits hight,
That through the waves one might the bottom see,
All pav'd beneath with jasper shining bright,
That seemd the fountaine in that sea did saile upright

And all the margent round about was set,
With shady laurell trees, thence to defend[18]
The sunny beames, which on the billowes bet,
And those which therein bathed, mote offend.
As Guyon hapned by the same to wend,

15. Games
16. Person
17. Basin
18. Ward off

Two naked damzelles he therein espyde,
Which therein bathing, seemed to contend,
And wrestle wantonly, ne car'd to hyde,
Their dainty parts from view of any, which them eyde.

Gervase Markham, *The English Husbandman*, On Grafting

Parts 3 and 5 introduce Gervase Markham as an expert on horses and farming, but he was also interested in horticulture. Like many other gardening experts, Markham was fascinated by the curious use of grafting, and in *The English Husbandman* (1613) he speculates about what wonders one might produce with grafting and other elaborate methods to alter nature, harking back to an earlier tradition represented in this anthology by Nicolas Bollard and Giambattista della Porta (Figure 26). He does retreat at the end to suggest that these techniques may not be entirely "wise." Such reservations are expressed more strongly in Shakespeare's *The Winter's Tale* and in Andrew Marvell's "The Mower Against Gardens." See also John Parkinson's reaction against boasts of changing the nature of a plant through such methods.

Now when you have made yourself perfect in the sowing, setting, planting and grafting of trees, you shall then learn to know the effects, wonders, and strange issues which do proceed from many quaint motions and helps in grafting, as thus: if you will have peaches, cherries, apples, quinces, medlars,[1] damsons,[2] or any plum whatsoever, to ripen early, as at the least two months before the ordinary time, and to continue at least a month longer than the accustomed course, you shall then graft them upon a mulberry stock; and if you will have the fruit to taste like spice, with a certain delicate perfume, you shall boil honey, the powder of cloves and soaxe [?] together, and being cold anoint the grafts therewith before you put them into the cleft; if you graft apples, pears, or any fruit upon a fig-tree stock, they will bear fruit without blooming. If you take an apple graft, and a pear graft, of like bigness, and having cloven them, join them as one body in grafting, the fruit they bring forth will be half apple and half pear, and so likewise of all other fruits which are of contrary tastes and natures; if you graft any fruit-tree, or other tree, upon the holly or upon the cypress, they will be green, and keep their leaves the whole year, albeit the winter be never so

Source: *The English Husbandman*, London, 1613, part 2, pp. 57–59.

1. A fruit like a small brown apple
2. A small dark plum

Figure 26. Figure of an "H" for a graft in a tree, suggesting the imprint of culture on nature. Gervase Markham, *The English Husbandman* (1613), p. 55. Call # STC 17355. Used by permission of the Folger Shakespeare Library.

bitter. If you graft either peach, plum, or any stone-fruit upon a willow stock, the fruit which cometh of them will be without stones.

If you will change the color of any fruit, you shall bore a hole slope-wise with a large auger into the body of the tree, even unto the pith, and then if you will have the fruit yellow you shall fill the hole with saffron dissolved in water: if you will have it red, then with saunders,[3] and of any other color you please, and then stop the hole up close, and cover it with red or yellow wax; also if you

3. The plant alexander, sometimes known as horse parsley

mix the color with any spice or perfume, the fruit will take a relish or taste of the same. Many other such like conceits and experiments are practiced amongst men of this art, but since they more concern the curious, then the wise, I am not so careful to bestow my labor in giving more substantial satisfaction, knowing curiosity loves that best which proceeds from their most pain,[4] and am content to refer their knowledge to the searching of those books which have only strangeness for their subject, resolved that this I have written is fully sufficient for the plain English husbandman.

William Shakespeare, *The Winter's Tale*

William Shakespeare's late romance *The Winter's Tale* (1610–11) represents the divisive effects of sexual jealousy, but it also celebrates the restorative powers of love. In the play's first half, the King of Sicilia, Leontes, accuses his wife Hermione of adultery with his friend Polixenes, the King of Bohemia; as a result, he rejects Hermione and their newborn daughter, and the baby daughter Perdita is carried secretly to Bohemia, where she is raised by a shepherd. There the prince of Bohemia, Polixenes's son Florizel, falls in love with her, not knowing who she really is. Perdita is introduced in a rustic sheep-shearing celebration that Polixenes attends incognito so as to see her, and there they discuss the ethics of grafting flowers. Perdita associates such practices with creating bastards and painting women with cosmetics, while Polixenes defends them. In this dialogue they continue a centuries-long debate about changing the plants into more exotic or valued varieties (see, for example, Nicolas Bollard, discussed above, and Giambattista della Porta, discussed in Part 1). Since in early modern literary texts, anxiety about grafting often codes concerns about social mobility and the mixing of classes, it is thus ironic that Polixenes defends the practice, since he opposes the marriage of his noble son to the shepherdess Perdita (who is of course really a princess in disguise). Later in the seventeenth century, writers express increasing resistance to any claims that the nature of plants can be altered by the human hand, as a threat to the natural order and, implicitly, to the social order (see also John Parkinson and Andrew Marvell on grafting).

Perdita. You're welcome, sir.
Give me those flowers there, Dorcas. Reverend sirs,
For you there's rosemary and rue; these keep

4. Effort
Source: William Shakespeare. *The Winter's Tale*, act 4, scene 4.

Seeming and savor all the winter long.
Grace and remembrance be to you both,
And welcome to our shearing!

Polixenes. Shepherdess,
A fair one are you—well you fit our ages
With flowers of winter.

Perdita. Sir, the year growing ancient,
Not yet on summer's death, nor on the birth
Of trembling winter, the fairest flowers o' the season
Are our carnations and streak'd gillyvors,[1]
Which some call nature's bastards: of that kind
Our rustic garden's barren; and I care not
To get slips of them.

Polixenes. Wherefore, gentle maiden,
Do you neglect them?

Perdita. For I have heard it said
There is an art which in their piedness[2] shares
With great creating nature.

Polixenes. Say there be;
Yet nature is made better by no mean
But nature makes that mean: so, over that art
Which you say adds to nature, is an art
That nature makes. You see, sweet maid, we marry
A gentler scion to the wildest stock,
And make conceive a bark of baser kind
By bud of nobler race: this is an art
Which does mend nature, change it rather, but
The art itself is nature.

Perdita. So it is.

Polixenes. Then make your garden rich in gillyvors,
And do not call them bastards.

Perdita. I'll not put
The dibble[3] in earth to set one slip of them;
No more than were I painted I would wish
This youth should say 'twere well and only therefore
Desire to breed by me.

1. Gillyflower, a form of carnations
2. Variegated colors
3. A pointed planting tool

William Lawson, *A New Orchard and Garden and The Countrie Housewife's Garden*, On Domestic Gardening

Part 2 introduces William Lawson's *A New Orchard and Garden* in which he compares trees to human beings, both to be cultivated for a long and profitable life. While not dismissing pleasure, Lawson's book mostly emphasizes hard work and discipline; the gardener must be ever vigilant, in particular when cultivating trees, because nature tends to run wild. Thus, "dressing" or pruning trees resembles moral reformation in humans, who will also degenerate if neglected. Plants can thus be shaped to any form that that the gardener requires; as Lawson boasts, "I can bring any tree (beginning by time) to any form" (Figure 27). Complementing *The New Orchard and Garden* and printed in the same book, Lawson's *The Countrie Housewife's Garden* represents the first printed gardening advice directed specifically at women, dividing the housewife's responsibility for the flower and kitchen garden from the husbandman's orchard tasks. In her realm, the country housewife may delight as well as "profit," for example, in the layout of her flowers in knot gardens (Figure 28), reflecting the assumption that gardening can be an art, even for country folk. The excerpt on separating the kitchen and ornamental garden does discourage the mingling of vegetables, herbs, and ornamental plants, which could disrupt a garden design; here art may conflict with practicality.

New Orchard and Garden

[INTRODUCTION]

The gardener had not need be an idle, or lazy lubber,[1] for to your orchard being a matter of such moment, will not prosper. There will ever be some thing to do. Weeds are always growing. The great mother of all living creatures, the earth, is full of seed in her bowels, and any stirring gives them heat of sun, and being laid near day, they grow; moles work daily, though not always alike. Winter herbs at all times will grow (except in extreme frost). In winter your young trees and herbs would be lighted of snow, and your alleys cleansed; drifts of snow will set deer, hares, and coneys,[2] and other noisome beasts over your walls and hedges, into your orchard. When summer clothes your borders with green and [s]peckled colors, your gardener must dress[3] his hedges, and

Source: William Lawson. *A New Orchard and Garden* (with *The Countrie Housewife's Garden*), pp. 1–3, 32–33; *Countrie Housewife*, pp. 3, 10–11, London, 1618.

1. A clumsy or idle man
2. Rabbits
3. To cultivate, set in order, or more specifically, prune

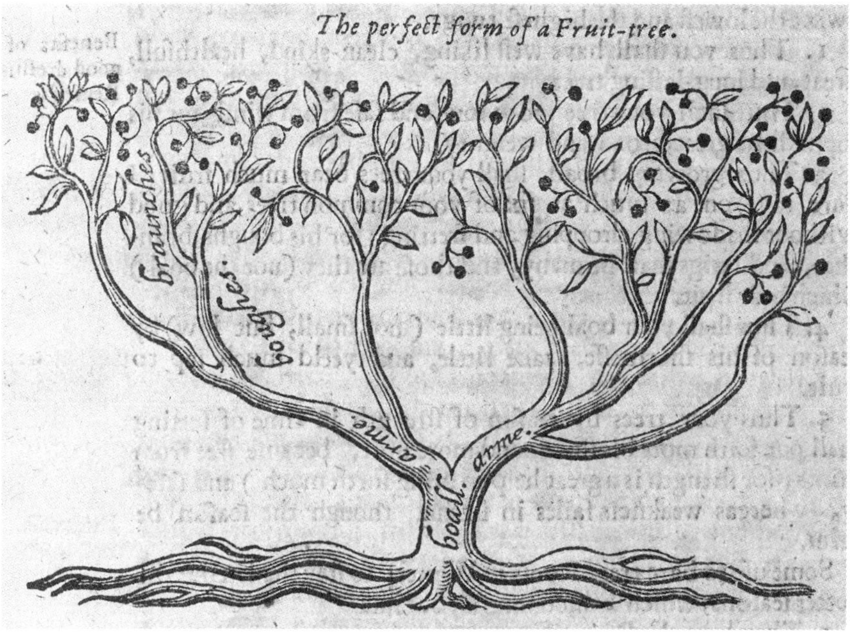

Figure 27. The rectangular image of "the perfect form of an apple tree," from William Lawson, *A New Orchard and Garden* (originally printed 1618; image from edition of 1660), p. 38. SB97 L39 1660. Kislak Center for Special Collections, Rare Books, and Manuscripts, University of Pennsylvania Libraries.

antic works[4]; watch his bees, and hive them; distill his roses and other herbs. Now begins summer fruit to ripe, and crave your hand to pull them.

[. . .]

Such a gardener as will conscionably, quietly and patiently, travail[5] in your orchard, God shall crown the labors of his hands with joyfulness, and make the clouds drop fatness[6] upon your trees; he will provoke your love, and earn his wages, and fees belonging to his place. [. . .]If you be not able, nor willing to hire a gardener, keep your profits to yourself, but then you must take all the pains.

CHAPTER 11. THE RIGHT DRESSING OF TREES

Of all these things aforesaid were indeed performed, as we have shewed them in words, you should have a perfect orchard in nature and substance, begun to

4. Elaborate or grotesque garden designs
5. Labor
6. Fertility

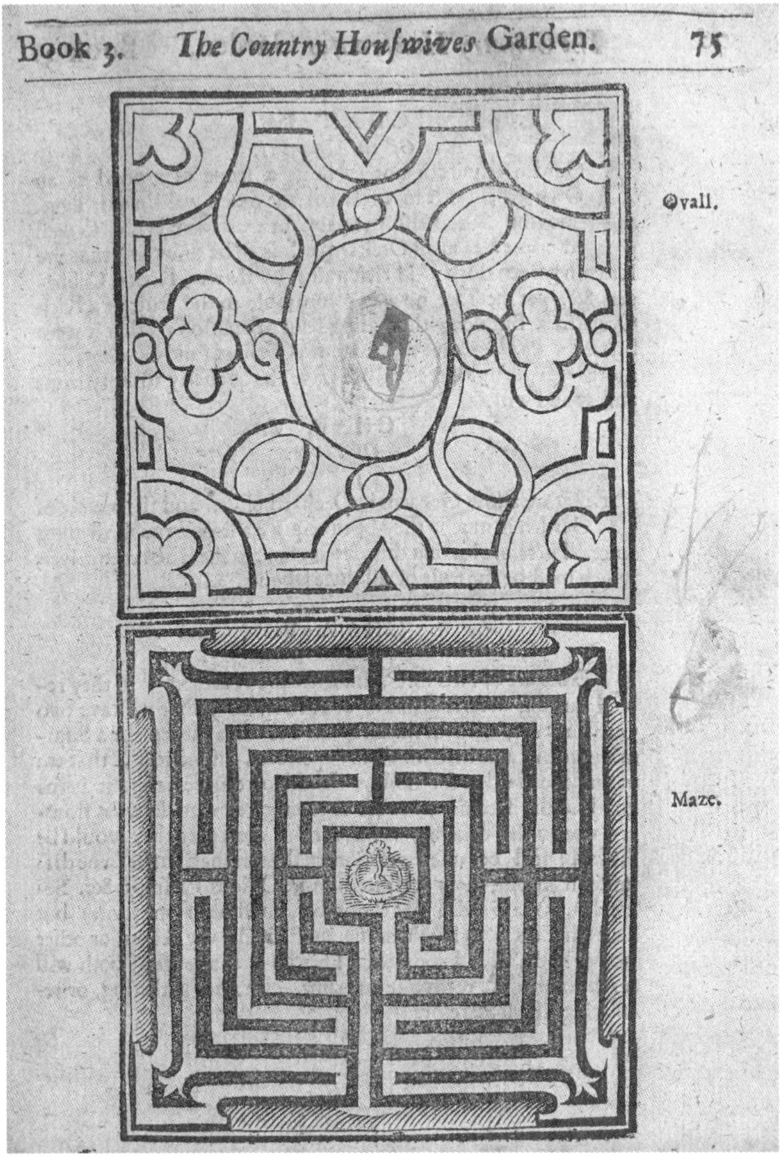

Figure 28. Elaborate garden knot designs for the country housewife, from William Lawson, *The Countrie Housewife's Garden* (originally printed 1618; image from edition of 1660). SB97 L39 1660. Kislak Center for Special Collections, Rare Books, and Manuscripts, University of Pennsylvania Libraries.

your hand. And yet are all these things nothing, if you want that skill to keep and dress your trees. Such is the condition of all earthly things, whereby a man receiveth profit or pleasure, that they degenerate presently without good ordering. Man himself left to himself, grows from his heavenly and spiritual generation, and becometh beastly, yea devilish to his own kind, unless he be regenerate.[7] No marvel then, if trees make their shoots, and put their sprays disorderly. And truly (if I were worthy to judge) there is not a mischief that breedeth greater and more general harm to all the orchard (especially if they be of any continuance) that ever I saw, (I will not except three) than the want of the skillful dressing of trees. [. . .]

Neither let any man ever so much as think, that it unprobable, much less unpossible, to reform any tree of what kind soever. For (believe me) I have tried it, I can bring any tree (beginning by time) to any form. The pear and holly may be made to spread, and the oak to close.

The Countries Housewife's Garden

CHAP. 3. OF THE FORM.

Let that which is said in the orchard's form, suffice for a garden in general, but for special forms in squares, they are as many, as there are devices in gardener's brains. Neither is the wit and art of a skillful gardener in this point not to be commended, that can work more variety for breeding of more delightsome choice, and of all those things, where the owner is able and desirous to be satisfied. The number of forms, mazes, and knots is so great, and men are so diversely delighted, that I leave every housewife to herself, especially seeing to set down many, had been but to fill much paper. Yet lest I deprive her of all delight and direction, let her view these few, choice, new forms, and note this generally, that all plots are square, and all are bordered about with privet, raisins,[8] fea-berries,[9] roses, thorn,[10] rosemary, bee-flowers,[11] hyssop, sage, or such like.

CHAP. 6. OF TWO GARDENS.

Herbs are of two sorts, and therefore it is meet (they requiring divers manners of husbandry) that we have two gardens: a garden for flowers, and a kitchen garden; or a summer garden, not that we mean so perfect a distinction, that the garden for flowers should or can be without herbs good for the kitchen, or the

7. Spiritually reborn
8. Grapevines
9. A kind of gooseberry
10. Likely, hawthorn
11. Flowers attractive to bees, perhaps wallflowers

kitchen garden should want flowers, nor on the contrary. But for the most part they would be severed: first, because your garden flowers shall suffer some disgrace, if among them you intermingle onions, parsnips, etc. Secondly, your garden that is durable, must be of one form, but that, which is for your kitchens use, must yield daily roots, or other herbs, and suffer deformity. Thirdly, the herbs of both will not be both alike ready, at one time, either for gathering, or removing.

Though your garden for flowers doth in a sort peculiarly challenge to it seize a profit, and exquisite form to the eyes, yet you may not altogether neglect this, where your herbs for the pot do grow. And therefore, some here make comely borders with the herbs aforesaid. The rather because abundance of roses and lavender yield much profit, and comfort to the senses: rose-water and lavender, the one cordial (as also the violets, borage, and bugloss),[12] the other reviving the spirits by the sense of smelling, both most durable for smell, both in flowers and water.

John Parkinson, *Paradisi in Sole: Paradisus Terrestris*, On Nature and Gardening

In writing his *Paradisi in Sole* (1629) (introduced in Part 2), John Parkinson attributed inherent values to plants, while also weighing in on other gardeners' efforts to transform them. The book's title page represents a paradise of plants, both exotic and familiar, which has existed since the Garden of Eden as God's creation (Figure 29). Parkinson resisted any claim that gardeners could change a plant's fundamental nature, proclaiming that earlier writers like Giambattista della Porta and Gervase Markham, who claimed to be able to control a plant's color, form, scent, or time of bloom, were simply telling "old wives' tales." In this excerpt he argues that a plant has an essential "spiritual" nature: no "corporeal" or artificial additions can alter it, for no "hetereogeneal things can be mixed naturally together." Parkinson's critique of such ideas is also reflected in the debate between Perdita and Polixenes in *The Winter's Tale*, which is clearly a coded conversation about mixing social ranks, and in Andrew Marvell's "The Mower Against Gardens," which associates tampering with plant reproduction with illicit sexual behavior.

The wonderful desire that many have to see fair, double, and sweet flowers, hath transported them beyond both reason and nature, feigning and boasting often of what they would have, as if they had it. And I think from this desire and

12. Plant with blue flowers related to borage

Source: John Parkinson. *Paradise in Sole: Paradisus Terrestris*, London, 1629, pp. 22–25.

Figure 29. John Parkinson's image of the Garden of Eden, mixing English and exotic plants (including a vegetable lamb), as the title page of *Paradisi in Sole: Paradisus Terrestris* (1629). Folio 630 P222. Kislak Center for Special Collections, Rare Books, and Manuscripts, University of Pennsylvania Libraries.

boasting hath risen all the false tales and reports, of making flowers double as they list, and of giving them color and scent as they please, and to flower likewise at what time they will; I doubt not, but that some of these errors are ancient, and continued long by tradition, and others are of later invention, and therefore the more to be condemned, that men of wit and judgment in these days should expose themselves in their writings, to be rather laughed at, then believed for such idle tales. [. . .] If any man shall say, that because there are many flowers double, whereof there are single also of the same kind, as for example, violets, marigolds, daisies, daffodils, anemones, and many other, that therefore those double flowers were so made by the art of man: viz. by the observation of the change of the moon, the constellations or conjunctions of planets, or some other stars or celestial bodies. Although I do confess and acknowledge that I think some constellations, and peradventure changes of the moon, etc., were appointed by the God of nature, as conducing and helping to the making of those flowers double, that nature hath so produced; yet I do deny, that any man hath or shall ever be able to prove, that it was done by any art of man, or that any man can tell the true causes and seasons, what changes of the moon, or constellations of the planets, wrought together for the producing of those double flowers, or can imitate nature, or rather the God of nature, to do the like. If it shall be demanded, from whence then came these double flowers that we have, if they were not so made by art? I answer, that assuredly all such flowers did first grow wild, and were so found double, as they do now grow in gardens, but for how long before they were found they became double, no man can tell; we only have them as nature hath produced them, and so they remain.

[. . .]

Concerning colors and scents, the many rules and directions extant in many men's writings, to cause flowers to grow yellow, red, green, or white, that never were so naturally, as also to be of the scent of cinnamon, musk, etc., would almost persuade any, that the matters thus set down by such persons, and with some show of probability, were constant and assured proofs thereof; but when they come to the trial, they all vanish away like smoke. I will in a few words show you the matters and manners of their proceedings to effect this purpose: first (they say) if you shall steep your seeds in the lees of red wine, you shall have the flowers of those plants to be of a purple color. If you will have lilies or gillyflowers to be of a scarlet red color, you shall put vermillion or cinnabar between the rind and the small heads growing about the root; if you will have them blue, you shall dissolve azure or bice[1] between the rind and the heads;

1. A blue pigment

if yellow, orpiment:[2] if green, verdigris, and thus of any other color. [. . .]. In the like manner for scents, they have set down in their writings, that by putting cloves, musk, cinnamon, benzoin,[3] or any other such sweet thing, bruised with rose water, between the bark and the body of trees, the fruit of them will smell and taste of the same that is put unto them; and if they be put onto the top of the roots, or else bound unto the head of the root, they will cause the flowers to smell of that scent the matter put unto them is of; as also to steep the seeds of roses, and other plants in the water of such like sweet things, and then to sow them, and water them morning and evening with such like liquor, until they be grown up; besides a number of such like rules and directions set down in books, so confidently, as if the matters were without all doubt or question, when as without all doubt and question I will assure you, that they are all but mere idle tales and fancies, without all reason or truth, or shadow of reason or truth. For scents and colors are both such qualities as follow the essence of plants, even as forms are also; and one may as well make any plant to grow of what form you will, as to make it of what scent or color you will; and if any man can form plants at his will and pleasure, he can do as much as God himself that created them. For the things they would add unto the plants to give them color, are all corporeal, or of a bodily substance, and whatsoever should give any color unto a living and growing plant, must be spiritual: for no solid corporeal substance can join itself with the life and essence of an herb or tree, and the spiritual part of the color thereof is not the same with the bodily substance, but is a mere vapor that riseth from the substance, and feedeth the plant, whereby it groweth, so that there is no ground or color of reason, that a substantial color should give color to a growing herb or tree; but for scent (which is a mere vapor) you will say there is more probability. Yet consider also, that what sweet scent so ever you bind or put unto the roots of herbs or trees, must be either buried, or as good as buried in the earth, or bark of the tree, whereby the substance will in a small time corrupt and rot, and before it can join itself with the life, spirit, and essence of the plant, the scent also will perish with the substance: for no heterogeneal things can be mixed naturally together, as iron and clay; and no other thing but homogeneal, can be nourishment or convertible into the substance of man or beast.

2. A bright yellow pigment
3. A fragrant resin

Mary Somerset, Duchess of Beaufort, Description of Her Garden

Mary Somerset, Duchess of Beaufort (1630–1715), was famous in her time as a botanist and a gardener. She collaborated with the most important horticulturalists of her time, including Hans Sloane and other members of the Royal Society. Drawing on an extensive network of travelers and other gardeners, Somerset gathered seeds and plants from the New World, South Africa, South Asia, China, and Japan. She was much sought after as an expert on exotic plants, which she cultivated in her own gardens and greenhouses. As a record of her work, she also compiled an impressive twelve-volume herbarium (a collection of dried plant specimens). For all her fame, she never published anything in her own lifetime, and her thinking about plants and gardening must be inferred from manuscript records. Among those records is an anonymous account of her garden in Chelsea, a rare description of a garden designed by a woman. The garden mixed exotics like yellow jessamines imported from the New World with more well-known English flowers like gillyflowers and fashionable ones like auriculas (on auriculas see John Parkinson and Samuel Gilbert, both in Part 2). The design of a more formal garden contrasts with that of the kitchen garden, which mixes flowers, herbs, and cauliflowers (compare with William Lawson, *The Countrie Housewife's Garden*).

[The Main Garden]

In the east aspect border under the wall, in [smudged page] and the border on the other side of the walk are planted in [smudged] of double pinks and the middle of the border is planted with flowering shrubs, as mezerions,[1] yellow jessamines, scorpion-sena, tree of St. John's wort, althaea,[2] dwarf almonds, and laurels.

On the outside of the border are lines of double feverfew, and double white matted pinks, a line of harewort[3] and a line of gillyflowers, these borders are the same all round the ground. The south aspect border under the wall, are planted two lines of gillyflowers and an edging of pinks.

Source: BL MS Sloane 4020, f. 267 [268] Chelsea, Middlesex, catalogues of plants in Sir H. Sloane's garden at 1693/4. (According to Jennifer Munroe, who transcribed this passage, the garden has been misidentified in the British Library record as belonging to Hans Sloane; however, it is clearly Somerset's Beaufort House in London.)

1. *Daphne mezereum*
2. Hollyhock
3. Hartwort?

The two borders on each side the terrace walk, that goes from the house to the road, betwixt the two bottoms, are planted in the middle with standard laurels, honeysuckles, syringas, and mezerions. And in the other part of the border are a line of tulips, a line of narcissus, and a line of crocus and anemones. The west aspect border under the wall are planted gillyflowers, as the other next the road. On the north aspect border under the wall are layers of bays.

And in a little bottom next the north wall are beds of hepatica and crocuses, a bed of gentianella and crocuses, and a bed of auriculas and crocuses, a bed of lilies of the valley and crocuses, a bed of tulips and crocuses, a bed of bachelors buttons and crocuses, and a bed of Star of Bethlehem and crocuses, and so it is mixed and planted throughout the whole bottom. And the loop next the sweet briar hedge shutting into the same bottom is planted with polyanthus.[4]

And on the mount walk that looks over into Mr. Wharton's garden, on each side of the gravel walks in the borders are tulips only, in the middle are planted standard laurels, and the border next the bays, are planted gentianellas and crocuses. At the end wall going down the steps is planted phylera.

The border on the north side are planted a line of polyanthus, a line of snow-drops, and a line of hepatica, and the wall is planted with honeysuckles. The borders under the house in the great garden are planted hepaticas and snow-drops.

[. . .]

The Parlor Garden

On the east aspect border, the wall is planted with polyanthus and the neat border that goes down by the other, betwixt the wall and the walk, are planted two lines of polyanthus and two lines of gentianellas. The [deleted word] aspect border under the wall, are planted stock gillyflowers. The south aspect border under the wall is a line of white matted pinks, and a line of gillyflowers.

On the north aspect border under the wall, are planted auriculas, and round the borders, that are round the grass in the same ground, are two edgings of green, and white abrotanums,[5] and at each corner in every border stands a yew, and the borders are tulips.

In the little piece of ground called the warren, on the south aspect border, under the wall, are planted gillyflowers, and in the other are polyanthus, and the middle of the ground is all asparagus.

[. . .].

4. A kind of primrose
5. Southernwood

In the Kitchen Garden

On the south aspect border under the wall, are planted gillyflowers to stand this winter.

On the west aspect border under the wall is sowed several small things. On the north aspect border under the stable wall are planted polyanthus. And in the piece of ground, that goes all along down by it are planted six beds of laurels, seven beds of seedling polyanthus. And in the other part of it, are several small things, as hollymus[6] and rows of scorpion-sena. The east aspect border under the wall, is planted with tansy, costmary, double sweet williams, and Roman lavender. The piece of ground next the south wall, are six beds of offsets of tulips, one bed of auriculas, nine beds of sweet marjoram, all the rest are cauliflowers. The rest of the ground is planted with plum-stocks and sweet herbs.

René Rapin, *Hortorum Libri IV*, or *Of Gardens*

The teacher and French Jesuit René Rapin (1621–87) wrote many theological treatises, but he also had a consuming interest in gardens. His most famous work on this topic was a Latin poem in four books, *Hortorum Libri* (1665), translated into English by John Evelyn's son as *Of Gardens* (1672). Rapin very self-consciously places his poem in the line of Virgil's *Georgics*, celebrating a life of rural retirement. However, his work was practical as well as celebratory, and the rest of the poem provides specific instructions for designing noble gardens, mixing classical myths with horticultural tips. In this excerpt, Rapin begins with advice on planting flowers and then turns to advocate the modern arts of ordered garden design that characterized French gardening defined by patterns, paths, and boxwood enclosures, contrasted with the gardens of a wild and bacchanalian mythical past, symbolized in a figure of Flora "unadorned" and "rude."

Now if both earth and air answer your ends,
(For earth upon air's influence depends)
Enlarge your prospect, nor confine your sight
To narrow bounds; flow'rs in no shades delight.
Break with the rake, if stiffer clods abound,
And with iron rollers level well the ground.
Nor yet make haste your borders to describe;

6. Halimus?

Source: *Of gardens: four books first written in Latine verse by Renatus Rapinus; and now made English by J. E.*, London, 1672, pp. 5–8.

But let the earth the autumn show'rs imbibe;
That after it hath felt the winter cold,
You may next spring turn up, and rake the mold.
This done, your box[1] in various forms dispose,
Such as were heretofore unknown to those,
Whose gardens nothing ow'd to modern art,
Deckt by what kinder Nature did impart,
Among ignobler plants you then might view,
Where blushing roses intermingled grew;
No spacious walks, no alleys were design'd,
Edg'd by green box, all yet was unrefin'd.
Flora at first was unadorn'd, and rude;
Happ'ning at Liber's[2] orgies to intrude.
The feast approch'd, the neighb'ring deities
Were present; thither old Silenus[3] hies,
Mounted on's ass; with whom the satyrs join
In drunken bacchanals, and sparkling wine.
Here Cybele[4] through Phrygia so rever'd.
And with the rest our Flora too appear'd:
Her hair upon her shoulders loosely played;
Or pride, or beauty this neglect had made.
How e're it was, the other goddesses
Laugh'd, and despis'd the rudeness of her dress.
This pity mov'd in Berecinthia's[5] heart,
Who griev'd to see her daughter want that art,
Which others us'd; and therefore to repair
Those imperfections, she adorn'd her hair
With various flow'rs; her temples these enclose,
And box which Nature on each field bestows.
Her mine's now alt'red, every charming grace
Strives to be most conspicuous in her face.
As this to Flora greater beauty gives;
So hence the gard'ner all his art derives.
The Romans, and the Grecians knew not how

1. Boxwood
2. Roman god of wine, fertility, and freedom
3. A satyr who was companion to Dionysus (or Bacchus)
4. Ancient Phrygian goddess of fertility
5. Another name for Cybele

To form their paths, and set their flowers as now.
Goodness of air and soil perhaps might be
Occasions of our curiosity
In gardens; and the genius too of France,
With time, this blest improvement might advance.
So that if you a villa do desire
With gardens, for a skillful man enquire;
Who with his pencil can on parchment draw
The form of your intended work. No flaw,
No error' scapes you; thus deformity
Timely appears to your considerate eye.
In thousand figures some their box enfold,
As was the Cretan labyrinth of old.
These artificial mazes some reject,
Who more the Phrygian flourishes[6] affect:
And these as many various textures taught,
As uncomb'd wool by Tyrian[7] virgins wrought.
Others with squares, less diff'rent, strive to please
Themselves, in which the fragrant flow'rs with ease,
And pleasure too, may stoop to the command
Of the spectator's eye, and gath'rers hand.
I will not divers knots to you suggest,
To choose of them which please your fancy best;
That is preferable beyond compare,
Which with the scantling[8] of your ground doth square.
When all things thus provided are, again
Level your ground, that, being smooth and plain,
Garden, and borders both may even be,
Admitting no irregularity.

Andrew Marvell, "The Mower Against Gardens"

While caught up in politics, Andrew Marvell (1621–1678) also wrote extraordinary poetry, and several of his poems (ca. 1650–52) participate in the pastoral and georgic traditions. His most famous poem, "The Garden," describes the

6. Elaborate curved designs
7. Tyre was an ancient Phoenician city
8. Proportion
Source: *Miscellaneous Poems by Andrew Marvell*, London, 1681, pp. 40–41.

experience of visiting a garden in solitude and contemplation, where the mind withdraws, "annihilating all that's made / To green thought in a green shade." But Marvell also wrote four poems featuring the persona of a mower that transform pastoral conventions. Unlike "The Garden," "The Mower Against Gardens" engages directly with contemporary gardening practices, and in particular, with efforts to manipulate the nature of flowers to create rarer and more desirable forms, including using manure to create a double carnation, cultivating multicolored tulips, and importing rarities from the New World. The poem characterizes the enclosed, private garden of adulterated plants in sexual terms as a "harem," in contrast to the "innocence" of open fields and "wild" nature (compare with the medieval and Renaissance gardens that are characterized erotically; see *Le roman de la rose* and Edmund Spenser's Bower of Bliss in *The Faerie Queene*). Not only does Marvell thus oppose the values of art and nature, but the poem also participates in a long-standing debate about the beliefs associated with grafting and other forms of hybridizing plants (see Nicolas Bollard, Gervase Markham, Shakespeare's *The Winter's Tale*, and John Parkinson, all discussed above).

Luxurious[1] man, to bring his vice in use,
  Did after him the world seduce,
And from the fields the flowers and plants allure,
  Where Nature was most plain and pure.
He first enclosed within the gardens square
  A dead and standing pool of air,
And a more luscious earth for them did knead,
  Which stupefied them while it fed.
The pink[2] grew then as double as his mind;
  The nutriment did change the kind.
With strange perfumes he did the roses taint,
  And flowers themselves were taught to paint.
The tulip white did for complexion seek,
  And learned to interline its cheek.
Its onion root they then so high did hold,
  That one was for a meadow sold.
Another world was searched through oceans new,
  To find the marvel of Peru.[3]

1. Luxury-loving, with a second meaning of lustful
2. The carnation: a double carnation was more sought after.
3. The flowers called the "four o'clock," imported from South America

And yet these rarities might be allowed
To man, that sovereign thing and proud,
Had he not dealt between the bark and tree,
Forbidden mixtures there to see.
No plant now knew the stock from which it came;
He grafts upon the wild the tame,
That the uncertain and adulterate fruit
Might put the palate in dispute.
His green seraglio[4] has its eunuchs too,
Lest any tyrant him outdo;
And in the cherry he does Nature vex,
To procreate without a sex.
'Tis all enforced, the fountain and the grot,[5]
While the sweet fields do lie forgot,
Where willing Nature does to all dispense
A wild and fragrant innocence;
And fauns and fairies do the meadows till
More by their presence than their skill.
Their statues polished by some ancient hand,
May to adorn the gardens stand,
But, howsoe'er the figures do excel,
The gods themselves with us do dwell.

Hester Pulter, "The Snail, the Tulip, and the Bee"

In Part 3 Hester Pulter's "The Ugly Spider" demonstrates some of Pulter's talent in using a range of sources, from natural histories like Pliny the Elder's and Edward Topsell's to theories of alchemy. However, she also included poems that reflect her own observations. In a long poem on her own garden at her country estate at Broadfield, "The Garden," she stages a debate as to which of her flowers "excel / In virtue, color, beauty, fashion, smell": the flowers she mentions include the woodbine (honeysuckle), wallflower, lily, rose, poppy, violet, heliotrope (sunflower), auricula, flower de luce (iris), gillyflower (carna-

4. Harem
5. Grotto
Source: "The Snail, the Tulip, and the Bee." *The Pulter Project: Poet in the Making*, edited by Wendy Wall and Leah Knight, 2018, http://pulterproject.northwestern.edu/poems/ee/the-snail-the-tulip-and-the-bee-emblem-53/.

tion), and the Adonis flower. Offering a moral about tyranny and resistance, this poem, "The Snail, the Tulip, and the Bee," also offers a glimpse of her own garden, suggesting Pulter herself cultivated the most fashionable flowers of the time and closely observed them. In this poem, she imagines a bee goes out to seek nectar in both poisonous plants and her garden flowers, where she names the "painted" tulip and the "curious auricula" (on auriculas, see John Parkinson and Samuel Gilbert, both in Part 2).

When fair Aurora, dressed with radiant light,
Had triumphed o'er the gloomy shades of night,
When she her virgin beauty first discloses,
Her dewy curls stuck full of half-blown roses,
Lapped in a robe of silver mixed with gray,
Which did prognosticate a glorious day,
Out flew the active Amazonian maid;[1]
The hills and dales not only she surveyed,
But out of every gold enameled cup
Her morning's draught of nectar she did sup.
Nay, where the toad and spider poisons found
Mel[2] she extracts; for this her wisdom's crowned.
On nightshade, henbane, hellish aconite,
On opium, hemlock, she doth safely light.[3]
Thus being with choice extractions loaded well
She turned to fly to her sexangular cell,[4]
But taking of my garden in her way,
Though full before, she could not choose but stay
To see the curious auriculas dressed
More variously than Iris' dewy breast.
Then were my tulips painted in their pride,
Which when this covetous insect espied
To carry home her wealth she'd not the power
Till she had searched the sweets of every flower.
The sun, from [whom] all influence receives,

1. A bee (Amazonian because Amazonian warriors had a queen in their matriarchy)
2. Honey
3. All poisonous plants
4. Six-sided honeycomb

Bid them decline; the tulip closed her leaves[5]
And in that painted prison shut the bee.
With her a snail who slid about to see
Where to get out upon her unctuous breast
But seeing no hope she laid her down to rest,
Whilst the angry bee did such a flutt'ring keep;
She nor her fellow pris'ner could not sleep.
But night being past, Delia[6] diffused his rays;
The tulip then her gilded leaves displays.
Out slid the snail, the bee did fainting lie,
And thus with beating of herself did die.
Then let impatient spirits here but see
What 'tis to struggle with their destiny.
So stout Biron[7] in prison was enraged,
Knowing his king was to his sword engaged.
When Belisarius[8] by a dog was led,
Being blind, he patiently did beg his bread.
So miscr'ant Bajazeth[9] did show his rage
When that proud tarter put him in a cage.
Scorning to be a footstool to his pride,
He dashed his curséd brains about and died.
When wise Callisthenes, used with greater scorn
Tyrannically mangled so was borne,
He, being unmoved, showed his philosophy;[10]
'Tis valianter by far to live than die.
Then if no hope of liberty you see
Think on the snail, the tulip, and the bee.

John Evelyn, *Elysium Britannicum*, or *The Royal Gardens*

John Evelyn (1620–1706) was both a gardener at his own estates at Wotton and Sayes Court and a prolific writer. Well traveled and infinitely curious about the

5. Petals
6. The sun
7. Charles, Duc de Biron
8. A Roman general punished by Emperor Justinian
9. Turkish emperor imprisoned by Tamburlaine the Great
10. A Greek historian punished by Alexander the Great by having his ears, nose, and lips cut off

Source: John Evelyn. *Elysium Britannicum, or The Royal Gardens*. Edited by John E. Ingram, University of Pennsylvania Press, 2001, pp. 60–65. (I have adapted and modernized the text.)

natural world, and a founding member of the Royal Society, he associated with many important scientists and thinkers of his day. In his time, he published several books on natural matters, including *Sylva: Or a Discourse of Forest-Trees and the Propagation of Timber in his Majesties Dominions* (1664), *Acetaria: A Discourse of Sallets* (1699), and *Kalendarium Hortense* (1664). However, this excerpt derives from the manuscript of Evelyn's unpublished masterwork, *Elysium Britannicum, or the Royal Gardens in Three Books* (as transcribed and edited by John Ingram). The manuscript contains three books: Book 1 covers principles and qualities of the seasons and environment; Book 2 addresses all aspects of garden design and features like waterworks; and Book 3 offers advice on the cultivation and the uses of flowers. It is an extraordinary compendium of both practical information based on experience and contemplation of the pleasures and wonders of nature. In this excerpt Evelyn often ecstatically and even erotically anthropomorphizes the earth as an ever-changing fertile female body enlivened by warmth and water, while he counsels the "industrious gardener" as to his mundane seasonal duties. In this sense the passage also harks back to centuries-old advice about adapting to the seasons, in both the body and the garden (see *Causae et curae* in Part 1, *Rams Little Dodoen* in Part 4, and *Secreta secretorum* in Part 4).

In the text below words in curly brackets represent Evelyn's interlineations, with words in square brackets being Ingram's notes or clarifications.

Of the four seasons

{It was truly said of our *annus fructificat, non tellus*; the earth and soil does much, but the seasons do more, it will therefore be of high importance that our gardener both observe and prepare for them because the {due} knowledge of them will instruct him how {he is} to entertain them when they happen to be either propitious or a sense, let him therefore understand briefly and plainly [the solar year].}

[. . .]

And in this order we commence with the spring as in which sundry divines (though all accord not) have supposed that the first garden was planted by God himself. We reckon it from the winter equinox to the summer solstice, at which season the sun ascends through [Aries] [Taurus] and [Gemini] the vernal signs. {and that all the astrations[1] are in efficacy} It is regularly of quality hot and humid, because which causes it to impart a gentle and gradual warmth, convenient for the opening of the pores of the earth, and her productions, which the severity of the winter had imprisoned and locked up; and if in

1. Astral factors [?]

this procedure of the spring anything impeach the nature of the season, as that instead of the pregnant, benign and supple showers, there comes down {descend} hail, frosts, and impetuous and piercing winds, which check and retard this delicious and promising season, we are to receive it as a chastisement from God, as a bridle to our intemperance, and may better prevent it by prayers, then precepts.

But otherwise the sun culminating over our horizon, daily heats the earth more and more, inciting and renewing her vegetative faculty, which accompanied with other virtuous and attractive constellations, exhales {causes her to exhale forth} the cold and superfluous moisture, which had lain in her bosom during the {his} absence of the sun concocting and converting it into showers, and a dew impregnated with the universal spirit, which descending in gentle irrigations upon her, becomes that powerful agent, the father {and life} of all productions. So that whenever we find a spring to be calm, warm and moist, we soon behold the effects of it to present us with the most glorious enamel, wherewith Nature is used to diaper and embroider our gardens with flowers and fruits in the greatest variety and perfection.

[. . .]

{Tis then} and the propitious Zephyr[2] tempering the fervor of the amorous planet,[3] courting the blossoms and flowers, kisses them open, expands their beauties and perfumes the air with their delicious and ravishing effluxes. It is now then that our industrious gardener should bestir himself in {stirring up the earth which was in autumn dug and extirpating weed there left, etc.} sowing and planting or else think no more of it till three months after for when once the sap creeps up by the bark of the trees, and that the bud begins th'annunciation of leaves and blossoms, it will be too late to betake himself {with success} to this employment. Now is the season of grafting, now likewise to prune and cut, disbranch, plash,[4] bind, and not whilst the rigorous frosts may endanger the destruction of our labors when the ignorant expose the wounds of their amputations to their tyranny; now may our gardener begin to open his tender plants and show them the air by degrees; but not expose them till the season be well advanced.

[. . .]

[In summer] our gardener is to lay aside all businesses and avocations whatsoever, to cultivate his ground, and pursue his employments. And the summer is the second period of the year, beginning from the estive[5] solstice to

2. West wind
3. Venus
4. Interlace branches to form a hedge
5. Summer

the autumnal equinox, in which the sun passes the three summer signs [Cancer, Leo, Virgo]. This season is hot and dry, and therefore the most proper for the concocting and ripening of the fruits, and gratifying the industry of our laborious gardener with the expectations of a bountiful and luxurious autumn. Now is the time of discreetly watering and refreshing his thirsty plants, to inoculate[6] the more curious, especially in the morning and evening, unless some extraordinary showers humectating[7] the earth, ferment, and produce a second spring, as it sometimes happens, irrigating the languishing plants and flowers, which now begin to put forth a fresh, in sign {token} of joy and gratitude. From this equinox to the winter solstice we calculate the autumn or third part of the year, in which the sun accomplishes the signs of [Libra, Scorpio, Sagittarius]. A season cold and moist, yet temperate, and agreeable, 'till towards its expiration, that the earth sensible of the unkind departure of her beloved begins to lay aside her festival robes and glorious mantling; in sign testimony whereof, the trees and the plants forsake their verdure and shed their ornaments. The continual sighing of the earth sending up her exhalations, they descend again in tears, which being (as at the spring) qualified by the sun, and other constellations, his companions, exceedingly refresh and abate those excessive heats which his conversation had raised excited in her during the summer ardor, embracements and more near embraces, which the earth receiving kindly from him, would, if the now approaching winter did not too much envy her fecundity, recompense in new productions both of flowers and fruits, as in some more propitious countries she does; however, she fails not bringing to maturity her present charge, perfecting both the fruits and the seeds {in} the vineyards, the orchards and the gardens; in fine where ever she has not been prevented by the unkindness {of the season}, or the ignorance of our gardener. And therefore from the very first approach of this grateful season, having gratefully received the effects of her bounty and his own industry, let our vigilant gardener begin to take up and prepare his nurseries for transplantation; especially, after a soaking rain, that they may yet root, and take hold of the ground before the frosts surprise him, for {now} after a while *Georgics*: [2.317]

Rura gelu tum claudit hyems
Winter locks up the ground with frost.

6. Graft
7. Watering

John Worlidge, *Systema Horticulturae*, or *The Art of Gardening in Three Books*

John Worlidge (d. 1693) published many books about husbandry, cider making, beekeeping, and horticulture, including *Systema Horticulturae, or, The Art of Gardening in Three Books* (first published in 1677 and reprinted in multiple editions thereafter). In this book, Worlidge professes that he writes "not only to excite or animate such as have fair estates, and pleasant seats in the country, to adorn and beautify them; but to encourage the honest and plain countryman in the improvement of his ville, by enlarging the bounds and limits of his gardens, as well as his orchards." In his advice about garden design, he instructs the reader to consider the garden's relationship to a manor house, and the experience of pleasure within its boundaries. In these two excerpts he lays out round and square designs for the garden (Figure 30). While considering the best layout for horticultural purposes, he also emphasizes symmetry and the optimal experience of walking the paths and seeing and smelling the plants.

Section I. Of the form of a garden.

As before was observed concerning the situation, so now may it be as to the form, that if ye are already limited and bounded, by reason of the situation of your house, and the contiguous parts about your intended plantation, you must cast it into as good a form and model as you can; but if you are at liberty, then may you make your election of what form pleaseth you best.

The round is very pleasant, and some curious gardens there are of that form in foreign parts. The walls about such a garden are very good for fruit, the winds being not so severe against a round, as against a straight wall. The walk also that circundates[1] that garden is not unpleasant, for that you may walk as long as you please in it, always forwards without any short turning; some straight walks there may be, that tend from the circumference to the center. The several quadrants may be sub-divided and planted with fruits; the borders of the round walk, and the cross walks being sufficient for flowers and plants of beauty and delight. At the center of this garden may be placed a fountain, or in defect of water a banqueting house, or house of pleasure. A rude draught[2] of such a form is here presented to your view [Figure 30], the outermost walk being adorned with cypress trees, the inner parts of the grass-plots with fir trees,

Source: John Worlidge. *Systema Horticulturae, or, The Art of Gardening in Three Books* [. . .], London, 1688, pp. 15–18.

1. Circumnavigates

2. Illustration

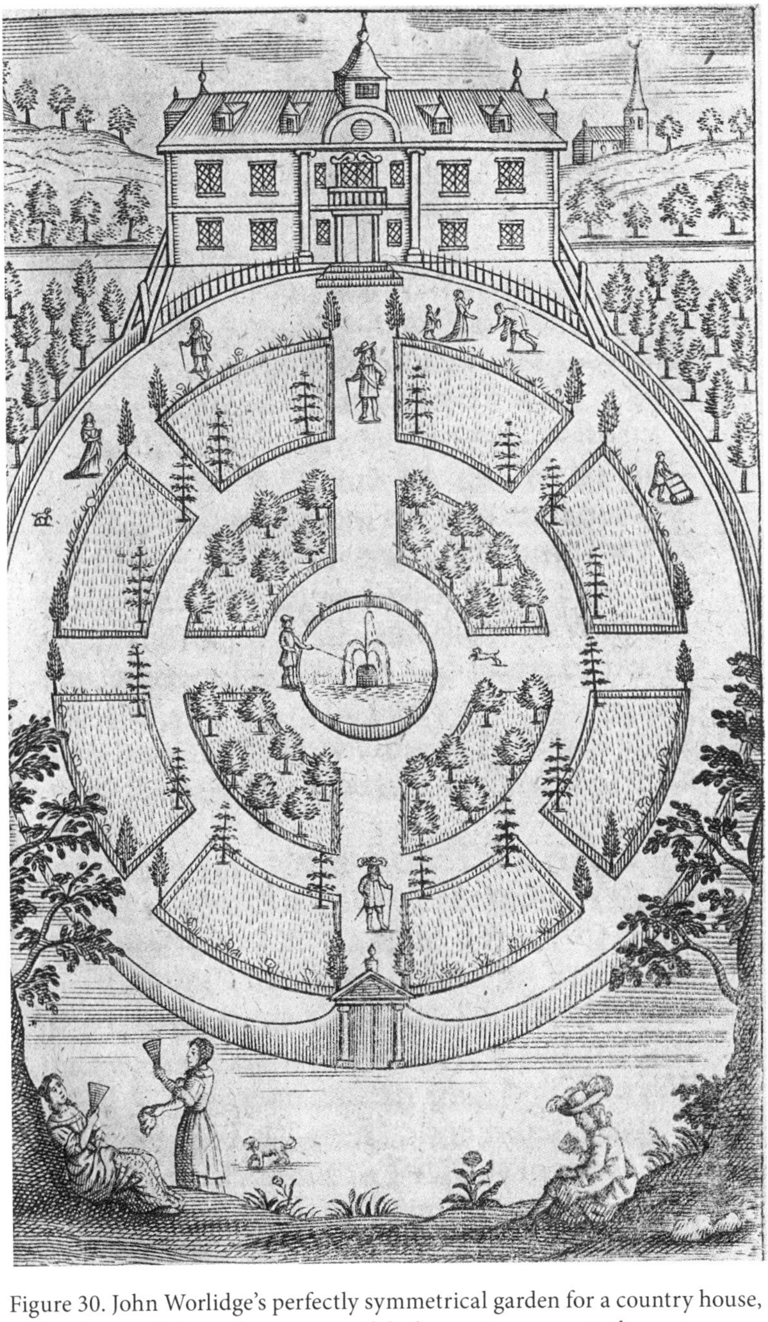

Figure 30. John Worlidge's perfectly symmetrical garden for a country house, oriented toward the main entrance of the house. It represents the gentry enjoying the gardens, while a lone worker rolls the garden paths, discreetly reminding the reader of the labor involved. From *Systema Horticulturae*, p. 17. 710 W88. Kislak Center for Special Collections, Rare Books, and Manuscripts, University of Pennsylvania Libraries.

and the quadrants within the lesser circle, planted with variety of fruit trees, and the principal walks round and straight, bordered with flowers and delightful shrubs and plants. Encompassed with a palisade[3] in the center of your garden, is a fountain of spring water always flowing, serving not only to refresh the spirits of such that delight in the sight of it, but is necessary in dry and hot seasons, to preserve your choicest plants from injury.

[. . .]

The square is the most perfect and pleasant form that you can lay your garden into, where your ground will afford it; every walk that is in it being straight, and every plant and tree standing in a direct line, represents it to your eye very pleasing. The delight you take in walking in it, being much the more as you are less careful: for when you walk in a round or circle, you are more subject to trespass on the borders, without continual thoughts and observation of your ground. You may divide the plot you intend for your gardens into three parts, by walls or palisades; the middle part may be sub-divided into gravel-walks, grass-plots, edged with borders, planted with your most select plants, shrubs, and flowers. If your partition-fences on the sides be walls, there may be raised the choicest wall-fruits: those that require most heat, on the most sunny-side; and fruits that require but little, on the most shady, as cherries and plums will thrive where there is not much of the sun; and currants flourish most where there is all shade; under such walls, that most pleasant fruit the raspberry delights to grow, it being a fruit wherewith that northern cold territory of Lapland abounds.

[. . .]

But if your partition-fences be of palisades, they may be adorned with perennial greens, and other hardy shrubs, and flower-bearing trees. The other two parts, you may convert the one of them into an orchard, the other into a kitchen-garden, which will be no small advantage or ornament to your seat, and middle garden of pleasure. But if you are willing to celebrate so fair a spot of ground, as the whole square, to the delights of Flora, then may you divide it into larger squares, and grass-plots, leaving only borders on their confines for your variety of plants. The new mode of gravel-walks and grass-plots is fit only for such houses or palaces, that are situated near cities, and great towns, although they are now become presidents[4] for many stately country residencies, where they have banished out of their garden's flowers, the miracles of nature, and the best ornaments that ever were discovered to make a seat pleasant. But

3. Fence
4. Precedents

'tis hoped that this new, useless, and unpleasant mode, will like many other vanities grow out of fashion.

[. . .]

The infinite variety of forms that might be drawn and here represented to you would but increase your charge, when perhaps every builder may better please himself in the shape and contrivance of his garden, than any other can do for him. But these few rules are not amiss to be observed, viz. that you endeavor to make the principal entrance into your garden, out of the best room in your house, or very near it, your walks being places of divertissement after a sedentary repast. The aromatic odors, they yield pleasant refreshments after a gross diet; such innocent exercises being the best digestive to weak stomachs. Let there be some other door into your garden, for gardeners, laborers, etc.. And let your principal walk extend itself as far as you can in length, directly from your house, adorned with the choicest plants for beauty and scent, and that there may be a succession of them through the year, not without flower-plots, which grace the best of gardens.

PART VII

Outlandish Natural Worlds

This anthology's parts on plants, animals, and weather and climate have already introduced elements of what Europeans encountered as the exotic natural world: for example, the crocodile, dragonswort, or Africa's hostile climate. The early English adjective for such phenomena was "outlandish," literally "not of our land." Only in the sixteenth century did the word fully gain the connotation of "bizarre," but from the beginning it still bore traces of the fear and wonder always generated by what was strange. The frontispiece of John Parkinson's *Paradisi in Sole*, representing the Garden of Eden, is replete with exotica, including the infamous "vegetable lamb," a legendary plant of the east that was believed to grow sheep (Figure 29). In the text itself, concerned with English gardening, John Parkinson still dwells lovingly on what he called "outlandish" flowers, imports that by that time had been naturalized and prized for their special beauty and rarity.

Such wonder at "outlandish" natural worlds have always accompanied history and literature reflecting travel and exploration for settlement and trade. In his history of the Greco-Persian wars, the Greek historian Herodotus included extended digressions on the landscape and fauna of Egypt and Scythia, and the growth of the Greek empire produced numerous comprehensive geographic works (while few survive today). Reaching even farther across Europe and the Near East, the Romans expanded knowledge of once-unknown territories in the interests of their dominion (Roller). While in the postclassical period much knowledge of ancient geography was neglected or lost, earlier information and lore about other lands did survive in encyclopedias and literature (Kimble). Works like Pliny the Elder's *Natural History* and Ptolemy's *Geographical Guide* could thus still influence much of medieval and Renaissance concepts of the extent and nature of the known world. Further, even if the formal study of geography declined, during the middle ages pilgrimage and trade routes to the east, including Asia Minor and South Asia, deepened connections between Europe and other regions (Keay; Verdon; Campbell 1988). The twelfth century did see a renewal of Western interest in geography with the infusion of classical texts via Arabic learning; however, it took the onset of what is now considered "the age of exploration" for the passion for global geographic knowledge to explode, especially with the momentous exploration of the Americas, which was to forever change both the Old World and the New (Greenblatt; Campbell 1988 and 1999; Mann; Schiebinger; Smith and Findlen).

The accounts of distant lands found in early geographic texts typically combine ethnography, geology, botany, and zoology, where writers sought to convey the exceptional nature of those unfamiliar places. While global natural histories as far back as Herodotus often based their claims to truth-telling on experience, generally their sources were other books or travelers' tales. Such texts thus characteristically try to balance the style of exact description with awe at the strangeness of it all. Often a report of an exotic creature, plant, or natural feature then slides into fantasy, where the merely different becomes extraordinary. Over time, the exotic could gradually become naturalized, as in Parkinson's "outlandish" flowers. Travel and exploration helped to transform global agriculture and husbandry, when plants and animals were both exported from and imported into Europe, profoundly changing the natural world across the globe (Grove; Schiebinger and Swan; Smith and Findlen).

In the Christian West, while trade, greed, and religious fervor may have motivated such exploration, many travelers also dreamed of finding the lost Eden or a paradise of the kind Parkinson's book represented. Such a concept of a return was not exclusive to Christianity, or to the age of exploration; long before, other cultures experiencing loss of land or the depredations of urbanization yearned to recapture a lost golden age, a time of verdant abundance without labor. Driven as it was by greed for gold, exotic goods, or spices, and by a desire for new lands to possess and conquer, exploration was thus intertwined with a vision of that return to a past nature: a poem like Michael Drayton's on the Virginian voyage collapses the two.

In reality, when it came to the New World, the hoped-for paradisiacal lands did not yield everything that was imagined or desired. When Walter Raleigh and his company ventured to Guiana, driven by the dream of discovering El Dorado, the fabled city of gold, they found instead an extraordinarily intractable and seductive natural world; it was verdant and bounteous, to be sure, but it was also disorienting and dangerous. The colonizers of that New World's nature sought a different kind of "commodity" or profit, whether through cultivating valuable crops like sugar or tobacco, which required slave labor, or through horticultural trade. The resulting "Columbian exchange"—the transfer of living things ranging from people to bacteria between Europe and the other continents—ended up transforming both worlds. In particular, the exchange decimated both the people and the landscape of the Americas (Mann; Grove), as the West left its everlasting imprint in the forests, jungles, and fields.

Pliny the Elder, *Naturalis historia*, or *Natural History*, On Arabia, Ethiopia, and the Fortunate Isles

In his massive *Naturalis historia*, or *Natural History* introduced in Part 1, Pliny the Elder also offered "an account of the countries, nations, seas, towns, havens, mountains, rivers, distances, and peoples who now exist, or formerly existed." Most of what he wrote was based on others' reports, mixing the fabulous with more realistic features. These three excerpts are derived from his accounts of three places: Arabia, Ethiopia, and the "Fortunate" or Canary Islands. The account of Arabia is more fact based, using recent information obtained from the Roman armies who ventured to those lands; as appropriate for the imperial project, it emphasizes the richness of that area's natural resources. In contrast, the description of Ethiopia extrapolates from the region's extreme weather an imagined monstrosity of its human and nonhuman inhabitants, reflecting the influence of climate theory (compare Hippocrates and Avicenna in Part 4). Finally, the excerpt on the Canary Islands anticipates later discourses about exotic islands that mixes both their natural riches and their strangeness.

On Arabia

Aelius Gallus, a member of the equestrian order, is the sole person who has hitherto carried the Roman arms into these lands, for Caius Caesar, the son of Augustus, only had a distant view of Arabia. In his expedition, Gallus destroyed the following towns, the names of which are not given by the authors who had written before his time, Negrana, Nestum, Nesca, Masugum, Caminacum, Labecia, and Mariva above-mentioned, six miles in circumference, as also Caripeta, the furthest point of his expedition. He brought back with him the following discoveries—that the nomads live upon milk and the flesh of wild beasts, and that the other nations, like the Indians, extract a sort of wine from the palm-tree, and oil from sesame. He says that the most numerous of these tribes are the Homeriae and the Minaei, that their lands are fruitful in palms and shrubs, and that their chief wealth is centered in

Source: Pliny the Elder. "On Arabia, Ethiopia, and the Fortunate Isles." *The Natural History of Pliny*, translated by John Bostock and Henry T. Riley, London: 1855, chaps. 32, 25, 27. *Perseus Digital Library*, http://www.perseus.tufts.edu/hopper/text?doc=Perseus%3Atext%3A1999.02.0137%3Abook%3D6%3Achapter%3D32.

their flocks. We also learn from the same source that the Cerbani and the Agraei excel in arms, but more particularly the Chatramotita; that the territories of the Carrei are the most extensive and most fertile; but that the Sabaei are the richest of all in the great abundance of their spice-bearing groves, their mines of gold, their streams for irrigation, and their ample produce of honey and wax.

On Ethiopia

The whole of this country has successively had the names of Etheria, Atlantia, and last of all, Ethiopia, from Ethiops, the son of Vulcan. It is not at all surprising that towards the extremity of this region the men and animals assume a monstrous form, when we consider the changeableness and volubility of fire, the heat of which is the great agent in imparting various forms and shapes to bodies. Indeed, it is reported that in the interior, on the eastern side, there is a people that have no noses, the whole face presenting a plane surface; that others again are destitute of the upper lip, and others are without tongues. Others again, have the mouth grown together, and being destitute of nostrils, breathe through one passage only, imbibing their drink through it by means of the hollow stalk of the oat, which there grows spontaneously and supplies them with its grain for food. Some of these nations have to employ gestures by nodding the head and moving the limbs, instead of speech. Others again were unacquainted with the use of fire before the time of Ptolemy Lathyrus, king of Egypt. Some writers have also stated that there is a nation of pygmies, which dwells among the marshes in which the river Nile takes its rise; while on the coast of Ethiopia, where we paused, there is a range of mountains, of a red color, which have the appearance of being always burning.

The Fortunate Isles [the Canaries]

Relative to the Fortunate Islands, Juba[1] has ascertained the following facts: that they are situated to the south in nearly a due westerly direction, and at a distance from the Purple Islands of six hundred and twenty-five miles, the sailing being made for two hundred and fifty miles due west, and then three hundred and seventy-five towards the east. He states that the first is called Ombrios, and that it presents no traces of buildings whatever; that among the mountains there is a lake, and some trees,[2] which bear a strong resemblance

1. Juba II (52/50 BCE–CE 23), king of Numidia and Mauretania and author of treatises on natural history

2. Possibly sugar cane

to giant fennel, and from which water is extracted; that drawn from those that are black is of a bitter taste, but that produced by the white ones is agreeable and good for drinking. He states also that a second island has the name of Junonia, but that it contains nothing beyond a small temple of stone: also that in its vicinity there is another, but smaller, island of the same name, and then another called Capraria, which is infested by multitudes of huge lizards. According to the same author, in sight of these islands is Ninguaria, which has received that name from its perpetual snows; this island abounds also in fogs. The one next to it is Canaria; it contains vast multitudes of dogs of very large size, two of which were brought home to Juba: there are some traces of buildings to be seen here. While all these islands abound in fruit and birds of every kind, this one produces in great numbers the date palm which bears the caryota,[3] also pine nuts. Honey too abounds here, and in the rivers papyrus, and the fish called silurus, are found. These islands, however, are greatly annoyed by the putrefying bodies of monsters, which are constantly thrown up by the sea.

John Mandeville, *Travels*

Medieval readers eagerly consumed travel narratives that shared stories and observations about a distant world that most would never see themselves. The most popular was the book of travel writing attributed to John Mandeville (the actual authorship of this text is still uncertain). It was first composed in French sometime during the mid-fourteenth century, and by 1500 it had spread across Europe and been translated into most vernaculars. For two centuries Mandeville's *Travels* dominated many accounts of the world beyond Europe, stretching to Africa, the Near East, Southeast Asia, and East Asia. While scholars still debate today how much was based on personal experience (the author makes some claims to that), most of the story does derive from the author's compiling and adapting the reports of multiple other writers. In his accounts of these "outlandish" places the author mixes information about human behavior with descriptions of the nonhuman environment and its creatures, both mundane and fabulous. These excerpts come from the *Travels*' accounts of Egypt and some of the island kingdoms of Southeast Asia. In Egypt the reader encounters both the then-exotic but real banana and the mythical phoenix; in the islands, we find a natural world that

3. A genus of palm trees

Source: *Travels of Sir John Mandeville*, Macmillan, 1900, chaps. 7, 21. *Project Gutenberg*, http://www.gutenberg.org/files/782/782-h/782-h.htm

is sweet, overabundant, and terrifying. (This version is based on the Cotton manuscript, a late Middle English translation dating to the early fifteenth century, with the spelling modernized.)

On Egypt

In Egypt there be two parts: the height, that is toward Ethiopia, and the lower, that is toward Arabia. In Egypt is the land of Rameses and the land of Goshen. Egypt is a strong country, for it hath many shrewd havens because of the great rocks that be strong and dangerous to pass by. And at Egypt, toward the east, is the Red Sea, that dureth unto the city of Coston; and toward the west is the country of Libya, that is a full dry land and little of fruit, for it is overmuch plenty of heat, and that land is clept Fusthe. And toward the part meridional is Ethiopia. And toward the north is the desert, that dureth unto Syria, and so is the country strong on all sides. And it is well a fifteen journeys of length, and more than two so much of desert, and it is but two journeys in largeness. And between Egypt and Nubia it hath well a twelve journeys of desert. And men of Nubia be Christian, but they be black as the moors for great heat of the sun.

In Egypt is the city of Heliopolis, that is to say, the city of the sun. In that city there is a temple, made round after the shape of the Temple of Jerusalem. The priests of that temple have all their writings, under the date of the fowl that is clept phoenix; and there is none but one in all the world. And he cometh to burn himself upon the altar of that temple at the end of five hundred year; for so long he liveth. And at the five hundred years' end, the priests array their altar honestly, and put thereupon spices and sulphur vif[1] and other things that will burn lightly; and then the bird phoenix cometh and burneth himself to ashes. And the first day next after, men find in the ashes a worm; and the second day next after, men find a bird quick and perfect; and the third day next after, he flieth his way. And so there is no more birds of that kind in all the world, but it alone, and truly that is a great miracle of God. And men may well liken that bird unto God, because that there ne is no God but one; and also, that our Lord arose from death to life the third day. This bird men see often-time fly in those countries; and he is not mickle more than an eagle. And he hath a crest of feathers upon his head more great than the peacock hath; and his neck is yellow after color of an oriel that is a stone well shining, and his beak is colored blue as indigo; and his wings be of purple color, and his tail is barred overthwart with green and yellow and red.

1. Virgin sulfur

And he is a full fair bird to look upon, against the sun, for he shineth full gloriously and nobly.

Also in Egypt be gardens, that have trees and herbs, the which bear fruits seven times in the year. And in that land men find many fair emeralds and enough; and therefore they be greater cheap. Also when it raineth once in the summer in the land of Egypt, then is all the country full of great mires.

[. . .]

Also in that country and in others also, men find long apples[2] to sell, in their season, and men clepe[3] them apples of Paradise; and they be right sweet and of good savor. And though ye cut them in never so many gobbets or parts, overthwart or endlong, evermore ye shall find in the midst the figure of the Holy Cross of our Lord Jesu. But they will rot within eight days, and for that cause men may not carry of those apples to no far countries; of them men find the mountance[4] of a hundred in a basket, and they have great leaves of a foot and a half of length, and they be convenably large. And men find there also the apple tree of Adam,[5] that have a bite at one of the sides; and there be also fig trees that bear no leaves, but figs upon the small branches; and men clepe them figs of Pharaoh.

On Java and South East Asia

But fast beside that isle, for to pass by sea, is a great isle and a great country that men clepe Java. And it is nigh two thousand mile in circuit. And the king of that country is a full great lord and a rich and a mighty, and hath under him seven other kings of seven other isles about him. This isle is full well inhabited, and full well manned. There grow all manner of spicery, more plenteously than in any other country, as of ginger, cloves-gilofre,[6] canell,[7] seedwall,[8] nutmegs and maces. And wit well, that the nutmeg beareth the maces; for right as the nut of the hazel hath an husk without, that the nut is closed in till it be ripe and that after falleth out, right so it is of the nutmeg and of the maces. Many other spices and many other goods grow in that isle. For of all things is there plenty, save only of wine. But there is gold and silver, great plenty.

[. . .]

2. Bananas
3. Name
4. Quantity
5. Melons
6. Cloves
7. Cinnamon
8. Setwal or zeodary

After that isle, in going by sea, men find another isle, good and great, that men clepe Pathen,[9] that is a great kingdom full of fair cities and full of towns. In that land grow trees that bear meal, whereof men make good bread and white and of good savor; and it seemeth as it were of wheat, but it is not allinges[10] of such savor. And there be other trees that bear honey good and sweet, and other trees that bear venom, against the which there is no medicine but [one]; and that is to take their proper leaves and stamp them and temper them with water and then drink it, and else he shall die; for triacle[11] will not avail, ne none other medicine. Of this venom the Jews had let seek of one of their friends for to empoison all Christianity, as I have heard them say in their confession before their dying; but thanked be Almighty God! they failed of their purpose; but always they make great mortality of people. And other trees there be also that bear wine of noble sentiment. And if you like to hear how the meal cometh out of the trees I shall say you. Men hew the trees with a hatchet, all about the foot of the tree, till that the bark be parted in many parts, and then cometh out thereof a thick liquor, the which they receive in vessels, and dry it at the heat of the sun; and then they have it to a mill to grind and it becometh fair meal and white. And the honey and the wine and the venom be drawn out of other trees in the same manner, and put in vessels for to keep.

In that isle is a dead sea, that is a lake that hath no ground; and if anything fall into that lake it shall never come up again. In that lake grow reeds, that be canes, that they clepe thaby,[12] that be thirty fathoms long; and of these canes men make fair houses. And there be other canes that be not so long, that grow near the land and have so long roots that endure well a four quarters of a furlong or more; and at the knots of those roots men find precious stones that have great virtues. And he that beareth any of them upon him, iron ne steel may not hurt him, ne draw no blood upon him; and therefore, they that have those stones upon them fight full hardily both on sea and land, for men may not harm [them] on no part. And therefore, they that know the manner, and shall fight with them, they shoot to them arrows and quarrels without iron or steel, and so they hurt them and slay them. And also of those canes they make houses and ships and other things, as we have here, making houses and ships of oak or of any other trees. And deem no man that I say it but for a trifle, for I have seen of the canes with mine own eyes, full many times, lying upon the river of that lake, of the which twenty of our fellows ne might not lift up ne bear one to the earth.

9. Possibly Borneo?
10. Entirely
11. Treacle
12. Bamboo

After this isle men go by sea to another isle that is clept Calonak.[13]

[. . .]

There be also in that country a kind of snails[14] that be so great, that many persons may lodge them in their shells, as men would do in a little house. And other snails there be that be full great but not so huge as the other. And of these snails, and of great white worms that have black heads that be as great as a man's thigh, and some less as great worms that men find there in woods, men make viand royal for the king and for other great lords.

Leo Africanus, *Della descrittione dell'Africa*, or *Description of Africa*

Born in Granada as al-Hasan ibn Muhammad al-Wazzan, Leo Africanus (ca. 1492–ca. 1550) moved to Fez and became an accomplished and well-traveled diplomat serving the Sultan. In 1518 he was captured and brought to Rome, where he enjoyed the patronage of Pope Leo X; he then converted to Christianity, taking the name Leo Africanus. While in Italy he wrote his immensely popular *Della descrittione dell'Africa*, or *Description of Africa* (probably composed in the 1520s but not published until 1550); this excerpt is taken from John Pory's 1660 English translation (based on the Latin version) entitled "A geographical history of Africa, written in Arabic and Italian by John Leo a Moor, born in Granada . . . gathered partly out of his own diligent observations, and partly out of the ancient records and chronicles of the Arabians and Moors." Like Pliny the Elder's ancient geography of Africa, it mixes the history of people with natural history. In contrast to earlier accounts, this description of Africa's natural world has far less of the fabulous, demonstrating the author's knowledge of the natural resources of "Barbary" and the extreme cold in the Atlas mountains.

Of the situation of Africa

As there are four parts in Africa, so the situation thereof is not in all places alike. That part which lieth towards the Mediterranean Sea, that is to say, from the straits of Gibraltar to the frontiers of Egypt, is here and there full of mountains. Southward it is extended about a hundred miles, albeit in some places it be larger and in some other narrower. From the said mountains unto Mount

13. Indo-China?

14. Likely giant tortoises

Source: *Leo Africanus, A geographical history of Africa, written in Arabic and Italian by John Leo a Moor, born in Granada, and brought up in Barbary . . .* Translated by John Pory, London, 1600, pp. 30–33.

Atlas there is a very spacious plain and many little hillocks. Fountains there are in this region great store, which meeting together at one head do send forth most beautiful rivers and crystal streams. Between the foresaid mountains and the plain country is situated the mountain of Atlas, which beginning westward upon the Ocean sea, stretcheth it self towards the east as far as the borders of Egypt. Over against Atlas lieth that region of Numidia which beareth dates, being everywhere almost sandy ground. Between Numidia and the land of Negros is the sandy desert of Libya situate, which containeth many mountains also; howbeit merchants travel not that way, when as they may go other ways with more ease and less danger. Beyond the Libyan desert beginneth the land of Negros, all places whereof are barren and sandy except those which adjoin upon the river of Niger, or through the which any river or stream runneth.

Of the unpleasant and snowy places in Africa

All the region of Barbary, and the mountains contained therein, are subject more to cold then to heat. For seldom cometh any gale of wind which bringeth not some snow therewith. In all the said mountains there grow abundance of fruits, but not so great plenty of corn.[1] The inhabitants of these mountains live for the greatest part of the year upon barley bread. The springs and rivers issuing forth of the said mountains, representing the quality and taste of their native soil, are somewhat muddy and impure, especially upon the confines of Mauritania. These mountains likewise are replenished with woods and lofty trees, and are greatly stored with beasts of all kinds. But the little hills and valleys lying between the foresaid mountains and mount Atlas are far more commodious, and abounding with corn. For they are moistened with rivers springing out of Atlas, and from thence holding on their course to the Mediterranean Sea. And albeit woods are somewhat more scarce upon these plains, yet are they much more fruitful, then be the plain countries situate between Atlas and the Ocean sea, as namely the regions of Morocco, of Duccala, of Tedles, of Tamesna, of Azgara, and the country lying towards the straits of Gibraltar. The mountains of Atlas are exceeding cold and barren, and bring forth but small store of corn, being woody on all sides, and engendering almost all the rivers of Africa. The fountains of Atlas are even in the midst of summer extremely cold; so that if a man dippeth his hand therein for any long space, he is in great danger of losing the same. Howbeit the said mountains are not so cold in all places: for some parts thereof are of such mild temperature, that they may be right commodiously inhabited: yea and sundry places thereof are well stored with inhabitants;

1. Grain

as in the second part of this present discourse we will declare more at large. Those places which are destitute of inhabitants be either extremely cold, as namely the same which lie over against Mauritania: or very rough and unpleasant, to wit, those which are directly opposite to the region of Tamesna. Where notwithstanding in summer time they may feed their great and small cattle, but not in winter by any means. For then the North wind so furiously rageth, bringing with it such abundance of snow, that all the cattle, which til then remain upon the said mountains, and a great part of the people also are forced to lose their lives in regard thereof: wherefore whosoever hath any occasion to travel that way in winter time, chooseth rather to take his journey between Mauritania and Numidia. Those merchants which bring dates out of Numidia for the use and service of other nations, set forth usually upon their journey about the end of October; and yet they are oftentimes so oppressed and overtaken with a sudden fall of snow, that scarcely one man among them all escapeth the danger of the tempest. For when it beginneth to snow over night, before the next morning not only carts and men, but even the very trees are so drowned and overwhelmed therein, that it is not possible to find any mention of them. Howbeit the dead carcasses are then found when the sun hath melted the snow.

Jean de Léry, *Histoire d'un voyage fait en la terre de Brésil*, or *History of a Voyage to the Land of Brazil*

In 1556 the French pastor Jean de Léry (1536–1613) found his way to what is now Brazil as part of a mission to set up a Calvinist colony there. When the colony dissolved, he spent several months living with the Tupinamba people, finally returning to France in 1558. Twenty years later, he published his *Histoire d'un voyage fait en la terre de Brésil*, or *History of a Voyage to the Land of the Brazil* (1578). The book advertised itself as an account of "the customs and strange ways of life of the American savages; together with the description of various animals, trees, plants, and other singular things completely unknown over here." It is now recognized as a groundbreaking work of ethnography and natural history of the New World. In his section on the indigenous flora and fauna, Léry, like many other early authors, dwells on the uses humans make of them, but his precise descriptions reflect his personal experience. In this excerpt he depicts mammals and reptiles, including tapirs, jaguars, and a gigantic terrifying lizard (which was likely an iguana) as sources of both food and danger. The animals are strange yet also recognizable as real creatures, not

Source: Jean de Léry. *History of a Voyage to the Land of Brazil*. Translated by Jane Whatley, University of California Press, 1993, pp. 82–83.

Figure 31. Illustration from Jean de Léry, representing a battle between two indigenous tribes, with a background of a natural scene with palm trees, a parrot, and a monkey, from *Histoire d'un voyage fait en la terre de Brésil, or History of a Voyage to the Land of Brazil* (1594) (fold-out illustration inserted between pp. 204 and 205). Dechert Collection. FC55 L5629 578h 1594. Kislak Center for Special Collections, Rare Books, and Manuscripts, University of Pennsylvania Libraries.

monsters. Léry also recounts sympathetically how the Tupinamba have come to manage their coexistence with them (Figure 31).

Concerning the four-footed animals, I will say first of all that in general and without exception there is not a single one in that land of Brazil in America that is in all respects exactly like any of ours; what is more, our Tupinamba rarely raise any domestic ones. So to describe the wild animals of their country—for which their generic name is *sóo*—I will begin with those that are edible. The first and most common one, which has a reddish and rather long coat, they call *tapiroussou.*[1] It is of about the height, bulk, and shape of a cow; however, it has no

1. A tapir

horns, and has a shorter neck, longer and more pendant ears, thinner and more agile legs, and an unsplit hoof shaped like that of a donkey. In fact, you could say that it partakes of both, and is half cow and half donkey. But it is entirely different from either, in its tail, which is very short (there are many animals in America that have almost none at all), and in its teeth, which are much more cutting and sharp; however, since it has no means of resistance other than flight, it is not at all dangerous. The savages kill it and various other animals with arrows, or else they catch it in traps and with other devices that they make quite skillfully. [. . .]

Our Tupinamba also have certain big toads, which when they are *boucané*[2] with the skin, tripe, and entrails, serve as food. Our physicians teach, and people back over here generally believe, that the flesh, blood, and whole body of the toad are deadly; however, from what I have said about those of Brazil, the reader can easily gather that either because of the temperature of the country, or perhaps for some other reason that I am unaware of, they are not vile, venomous or dangerous as ours are.

They also eat snakes as big as your arm and about three feet long; and (as I said they do with crocodiles) I have seen the savages drag back some of them that are streaked with black and red, which they would throw alive in the middle of their houses among their wives and children, who instead of being afraid of them would grasp them with both hands. They prepare and cook these big terrestrial eels in sections; but from what I know of it, the meat has an insipid, sweetish taste.

It isn't that there are no other kinds of snakes: especially in the rivers one finds certain longer, slender ones, as green as a beet, whose sting is extremely venomous; and in the story I am about to tell, you will hear that, besides these *touous*[3] I just spoke of, there are other and larger lizards in the forest that are very dangerous.

One day two other Frenchmen and I were rash enough to set forth to visit the region without the savages whom we customarily had along as guides. Having lost our way in the woods, as we were going along a deep valley, we heard the sound of a beast making its way toward us. Thinking that it was some savage, we continued on our path without disquiet and thought no more about it. But suddenly on our right, and about thirty feet from us, we saw on a little rise a lizard much bigger than a man's body, six or seven feet long, which seemed covered with whitish scales, as sharp and rough as oyster shells; with one of its front feet lifted, its head raised high and its eyes gleaming, it

2. Smoked
3. A kind of lizard

stopped short to look at us. We had not a single harquebus[4] or pistol among us, but only our swords, and, savage-fashion, each a bow and arrows in hand—weapons that could not serve us very well against such a furious and well-armed animal. Seeing him, and fearing that if we took flight he would outrun us and, having caught us, would swallow us up and devour us, we looked at each other stunned, and remained stock-still. This monstrous and terrible lizard opened its maw; because of the great heat (for the sun was shining and it was about noon), it was breathing so hard that we could easily hear it. After it had stared at us for about a quarter of an hour, it suddenly turned around; crashing through the leaves and branches where it passed—with a noise greater than that of a stag running through a forest—it fled back uphill. As for us, we had had such a scare that we had no desire to run after it; praising God for delivering us from this danger, we went on our way. It has occurred to me since, in accord with the opinion of those who say that the lizard takes delight in the human face, that this one had taken as much pleasure in looking at us as we had felt fear in gazing upon it.

There is also in that country a predatory beast that the savages call *jan-ouare*,[5] which is almost as long-legged and light-footed as a greyhound. It has long hairs around the chin, and a beautiful spotted skin like that of a lynx, which in general it closely resembles. The savages have great fear of this beast, and not without cause; for since it lives off its prey, like the lion, if it catches them it does not fail to kill them and then to tear them to pieces and eat them. And for their part, too, being cruel and vindictive against anything that hurts them, when they can catch one in a trap (which they do often), they do their worst: they pierce and wound it with arrows, and make it linger in its misery for a long while in the pit where it has fallen, before they finish it off. So that you can better understand how this beast deals with them: one day when five or six other Frenchmen and I were passing by the big island, the savages warned us to look out for the *jan-ouare*, which, that very week, had eaten three people in one of their villages.

Thomas Harriot, *Brief and True Report of the New Found Land of Virginia*

Thomas Harriot (1560–1621) was the most accomplished English mathematician and expert in navigation and astronomy of his time. From an early age he

4. Firearm like a rifle

5. Jaguar

Source: Thomas Harriot. *A briefe and true report of the new found land of Virginia*, Frankfurt, 1590, pp. 14, 16.

was part of the household of Sir Walter Raleigh and shared Raleigh's commitment to natural philosophy and exploration. Because of his scientific expertise, Harriot was asked to join Sir Richard Greville's 1585–86 expedition to Virginia, which was promoted by Raleigh. The voyagers ended up in what is now Roanoke; although they attempted to settle there, they failed to provide for themselves because they lacked proper leadership and training. Desperate for supplies, they were eventually rescued by Sir Francis Drake. After their return, Harriot wrote this *Brief and True Report of the New Found Land of Virginia*, advertising the natural resources and the character of the indigenous population that would make Virginia favorable for settlement and colonization. While the report's style implies scientific accuracy, it omits any of the settlers' hardships or eventual conflicts with the native tribes. First published in 1587, the report was reprinted by Richard Hakluyt in his 1589 edition of *Principal Navigations* and later published by the German Theodore de Bry as part of a series called *America* (1590), which included illustrations by John White, a trained surveyor who accompanied the expedition. While scholars now study Harriot's report for his ethnography, its description of the New World plants is revealing, especially insofar as Harriot attempts to make them appealing through analogy to English plants. Harriot also describes the typical garden of the "town" of Secota, which is both exotic and familiar in its features of groves, gardens, and fields, as Harriot naturalizes the otherwise outlandish vegetation and gardening practices (Figure 32).

The second part of such commodities as Virginia is known to yield for victual and sustenance of man's life, usually fed upon by the natural inhabitants: as also by us during the time of our abode. And first of such as are sowed and husbanded.

Pagatowr, a kind of grain so called by the inhabitants: the same in the West Indies is called maize; English men call it guinea wheat or turkey wheat, according to the names of the countries from whence the like hath been brought. The grain is about the bigness of our ordinary English peas and not much different in form and shape, but of divers colors: some white, some red, some yellow, and some blue. All of them yield a very white and sweet flour; being used according to his kind it maketh a very good bread. We made of the same in the country some malt, whereof was brewed as good ale as was to be desired. So likewise by the help of hops thereof may be made as good beer. It is a grain of marvelous great increase; of a thousand, fifteen hundred and some two thousand fold. [. . .]

Okindgier, called by us beans, because in greatness and partly in shape they are like to the beans in England, saving that they are flatter, of more divers col-

Figure 32. Illustration of the gardens of the town of Secota, mapping English plantation practices on the indigenous gardens. Drawing by John White, in Thomas Harriot, *A Briefe and True Report of the New Found Land of Virginia* (1580), plate 20. Call # STC 12786. Used by permission of the Folger Shakespeare Library.

ors, and some pied. The leaf also of the stem is much different. In taste they are altogether as good as our English peas.

Wickonzówr, called by us peas, in respect of the beans for distinction sake, because they are much less; although in form they little differ; but in goodness of taste much, and are far better than our English peas. Both the beans and peas are ripe in ten weeks after they are set. They make them victual either by boiling them all to pieces into a broth; or boiling them whole until they be soft and begin to break as is used in England, either by themselves or mixtly[1] together: Sometimes they mingle of the wheat with them. Sometime also being whole sodden,[2] they bruise or pound them in a mortar, and thereof make loaves or lumps of dowish[3] bread, which they use to eat for variety.

Macóqwer, according to their several forms called by us, pompions,[4] melons, and gourds, because they are of the like forms as those kinds in England. In Virginia such of several forms are of one taste and very good, and do also spring from one seed. There are of two sorts; one is ripe in the space of a month, and the other in two months.

There is an herb which in Dutch is called *Melden.* Some of those that I describe it unto, take it to be a kind of orage;[5] it groweth about four or five foot high: of the seed thereof they make a thick broth, and pottage of a very good taste; of the stalk by burning into ashes they make a kind of salt earth, wherewithal many use sometimes to season their broths; other salt they know not. We ourselves, used the leaves also for potherbs.

There is also another great herb in form of a marigold, about six foot in height; the head with the flower is a span in breadth. Some take it to be *Planta Solis:*[6] of the seeds hereof they make both a kind of bread and broth.

The Town of Secota

Their towns that are not enclosed with poles are commonly fairer. Then such as are enclosed, as appeareth in this figure [Figure 32] which lively expresseth the town of Secota. For the houses are scattered here and there, and they have garden expressed by the letter E. wherein groweth tobacco which the inhabitants call *Uppowoc.* They have also groves wherein they take deer, and fields wherein they sow their corn. In their corn fields they build as it were a scaffold whereon they set a cottage like to a round chair, signified by F. wherein they place one to

1. Mixed
2. Boiled
3. Doughy
4. Pumpkins
5. Orache, mountain spinach
6. Sunflower

watch for there are such number of fowls, and beasts, that unless they keep the better watch, they would soon devour all their corn. For which cause the watchman maketh continual cries and noise. They sow their corn with a certain distance noted by H. otherwise one stalk would choke the growth of another and the corn would not come unto his ripeurs[7] G. For the leaves thereof are large, like unto the leaves of great reeds. They have also a several broad plot C. where they meet with their neighbors, to celebrate their chief solemn feasts as the 18th[8] picture doth declare: and a place D. where after they have ended their feast they make merry together. Over against this place they have a round plot B. where they assemble themselves to make their solemn prayers. Not far from which place there is a large building A. wherein are the tombs of their kings and princes, as will appear by the 22th. figure likewise they have garden noted by the letter I. wherein they use to sow pompions. Also a place marked with K. wherein the make a fire at their solemn feasts, and hard without the town a river L. from whence they fetch their water. This people therefore void of all covetousness live cheerfully and at their hearts ease. But they solemnize their feasts in the night, and therefore they keep very great fires to avoid darkness, and to testify their joy.

Walter Raleigh, *Discovery of the Large, Rich, and Beautiful Empire of Guiana*

While not born into the aristocracy, Walter Raleigh (1552–1618) rose to an influential position in the courts of Elizabeth I and James I (although his life ended in disgrace). A man of many talents, he fought in wars on lands and sea, wrote poetry and prose, and experimented with natural philosophy. He was also actively involved in England's early efforts in colonization; he first sponsored a failed expedition to Virginia in 1585–86 (see Thomas Harriot, *Brief and True Report of the New Found Land of Virginia*, above), and a decade later he made his own first voyage to Guiana (now in Venezuela) and the jungle between the mouths of the Orinocco and Amazon rivers. Raleigh was chasing the myth of El Dorado, a city called Manoa near the Orinocco, where everything was said to be made of gold. The journey was arduous and ultimately disappointing, since he returned to England with nothing but a few gold samples, a large quantity of fool's gold, and some marcasite. After he returned in 1596, he composed his

7. Ripeness

8. Refers to another picture in the text

Source: Walter Ralegh. *The Discoverie of the Large, Rich, and Beautiful Empire of Guiana*, London, 1596, pp. 48, 67–68, 84.

Discovery of the Large, Rich, and Beautiful Empire of Guiana, an effort to justify the journey and encourage further exploration. This was an extraordinarily popular book, with scores of English, Dutch, and French editions printed throughout the seventeenth century. In these excerpts, Raleigh paints a complex portrait of the nature of this new world: the land is both strange and beautiful, resistant and inviting, in his words, a "country that hath yet her maidenhead." At points he wonders at its sublime beauty, even as he never ceases to seek for precious metals and stones, which always lie just out of his reach. At the same time, like Harriot's, Raleigh's prose often reaches to domestic analogies as a way of familiarizing that new world and rendering it less hostile in appearance; for example, in the experience described in the first excerpt, he contrasts the violence of an alligator attack with a sylvan landscape (Figure 33).

On both sides of this river, we passed the most beautiful country that ever mine eyes beheld; and whereas all that we had seen before was nothing but woods, prickles, bushes, and thorns, here we beheld plains of twenty miles in length, the grass short and green, and in divers parts groves of trees by themselves, as if they had been by all the art and labor in the world so made of purpose; and still as we rowed, the deer came down feeding by the waters side, as if they had been used to a keeper's call. Upon this river there were great store of fowl, and of many sorts; we saw in it divers sorts of strange fishes, and of marvelous bigness, but for lagartos[1] it exceeded, for there were thousands of those ugly serpents, and the people call it for the abundance of them the river of Lagartos, in their language. I had a negro a very proper young fellow, that leaping out of the galley to swim in the mouth of this river, was in all our sights taken and devoured with one of those lagartos.

[. . .]

Upon this river one Captain George, that I took with Berreo told me there was a great silver mine, and that it was near the banks of the said river. But by this time as well Orinocco, Caroli, and all the rest of the rivers were risen four or five foot in height, so as it was not possible by the strength of any men, or with any boat whatsoever to row into the river against the stream. I therefore sent Captain Thin, Captain Greenvile, my nephew John Gilbert, my cousin Butshead Gorges, Captain Clark, and some 30 shot more to coast the river by land, and to go to a town some twenty miles over the valley called Amnatapoi, and they found guides there, to go farther towards the mountain foot to another great town, called Capurepana, belonging to a Cassique called Hahara-

1. Alligators

382 West-Indianischer Historien Ander Theil

schnappen/daß die Spanier/so auß Trinidado geflohen/ vnd in Emereja bey dem Carapana blieben/ jrgendt in einem Dorff an diesem Wasser gelegen/solten zusammen seyn kommen/ Wie nun die Nacht mit gewalt einher fiel/vnd sie noch ernstlicher nach dem Dorff frageten/sagete der Pilot/ es were ein wenig besser hinauff/vnd wolte sich doch nichts ereugen/vnd war das Volck für Mattigkeit schier vergangen/ zu
Piloten gefahr. dem waren sie in die viertzig Englische Meil allbereit von der Galleen. Hierüber würde der Pilot gewiß seyn auffgeknüpffet worden/wann sie bey Nacht den Weg widerumb zurück gewust/ dann es war stickfinster/vnd fieng das Wasser an enger zu werden/vnd waren die Bäum auff beyden seiten so dick in einander gewachsen/daß sie mit jhren Wehren einen Paß dadurch machen musten. Da sie nun jhrem Alten Piloten je lenger je minder vertraweten/ vnd im Zweiffel stunden/ ob sie für oder zurück wolten/ ließ sie der Pilot dennoch allzeit auff der Meinung/daß es nur noch ein klein wenig weiter were/ biß sie entlich vmb ein
Kommen entlich ins Dorff. Vhr nach Mitternacht ein Liecht ersahen/vnd die Hunde bellen höreten. Also ruderten sie geschwind darauff zu/lendeten an/funden aber nicht viel Volcks/dann der Herr des Orts war wol vierhundert Englische Meilweges von dannen/zu den Canibalibus verreiset/ mit Gold zuhandlen/ vnd Weiber von jnen zuerkauffen/ Sie bekamen aber in seiner Behausung viel Brodt/ Fisch/ Hüner/ Indianischen Wein/vnd ruheten die Nacht folgendts auß/des morgens handelten sie mit den Einwohnern vmb gedachte Proviant/ vnd fuhren damit wider zu jhrer Galleen.

Oberauß schöne Landschaften. Auff beyden seiten des Wassers sahen sie die schöneste Landschafft die in der gantzen Welt zufinden/ es waren auff die zwantzig Englische Meil die schönesten Thäler/das Graß war kurtz vnnd grün/ vnnd an vielen Orten mit Bäumen so ordentlich besetzt/als ob sie also mit fleiß dahin gepflantzet worden/ Sie sahen auch weiter hinab das Wild am Vfer des Wassers vmbher spatzieren/als ob es zahm Viehe gewesen/deßgleichen ein grosse menge von allerley Vögel vnd vnterschiedlicher Farben: In dem Wasser sahen
Schlangen Lagartos. Ein Mohr von einer Schlangen gefressen. sie allerley frembde vnd wunderliche grosse Fische/auch eine vnzehenliche menge der vnflätigen Schlangen/die sie Lagartos nennen/des Herrn Ralegs Mohr/ein feiner Jüngling/ sprang daselbst ins Wasser/ vnd wolt an den Einfluß schwimmen/dieser ward in Angesicht der Engelländer von einer solchen Schlangen verschlungen.

Figure 33. Illustration from Walter Raleigh, *Discoverie of Guiana*, representing alligators devouring a man, with an otherwise peaceful background. From an edition of Theodor de Bry's *America*, part 13, published in German by Johan Ludwig Gottfried (1631). Courtesy of the John Carter Brown Library.

cea (that was a nephew to old Topiawari king of Arromaia our chiefest friend) because this town and province of Capurepana adjoined to Macureguarai, which was a frontier town of the empire: and the meanwhile myself with Captain Gifford, Captain Calfield, Edward. Hancocke, and some half a dozen shot marched over land to view the strange overfalls of the river of Carols which roared so far of, and also to see the plains, adjoining and the rest of the province of Canuri. I sent also Captain Whiddon, W. Connock and some eight shot with them, to see if they could find any mineral stone alongst the river side, When we ran to the tops of the first hills of the plains adjoining to the river, we beheld that wonderful breach of waters, which ran down Caroli; and might from that mountain see the river how it ran in the parts, above twenty miles of, and there appeared some ten or twelve overfalls in sight, every one as high over the other as a church tower, which fell with that fury, that the rebound of water made it seem, as if it had been all covered over with a great shower of rain; and in some places we took it at the first for a smoke that had risen over some great town. For mine own part I was well persuaded from thence to have returned, being a very ill footman,[2] but the rest were all so desirous to go near the said strange thunder of waters, as they drew me on by little and little, until we came into the next valley where we might better discern the same. I never saw a more beautiful country, nor more lively prospects, hills so raised here and there over the valleys, the river winding into divers branches, the plains adjoining without bush or stubble, all fair green grass, the ground of hard sand easy to march on, either for horse or foot, the deer crossing in every path, the birds towards the evening singing on every tree with a thousand several tunes, cranes and herons of white, crimson, and carnation perching in the rivers side, the air fresh with a gentle easterly wind, and every stone that we stooped to take up, promised either gold or silver by his complexion.

[. . .]

In this branch called Cararoopana were also many goodly islands, some of six miles long, some of ten, and some of twenty, when it grew towards sun set, we entered a branch of a river that fell into Orenoque called Winicapora: where I was informed of the mountain of crystal, to which in truth for the length of the way, and the evil season of the year, I was not able to march, nor abide any longer upon the journey; we saw it a far off and it appeared like a white church tower of an exceeding height. There falleth over it a mighty river which toucheth no part of the side of the mountain, but rusheth over the top of it, and falleth to the ground with a terrible noise and clamor, as if 1000 great

2. Poor walker

bells were knocked one against another. I think there is not in the world so strange an overfall, nor so wonderful to behold. Berreo told me that it hath diamonds and other precious stones on it, and that they shined very far off: but what it hath I know not, neither durst he or any of his men ascend to the top of the said mountain, those people adjoining being his enemies (as they were) and the way to it so impassible.

Michael Drayton, "Ode: To the Virginian Voyage"

A commoner by birth, Michael Drayton (1563–1631) was in London by the 1590s seeking aristocratic patronage to make a living as a prolific writer of poetry, especially heroic, historical, and amorous verses. His *Poly-Olbion, or, A chorographical description of all the tracts, rivers, mountains, forests, and other parts* [. . .] *of Great Britain* (1612) extended his sense of heroism to praise the variety and glory of Britain's land and waters. A year before the venture to found Jamestown in Virginia, Drayton also published an ode, "To the Virginian Voyage," as a stirring call to settlers of the New World lands, offering them the status of heroes and tempting them with visions of pearls, gold, and a fertile country that yields fruit without labor. While Drayton's representation of Virginia borrows from Richard Hakluyt's description of the 1584–86 Virginian voyages, here Drayton also evokes a Golden Age of human harmony with the natural world now present (compare with Virgil's *Georgics* in Part 4). It contrasts sharply with more down-to-earth if still propagandistic accounts of Virginia offered in Thomas Harriot's *Brief and True Encounter of the New Found Land of Virginia* and Walter Raleigh's *Discovery of Guiana*.

You brave heroic minds,
Worthy your country's name,
That honor still pursue,
Go, and subdue,
Whilst loit'ring hinds[1]
Lurk here at home, with shame.

Britons, you stay too long,
Quickly aboard bestow you,
And with a merry gale
Swell your stretch'd sail,

Source: *Poems: By Michael Drayton Esquire*, London, 1619, pp. 295–96.
1. Deer

With vows as strong,
As the winds that blow you.

Your course securely steer,
West and by south forth keep,
Rocks, lee-shores, nor shoals,
When Eolus[2] scowls,
You need not fear,
So absolute the deep.

And cheerfully at sea,
Success you still entice,
To get the pearl and gold,
And ours to hold,
Virginia,
Earth's only Paradise.

Where nature hath in store
Fowl, venison, and fish,
And the fruitful'st soil,
Without your toil,
Three harvests more,
All greater than your wish.

And the ambitious vine
Crowns with his purple mass,
The cedar reaching high
To kiss the sky,
The cypress, pine
And useful sassafras.

To whose, the Golden Age
Still Nature's laws doth give,
No other cares that tend,
But them to defend
From winter's age,
That long there doth not live.

2. God of the winds

When as the luscious smell
Of that delicious land,
Above the seas that flows,
The clear wind throws,
Your hearts to swell
Approaching the dear strand.[3]

In kenning[4] of the shore,
(Thanks to God, first given,)
O you, the happi'st men,
Be frolic then,
Let cannons roar,
Frighting the wide heaven.

And in regions far
Such heroes bring ye forth,
As those from whom we came,
And plant our name,
Under that star
Not known unto our north.

And as there plenty grows
Of laurel every where,
Apollo's sacred tree,
You it may see,
A poet's brows
To crown, that may sing there.

Thy voyage attend,
Industrious Hakluyt
Whose reading shall inflame
Men to seek fame,
And much commend
To after-times thy wit.

3. Beach
4. Discerning

John Parkinson, *Theatrum Botanicum*

Parts 2 and 5 introduce John Parkinson (1567–1650) with excerpts from his *Paradisi in Sole* (1629), focused on English gardening. Later in his career, having ascended to the status of apothecary to King Charles I, Parkinson dedicated his efforts to compiling an herbal, his massive *Theatrum Botanicum* (1640). Covering approximately 3,800 plants organized in seventeen "tribes," the herbal was advertised as "The theater of plants, or, an herbal of a large extent containing therein a more ample and exact history and declaration of the physical herbs and plants that are in other authors, increased by the access of many hundreds of new, rare, and strange plants from all the parts of the world." Its title page advertises its reach to the four continents of worlds (Figure 34). Whereas he limited *Paradisi in Sole*'s coverage of "outlandish" or non-native plants to those that would prosper in English climates, in the *Theatrum* Parkinson considered a much wider variety of which he had reports from around the globe. In these excerpts on the "sorrowful tree," night-flowering jasmine, and the "fountain tree of water," Parkinson includes others' accounts of those trees' features, derived from other herbals and travelers' reports. He strives to precisely describe their physical features and uses but also betrays some of the wonder that such exotica inspire. The fountain tree of water (Figure 35) is now thought to be either a myth or an exaggerated version of the palm tree, from which a liquor can be extracted. At the end of this entry Parkinson does note that he is not so credulous as to speak of the barnacle tree, a tree once thought to generate barnacle geese (and reported by John Mandeville in his *Travels*, above).

Arbor Tristis. The sorrowful tree.

The tree that beareth this name[1] from the properties riseth to be a reasonable tall, spreading sundry slender branches and fair leaves set by couples on them, very like unto the large or great myrtle leaves and smaller than those of the plum tree, little or nothing snipped about the edges, a little rough, and green on the upper side and gray underneath. At each joint with the leaves towards the ends of the branches on both sides come forth slender reddish yellow footstalks wherewith they color their broths and meats yellow like saffron, bearing three or four, or more flowers together thereon, composed of sundry small white leaves pointed at the ends, making a double flower, with divers small threads in the middle, smelling so sweet that they are thought to exceed either

Source: John Parkinson. *Theatrum Botanicum*, London, 1640, p. 1645.

1. This is the parijaat tree or night flowering jasmine.

Figure 34. John Parkinson, *Theatrum Botanicum*, title page depicting exotic flora and fauna from different regions of the world. Folio 581.63 P232. Kislak Center for Special Collections, Rare Books, and Manuscripts, University of Pennsylvania Libraries.

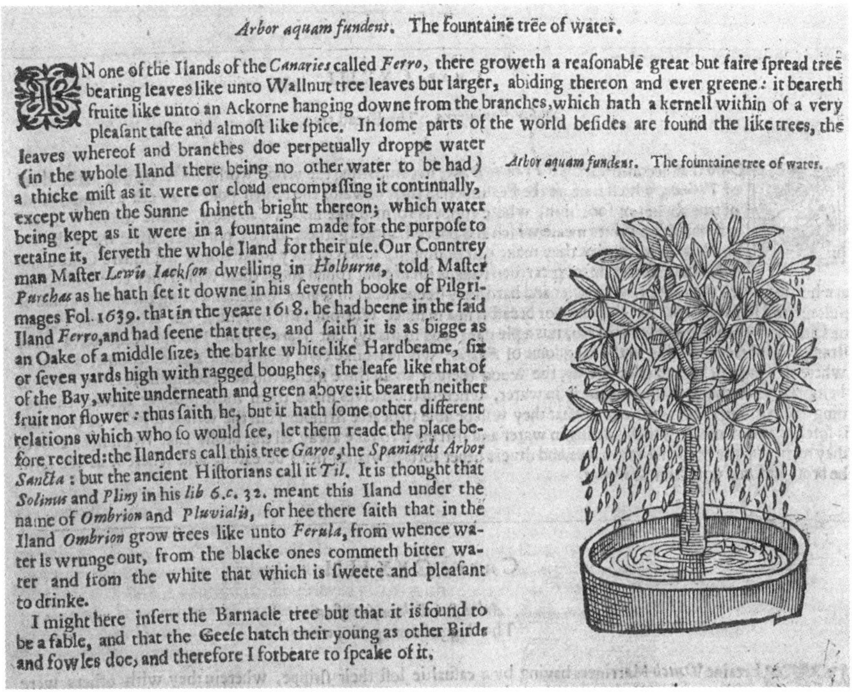

Arbor aquam fundens. The fountaine tree of water.

IN one of the Ilands of the *Canaries* called *Ferro*, there groweth a reasonable great but faire spread tree bearing leaves like unto Wallnut tree leaves but larger, abiding thereon and ever greene: it beareth fruite like unto an Ackorne hanging downe from the branches, which hath a kernell within of a very pleasant taste and almost like spice. In some parts of the world besides are found the like trees, the leaves whereof and branches doe perpetually droppe water (in the whole Iland there being no other water to be had) a thicke mist as it were or cloud encompassing it continually, except when the Sunne shineth bright thereon; which water being kept as it were in a fountaine made for the purpose to retaine it, serveth the whole Iland for their use. Our Countrey man Master *Lewis Iackson* dwelling in *Holburne*, told Master *Purchas* as he hath set it downe in his seventh booke of Pilgrimages Fol. 1639. that in the yeare 1618. he had beene in the said Iland *Ferro*, and had seene that tree, and saith it is as bigge as an Oake of a middle size, the barke white like Hardbeame, six or seven yards high with ragged boughes, the leafe like that of the Bay, white underneath and green above: it beareth neither fruit nor flower: thus saith he, but it hath some other different relations which who so would see, let them reade the place before recited: the Ilanders call this tree *Garoe*, the *Spaniards Arbor Sancta*: but the ancient Historians call it *Til*. It is thought that *Solinus* and *Pliny* in his *lib 6.c.* 32. meant this Iland under the name of *Ombrion* and *Pluvialis*, for hee there saith that in the Iland *Ombrion* grow trees like unto *Ferula*, from whence water is wrunge out, from the blacke ones commeth bitter water and from the white that which is sweete and pleasant to drinke.

I might here insert the Barnacle tree but that it is found to be a fable, and that the Geese hatch their young as other Birds and fowles doe, and therefore I forbeare to speake of it,

Arbor aquam fundens. The fountaine tree of water.

Figure 35. John Parkinson, *Theatrum Botanicum*, woodcut of the fountain tree of water, p. 1645. Folio 581.63 P232. Kislak Center for Special Collections, Rare Books, and Manuscripts, University of Pennsylvania Libraries.

the orange or jasmine flowers, whose property is never to blow open in the day time, but in the night only (when its time of flowering is), for so soon as the sun shineth thereon in the morning, they all for the most part fall down under the tree, and the whole tree with the branches seem as withered and dead until the evening, either through the tenderness of the stalk, or by a natural antipathy unto the sun, not to abide the shining face thereof, for some of the flowers do abide on these branches that are most shadowed from the sun. The following fruit they give is flat somewhat like a lupine with a thick skin (it must be but small store, for what quantity of fruit can this tree bear if all or the most of the flowers do fall away) yet heart fashion, and of a greenish ash color, with a division in the middle, in each part whereof is contained small flat beans or kernels, like unto those of the sweet bean or carob tree, heart fashion likewise, and covered with a greenish skin or peeling, the inner kernel being white and somewhat bitter. This tree hath been much desired to be transplanted into our Christian world, but as some have said it would not abide, notwithstanding all the care of earthen and wooden vessels, wherein it was planted to be brought into Spain or Portugal, neither ever would the seed spring as it is affirmed, but I have lately understood by a catalogue of the plants growing in the garden of Signor Corvino of Rome that it groweth there, being one of the plants named therein. It plentifully groweth in Malabar and brought thence to Goa, and sundry other places of the Indies, where every branch being put into the ground will take root and grow. It is called in Malabar Mogli, in Malaya Singadi, in Decan Pul, of the Arabians Guart, of the Persians and Turks Gul, but at Goa and Canarin Parizataco from a certain nobleman so called (as the natives think and therein very near intimating one of Ovid's fabulous metamorphosis) whose fair daughter the sun having espied fell in love withal, and having deflowered her aforsaken, for another, she slew herself; from whose ashes of her burnt carcass rose up this tree, which is ever since ashamed to behold the face of the sun. In many places of the Indies they distill the flowers for their sweet scent's sake, and keep it for use; which in Malabar they call the water of Mogli after the tree's name. The said water is good for sore eyes to cool their heat and redness, if linen clothes being dipped therein be laid upon them. The Indian physicians do hold opinion that both flowers and fruit do comfort the heart, and refresh the fainting spirits thereof, for they have some bitterness in them; it hath not been observed that the Indians apply this tree to any other use then is formerly expressed, and the coloring of their meats like as saffron is used for the same purpose in Spain and other countries.

The fountain tree of water.

In one of the islands of the Canaries called Ferro, there groweth a reasonable great but faire spread tree bearing leaves like unto walnut tree leaves but larger, abiding thereon and ever green: it beareth fruit like unto an acorn hanging down from the branches, which hath a kernel within of a very pleasant taste and almost like spice. In some parts of the world besides are found the like tree, the leaves whereof and branches do perpetually drop water (in the whole island there being no other water to be had), a thick mist as it were or cloud accompanying it continually, except when the sun shineth bright thereon, which water being kept as it were in a fountain made for the purpose to retain it, serveth the whole island for their use. Our countryman Master Lewis Jackson dwelling in Holborn told Master Purchas as he hath set it down in his seventh book of *Pilgrimages* Fol. 1639, that in the year 1618 he had been in the said island Ferro, and had seen that tree, and saith it is as big as an oak of a middle size, the bark white like hardbeam, six or seven yards high with ragged boughs, the leaf like that of the bay, white underneath and green above. It beareth neither fruit nor flower: thus saith he, but it hath some other different relations which who so would see, let them read the place before recited [. . .] I might here insert the barnacle tree but that it is found to be a fable, and that the geese hatch their young as other birds and fowls do, and therefore I forbear to speak of it.

Thomas Sprat, *History of the Royal Society*, Observations on Java

Parts 1 and 4 introduce Thomas Sprat's *History of the Royal Society for Improving Natural Knowledge* as testimony to the early efforts in England to bring together men committed to experimentation and observation of the natural world. Many of the experiments described their focus on familiar natural phenomena, but the fellows were also clearly interested in travelers' reports of exotica from across the globe. The *History* includes an interchange between the Society and Philiberto Vernatti, resident of Batavia, or what was the Dutch East Indies and is now Jakarta in Indonesia. The excerpts from this exchange emphasize the Society's concern with verifying reports of natural marvels through observation by a reliable witness, where some reports were dismissed as jests or foolishness. At the same time, Vernatti still expressed wonder at the outlandish life he had encountered, while maintaining his rational approach.

The history of the answers return'd by Sir Philiberto Vernatti, Resident in Batavia in Java Major, to certain inquiries sent thither by order of the *Royal Society*, and recommended by Sir Robert Moray.

Q. 3. *Whether there be a hill in Sumatra which burneth continually, and a fountain which runneth pure Balsam.*[1]

A. There is a hill that burneth in Sumatra near Endrapoer; but I cannot hear of any such fountain; and I believe that the like hill is upon Java Major opposite to Batavia: for in a clear morning or evening, from the road a man may perfectly perceive a continual smoke rise from the top and vanish by little and little. I have often felt earthquakes here, but they do not continue long; in the year 1656 or (I do not remember well the time) Batavia was covered in one afternoon, about two of the clock, with a black dust, which being gathered together, was so ponderous, that it exceeded the weight in gold. I, at that time,

Source: Thomas Sprat. *The History of the Royal-Society of London for the Improving of Natural Knowledge*, London, 1667, pp. 158–64.

1. An aromatic resin

being very ill, did not take much notice of it, but some have gathered it, and if I light upon it shall send you some. It is here thought, it came out of the hill: I never heard of any that had been upon this hill's top: Endrapeor is counted a mighty unwholesome place, as likewise all others where pepper grows, as Jamby Banjar, Balingtoan, etc. though some impute it to the hill's burning.

As for the fountain it is unknown to us, except *Oleum Terrae*[2] is meant by it, which is to be had in Sumatra, but the best comes from Pegu.[3]

Q. 4. *What river is that in Java Major that turns wood into stone?*

A. There is none such to our knowledge; yet I have seen a piece of wood with a stone at the end of it, which was told me, that was turned into stone by a river in Pegu; but I took it but for a foppery;[4] for divers arbusta[5] grow in rocks, which being appropriated curiously, may easily deceive a too hasty believer.

Q. 6. *Whether in the island of Sambrero, which lieth Northwards of Sumatra, about eight degrees northern latitude, there be found such a vegetable as Master James Lancaster relates to have seen, which grows up to a tree, shrinks down when one offers to pluck it up into the ground, and would quite shrink unless held very hard? And whether the same, being forcibly plucked up, hath a worm for its root, diminishing more and more; according as the tree groweth in greatness; and as soon as the worm is wholly turned into the tree, rooting in the ground, and so growing great? And whether the same plucked up young turns, by that time it is dry, into a hard stone, much like to white coral.*

A. I cannot meet with any that ever have heard of such a vegetable.

Q. 7. *Whether those creatures that are in these parts plump and in season at the full moon, are lean and out of season at the new, find the contrary at the East-Indies.*

A. I find it so here, by experience at Batavia, in oysters and crabs.

Q. 8. *What ground there may be for that relation, concerning horns taking root, and growing about Goa?*

2. Oil of the earth, or petroleum
3. Now Bago, Myanmar
4. Foolishness
5. Arbutus

A. Inquiring about this, a friend laughed, and told me it was a jeer put upon the Portuguese, because the women of Goa are counted much given to lechery.

[. . .]

Q. 13 *Whether the Arbor Triste sheds its flowers at the rising of the sun, and shut them again at the setting of the sun? And whether the distilled water thereof (called Aqua di Mogli by the Portugals) may not be transported to England? And whether at the rising of the sun the leaves of the Arbor Triste drop off as well as the flowers?*[6]

A. There are two sorts of the Arbor Triste; one is called by the Portugals *Triste de Die*, the other *Triste de Nocte*; the one sheds his flowers at the rising, the other at the setting of the sun; but neither of them shed their leaves. There is nobody here that understands the distilling of waters; some say this *Aqua di Mogli* is to be had at Malaca, for which I have writ, and shall send it if procurable.

Q. 14. *Whether the Arbor de Rays, or Tree of Root, propagate itself in a whole forest, by shooting up and letting fall roots from its branches into the ground, that spring up again, and so on?*

A. This is true. And we have divers trees about Batavia, and the like adjacent islands, above fifty foot in the diameter.

Q. 15. *What kind of fruit is that in Jucca, which grows immediately out of the tree's body; and is said to breed the plague if eaten immoderately?*

A. It is a fruit much like to durian, which groweth in the same manner; hath a faint smell, and sweet waterish taste; for my part I do not affect them: The plague is a disease unknown amongst the Indians; but this fruit, as most others do, immoderately eaten, causes a diarrhea,[7] which easily degenerates to a tenasmus,[8] by us called peirsing, a dangerous sickness, and worse than the plague.

[. . .]

Q. 20. *Whether the animal call'd abados, or* rhinoceros, *hath teeth, claws, flesh, blood, and skin yea his very dung and water, as well as his horns, antidotal? And whether the horns of those beasts be better or worse, according to the food they live upon.*

6. See John Parkinson on the "arbor triste," above.

7. Diarrhea

8. A continuous desire to empty the bowels

A. Their horns, teeth, claws, and blood are esteemed antidotes, and have the same use in the Indian pharmacopeia as the therieca[9] hath in ours; the flesh I have eaten is very sweet and short; some days before the receipt of your letter, I had a young one no bigger than a spaniel dog, which followed me wherever I went, drinking nothing but buffalo milk, lived about three weeks, then his teeth began to grow, and got a looseness,[10] and died. 'Tis observed, that children (especially of European parents) at the breaking out of their teeth are dangerous sick, and commonly die of the scouring in these parts. His skin I have caused to be dried, and so present it unto you, since fate permits not to send him you living; such a young one was never seen before. The food I believe is all one to this animal, being that they are seldom seen but amongst withered branches, thistles and thorns; so that the horn is of equal virtue.

[. . .]

Q. 28. *Whether at Hermita, a town in Ethiopia, there are tortoises, so big, that men may ride upon them?*

A. It is reported, that there be extraordinary great ones there; I have seen some sea-tortoises here, of four foot broad, in oval form, very low legged, but of that strength, that a man may stand on one. The manner of catching them, is to turn them with a fork upon their backs.

Q. 29. *Whether there be a tree in Mexico, that yields water, wine, vinegar, oil, milk, honey, wax, thread and needles?*

A. The cokos[11] trees yields all this and more; the nut, while it is green, hath very good water in it, the flower being cut, drops out great quantity of liquor, called sury, or taywack, which drank fresh, hath the force, and almost the taste of wine; grown sour, is very good vinegar; and distilled, makes very good brandy, or arrack. The nut grated, and mingled with water, tasteth like milk: pressed, yields very good oil; bees swarm in these trees, as well as in other; thread and needles are made of the leaves and tough twigs. Nay, to add something to this description: in

9. An antidote to poison
10. In the bowels
11. Coconut

Amboina,[12] they make bread of the body of the tree, the leaves serve to thatch houses, and likewise sails for their boats.

Aphra Behn, *Oroonoko, or The Royal Slave: A True History*

Aphra Behn (1640?–1689) began her career as a prolific playwright, translator, and novelist in the 1670s. She was to write nineteen adventurous plays exploring issues of gender, marriage, and politics, as well as several highly successful works of prose fiction, a remarkable record for a time when few women published their writing. Her most famous work is her short novel, *Oroonoko, or The Royal Slave: A True History* (1688), a story of a noble African prince who is sold into slavery. The tale portrays his life in Africa and transportation to Surinam on the coast of the Guianas, his organization of a slave revolt there, his tragic love for Imoinda, and his eventual hideous death. Most of the story is set in Surinam when it was still under British rule before being captured by the Dutch in 1667. The story's narrator represents herself as an "eyewitness" to the events and thus as having experienced Surinam's environment (it is possible that Behn herself lived there around 1663–64). The description of the colony's indigenous inhabitants paints them as living in complete harmony with the natural world, as well as with their colonial occupiers. Animals and things derived from animals and plants become articles of clothing or the stuff of congenial trade. This golden age-like setting is then abruptly undermined by the mention of the African slave trade that actually sustains the colony's economy; the rest of the story portrays the British governors as cruel overlords of the slave population.

The scene of the last part of [Oroonoko's] adventures lies in a colony in America, called Surinam, in the West Indies. But before I give you the story of this gallant slave, 'tis fit I tell you the manner of bringing them to these new colonies; those they make use of there not being natives of the place. For those we live with in perfect amity, without daring to command 'em; but, on the contrary, caress 'em with all the brotherly and friendly affection in the world, trading with them for their fish, venison, buffalo's skins, and little rarities; as marmosets, a sort of monkey, as big as a rat or weasel, but of marvelous and delicate shape, having face and hands like a human creature; and cousheries, a little beast in the form and fashion of a lion, as big as a kitten, but so exactly made in all parts like that noble beast that it is it in miniature. Then for little

12. Island in Indonesia

Source: *Oroonoko, or, The Royal Slave: A True History*, London, 1688, pp. 3–13.

paraketoes,[1] great parrots, mackaws, and a thousand other birds and beasts of wonderful and surprising forms, shapes, and colors. For skins of prodigious snakes, of which there are some threescore yards in length, as is the skin of one that may be seen at his Majesty's Antiquary's, where are also some rare flies, of amazing forms and colors, presented to 'em by myself, some as big as my fist, some less; and all of various excellencies, such as art cannot imitate. Then we trade for feathers, which they order into all shapes, make themselves little short habits of 'em and glorious wreaths for their heads, necks, arms, and legs, whose tinctures are unconceivable. I had a set of these presented to me, and I gave 'em to the King's Theater, and it was the dress of the Indian Queen, infinitely admired by persons of quality; and was unimitable. Besides these, a thousand little knacks and rarities in nature; and some of art, as their baskets, weapons, aprons, etc. We dealt with 'em with beads of all colors, knives, axes, pins, and needles, which they used only as tools to drill holes with in their ears, noses, and lips, where they hang a great many little things; as long beads, bits of tin, brass or silver beat thin, and any shining trinket. The beads they weave into aprons about a quarter of an ell long, and of the same breadth; working them very prettily in flowers of several colors, which apron they wear just before 'em, as Adam and Eve did the fig-leaves, the men wearing a long stripe of linen, which they deal with us for. They thread these beads also on long cotton threads, and make girdles to tie their aprons to, which come twenty times, or more, about the waist, and then cross, like a shoulder-belt, both ways, and round their necks, arms, and legs. This adornment, with their long black hair, and the face painted in little specks or flowers here and there, makes 'em a wonderful figure to behold. Some of the beauties, which indeed are finely shaped, as almost all are, and who have pretty features, are charming and novel, for they have all that is called beauty, except the color, which is a reddish yellow; or after a new oiling, which they often use to themselves, they are of the color of a new brick, but smooth, soft, and sleek. They are extreme modest and bashful, very shy, and nice of being touched. And though they are all thus naked, if one lives forever among 'em there is not to be seen an undecent action, or glance; and being continually used to see one another so unadorned, so like our first parents before the Fall, it seems as if they had no wishes, there being nothing to heighten curiosity; but all you can see, you see at once, and every moment see; and where there is no novelty, there can be no curiosity. Not but I have seen a handsome young Indian dying for love of a very beautiful young Indian maid, but all his courtship was to fold his arms, pursue her with his eyes, and sighs were all his

1. Parakeets

language; while she, as if no such lover were present, or rather as if she desired none such, carefully guarded her eyes from beholding him, and never approached him but she looked down with all the blushing modesty I have seen in the most severe and cautious of our world. And these people represented to me an absolute idea of the first state of innocence, before man knew how to sin. And 'tis most evident and plain that simple Nature is the most harmless, inoffensive, and virtuous mistress. 'Tis she alone, if she were permitted, that better instructs the world than all the inventions of man. Religion would here but destroy that tranquility they possess by ignorance; and laws would but teach 'em to know offense, of which now they have no notion.

[. . .]

With these people, as I said, we live in perfect tranquility and good understanding, as it behooves us to do; they knowing all the places where to seek the best food of the country, and the means of getting it; and for very small and unvaluable trifles, supply us with that 'tis impossible for us to get; for they do not only in the woods, and over the savannahs, in hunting, supply the parts of hounds, by swiftly scouring through those almost impassable places, and by the mere activity of their feet run down the nimblest deer and other eatable beasts; but in the water, one would think they were gods of the rivers, or fellow-citizens of the deep, so rare an art they have in swimming, diving, and almost living in water, by which they command the less swift inhabitants of the floods. And then for shooting, what they cannot take, or reach with their hands, they do with arrows, and have so admirable an aim that they will split almost an hair, and at any distance that an arrow can reach. They will shoot down oranges and other fruit, and only touch the stalk with the dart's point, that they may not hurt the fruit. So that they being on all occasions very useful to us, we find it absolutely necessary to caress 'em as friends, and not to treat 'em as slaves, nor dare we do other, their numbers so far surpassing ours in that continent.

Those then whom we make use of to work in our plantations of sugar are negroes, black slaves altogether, who are transported thither in this manner. Those who want slaves make a bargain with a master or a captain of a ship, and contract to pay him so much apiece, a matter of twenty pound a head, for as many as he agrees for, and to pay for 'em when they shall be delivered on such a plantation: so that when there arrives a ship laden with slaves, they who have so contracted go aboard, and receive their number by lot; and perhaps in one lot that may be for ten, there may happen to be three or four men, the rest women and children. Or be there more or less of either sex, you are obliged to be contented with your lot.

Recommended Reading and Bibliography

While by no means a comprehensive bibliography, this list of recommended readings directs interested readers to texts to expand their understanding of categories covered by each part of this anthology. As with the parts themselves, there is considerable overlap; for example, people interested in plant culture should consult several of the sections, including Gardens and Gardening, Inhabiting the Land, and Outlandish Natural Worlds. The bibliography ends with recent books of ecocriticism focused on premodern literature and culture, which address many of the areas covered by the various parts. Because of the state of ecocriticism in the various fields, the overall list tilts heavily toward early modern English literature, but one can hope that will change in the future.

Natural Philosophy and Natural Knowledge

Beagon, Mary. *Roman Nature: The Thought of Pliny the Elder.* Clarendon, 1992.

Collingwood, R. G. *The Idea of Nature.* Clarendon, 1945.

Crombie, A. C. *Medieval and Early Modern Science.* Harvard University Press, 1967.

Daston, Lorraine, and Katherine Park. *Wonders and the Order of Nature: 1150–1750.* Zone, 1998.

Eamon, William. *Science and the Secrets of Nature: Books of Secrets in Medieval and Early Modern Culture.* Princeton University Press, 1994.

Economou, George. *The Goddess Natura in Medieval Literature.* Harvard University Press, 1972.

Elyot, Thomas. *The Boke Named the Governour.* London, 1531.

Findlen, Paula. *Possessing Nature: Museums, Collecting, and Scientific Culture in Early Modern Italy.* University of California Press, 1994.

Foucault, Michel. *The Order of Things: An Archaeology of the Human Sciences* (1966). Pantheon Books, 1970.

French, Roger. *Ancient Natural History.* Routledge, 1984.

Glacken, Clarence J. *Traces on the Rhodian Shore: Nature and Culture in Western Thought from Ancient Times to the End of the Eighteenth Century.* University of California Press, 1967.

Grant, Edward. *A History of Natural Philosophy: From the Ancient World to the Nineteenth Century.* Cambridge University Press, 2007.

Harkness, Deborah E. *The Jewel House: Elizabethan London and the Scientific Revolution.* Yale University Press, 2007.

Hesiod. "Works and Days." *The Homeric Hymns and Homerica*, translated by Hugh G. Evelyn-White, Harvard University Press / William Heinemann, 1914. https://www.gutenberg.org/files/348/348-h/348-h.htm.

Hoeniger, F. D., and J. F. M. Hoeniger. *The Development of Natural History in Tudor England*. Folger Shakespeare Library / University Press of Virginia, 1969.

———. *The Growth of Natural History in Stuart England from Gerard to the Royal Society*. Folger Shakespeare Library / University Press of Virginia, 1969.

Jardine, Nicolas, James Secord, and Emma Spary, editors. *Cultures of Natural History*. Cambridge University Press, 1996.

Lindberg, David. *The Beginnings of Western Science: The European Scientific Tradition in Philosophical, Religious, and Institutional Context, 600 BC to AD 1450*. University of Chicago Press, 1992.

———. *Science in the Middle Ages*. University of Chicago Press, 1978.

Lloyd, G. E. R. *Science, Folklore and Ideology: Studies in the Life Science in Ancient Greece*. Cambridge University Press, 1983.

Lovejoy, Arthur O. *The Great Chain of Being: A Study of the History of an Idea*. Harvard University Press, 1936.

Newman, William R., and Anthony Grafton, editors. *Secrets of Nature: Astrology and Alchemy in Early Modern Europe*. MIT Press, 2001.

Nicholson, Marjorie. *The Breaking of the Circle. Studies in the Effect of the "New Science" upon Seventeenth Century Poetry*. Northwestern University Press, 1950.

Robertson, Kellie. *Nature Speaks: Medieval Literature and Aristotelian Philosophy*. University of Pennsylvania Press, 2017.

Schoenfeldt, Michael. *Bodies and Selves in Early Modern England: Physiology and Inwardness in Spenser, Shakespeare, Herbert, and Milton*. Cambridge University Press, 1999.

Shank, Michael H. "Natural Knowledge in the Latin Middle Ages." In *Wrestling with Nature: From Omens to Science*, edited by Peter Harrison, Ronald L. Numbers, and Michael H. Shank, University of Chicago Press, 2011, pp. 83–115.

Siriasi, Nancy. *Medieval and Early Renaissance Medicine*. University of Chicago Press, 1990.

Thomas, Keith. *Man and the Natural World: A History of the Modern Sensibility*. Pantheon, 1983.

Tillyard, Eustace M.W. *The Elizabethan World Picture: A Study of the Idea of Order in the Age of Shakespeare, Donne and Milton*. Chatto and Windus, 1943.

Wall, Wendy. *Recipes for Thought: Knowledge and Taste in the Early Modern English Kitchen*. University of Pennsylvania Press, 2016.

Yamamoto, Dorothy. *The Boundaries of the Human in Medieval English Literature*. Oxford University Press, 2000.

Plants

Anderson, Frank J. *An Illustrated History of the Herbals*. Columbia University Press, 1977.

Arber, Alice. *Herbals: Their Origin and Evolution. A Chapter in the History of Botany, 1470–1670*. 3rd ed., Cambridge University Press, 1986.

Bellamy, Liz. *The Language of Fruit: Literature and Horticulture in the Long Eighteenth Century*. University of Pennsylvania Press, 2019.

Collins, Minta. *Medieval Herbals: The Illustrative Traditions*. British Library, 2000.

Duthie, Ruth. *Florists' Flowers and Societies*. Shire Publications, 1988.

Feerick, J. "Botanical Shakespeares: The Racial Logic of Plant Life in *Titus Andronicus*." *South Central Review* vol. 26, 2009, pp. 82–102.

Goody, Jack. *The Culture of Flowers*. Cambridge University Press, 1993.

Henrey, Blanche. *British Botanical and Horticultural Literature before 1800*. Vol. 1. Oxford University Press, 1975.

Hyde, Elizabeth. *Cultivated Power: Flowers, Culture, and Politics in the Reign of Louis XIV.* University of Pennsylvania Press, 2005.

Knight, Leah. *Of Books and Botany in Early Modern England: Sixteenth-Century Plants and Print Culture.* Ashgate, 2009.

Laroche, Rebecca. *Medical Authority and Englishwomen's Herbal Texts, 1550–1650.* Aldershot: Ashgate, 2009.

Marder, Michael. *The Philosopher's Plant: An Intellectual's Herbarium.* Columbia University Press, 2014.

Morton, A. G. *History of Botanical Science: An Account of the Development of Botany from Ancient Times to the Present Day.* Academic, 1981.

Nardizzi, Vin, editor. "Premodern Plants." Special issue, *Postmedieval* vol. 9, no. 4, 2018.

Pavord, Anna. *The Naming of Names: The Search for Order in the World of Plants.* Bloomsbury, 2005.

———. *The Tulip.* Bloomsbury, 1999.

Rohde, Eleanour Sinclair. *The Old English Herbals.* Longmans, 1922.

Saunders, Gill. *Picturing Plants: An Analytical History of Botanical Illustration.* Berkeley: University of California Press, 1995.

Van Arsdall, Anne. *Medieval Herbal Remedies: The Old English Herbarium and Anglo-Saxon Medicine.* London: Routledge, 2012.

Zirkle, Conway. *The Beginnings of Plant Hybridization.* 1935. University of Pennsylvania Press, 2019.

Animals

Bach, Rebecca. *Birds and Other Creatures in Renaissance Literature: Shakespeare, Descartes, and Animal Studies.* Routledge, 2018.

Boehrer, Bruce. *Animal Characters: Nonhuman Beings in Early Modern Literature.* University of Pennsylvania Press, 2010.

———. *Shakespeare Among the Animals: Nature and Society in the Drama of Early Modern England.* Palgrave / St. Martin's Press, 2002.

Cavendish, Margaret. *Poems and Fancies: A Digital Edition edited by Liza Blake.* http://library2.utm.utoronto.ca/poemsandfancies/.

Clark, Wilene B. *A Medieval Book of Beasts: The Second-Family Bestiary: Commentary, Art, Text and Translation.* Boydell Press, 2006.

Crane, Susan. *Animal Encounters: Contacts and Concepts in Medieval Britain.* University of Pennsylvania Press, 2012.

Fudge, Erica. *Brutal Reasoning: Animals, Rationality, and Humanity in Early Modern England.* Cornell University Press, 2006.

———. *Perceiving Animals: Humans and Beasts in Early Modern English Culture.* University of Illinois Press, 2002.

Hölfele, Andreas. *Stage, Stake, and Scaffold: Humans and Animals in Shakespeare's Theatre.* Oxford University Press, 2011.

Paster, Gail Kern. "Melancholy Cats, Lugged Bears, and Other Passionate Animals: Reading Shakespeare's Psychological Materialism across the Species Barrier." *Humoring the Body: Emotions and the Shakespearean Stage.* University of Chicago Press, 2004, pp. 135–188.

Raber, Karen. *Animal Bodies, Renaissance Culture.* University of Pennsylvania Press, 2013.

———. "From Sheep to Meat, From Pets to People: Animal Domestication 1600–1800." *A Cultural History of Animals,* vol. 4, *1600–1800,* edited by Matthew Senior, Berg, 2007, pp. 73–99.

———. "How to Do Things with Animals: Thoughts on/with the Early Modern Cat." *Early Modern Ecostudies: From Shakespeare to the Florentine Codex*, edited by Tom Hallock, Ivo Kamps, and Karen Raber. Palgrave, 2009, pp. 93–114.

Salisbury, Joyce E. *The Beast Within: Animals in the Middle Ages*. 2nd ed., Routledge, 2011.

Shannon, Laurie. *The Accommodated Animal: Cosmopolity in Shakespearean Locales*, University of Chicago Press, 2013.

Steel, Karl. *How to Make A Human: Animals and Violence in the Middle Ages*. Ohio State University Press, 2011.

Toynbee, J. M. C. *Animals in Roman Life and Art*. Cornell University Press, 1973.

Weather, Climate, and Seasons

Blom, Philip. *Nature's Mutiny: How the Little Ice Age of the Long Seventeenth Century Transformed the West and Shaped the Present*. London: Liveright, 2019.

Brayton, Dan. *Shakespeare's Ocean: An Ecocritical Exploration*. University of Virginia Press, 2012.

Duckert, Lowell. *For All Waters: Finding Ourselves in Early Modern Wetscapes*. University of Minnesota Press, 2017.

Fagan, Brian, *The Little Ice Age: How Climate Made History, 1300–1850*. Basic Books, 2007.

Feerick, Jean E. *Strangers in the Blood: Relocating Race in the Renaissance*. University of Toronto Press, 2010.

Floyd-Wilson, Mary. *English Ethnicity and Race in Early Modern Drama*. Cambridge University Press, 2003.

Jones, Gwilym. *Shakespeare's Storms*. Manchester University Press, 2014.

Mentz, Steve. *At the Bottom of Shakespeare's Ocean*. Continuum Press, 2009.

———. *Shipwreck Modernity: Ecologies of Globalization, 1550–1719*. University of Minnesota Press, 2015.

———. "Strange Weather in King Lear." *Shakespeare* vol. 6, no. 2, 2010, pp. 139–52.

Totoro, Rebecca. *Meteorology and Physiology in Early Modern Culture: Earthquakes, Human Identity, and Textual Representation*. Routledge, 2018.

Tuve, Rosamond. *Seasons and Months: Studies in a Tradition of Middle English Poetry*. Librarie Universitaire, 1933.

Inhabiting the Land

Alpers, Paul J. *What is Pastoral?* University of Chicago Press, 1996.

Ambrosoli, Mauro. *The Wild and the Sown: Botany and Agriculture in Western Europe 1350–1850*. Cambridge University Press, 1977.

Dolan, Frances E. *Digging the Past: How and Why to Imagine Seventeenth-Century Agriculture* University of Pennsylvania Press, 2020.

Hiltner, Kent. *What Else is Pastoral? Renaissance Literature and the Environment*. Cornell University Press, 2011.

Kermode, Frank, editor. *English Pastoral Poetry from the Beginnings to Marvell: An Anthology*. 1952. W. W. Norton, 1972.

Leslie, Michael, and Raylor, Timothy, editors. *Culture and Cultivation in Early Modern England: Writing and the Land*. Leicester University Press, 1992.

Low, Anthony. *The Georgic Revolution*. Princeton University Press, 1985.

McRae, Andrew. *God Speed the Plough: The Representation of Agrarian England, 1500–1660*. Cambridge University Press, 1996.

Nardizzi, Vin. *Wooden Os: Shakespeare's Theatres and England's Trees.* University of Toronto Press, 2013.

Saunders, C. J. *The Forest of Medieval Romance: Avernus, Broceliande, Arden.* D. S. Brewer, 1993.

Theis, Jeffrey S. *Writing the Forest in Early Modern England: A Sylvan Pastoral Nation.* Duquesne University Press, 2005.

Turner, James. *The Politics of Landscape: Rural Scenery and Society in English Poetry 1630–1660.* Blackwell, 1979.

Wall, Wendy. "Renaissance National Husbandry: Gervase Markham and the Publication of England," *Sixteenth Century Journal* vol. 27, 1996, pp. 767–85.

White, K. D. *Roman Farming.* Cornell University Press, 1970.

Williams, Raymond. *The Country and the City.* Oxford University Press, 1973.

Gardens and Gardening

Bowe, Patrick. *Gardens of the Roman World.* J. Paul Getty Museum, 2004.

Bushnell, Rebecca. *Green Desire: Imagining Early Modern English Gardens.* Cornell University Press, 2003.

Carroll, Maureen. *Earthly Paradises: Ancient Gardens in History and Archaeology.* British Museum Press, 2003.

Comito, Terry. *The Idea of the Garden in the Renaissance.* Rutgers University Press, 1978.

Crisp, Frank. *Medieval Gardens.* 2 vols., Bodley Head / Hackett, 1979.

Gleason, Kathryn, editor. *A Cultural History of Gardens in Antiquity.* Bloomsbury, 2013.

Hadfield, Miles. *A History of British Gardening,* 2nd revised ed.. Penguin, 1985.

Hoyles, Martin. *The Story of Gardening.* Pluto Press, 1991.

Hunt, John Dixon. *Garden and Grove: The Italian Renaissance Garden in the English Imagination, 1600–1750.* University of Pennsylvania Press, 1996.

———. *Greater Perfections: The Practice of Garden Theory.* University of Pennsylvania Press, 2000.

———. *A World of Gardens.* Reaktion Books, 2012.

Hunt, John Dixon, and Peter Willis, editors. *The Genius of the Place: The English Landscape Garden 1620–1820.* Elek Books, 1975.

Hyde, Elizabeth, editor. *A Cultural History of Gardens in the Renaissance.* Bloomsbury, 2013.

Leslie, Michael, editor. *A Cultural History of Gardens in the Medieval Age.* Bloomsbury, 2013.

———. "Spenser, Sidney, and the Renaissance Garden." *English Literary Renaissance* vol. 22, 1992, pp. 3–36.

Miller, Mara. *The Garden as an Art.* State University of New York Press, 1993.

Munroe, Jennifer. *Gender and the Garden in Early Modern English Literature.* Ashgate, 2008.

———. *Making Gardens of Their Own: Advice for Women, 1550–1750.* Essential Works for the Study of Early Modern Women, series 3, part 3, vol. 1. Routledge, 2016.

O'Malley, Therese, and Joachim Wolschke-Bulmahn. *John Evelyn's "Elysium Britannicum" and European Gardening.* Harvard University Press, 1998.

Prest, John. *The Garden of Eden: The Botanic Garden and the Re-Creation of Paradise.* Yale University Press, 1981.

Stokstad, Marilyn, and Jerry Stannard. *Gardens of the Middle Ages.* University of Kansas Press, 1983.

Strong, Roy. *The Renaissance Garden in England.* 1979. Thames and Hudson, 1998.

Thacker, Christopher. *The History of Gardens.* University of California Press, 1979.

Tigner, Amy L. *Literature and the Renaissance Garden from Elizabeth I to Charles II: England's Paradise*. Ashgate, 2012.

Outlandish Natural Worlds

Albanese, Denise. *New Science, New World*. Duke University Press, 1996.

Campbell, Mary B. *The Witness and the Other World: Exotic European Travel Writing 400–1600*. Cornell University Press, 1988.

———. *Wonder and Science: Imagining Worlds in Early Modern Europe*. Cornell University Press, 1999.

Greenblatt, Stephen. *Marvelous Possessions: The Wonder of the New World*. University of Chicago Press, 1991.

Grove, Richard. *Green Imperialism: Colonial Expansion, Tropical Island Edens and the Origins of Environmentalism, 1600–1860*. Cambridge University Press, 1994.

Keay, John. *The Spice Route: A History*. University of California Press, 2006.

Kimble, George H. T. *Geography in the Middle Ages*. Methuen, 1938.

Mann, Charles. *Uncovering the New World Columbus Created: 1493*. Knopf, 2011.

Reveal, James L. *Gentle Conquest: The Botanical Discovery of North America, with Illustrations from the Library of Congress*. Starwood, 1991.

Roller, Duane. *Ancient Geography: The Discovery of the World in Classical Greece and Rome*. I. B. Tauris, 2015.

Schiebinger, Londa. *Plants and Empire: Colonial Bioprospecting in the Atlantic World*. Harvard University Press, 2007.

Schiebinger, Londa, and Claudia Swan, editors. *Colonial Botany: Science, Commerce, and Politics in the Early Modern World*. University of Pennsylvania Press, 2005.

Smith, Pamela H., and Paula Findlen, editors. *Merchants and Marvels: Commerce, Science and Art in Early Modern Europe*. Routledge, 2002.

Test, Edward Mclean. *Sacred Seeds: New World Plants in Early Modern English Literature*. University of Nebraska Press, 2019.

Tigner, Amy. "The Colonial Garden." *Literature and the Renaissance Garden from Elizabeth I to Charles II: England's Paradise*. Ashgate, 2012, pp. 159–194.

Verdon, Jean. *Travel in the Middle Ages*. Translated by George Holoch, University of Notre Dame Press, 2003.

Ecocriticsm

Borlik, Todd. *Ecocriticism and Early Modern English Literature: Green Pastures*. Routledge, 2012.

———. *Literature and Nature in the English Renaissance: An Ecocritical Anthology*. Cambridge University Press, 2019.

Bowerbank, Sylvia. *Speaking for Nature: Women and Ecologies of Early Modern England*. Johns Hopkins University Press, 2004.

Bruckner, Lynne, and Daniel Brayton, editors. *Ecocritical Shakespeare*. Ashgate, 2011.

Cohen, Jeffrey Jerome, editor. *Animal, Vegetable, Mineral: Ethics and Objects*. Oliphaunt Books, 2012.

———. *Medieval Identity Machines*. University of Minnesota Press, 2003.

Crane, Mary Thomas. *Losing Touch with Nature: Literature and the New Science in Sixteenth-Century England*. Johns Hopkins University Press, 2014.

Duckert, Lowell, and Jeffrey Jerome Cohen, editors. *Elemental Ecocriticism: Thinking with Earth, Air, Water, and Fire*. University of Minnesota Press, 2015.

Egan, Gabriel. *Green Shakespeare*. Routledge, 2006.

———. *Shakespeare and Ecocritical Theory*. Bloomsbury, 2013.

Feerick, Jean E., and Vin Nardizzi. *The Indistinct Human in Renaissance Literature*. Palgrave Macmillan, 2012.

Floyd-Wilson, Mary, and Garrett A. Sullivan Jr., editors. *Environment and Embodiment in Early Modern England*. Palgrave Macmillan, 2007.

Hallock, Thomas, Ivo Kamps, and Karen R. Raber, editors. *Early Modern Ecostudies: From the Florentine Codex to Shakespeare*. Palgrave Macmillan, 2009.

Hanawalt, Barbara A., and Lisa J. Kiser, editors. *Engaging with Nature: Essays on the Natural World in Medieval and Early Modern Europe*. University of Notre Dame Press, 2008.

Keegen, Bridget, and James C. McKusick, editors. *Literature and Nature: Four Centuries of Nature Writing*. Prentice Hall, 2002.

Kiser, Lisa. "Chaucer and the Politics of Nature." *Beyond Nature Writing: Expanding the Boundaries of Ecocriticism*, edited by Kathleen R. Wallace and Karla Armbruster. University of Virginia Press, 2001, pp. 41–56.

Knight, Leah. *Reading Green in Early Modern England*. Routledge, 2014.

Macfaul, Tom. *Shakespeare and the Natural World*. Cambridge University Press, 2015.

Martin, Randall. *Shakespeare and Ecology*. Oxford University Press, 2015.

McColley, Diane Kelsey. *Poetry and Ecology in the Age of Milton and Marvell*. Aldershot / Ashgate, 2007.

Meeker, Joseph. *The Comedy of Survival: Studies in Literary Ecology*. Scribner, 1974.

Merchant, Carolyn. *The Death of Nature: Women, Ecology, and the Scientific Revolution*. 1980. Harper Collins, 1990.

Munroe, Jennifer, and Rebecca Laroche, editors. *Ecofeminist Approaches to Early Modernity*. Palgrave Macmillan, 2011.

Munroe, Jennifer, and Rebecca Laroche. *Shakespeare and Ecofeminist Theory*. Bloomsbury, 2017.

Rudd, Gillian. *Greenery: Ecocritical Reading of Late Medieval Literature*. Manchester University Press, 2011.

Schliephake, Christopher, editor. *Ecocriticism, Ecology and the Cultures of Antiquity*. Lexington Books, 2017.

Scott, Charlotte C. *Shakespeare's Nature: From Cultivation to Culture*. Oxford University Press, 2013.

Stanbury, Sarah. "Ecochaucer: Green Ethics and Medieval Nature." *Chaucer Review*, vol. 39, 2004, pp. 1–16.

Torrance, Robert M., editor. *Encompassing Nature: A Sourcebook*. Continuum, 1998.

Watson, Robert. *Back to Nature: The Green and the Real in the Late Renaissance*. University of Pennsylvania Press, 2006.

Permissions to Reprint

Copyrighted material from the following texts has been included by permission. A good faith effort has been made to contact all relevant copyright holders.

Thomas Aquinas. *The Power of God*. Translated by Richard J. Regan. Oxford: Oxford University Press: 2012. Reproduced with permission of the licensor through PLSclear.

Aristotle. *Physics* (translated by R. P. Hardie and R. K. Gaye), *De Anima* (translated by J. A. Smith), and *On Meteorology* (translated by E. W. Webster). *The Complete Works of Aristotle: The Revised Oxford Translation*, edited by Jonathan Barnes. Volume 1. Princeton: Princeton University Press, 1984. Bollingen Series 70. Permission conveyed through Copyright Clearance Center.

Roger Bacon. *Opus Majus*. Vols. 1–2. Translated and edited by Robert Belle Burke. Philadelphia: University of Pennsylvania Press, 1928. Reprinted with permission of the publisher.

Johanna Bauman. "Tradition and Transformation: The Pleasure Garden in Piero de' Crescenzi's *Le Livre des Prouffitz champestres et ruraulx*." *Studies in the History of Gardens & Designed Landscapes*, vol. 22, no. 2, 2002, pp. 99–141. Published by Taylor & Francis, Ltd. Reprinted by permission of the publisher. Permission conveyed through Copyright Clearance Center.

Nicholas Bollard, from W. L. Braekman. "Bollard's Middle English Book of Planting and Grafting and Its Background." *Studia Neophilogica* vol. 57, 1985, pp. 19–39. Reprinted with permission of journal editor.

Wilene B. Clark. *A Medieval Book of Beasts: The Second-Family Bestiary: Commentary, Art, Text and Translation*. 9780851156828. The Boydell Press 2006. Reprinted by permission of Boydell & Brewer Ltd.

Columella. *On Agriculture*. Vol. 1. Translated by Harrison Boyd Ash. Loeb Classical Library ® Volume 361. Cambridge, Mass.: Harvard University Press. First published 1941. Loeb Classical Library ® is a registered trademark of the Fellows of Harvard College. Reprinted with permission.

Columella. *On Agriculture*. Vol. 3. Translated by E. S. Forster and Edward H. Heffner. Loeb Classical Library ® Volume 408. Cambridge, Mass.: Harvard University Press. First published 1955. Loeb Classical Library ® is a registered trademark of the Fellows of Harvard College. Reprinted with permission.

John Evelyn. *Elysium Britannicum, or The Royal Gardens*. Edited by John E. Ingram. Philadelphia: University of Pennsylvania Press, 2001. Reprinted by permission of the publisher.

Carl I. Hammer. *Charlemagne's Months and their Bavarian Labors: The Politics of the Seasons in the Carolingian Empire*. Archaeopress, 1997. BAR International Series 676. Used by permission of Carl I. Hammer.

Hildegard of Bingen. *On Natural Philosophy and Medicine: Selections from Cause et Cure*. Translated by Margret Berger. 9780859915519, D. S. Brewer, 1999. Reprinted by permission of Boydell & Brewer Ltd.

William Langland. Excerpt from *Piers Plowman: A Norton Critical Edition*. Edited by Elizabeth Robertson and Stephan H. A. Shepherd, translated by E. Talbot Donaldson. Copyright © 2006 by W. W. Norton & Company, Inc. Translation of the B text of *Piers Plowman* by E. Talbot Donaldson copyright © 1990 by W.W. Norton & Company, Inc. Used by permission of W. W. Norton & Company, Inc.

Guillaume de Lorris and Jean De Meun. *The Romance of the Rose*. Translated by Frances Horgan. Oxford: Oxford University Press, 1994, pp. 21–22. Reproduced with permission of the licensor through PLSclear.

Frederick Meyer, Emily Emmart Trueblood, and John L. Heller, editors. *The Great Herbal of Leonhart Fuchs*. Copyright © 1999 by the Board of Trustees of the Leland Stanford Jr. University. All rights reserved. Used by permission of the publisher, Stanford University Press.

William Harrison. *The Description of England: The Classic Contemporary Account of Tudor Social Life*. Edited by Georges Edelen. Copyright © 1994 Folger Shakespeare Library. Reprinted with permission.

Jean De Léry. *History of a Voyage to the Land of Brazil*. Translated by Janet Whately. Berkeley: University of California Press, 1993. Permission conveyed through the Copyright Clearance Center.

Marie De France. "The Eagle and the Crow." *Fables*, edited and translated by Harriet Spiegel, pp. 61–62. © University of Toronto Press, 1987. Reprinted with permission of the publisher.

Physiologus: A Medieval Book of Nature Lore. Translated by Michael J. Curley. Chicago: University of Chicago Press, 1979. © Michael J. Curley. Used by permission of Sandy Plann on behalf of the estate of Michael J. Curley.

Jacopo Sannazaro. *Arcadia and Piscatorial Eclogues*. Translated with an introduction by Ralph Nash. Detroit: Wayne State University Press. 1966. Reprinted with permission of the publisher.

Sor Juana Inés de La Crus. *A Sor Juana Anthology*. Translated by Alan S. Truebood. Foreword by Octavio Paz. Cambridge, Mass.: Harvard University Press. Copyright © 1988 by the President and Fellows of Harvard College. Reprinted with permission of the publisher.

Theocritus. *Idylls*. Translated by Anthony Verity with an introduction and notes by Richard Hunter. Oxford: Oxford University Press, 2008. Reproduced with permission of the licensor through PLSclear.

Theophrastus. *De Causis Plantarum*: Vol 1. Translated by Benedict Einarson and George K. K. Link. Loeb Classical Library ® Volume 471. Cambridge, Mass.: Harvard University Press. Copyright © 1976 by the President and Fellows of Harvard College. Loeb Classical Library ® is a registered trademark of the Fellows of Harvard College. Reprinted with permission.

Anselm Turmeda. "The Disputation of the Donkey." Translated by Neil Kenny. *Cambridge Translations of Renaissance Philosophical Texts*, vol. 1, *Moral Philosophy*, edited by Jill Kraye.

Cambridge: Cambridge University Press, 1997. Reproduced with permission of the licensor through PLSclear.

Anne Van Arsdall. *Medieval Herbal Remedies: The Old English Herbarium and Anglo-Saxon Medicine*. New York and London: Routledge, 2002. Permission conveyed through Copyright Clearance Center.

Virgil. *Eclogues*. Translated by Len Krisak with introduction by Gregson Davis. Philadelphia: University of Pennsylvania Press, 2012. Reprinted with permission of the publisher.

Virgil. *Georgics: A Poem of the Land*. Translated and edited by Kimberly Johnson. London: Penguin, 2009. Reprinted with permission of the publisher.

Excerpts from *The Wakefield Mystery Plays*. Edited by Martial Rose, copyright © 1961 by Martial Rose, pp. 207–9. Used by permission of Doubleday, an imprint of the Knopf Doubleday Publishing Group, a division of Penguin Random House LLC. All rights reserved.

Index

Page numbers in italic type indicate illustrations.